THE ESSENTIAL GUIDE TO NATURE WALKING IN THE UNITED STATES

ALSO BY CHARLES COOK

The Essential Guide to Hiking in the United States

The Essential Guide to Wilderness Camping and Backpacking in the United States

THE ESSENTIAL GUIDE TO NATURE WALKING IN THE UNITED STATES

Charles Cook

An Owl Book
Henry Holt and Company
New York

For Rosemary

Henry Holt and Company, Inc.
Publishers since 1866
115 West 18th Street
New York, New York 10011

Henry Holt® is a registered
trademark of Henry Holt and Company, Inc.

Published in Canada by Fitzhenry & Whiteside Ltd.,
195 Allstate Parkway, Markham, Ontario L3R 4T8

Library of Congress Cataloging-in-Publication Data
Cook, Charles.
The essential guide to nature walking
in the United States
Charles Cook. — 1st ed.
p. cm.
"An Owl book."
Includes index.
1. Walking—United States—States—Guidebooks. 2. Natural history—United States—States—Guidebooks. I. Title.
GV199.4.C665 1997 96-23411
796.5'1'0973—dc20 CIP

ISBN 0-8050-4111-7

Henry Holt books are available for special
promotions and premiums. For details contact:
Director, Special Markets.

First Edition—1997

DESIGNED BY PAULA R. SZAFRANSKI
MAPS DESIGNED BY G & H SOHO, INC.

Printed in the United States of America
All first editions are printed on acid-free paper. ∞

1 3 5 7 9 10 8 6 4 2

CONTENTS

INTRODUCTION

One foot goes before the other, and the movement comes easily and naturally. Your arms swing gently, your lungs fill with fresh air, and—if you're a regular walker—your legs carry you forward almost effortlessly out into the world.

Soon you're covering ground: traversing some rolling rural countryside, or exploring a wild forest, or following a slow-flowing stream to its source. Your surroundings are superbly scenic. You feel increasingly relaxed, free . . . and filled with contentment.

Walking is simple and second nature for most of us. It's an everyday kind of activity, not something that's frequently the rage of fashion or touted for its sex appeal. Yet few physical pursuits in this life are ultimately as rewarding. It's a wonderfully satisfying way to spend an hour, an afternoon, a day, or longer.

Walking is the oldest, most tried-and-true, least complicated, and least expensive form of outdoor recreation you'll find. You need little equipment and no instruction to be on your way. It predates all other forms of transportation, and when you don't have far to travel, walking remains superior to most of the alternatives.

There's no better way to get to know an area than on foot. Cities, towns, and villages have long been interesting places to walk, even with their hazards and distractions (vehicles, noise, air pollution). You could also leave the trappings of civilization to walk in nature, which is what this book is about.

Everyone who can walk will benefit from walking in nature. It doesn't matter whether your limit is a fifteen-minute stroll or an all-day trek. You don't have to be physically fit, there are no age requirements, and you don't need to challenge yourself unless you want to. Walking can be done at any pace or level, and for any distance.

The most recommended way of walking? Do it *your* way. With walking there's plenty of room for individuality, personal proclivities, and changes in your energy level from one time to another. Walk the way that works best for you.

And what exactly is nature walking? It's any and every kind of walking you can do in the natural world. The activity encompasses strolling, striding, sauntering, stepping, treading, tramping, traipsing, traversing, rambling, roving, roaming, racewalking, hiking, meandering, wandering, wending, pacing, peregrinating, perambulating . . . in natural surroundings.

Why walk in nature? Here are some reasons: First, the natural world is a beautiful and sometimes spectacular place that most of us love to visit. Not many of us can claim to suffer from a surfeit of esthetic beauty in our lives. Nature's loveliness gives a nearly instantaneous lift.

Second, natural areas are healthier places to walk than most cities, towns, and suburbs. The air tends to be much cleaner, the sounds more appealing, and periodically it's even possible to experience that rarest of riches in this frenetic era: silence!

Third (following directly from the second), nature tends to be a much more relaxing place than the rest of our too often chaotic world. As long as you don't overdo it physically, nature walking is likely to leave you feeling de-stressed, calm, peaceful, refreshed.

Fourth, parks and other unspoiled places offer a profusion of interesting flora and fauna. If you want to learn more about your myriad "relatives" in the living community, there's no limit to the studies (formal or informal) you can undertake. Walking will bring you in direct contact with "the rest of the family."

Fifth, walking on soft or hard earth, sand, stones, rocks, tree roots, and other natural material is infinitely more interesting and physically appealing than walking on the flat sidewalks and floors that make up our ordinary, semi-artificial, and overly predictable human environment. Your body will enjoy contact with the earth.

Sixth, the natural world presents many opportunities for meeting with the new and the unexpected. Such experiences will sometimes make for a memorable day, are rarely grim, and come with few hassles if you're properly prepared. Not knowing what you'll encounter each time can keep you alert, on your toes, and feeling fully alive.

Seventh, nature walking furnishes chances for developing self-sufficiency and self-reliance. When you're away from telephones and immediate assistance, the responsibility for dealing with any potential problems, including inclement weather, is strictly your own. Under such conditions you soon learn to take care of yourself in the natural world, which helps build a special kind of grounded confidence and maturity.

Eighth, nature offers a nonlinear universe that allows you to take a vacation from human design and thought. Here it's easier to find a fresh perspective on many things, including possible solutions to personal problems. You may even begin to achieve clarity about what you want out of life, how you wish to live, who you really are.

Ninth, the natural world has long been known for its capacity to inspire, to enrich human life in ways that aren't always easily understood, and to help heal or soothe troubles of the heart or soul. While there are no guarantees, spending time in nature on a regular basis is part of a prescription for sanity.

Tenth, contact with nature helps you feel whole, rooted, and connected to the planet you live on. Can a person be mature, balanced, and physically and emotionally healthy without having a relationship with nature? Doubtful! Since we all are part of the intricate web of life on the planet, something important is missing if you don't spend time in direct contact with nature and the earth.

Other reasons to go nature walking? Add your own. Mention should be made of the fact that most of us do it, above all else, because we've learned to love it. Walking in nature almost always feels good and it's something the body shows every sign of "wanting us to do" on a regular basis.

But be forewarned: as you probably already know or suspect, nature walking and other healthy outdoor pursuits are habit-forming. Once you start you probably won't want to stop. In fact, a day can come to seem incomplete or intolerable without a walk. Yes, you might easily become a life-long nature walker. But you aren't likely to regret that fate, and the rewards will be yours to relish.

HOW TO USE THIS BOOK

Read Part I for suggestions, reflections, and basic information about walking in nature and how to make it as rewarding as possible. Topics covered include walking benefits, safety and comfort, what to wear and bring, how to develop a walking habit, and keeping our earth walkable.

In Part II you'll find the most comprehensive country-wide guide to locations for nature walks available in a single volume. There's a chapter for each of the fifty states, with listings and descriptions of five hundred of the best natural places for walks in the United States, or ten for each state.

Use this part of the book to find new locations to walk near your home, elsewhere in your state, in nearby states, or on trips to other parts of the country. (You could use this book to devise an extended nature-walking vacation, visiting from a few to dozens of the finest natural areas for walking.) Consult the overview map to identify the places that would be most convenient to visit or to locate other areas of interest.

Read through the descriptions of areas that sound like good candidates to visit. Using the phone number or address provided, call or write the location to request up-to-date information, including a trail map if one is available (there may or may not be a charge for it), as well as directions. You may also be able to obtain a map on the premises, especially if there's a visitor center, but this won't always be the case.

It's always best to contact a park in advance of a visit, rather than show up unannounced—and perhaps discovering that the trail system or the entire area is closed (for reasons, usually temporary, which include budget cuts, fire hazard during a dry season, flooding, or scheduled hunting seasons).

In the final paragraph of each listing are "Suggested Trails for Nature Walks," listing up to ten of the easiest trails at a location. Sometimes you'll be able to find these on a trail map or described in a trail guidebook, or it may be necessary to obtain directions from a ranger or other park employee.

Not all easy trails may have been included here, especially if there are more than ten in a particular area, and complete information could not be obtained from some parks and preserves. If you're in search of more challenging trails, request information about these directly from the park.

Using the suggested trails as a starting point, ask for additional recommendations from park employees. Be sure to read the discussion at the beginning of Part II about trail ratings and the criteria used in selecting locations. Some "easy" trails will be more difficult than others with the same rating.

Each state chapter concludes with a brief resource section of "Other Suitable Locations for Nature Walks," which you can use to find information about other parks, forests, sanctuaries, and preserves appropriate for nature walks. This section may be especially useful if few or none of the recommended locations happen to be near where you live.

Many smaller county, suburban, urban, and other local parks have not been included among the recommended areas, and some of these will be well worth a visit. Phone the county or local parks department for further information.

Part I

NATURE WALKING BASICS

· 1 ·

Life on Foot

Imagine life without walking. What if you were suddenly unable to walk? Would it be a major hardship, a traumatic event? Many of us are very attached to our ability to walk, which makes up an important part of our identity and serves us in a multitude of ways. At the same time, unless we've been incapacitated, it's all too easy to take walking for granted.

If we take good care of ourselves—and regular walks can constitute one part of a healthy regimen—the majority of us should be able to walk throughout our lives. If we're lucky we'll walk to a ripe old age, and maybe even till our dying day.

Not everyone appreciates walking, to be sure. Some who have succumbed to the seductions of the sedentary life walk as little as possible, hopping in a car or taking public transportation at every possible opportunity. These people have presumably forgotten or never known the pleasures of walking.

It's true that the activity isn't always memorable. Much everyday walking is functional and routine: running errands, shopping, cleaning house, or taking care of other business on foot. We all know about this kind of walking, which sometimes occurs amid distractions and under time pressure. It isn't inherently rewarding.

For a great many of us, however—including a growing segment of the population—walking offers much more than just a way to get around. We walk for recreation and pleasure, for exercise and relaxation, for the freedom and pure joy of it, and try to get out on our feet as often as we can. We walk in parks, forests, preserves, other natural areas, and sometimes in our own neighborhood—and we wouldn't be inclined to give it up for anything.

Walking and the Body

The human body is perfectly suited for walking, an activity that dates all the way back to our origins as a species—our evolution into upright, bipedal, walking animals. Thousands of generations of our ancestors hunted, gathered, traveled, migrated, and carried out everyday activities on foot.

Walking has always been a vital part of human life. As children we don't need to be taught to walk. Like talking, the activity is largely instinctive for us, although it takes some initial practice to get it right.

Walking remained an integral part of human existence until extremely recently. The development of the automobile and other modern transportation made it easy, for the first time, to get from one place to another without walking. Sedentary lifestyles have since become an unfortunate fact of life for many people.

Life is movement. This is true for all animals, and certainly so for human beings. It's no accident that most of us don't feel comfortable remaining in one position for long, whether sitting, standing, or even lying in bed. The body isn't built to stay put. And since the systems of the body have "been designed" or evolved for an active animal, a body that doesn't move much is unlikely to stay healthy or in balance.

Human beings move around mainly by walking. To maintain optimal health and well-being, it's clear that we need to overcome the inertia induced by civilized comforts and walk—as well as pursue other physical activities—as often as possible.

Becoming a Recreational Walker

If you're not already a recreational walker, now's the time to become one. How to get started? Nothing could be easier: take a walk! No activity requires less preparation, less in the way of knowledge, background, instruction, or "psyching yourself up."

Enjoying a walk shouldn't be a problem, but having a good time of it isn't automatic if you're someone who's out of shape and unaccustomed to exercise, or who has workaholic tendencies and finds it difficult to relax and do something "unproductive." If that's the case for you, be patient with yourself, but try a leisurely walk that leaves behind expectations and demands.

Indeed, walking is most likely to be pleasurable if you can let go of worries, responsibilities, and goals for the moment and simply *be* in the activity. Allow your feet and legs to carry you along, and abandon yourself to the flow of movement. Good feelings will usually follow soon enough if you permit them to.

Notice the sensations in your body as you walk. Exactly how do you feel? Is there pain or discomfort? Are you enjoying yourself? If not, do you know why? Could it be that you're preoccupied with other matters? Are you short on energy? (If so, have you had enough rest, sleep, and food lately?) Do you feel pressure to be accomplishing something?

If you experience recurring pain or other physical symptoms, before embarking on a walking program be sure to see a physician—preferably someone who has experience with sports or exercise, and who won't simply tell you to "lay off the activity."

If you're having a tough time getting into a walk, feeling tired, or you're otherwise not having a good time of it, bring the walk to a close and continue another day. If you're out of shape, keep the walks short and sweet at first. It may take weeks or even months to work up to longer distances, but if you persist, know that the rewards will come.

Walking Companionship and Solitude

Solitude and companionship have different attractions and benefits to a walker. Solitary walking is great for thinking, problem solving, reflecting, ruminating, meditating, and just letting your mind wander aimlessly. We all need to be alone sometimes, and nature's a great place for solitude.

Companionship, on the other hand, has the potential for making a walk a warm, communal experience. Good conversation is common, friendships may become deeper, and it's often more gratifying to be able to talk about what we witness along the way. Also, most physical activities feel easier, with fatigue less noticeable, when the exercise is shared with others.

It's important to have some compatibility between walking partners or among the members of a group. (If one person wants to go slowly and stop frequently, and the other is a speedwalker, the potential conflict is clear.) Although it's not necessary to have a perfect match, try to find friends who share your intentions, pace, and relative level of fitness.

Walking Clubs and Groups

If you don't know other walkers, find out if there are any walking clubs in your area. Such groups exist in many communities throughout the country. Some are well organized, have meetings, charge annual dues, publish a newsletter or trip schedule, and offer walks or hikes of varying lengths and levels of difficulty as often as every weekend. Other groups are much more informal.

Although not all walking clubs sponsor nature walks (some engage in urban, mall, or indoor fitness walking), the majority do organize trips to parks and natural areas. If you participate you will surely become more acquainted with a number of natural places to walk in your area. In some cases the social experience may be as rewarding as the walk itself. If you don't have walking friends and prefer not to walk alone, you're certain to benefit from the services of a club.

The best way to find such a group is to ask at your local outdoor supply store, nature center, or environmental center. Also, check bulletin boards at sporting goods stores, health clubs, schools, and your workplace, and call any outdoor organizations in your area. Another avenue is to contact the Sierra Club, which has chapters in many states (their headquarters are located at 730 Polk Street, San Francisco, California 94109).

Walking Away Your Worries

We all know that life can be complicated, difficult, and stressful at times. Few of us are immune to occasionally feeling irritable, frustrated, angry, discouraged, or depressed. While causes shouldn't be ignored (when in doubt, it's worth talking with someone about what's going on), there's a completely safe, temporary, effective, nontoxic treatment available. Take a long walk in nature. See if your mood doesn't begin to lift.

It could also be that you have insomnia, or you just aren't sleeping well, or are sleeping too much. Or maybe you're having trouble making a decision or solving a problem. Or you're stuck for a fresh idea or concept, your creative juices seem to have dried up, or you find yourself in the throes of writer's block.

While it won't offer a magic cure, walking in the natural world almost always seems to lighten loads and ease troubles—presumably because it "takes us out of ourselves," temporarily removes us from stress, ushers us into a more nourishing and healthy environment, and gives our body the exercise it needs. It's almost certain to serve as good preventive medicine.

But what if we're currently lucky enough to be spared such challenges? What if we actually feel content, terrific, on top of the world? These can't possibly be grounds for staying at home. Walking couldn't be better than when we feel at one with the world.

Walking as Participation in Life

Walking takes us out of our private spaces and allows us to explore, participate, and interact with our community, the environment, the world at large. If we don't feel sufficiently a part of the planet we live on, becoming a regular walker is a good start.

Walking energizes us. It induces the heart to beat faster, the blood to flow more rapidly, the lungs to take in more oxygen. The body assumes a state of greater activity, the brain achieves heightened alertness, the senses open and are ready to absorb the stimuli we're going to encounter as we walk. Some of the extra energy we accumulate will be of use to us in daily life.

And walking provides the perfect means to experience first-hand the sights, sounds, smells, tastes, and sensations of the world, natural and otherwise. Film and video and photography only hint at the realities. When it comes to nature, we know pathetically little if we don't go and experience it in person.

It's impossible to remain unaffected by what we see and encounter as we walk. We may be moved by the extraordinary beauty of pristine places, and possibly disturbed by the all-too-ubiquitous eyesores of the world. In nature we may be inspired to study or learn more about wildlife, plant life, and natural processes. Some of us will feel an urgency to take action to help protect and preserve unspoiled areas. And we could be provoked to ponder just how, personally as well as societally, we might use fewer of the earth's resources and learn to live more in harmony with nature.

Walking allows us to mingle with other human beings—and when we walk and spend time in nature we're also able to interact, to a lesser or greater extent, with wildlife—all the other "citizens" of the living green world. Most animals will give us a wide berth, but some will be as curious as we are, and they may come close if we stop and stand or sit quietly.

Some of us will travel to natural areas far and wide, or we may limit our explorations to places closer to home. In spite of past harm and current threats to the environment, we can be grateful that in this country it's still possible to find an amazing range of relatively wild and unspoiled places to walk.

Ultimately, it could be said that by becoming committed walkers, we make a statement that "we're not going to take life lying down." Some of us want to see and know and experience as much as we can within the limits of a lifetime, and long to let our legs take us to the horizons. And in walking through life we're likely to discover that our participation makes a positive difference.

· 2 ·

Walking Rewards

We walk in nature for many reasons and rewards. Aside from the enjoyment involved, most of us presumably know that it's also good for us. Who would imagine or claim otherwise? Evidence for the physiological benefits of walking is overwhelming—and at the same time, what we have to gain extends far beyond the physical.

If you're already a confirmed nature walker you don't need convincing. If you don't walk often, what are the obstacles? Think you can't find the time? Is it a matter of motivation? If so, consider some of the wide-ranging rewards and benefits you'll reap if you make nature walking a regular practice:

Walking as Exercise

For optimal health it's absolutely clear that human beings need exercise on a regular basis, and walking is one of the best forms of exercise you can engage in. It will benefit your cardiovascular system, your respiratory system, and virtually all other systems of the body. It's also safer, gentler, and less likely to lead to an injury than most other kinds of exercise.

Walking is especially good for your body when practiced aerobically (at a relatively fast, vigorous pace for a sustained period). And since the more you do, the more calories you'll burn, regular aerobic walking can help you keep trim.

If walking becomes your primary mode of exercise, you don't really have to go to a gym, join a health club, or invest in body-building machines (although you may still want to do other exercises, including upper body work, to achieve the most complete level of fitness). You can enjoy your workout almost anywhere, at any time, at absolutely no cost.

Walking for Pleasure

Pleasure is a major motivator in life, and walking is as reliable a source of gratification and good feelings as can be found. There are many other reasons why we become nature walkers, but physical pleasure is one of the best incentives.

Unless you're injured, ill, overly tired, or out of shape, the act of walking should feel good from beginning to end. Sometimes you'll experience a real high—a feeling of elation, or a warm inner glow. Such natural highs sometimes last for hours or days, and there's never a corresponding letdown later.

Walking as Release

Given all the stresses of modern life—the difficulties, dangers, unhealthy conditions, and the way we overload ourselves with work and other responsibilities—it's amazing most of us actually maintain a semblance of sanity. To lead a reasonably healthy and balanced life it's essential to find ways to relax and let go of stress.

While there are a number of things you can do to release tension, walking is unbeatable on this count. It can't fail to help you unwind. There's nothing you need to do except . . . walk.

If you're someone who spends long hours at work, or are involved in other demanding and stressful situations, it's easy to find yourself knotted up inside and feeling irritable at times. You can begin to walk the tension away in a matter of minutes. To fully unwind, the longer the walk, the better.

Walking as Leisure

Leisure has become a scarce commodity in our culture. Although the art of relaxing and enjoying life has not been lost, most of us don't schedule enough free time for ourselves. Aside from the demands of daily life, some of us find it difficult to just "be," to enjoy a day without accomplishing something. Yet we all need a respite sometimes.

Walking in nature is one way to revive an atrophied sense of leisure. Take an easy stroll and forget about the time, any previous plans, or thoughts about what you should be doing. Enjoy the moment. Appreciate the beauty of nature.

If you're a walker who enjoys physical challenges, who likes to push yourself and perhaps accumulate accomplishments, try doing it differently for once. Let go of your ambitions. Relax, breathe deeply, and set off on a slow, leisurely walk.

Walking as Immersion in Nature

We all know what it's like to be immersed in a job, in school, in a book, in watching television, in a movie, in music, in traffic, in conversation, in good company. What about being immersed in nature? The overcivilized among us might find this a frightening prospect, but to those of us who love nature it's bliss: being enveloped in a world where nothing's man-made; almost everything's easy on the eyes, ears, and olfactory nerves; and most things seem to be just the right scale. To those who are open to it, few places are more comforting or nourishing.

Even though the scenery is moving by, it's easy to be absorbed and engrossed in nature as we walk. There's almost no feeling of separation from our surroundings in the way that's so common in most cities, suburbs, and other "civilized places."

Walking as Sensory Smorgasbord

The natural world is in some respects the most restful and unstressful place imaginable, and at the same time there's an endless array of life forms, geological forms, and natural phenomena. These are extremely interesting, incredibly varied, and ceaselessly stimulating to our senses. And it all keeps changing as we walk from one natural "neighborhood" to another.

Human beings are born with exceptional sensory acuity, but we begin to lose it quickly in the man-made world—which along with its many unique wonders, includes a bombardment of often unpleasant stimuli. Some of these we quickly learn to ignore and shut out, and others we simply numb ourselves to.

The more time we spend in nature, the more our senses begin to mend, open, and receive a widening range of input. To experience the extraordinary sensory world of which we're a part can be like feasting at a natural banquet.

Walking as Exploration

Nature walking can be an entry into exploration of the earth. Are you someone who finds it exciting to think about venturing into "new," unknown, wild, beautiful, interesting, exotic places? If so, then walking offers you myriad possibilities of things to experience or discover.

There are no limits to the potential pleasure and fun that may await you when you walk in nature (it's even possible to play like a kid again, if you want—great therapy for overworked adults). If you're a nature novice, simply following unfamiliar trails may suffice at first.

Experienced nature walkers can graduate to more rugged trails or get off the beaten path. Expert "explorers" may push their way (carefully) through bushes, tangled vines, or tall grasses, or work their way around a remote pathless pond or lake—or (with the greatest caution) poke into crevices and caves, descend into canyons, and climb up to cliffs or knobs.

As long as you're moving with alertness and care, and within the limits of your ability, you should be able to proceed safely. If you're lucky you'll see some things you've never encountered before (wild animals in close proximity, interesting plants, striking rock formations). You'll almost certainly have some stories to tell by the end of the day.

This kind of exploratory walking is definitely not for everyone. It is a good idea to leave designated paths or walkways only if you know exactly what you're doing, are thoroughly experienced in nature or wilderness travel, and have a map and compass along.

Walking as Adventure

Exploration and adventure are close companions. Almost any walk or experience in nature can become an adventure, and on occasion a thrillingly memorable one. The presence of the unknown, the fact that you may be doing something new and have to stretch yourself, or that you're visiting a new place—all can contribute to a sense of adventure.

Adventure often implies that risk and danger are involved. You may fear or imagine something going wrong, especially when trying a new activity, although the actual risks in nature walking are small. There are no guarantees in the natural world or anywhere else, but proper preparation and awareness help obviate danger without losing the thrill of adventure.

Some situations call for extreme caution: walking or hiking on a rough or steep trail, or wading across a rushing stream, or negotiating icy or otherwise slippery rocks. It's vital to rely on common sense and be willing to turn back when necessary.

Awareness of our physical vulnerability—and our inability to control the forces of nature or life—can add to the feeling of adventure when we're walking in the wilds. It can also lead to greater humility and respect for our limitations. This lesson can be a painful one at first, but it's an essential part of human growth and maturity.

If you're relatively new to walking in nature, just following an easy trail into the woods alone or with a companion may be more than enough adventure for you. No problem. Most of us aren't inclined or equipped to be world-class adventurers the first time out. It's perfectly acceptable to seek a quiet, comfortable experience in nature over an adventurous one.

Walking as Challenge

Some of us like to set difficult goals for ourselves. If choosing to take on walking challenges helps you enjoy the activity and motivates you to walk more, by all means do so. It's healthy as long as you don't get so caught up in the goals that you overdo it and run (walk) yourself into the ground.

Does the idea of a long-distance walk or a hike over difficult terrain attract you? Then go for it—if you're physically fit and prepared. It can be gratifying to set a difficult goal for yourself, plan an itinerary, make preparations, and then accomplish what you've set out to do.

Know your limitations. It's obviously foolish to attempt walking fifteen or twenty miles if you're not a regular long-distance trekker. Refrain from biting off so much that you might be risking exhaustion, an injury, or getting stranded overnight.

Goals need not be ambitious to be rewarding. For someone unused to exercise, just committing to taking walks on a regular basis will probably provide more than enough of a challenge. If you want to time yourself or keep track of distances to measure progress, that's fine. May you succeed beyond your expectations—but don't forget to enjoy yourself in the process.

Walking as Freedom

It's not easy to feel like a free agent in this world. The requirements, obligations, and demands of modern life can become overwhelming at times, and seem to leave us with too little room to be ourselves. An unfortunate number of us feel confined, controlled, or trapped by work or life circumstances.

Few activities will help restore a feeling of freedom to your life more effectively than walking in nature, which is one of the many reasons it's so satisfying. Here you can allow yourself to be physically, mentally, emotionally, and spiritually free. You can be who you are without compromise, free of ordinary external constraints.

Nature walking can help connect you with a sense of your personal power, energy, strength, and creativity. It can permit you to experience deeply the freedom of life itself.

Allow your body to unwind as you walk. Let your arms swing, eyes wander, and worries fade away. Nature's extraordinary gifts are available to you. Enjoy your independence, autonomy, liberty. On foot you're free!

· 3 ·

What to Carry and Wear

Unlike most other forms of outdoor recreation, nature walking requires very little in the way of gear. In warm weather and on dirt trails it would even be possible for us to walk barefoot, not wear clothing, and go without any gear at all if we wanted to, which is the way our ancient ancestors lived.

We've long been separated from nature and softened by civilization, however, so our bodies need protection from the elements, as well as from any rough ground under our feet. With experience we'll start to toughen up and at least partially acclimate to the outdoors, but we still need some clothing and a bit of extra gear for safety and comfort as we walk.

What you'll bring usually depends on where you're going, how long you'll be outside, and how far you plan to walk. Few extras are required if you're sticking close to home, your car, or park facilities. On an extended outing, however, or whenever you'll be away from roads, always carry the following items (for safety's sake, it's wise to bring them along on shorter walks as well):

Water

Intake of water is important while walking or exercising. If you don't drink adequate amounts of water you'll risk becoming dehydrated, which can lead to such symptoms as headaches, dizziness, or lack of energy. On a hot day you could be courting heat exhaustion or heat stroke. Avoid the possibility of such problems by drinking *plenty* of water.

Except on the briefest walks, carry a plastic bottle or canteen filled with water and drink frequently along the way. On a short to medium walk, bring a minimum of a pint and preferably a quart (or liter), with even more when on a longer outing. Double these amounts in warm weather, and quadruple them on a hot day (although it's advisable to limit exercise in the heat). In such weather you're best off taking frequent sips along the way, rather than gulping it all down in a couple of shots. Also, be sure to take in lots of additional water in the hours after returning home if you have been on a particularly long walk or the day was especially hot.

Although your body obviously requires more water in warm or hot weather, don't forget to drink when walking in the cold, even if you don't feel thirsty. The risk of dehydration isn't limited to summer. One option on a chilly day is to bring a hot drink in an unbreakable thermos.

Food

Consider carrying lunch or other food on a long walk, since your body needs nourishment and energy for the exercise. Even on a short outing it wouldn't hurt to bring a snack, just in case you get hungry or you're out longer than expected. Never plan to fast or diet on a day that includes a significant amount of walking. Skip eating only if you're truly not hungry and have energy to spare.

What should you bring? Preferably food that's convenient to carry, such as a sandwich, some "trail mix," and a piece of fruit. Practically anything can be brought in plastic containers, however, so the possibilities are almost unlimited.

If you choose to bring messy foods, be sure to pack them carefully to avoid leakage. The safest way is in sturdy plastic containers, which should then go inside sealed (double) plastic bags. Remember that some foods are quickly perishable in warm weather (fresh meats, dairy products, as well as certain fruits and vegetables).

Finally, if you're planning on a long walk, have a good breakfast or otherwise eat something before you start out. But refrain from stuffing yourself.

Day Pack or Fanny Pack

The easiest way to carry water, food, extra clothing, and other items is in a small pack—a so-called day pack, which is held on your back by two shoulder straps. Day packs come in many sizes. Try to get one that's large enough to carry extra clothing and other gear for a variety of seasons and conditions of weather. It should be made of nylon and coated with waterproofing.

Another option for shorter walks, or other times when little has to be carried, is a fanny pack. This is a mini-pack that fastens around your waist. It'll have enough room for a few small items, but not for much food or a large water bottle.

Rain Gear

Walking in the rain is not the experience of choice for many walkers, although it's much less problematic than some imagine. It can even be surprisingly enjoyable at times—that is, as long as you're wearing rain gear. Since weather forecasts are extremely fallible and untrustworthy, it's wise to carry rainwear whenever there's even the remotest chance of rain, especially if you'll be venturing well away from your home, car, or possible shelter.

Temperatures may plunge during a storm, making things quite a bit colder, even in the summer. Don't risk getting soaked to the skin. A small collapsible umbrella does in a pinch, but walking any distance with an umbrella is awkward and tiring, especially on a windy day. Carrying and wearing rain gear is your best bet.

There are many kinds of rain wear to choose from, but ideally you should get something that's made of lightweight, waterproof nylon—which will weigh little and take up minimal space in your pack—rather than a heavy rubberized garment. Options include a poncho, an anorak, a rain parka, a rain jacket, or a rain suit with pants. Sporting goods and outdoor supply stores stock most of these items. Avoid inexpensive vinyl rainwear, which is totally unreliable.

Walking Shoes

Few items are more important than footwear. Wearing the right shoes can make the difference between a walk being a delightful or a distressing experience, as those of us who have ever endured poor-fitting shoes know. Getting a good fit is critical. Avoid uncomfortable shoes at all costs.

Shoes designed especially for walking are best, and these have been vastly improved over the years. There's usually padding in just the right places, and the sturdy soles are suitable for a variety of surfaces. Running or cross-training shoes will also sometimes do.

By definition, a shoe doesn't come up above your ankles; anything that does is a boot. If you'll be walking or hiking on rough trails, you may want to get hiking boots. These are less flexible but offer more stability than walking shoes, reducing the risk of an injury if you stumble. They're better on rocks, and provide the best protection in mud or deep water.

Assuming, however, that you'll be doing most of your walking on relatively easy, unrugged nature trails, paths, or roads, go with walking shoes. Get some advice from a salesperson and try on lots of pairs, if necessary, before buying. They should fit beautifully from the start, without any breaking in required.

Walking Socks

What you wear on your feet inside the shoes is also important. If you will be out in cool or cold temperatures, and/or possible rain, avoid cotton socks. Cotton provides no insulation when wet from sweat or rain, meaning you may get cold feet.

Wool ragg socks or thick synthetic socks are most recommended. Heavy socks provide a layer of cushioning and extra protection from rough ground, as well as additional warmth in cool weather.

Some walkers wear thin liner socks inside a regular pair of heavy socks. These finely woven socks help reduce any friction between your skin and footwear, thus diminishing the chances of getting blisters. They also add a bit of warmth and help wick away moisture.

Other Walking Clothing

There's no one way to dress for walking. The temperature, weather, season, climate, local environment, and personal preference all enter into a decision about what to wear. On a warm or hot day your entire outfit could consist of a T-shirt and shorts, whereas in subfreezing temperatures you'll need multiple layers of clothing. Dry or wet, cold or hot climates call for completely different outfits.

Avoid tight clothing under all circumstances. Garments should be loose-fitting for maximum circulation, comfort, and freedom of movement. If cold and/or wet conditions are possible, avoid wearing cotton, especially next to your skin (since cotton loses its insulating properties when wet). Choose wool or synthetics instead. Dress in layers, rather than wearing one or two bulky items. Add clothing at the first sign of feeling cold, and remember to remove layers if and when you start to overheat.

Wear anything you want to when it's warm. But anytime you're walking well away from your car or potential shelter, always carry extra clothing—if there's even the slightest chance of a storm, a drop in temperature, or any other reason you might get cold. Never forget that weather sometimes springs surprises, so don't risk your well-being by cutting corners on clothing.

Bug Repellant

Depending on the season and local conditions of weather and temperature, you may encounter bugs on your walk. While often no more than a minor annoyance (many varieties don't bite human beings), in a few locales insects can present a problem when it's warm. If you're going to a place where temperatures are mild, it's best to carry a small container of repellant.

In recent years there's been growing concern about the safety of commercial repellants, most of which contain chemicals that cause a skin reaction in some people. Use them sparingly and only when needed. Probably your wisest and safest choice is to seek out one of the "all natural" bug repellants now available.

Sunscreen

Although sunlight in limited doses has healthy and important benefits for the human body (and this isn't emphasized enough), we all know about the hazards of excess exposure.

Sun need not be a concern if you'll be walking in forested areas, which constitute major portions of many parks. If there are trees to shade you from the sun's rays, you most likely won't need sunscreen or other protection—

unless, that is, you'll also be spending time at lakes, ponds, or meadows, on mountaintops, or in other open areas (including deciduous forests when the leaves are down).

Apply sunscreen whenever you'll be in direct sunlight for more than a few minutes. Protection is especially critical when you're walking entirely in the open, such as in the desert, above treeline, or in other unshaded places. Consider also wearing a wide-brimmed hat where it's sunny. Don't forget that you can receive a burn when it's cloudy, so if you'll be out in the open, bring and use the sunscreen even on a gray day.

Toilet Paper

Many parks and natural areas provide public restrooms or outhouses, but such facilities are often few and far between, especially when you get away from roads. Where they exist, you won't always find toilet paper inside. To be safe, it's smart to bring a small roll of toilet paper or a packet of tissues. See Chapter 8 for a brief discussion of how to follow responsible sanitation practices in the natural world.

Optional: A Walking Stick

You'll hear a variety of opinions about walking sticks. Some walkers love them and wouldn't be caught on a path or trail without them. Others are less enamored of them, preferring to have both hands and arms completely free as they walk.

A stick is unquestionably useful in lending additional balance whenever footing is rough or unstable, as on a rocky trail or when wading a stream. A makeshift walking stick can be obtained from nature—picked up along the path. Attractive carved sticks can also be purchased at many outdoor supply stores. Some walkers use ski poles for the same purpose.

Items to Bring When Venturing off the Beaten Path

The following items should be considered mandatory for longer walks or whenever you'll be getting off the beaten path, especially in large or remote natural areas. Since you never know when one of these items will come in handy or could even prove critical, it's a good idea to bring them on *all* nature walks.

Map

The importance of having a map cannot be overstated, especially when visiting larger parks and forests or where some of the paths and walkways might not be marked. The only reason to be without a map in such an area is if you're with others who know the way.

Obtain your map in advance, whenever possible, since one won't always be available at the location itself (especially at lesser-known parks or forests, which may not have a visitor center or park office on the premises). Many sporting goods and outdoor supply stores sell maps, which are also sometimes included in walking and hiking guidebooks.

If you're not able to get hold of a map in advance, ask at the park entrance or visitor center, if there is one. Free maps are frequently inadequate for route finding. A suitable high-quality map, which is usually going to cost a few dollars, will indicate all of the important trails, paths, other routes, and geographical features.

Compass

A compass is a handy little item that will help you avoid ever getting seriously lost, and could even save your life someday. Most commonly you'll use it simply to verify where you are and the direction you're heading in. With it you shouldn't ever find yourself in the predicament of not knowing where you are.

When you're following clearly marked paths or trails you probably won't have to consult your compass often. Then again, it's impossible to know when you'll need it. Learn how to use the compass from an experienced friend or read a book on the subject.

Guidebook

A good guidebook can give you leads, suggestions, and other information useful in planning walks. Hiking and walking guidebooks that offer descriptions of paths or trails are available for some natural areas, and other guidebooks provide more general information about a park or preserve. Any guidebook that discusses and describes walking options is probably worth owning. Bring it along on the walk itself if trail data are included, since that information could help you find your way. Some also include useful information on flora and fauna, geological formations, and other interesting sights that can enhance your walk.

First Aid Kit

Carry a first aid kit in your day pack whenever you'll be away from possible assistance. Include such items as adhesive bandages, gauze, tape, antiseptic cream, moleskin, molefoam, and a large elastic bandage in case of a twisted ankle. Even though walking injuries are uncommon, getting hurt in a remote area is a serious business. Since it's impossible to predict when the first aid kit might prove important, always bring it. Purchase one from any pharmacy or put together your own.

Whistle

Bringing a small, inexpensive whistle will provide a bit of additional security when walking or hiking in a large natural area. If you should somehow become lost (which you can help avoid by using your compass and map, but given human fallibility, should never be considered beyond the realm of possibility), the piercing sound of the whistle is likely to be heard much farther than your voice. It could assist others in locating you.

Flashlight

When taking an all-day walk, or a shorter walk in late afternoon or early evening, carry a small, dependable flashlight in your pack. Although you presumably have no intention of staying out after dark, there's always the possibility that an injury, getting lost, or some other unforeseen circumstance could delay you. Having a flashlight might make the difference between getting out safely and spending an unplanned night in the woods, which in cold weather could be life-threatening. Bring extra (alkaline) batteries and a spare bulb.

Matches

Matches must be included on any list of potential "life savers." In the unexpected event that you should find yourself lost, hurt, or stranded, with the prospect of spending a night in the woods minus appropriate gear, matches would enable you to start a fire for warmth or to signal for help.

To protect them from getting wet, pack the matches securely in small, doubled-up plastic bags or inside a waterproof matchsafe. Or you could bring waterproof matches, which are available in camping stores. A lighter is another option (keep in mind that such an item is capable of malfunctioning).

Pocket Knife

A knife will occasionally come in handy on an outing, and it can prove important in an emergency, helping you to cut kindling for a fire or perhaps rig a temporary shelter. Swiss Army knives, with their assortment of nifty tools, are especially popular. It goes without saying that a knife should never be used to cut live branches, make markings on trees, or harm vegetation in any way.

· 4 ·

Ways of Walking in Nature

Nature walking encompasses a wide range of possibilities, and there are numerous ways to go about it. How you proceed will inevitably reflect your interests, inclinations, inspirations, abilities, previous experience, and level of fitness. Someone else's way shouldn't necessarily be yours. In this chapter we survey some of your options.

Taking It Slow and Easy

There are many reasons why you might want to go slowly. This may be your natural pace, which is true for more than a few seasoned and fit walkers. Or you may find a slow, leisurely walk the most appealing way to enjoy the surroundings and scenery.

It could also be that you're out of shape and therefore need to take it easy. Or perhaps you have a physical condition that limits your ability. Whatever your reasons, go as slowly as you need or want to. Don't let someone else's lack of understanding or impatience lead you to feel inadequate about it. Walking with others who want to go fast may leave you continuously behind, constantly trying to catch up, and probably feeling rushed and frustrated. You won't enjoy such a walk. Try to find compatible or at least accommodating partners.

We live in a speed-obsessed culture, and practically everyone can benefit from slowing down sometimes. We don't get more out of life by rushing through it. If you happen to be someone who always seems to be in a hurry, try walking much more slowly than usual. This may be hard at first, but you'll be rewarded. Take your time. Soak in the scenery and savor it.

Walking to Observe or Identify Wildlife and Plants

Viewing flora and fauna is important to many people who visit the natural world. For more than a few, walking is a way to get around in nature while searching for subjects or objects of interest. Some walkers roam through the outdoors with binoculars, identification books, and sometimes checklists—looking for birds, animals, plants, flowers, or rocks to view or identify.

In most natural areas there's no scarcity of fascinating subjects to discover. An enduring hobby or pursuit can easily evolve out of an interest in observation or identification. Unless you know an area extremely well, there's no predicting what you'll find on any one day or along a particular path.

Walking at a very leisurely pace allows you to see the most. A faster walk will frighten away birds and animals, and you'll miss much flora. The greatest rewards usually go to those who are willing to stop every now and then and tune in to what's around them.

Wandering

Wandering (or rambling or meandering) suggests an undirected, "purposeless" way of walking. Such an "unproductive" activity will never win widespread approval in our culture, but it can be wonderfully therapeutic. This way is most recommended for the overworked, overstressed, overscheduled, overprogrammed among us.

If you're inclined to give it a try, experiment with allowing your feet to carry you where they want to go. Forget about plans, goals, itineraries, and ideas about how you should walk. While it's important to keep from becoming utterly oblivious of where you are and where you're going (so you don't get lost), the ideal is turn off the internal controls—so there's nothing else to do but let yourself walk and stop whenever you want to.

To some in our society, including many workaholics and overachievers, it is undoubtedly scary to contemplate a walk without preconceived notions. Yet there's no freer way to walk. Give it a try when you're feeling unusually adventurous. Simply toss out any plans you had, and just wander aimlessly. While it won't work for everyone, for some this can be a refreshingly liberating practice.

Walking Aerobically

Aerobic walking provides a totally different experience from meandering in nature. Moving at a moderately fast and steady pace for an extended period can be a great workout. And the natural world is unquestionably the loveliest, most appealing environment you could chose for such exercise. A drawback in walking this way is that you won't see as much up close as you will on a leisurely walk, and your experience of nature is likely to be less intimate. At the same time, the physical exhilaration of such a walk can be extraordinary.

If you're not an aerobic walker but aspire to become one, take some time to work your way up gradually to a faster pace and longer distances. Walking aerobically for a good distance every day puts considerable demands on your body (three or four times a week will be enough for some walkers), but it's a great way to achieve a high level of fitness and well-being.

Owing to the physical stress involved, those who walk in this way need to be extra careful to avoid injuries. Pay close attention to any hints of discomfort or pain. Stop immediately if something doesn't feel right, and don't push hard when you're tired. Quit for the day whenever it ceases to be enjoyable.

Racewalking

Racewalking is a fast aerobic walk done in such a way that one of your feet always remains fully in contact with the ground. It looks to the uninitiated like an unusual, swaying hybrid of walking and jogging. Commonly practiced competively, racewalking has recently experienced phenomenal growth in popularity with recreational walkers because it's an outstanding workout, and isn't as jarring on the knees, feet, and back as running and jogging.

You can racewalk almost anywhere, but as with other kinds of walking it's especially enjoyable in the natural world. Rough trails aren't suitable. Best for racewalking are paved or unpaved walkways, trails, or dirt paths on relatively level terrain.

Hiking

Hiking usually refers to a rather directed and often rigorous kind of walking that one does in the natural world—typically involving distances of several miles or more, and usually on hiking trails, which range from easy paths to rugged, precipitous routes. Hiking trails are found in all states, but they're especially common in the country's mountain regions, and elsewhere in the larger parks, forests, and wilderness areas.

A typical hike has a geographical goal involved: getting to one or more destinations, which can include a mountaintop, canyon, geological formation, waterfall, river, lake, or other scenic location. It's also possible to hike in a less goal-oriented way and simply enjoy exploring nature.

Some hikers camp out as well. When you go on an overnight hiking trip and carry everything you need in a large backpack, it's usually called a backpacking trip. For more information about hiking and backpacking, see my books *The Essential Guide to Hiking in the United States* and *The Essential Guide to Wilderness Camping and Backpacking in the United States*.

Bushwhacking

Bushwhacking refers to leaving all roads, walkways, trails, and paths to walk "cross country." Some bushwhackers explore remote trail-less areas where few human beings ever venture. Others simply prefer to get off the beaten path. Route-finding skills are obviously critical here, so don't even think of trying bushwhacking until you're an expert with map and compass.

In regions where vegetation is dense, bushwhacking can be extremely difficult. As it's no longer acceptable to "whack" or cut bushes as you go, you basically have to ease your way through and try to minimize the number of scrapes and scratches you get. Bushwhacking is infinitely easier across an open landscape, such as in the desert or above treeline in a mountain region.

Bushwhackers see few other people, which is a major appeal to those who love solitude or otherwise want to avoid crowds. This also means that if you get lost or injured, it's highly unlikely that anyone will happen by to help. In other words, the risks are much greater than with other kinds of walking. Bushwhacking is serious business. Do it with others who are highly skilled, or consider trying it alone only after accumulating extensive wilderness experience. Also, make sure you are either traveling on public lands or have permission to cross private property.

Long-Distance Walking

What's the appeal of walking long distances? For one thing, there's an extended, exceptional workout and a great sense of accomplishment. You also take in huge doses of scenery over the course of a day, as much or more than others would see on several walks—a larger view of the lay of the land, of the bigger geographical picture, rather than just a small segment.

What are the possibilities? Some walkers cover fifteen, twenty, twenty-five, and even thirty miles or more at a stretch (a few go even farther). You'll naturally need to keep a good pace to walk such distances in a day. Taking regular breaks is highly recommended.

Most long-distance walkers are extremely fit, of course. By progressively lengthening your walks you may be able to achieve such a level of fitness, assuming your body is suited for it. A small number of ambitious walkers take extended trips involving hundreds or even thousands of miles, even walking the length or breadth of the United States. For hikers and backpackers, there are several supertrails in this country—National Scenic Trails that run 2,000 to 3,000 miles or more. The majority of these are strenuous, traversing rugged stretches of mountainous terrain.

Stopping and Resting

On a long walk it's important to remember to take breaks. The body requires periodic rest, although individual needs vary enormously. Some especially fit walkers take few breaks and continue comfortably for considerable stretches without stopping. More common and recommended is to rest at regular intervals, as often as every hour or so. Other walkers prefer to pause or stop frequently, especially when encountering something of interest.

With experience you'll find what works best for you. Pay attention to how your body feels. When it seems like time for a break, take one. Some days you may need more rest than others. The terrain also enters in: you'll probably need to stop, or at least catch your breath, much more often when it's steep and rough than when you're walking on easy, level ground.

A good place to take a break is any scenic spot that calls out to you. Likely locations include lakeshores, waterfalls, ponds, meadows, clifftops, and mountaintops offering panoramic vistas. It doesn't have to be a spectacular area, however. Sometimes the banks of a little brook or a patch of open grass will present themselves as the perfect place to rest.

· 5 ·

Cultivating a Life-Long Practice

You'll get the most out of nature walking by doing it on a regular basis, integrating the activity into your life, and pursuing it as a life-long practice. If frequent walks in nature aren't already part of your routine, find the time for them now. Keep in mind what you stand to gain—how good you'll feel, how your life will benefit—and you should find the motivation.

Developing a Walking Habit

Given all the competition for our time and attention, it's fortunate that walking is very habit-forming. If you're not a regular walker and have a history of semisedentary living, the habit may take a few months to become firmly established. Initially it may require a modicum of resolve, determination, and self-discipline to get going. You'll know you're hooked when a day doesn't feel right without a walk. Doing it daily is ideal. Every other day is next best.

If you already walk regularly and you're in decent shape, nature walking should come easily to you. The biggest change will be the shift from walking on smooth surfaces to the sometimes rougher ground of wild nature.

A healthy activity like walking can be quite addictive, but there shouldn't be any negative side effects unless you go seriously overboard. You're clearly overdoing it if your walks begin to crowd out other important things, or you find yourself repeatedly injured or exhausted. As with other good things in life, it's best to strive for moderation and balance.

Scheduling Walks

Should walks be scheduled in advance? For a busy person the answer is probably yes. A schedule can help keep your walks from getting bumped by competing interests and obligations. Try to set aside a certain time every day (or two), and resolve that nothing will interfere except extreme weather or emergencies.

Simultaneously, don't rule out the possibility of unplanned walks when the impulse strikes and time permits. If you're fortunate enough to have a surfeit of free time or a flexible worklife, you may not need a walking schedule at all.

Assuming you have to work or attend school during daytime hours, the most obvious times for walks are early morning and early evening (and perhaps your lunch hour, if there's a suitable natural area nearby). Even with an overloaded schedule, you should be able to find fifteen minutes to an hour or more each day for a walk.

Remember, nature walking has the potential to relax as well as energize you, and can help clear your mind and allow you to be more effective at work. A walk may more than pay for itself in improved efficiency and heightened spirits. Avoiding a healthy activity because of a supposed lack of time is self-defeating.

It's quite true that for some of us there simply aren't enough hours in a day, especially those of us who are working extra hours or attempting to juggle work, school, raising children, and perhaps trying to satisfy other interests. Do you currently allot any time in your day to less satisfying diversions (like TV) which could instead be devoted to walking?

Weekends and holidays offer obvious occasions for extended walks. With a full day you have the freedom to travel farther from home and walk to your heart's content. Just don't reserve walking for weekends alone. Doing it several times a week will make the biggest, most positive difference in your life.

Developing Other Interests That Include Walking

You can create additional incentives and opportunities for foot travel by taking up nature-related studies and hobbies like birdwatching or plant and wildflower identification. These activities will not only enhance your walks, but they quite often are enjoyable and satisfying in themselves.

How to get started? Some of the best ways are to enroll in a nature class at your school, botanical garden, zoo, environmental center, or adult education center; join a local chapter of the Audubon Society or Sierra Club, and attend outings and lectures; or sign up for guided walks that focus on flora, fauna, geology, and ecology.

Assuming you become increasingly interested in, fascinated by, and passionate about nature in its myriad forms, you're sure to want to spend as much time as possible in the wilder places. Not only won't you have to coax yourself into taking nature walks, rather it's likely that you won't be able to get enough of them.

Developing a Walking Library

Another useful project for novice nature walkers is to collect relevant writings and resources, including walking guidebooks, as well as bird, animal, and plant identification field guides. These will probably help inspire you to walk more in nature and perhaps discover new locations to visit.

Subscribe to *Walking* magazine (9–11 Harcourt Street, Boston, Massachusetts 02116; (617)266-3322) to help keep yourself informed about what's happening in the walking world. You can also develop your own files for maps, magazines, and articles you've clipped. Your sporting goods, outdoor, or book store may have guidebooks to local as well as distant parks, including locations where you've already walked and those you'd like to visit at some future time. Before you know it you'll fill a few bookshelves.

Recruiting Friends

While the joys of solo walking must not be discounted, it's great to share walks with friends. If you're relatively new to nature walking, some good company will help reinforce the habit—and if you have any hesitancy or resistance, and should be tempted to stay at home, your friends can help keep you on track.

If you don't already have walking companions, try to recruit a friend or two to join you. But never attempt to coax or drag someone along who doesn't really want to go (whether a friend, acquaintance, spouse, or child). Not only is it unfair to them but if they resent it, the walk may end up not being fun for anyone. Better to join a walking club (see Chapter 1).

Walking Vacations

Those who love walking are not only unlikely to need a break from it, but will often plan vacations with walking specifically in mind. Is there a well-known park, scenic area, or region of the country you'd love to visit? Why not make it the destination for a walking vacation?

If it's a location listed in Part II of this book, you've already got a phone number to call or an address to write to. Request general information and ask about accommodations or camping options, and whether a local guidebook is available. Do this as far in advance of your intended trip as possible, so you'll have ample time for planning and making any required reservations.

Unless you prefer to stay at a fancy resort with plush accommodations, a walking vacation can be extremely inexpensive. Indeed, staying at a low-cost bed-and-breakfast or camping out can make your vacation very affordable. The walking part is, of course, absolutely free.

A walking vacation will likely confirm and even intensify your appreciation or love of nature walking. One trip often leads to another, and the wonders of such a getaway make a "nonnatural," nonphysical vacation—no matter how restful or fun—pale in comparison.

Living Near the Natural World

It couldn't be easier to take daily or regular nature walks if you reside right next to a park, forest, or other natural area. Needless to say, not all of us are so fortunate, including those of us who are ensconced in a metropolis or other densely populated, highly developed region.

Living a short walk, drive, or bus or train ride away from a natural environment is next best. But what if the nearest park isn't close and is inconvenient to reach? First, make sure there are indeed no natural areas nearby. Some state forests, other public lands, and private preserves are minimally identified, if at all, but open to walking (state parks are usually the most publicized, whereas state forests may be largely unknown except to next-door neighbors). If your state has a department of conservation or environmental protection, call to request a complete listing of the state's parks and natural areas. There may also be sizable county or local parks in your region.

If all you can get to on a regular basis is a small urban or suburban park, make that do for now. Nature does indeed survive in cities as well as suburbs—in some cases beautifully so—but as often with a degree of deterioration and amid noise as well as air pollution. At the same time, it must be acknowledged that no natural area, however remote, is totally free of civilization's unhealthy side effects. Appreciate that green oases do thankfully exist in most cities and suburbs. Walk and enjoy.

Walking as You Age

No physical activity is suitable for a wider age range than walking. Virtually all ages are fully qualified. It's wonderful for children, an ideal habit for adults, and a superb way for seniors to stay in shape.

Keeping physically active is especially important for good health and longevity as we grow older. Since it's safe and easy on the body, walking remains one of the most recommended forms of exercise for middle-aged and older people.

You're never too old to walk, unless you have a condition that immobilizes you or makes movement too painful. Cut back if you have to because of infirmity or shortness of breath, but continue as long as you can on some level. If it's necessary to go very slowly and stop constantly, that's fine. Your body is still benefiting, and you should feel better because of it.

A life-long walking habit is one of the best possible forms of health insurance you can get. None of us will live forever, but an active and fit body is likely to be less susceptible to disease and decline, and the quality of your life in later years could well be enhanced.

Walking with Children

Children love nature, especially when they're introduced to it properly. Take them on walks and you'll help promote their life-long appreciation for the natural world. The earlier you get them out, the better. Some parents carry their babies on nature walks.

Since young children can walk only short distances, the outing needs to be tailored to their ability. Stop when a child is tired and no longer enjoying herself or himself. In due course, you might find yourself pleading with them to slow down. Older children won't always want to walk with their parents, but it's more likely if you've established a tradition of family walks and they've learned to love the activity.

Walking in nature with other family members helps foster a feeling of cohesion and togetherness. It can be more fun, interesting, and exciting for children than a sedentary picnic. You'll be helping them discover a new world and giving them great memories of their family, as well as the outdoors. And through your child's eyes you might even learn to see nature freshly again.

· 6 ·

Walking Safely and Comfortably

Walking is as safe as physical activities get. Yet no activity is entirely without risks or possible discomforts. Walking mishaps and injuries do occasionally occur. It's important to stay alert and attentive whenever you're on foot.

Fortunately, most potential problems are minor, correctable, and often avoidable. In this chapter we survey some of the hazards that you could encounter along the path. Knowing what to watch out for will help you stay out of harm's way and keep any troubles from interfering with your enjoyment.

Walking Injuries

Although human beings are mortal and have physical vulnerabilities, not everyone behaves accordingly. It's important to remember that no matter how strong and healthy you are, or how relatively safe walking is, you're never immune to being injured. Failing to recognize risks and exercise caution can mean trouble.

The easiest way to get hurt walking is simply to trip and fall. Taking a sudden, unexpected spill onto hard pavement or rocks could easily result in an injury, possibly even broken bones. However tempting it may be to become lost in reverie on a nature walk, it's vital to stay conscious of what's underfoot. If you're attentive you'll be much less likely to trip or stumble over a rock, tree root, or other obstacle. Get in the habit of glancing down frequently at the ground and at your feet, especially when walking at a brisk pace. If you want to gaze off into the distance or study the trees, it's wisest to do so standing still or sitting.

Rougher terrain calls for a slower pace. Most people have the sense to proceed cautiously when the footing is rocky or steep, since that's where a fall would be most dangerous. But it's also important to pay attention when the terrain is easy, as this is where you're actually more likely to fall—since it usually feels safer, you may be inclined to let your guard down, and little impediments may escape your notice and trip you up.

If you lose your balance and start to fall, don't fight gravity; tightening up and resisting will leave you more prone to injury. Allow your body to crumple loosely to the ground, and use your hands to soften the impact. If at all possible, plop down gently on your rear end, which is ideally suited for such purposes.

Taking a bad step and stumbling (which happens to every walker on occasion) can result in a twisted or sprained ankle, which is probably the most common walking injury. You're more likely to turn an ankle on rough, rocky ground, but it can happen anywhere. By staying alert and being ready to shift your weight in an instant, it's possible to pull out of a stumble and avert an accident. Wearing good, sturdy walking shoes will also reduce the chances of an injury. Hiking boots give the most complete ankle protection of any footwear, which is why they are especially recommended for walking on rugged trails.

Always be prepared for surprises underfoot. A rock or stone may shift as you step on it. Fallen leaves could conceal stones, small branches, holes, or crevices. When walking in dense leaves or other vegetation, or any time light is limited and you can't see the ground clearly, step slowly and carefully, ready for a hidden object or hole.

Carry an elastic bandage, which would help support your ankle in the event of an injury. While a serious sprain can leave you incapacitated, most walking injuries are thankfully minor. If it's just a slightly pulled muscle you may be able to continue on your way.

Always rest for a few minutes if you seem to have hurt yourself. If there's significant pain and/or swelling after this time, terminate the walk immediately (unless you're stranded and have absolutely no alternative). Walking on an injury may multiply the damage. Seek assistance. When in doubt, head right for your doctor's office or the nearest hospital emergency room.

If you'll be walking in wild areas and venturing off the beaten path, consider taking a first aid course and learning more about medical self-care. Be prepared to take full responsibility for any possible mishap, and realize that you won't necessarily be rescued if you sustain an injury in a remote area (there may be no way to summon help). If you feel unwilling to assume such responsibility, you shouldn't walk alone in a large park or natural area; if you choose to go, take every possible safety precaution.

Blisters

While they're by no means life-threatening, blisters will take the joy out of any walk. Common causes of blisters include wearing shoes or boots that don't fit properly; letting feet get too hot and sweaty; and attempting to walk too far on feet that haven't been toughened by regular walking.

Once there's a hint of a problem, a blister can still be nipped in the bud by the timely use of moleskin or molefoam. These materials, which are available in pharmacies, have adhesive on the back and are applied directly to your skin. They'll reduce or eliminate any blister-creating friction against the skin.

The most important thing to do—and a difficult lesson for many to master—is to stop at the *first* sign or sensation of discomfort, rubbing, or overheating inside your shoes. Don't wait a moment more to do something about it, even though it may not hurt yet. Sit down, remove your shoes and socks, and examine your feet. Any area that's even slightly red or sore from rubbing or chaffing needs immediate attention. Allow the feet to dry and cool off and then, using scissors or knife, cut a piece of moleskin to fit the problem area. Assuming there's room, use thicker molefoam on your heel or anywhere else there's been uncomfortable pressure.

If you wait till there's pain before stopping to survey the damage, it's almost certainly too late. Moleskin or molefoam won't save the day once blisters are formed, and the rest of your walk could be uncomfortable or worse. Recurring blister problems are usually a sign that your footwear is failing you. Do yourself a favor and replace it. When you do get new shoes or boots, it's always a wise idea to try them out close to home before wearing them on an extended walk.

Aching Feet and Sore Muscles

Feet and muscles eventually get tired and sore, and will begin to ache if you keep walking long enough. Unless you've seriously exceeded your capacity, most discomforts don't indicate serious problems and will normally disappear in a day or two.

Such symptoms will be less severe if you're a regular walker, but we all have our limits. Listen to your body. Unless you're out to prove something (as some long-distance walkers and other physically ambitious people admittedly are), take it as a sign that it's time to quit when muscles or feet start to ache.

Pain

Real pain conveys an important message. Never ignore it! A cramp in your leg or side that vanishes in a couple of minutes may be insignificant, yet it could also mean that you're going too fast, have walked far enough, or have been overdoing it in recent days.

When pain doesn't go away or keeps recurring, it can be a sign of a serious condition. See a doctor as soon as possible to have the problem checked out. A minor injury could become a major one if unattended to.

If you've somehow sustained an injury, don't let this or any other difficulty discourage you from resuming walking. And under the care of a good "walking doctor," you won't be encouraged to remain inactive for any longer than is absolutely necessary.

Walking in the Heat

In much of the country, waiting for perfect weather would practically eliminate the possibility of regular walks. Even extremes of weather or temperature shouldn't preclude walking, but it's important to know how to walk safely at such times.

During a hot spell it's wise to walk in the cooler hours of early morning or evening whenever you can. Wear the lightest, most breathable clothing you own. If you'll be in the sun for more than short periods, protect your skin with sunscreen and wear a sun hat and possibly a long-sleeved shirt or pants.

On a hot, humid day it's critical to carry and drink large amounts of water. Bring one to two quarts (liters) for a short to medium-length walk, and as much as a gallon if you'll be out all day or in the desert. Drink often and take frequent breaks.

Stop immediately if you start to feel even slightly weak, dizzy, or nauseated. Take a long rest in the shade, sip water, and continue walking only when you feel completely restored. Don't proceed if you're not feeling well. Be ready to shorten any walk when conditions warrant it.

Letting your body overheat puts you at risk for heat cramps, heat exhaustion, or heat stroke. Cramps in legs or elsewhere can be an early sign of trouble. A feeling of exhaustion may mean you've already overdone it. Pushing on might invite heat stroke, which is a life-threatening condition. These problems can be completely averted by exercising restraint in hot weather.

Walking in the Cold

Many people stay home in winter or during spells of frigid weather rather than brave the bitter winds. However, if you know how to dress for it, keep exposed skin to a minimum, and stay attuned to your body's need for warmth, you can walk safely even in subzero temperatures—which is generally a healthier practice than staying cooped up indoors for days or weeks on end.

As long as you wear a sufficient amount of the right clothing (see Chapter 3), you can stay toasty warm in even the coldest of weather. Extremely low temperatures call for insulated shoes or boots, and often a face mask, especially on windy days.

A brisk walk will generate lots of heat, so you'll sometimes need less clothing than expected. Remember to remove layers to avoid getting soaked in perspiration, which will leave you more vulnerable to chilling when you stop to rest, or the wind picks up, or the temperature drops. Always bring extra clothing for rest breaks or in case it's colder than anticipated.

Whenever you feel uncomfortably cold or chilled, or any part of your body becomes numb, take direct and immediate action. Never ignore these warning signs and try to "tough it out." Put on more clothing (borrow some from friends, if necessary). If you can't warm up, head quickly for your car or the nearest shelter.

Two cold-weather conditions that can befall the careless are hypothermia and frostbite, which most frequently occur because of inadequate clothing. In hypothermia, which is occasionally fatal, your core body temperature drops dangerously low. It's sometimes known to occur in temperatures as warm as 50 to 60 degrees F. Frostbite involves the freezing of flesh, and can lead to the loss of extremities. You'll never encounter either condition if you're conscientious about taking care of yourself in the cold.

Walking in the Rain

Would anyone in their right mind want to walk in the rain? Yes, some of us actually enjoy it at times. While most of us have a very negative view of life-giving precipitation, rain can be wonderfully refreshing.

A wet and misty day in the mountains can be beautifully atmospheric. Flowers and plants glisten, and the scents are never sweeter. Walking in the rain is potentially most pleasurable in warm weather, and least so when it's cold.

However you feel about it, you're almost certain to get caught in rain every now and then, especially if you take long walks in wild areas. And with rainwear and sufficient clothing to keep you warm (see Chapter 3), walking in the rain shouldn't be a problem.

Since forecasts are frequently wrong, it's a big mistake to cancel your plans and stay home whenever precipitation is a possibility. You're sure to miss out on some great walks. Also, many so-called rainy days involve just a little light drizzle or an occasional shower.

Most avid walkers learn to accommodate the rain and aren't easily discouraged by it. If you're still doubtful that you could enjoy yourself, just try a short rainy-day walk and see what happens.

Storms and Lightning

Whereas rain need not really dampen your spirits or risk your well-being, severe storms have more potential for danger. An ordinary afternoon thunderstorm will usually leave you unscathed, but high winds, flooding, or other other severe conditions are another matter. When such a storm is forecast and seems probable, you may want to stay home. If you're taken by surprise in the woods, be ready to head quickly toward shelter or your car.

No one needs to be told that lightning is dangerous, but risks are extremely small in a forested area. Nevertheless, in an electrical storm you don't want to remain at an exposed high elevation, in an open meadow or clearing, or at a lakeshore. Never be one of the tallest objects around. If you're in an open area, head quickly for a lower elevation and/or a dense forest as the storm approaches (you usually have a few minutes' warning). Never seek shelter under a lone exposed tree or cluster of trees.

Stream Crossings

Streams and rivers of all sizes are to be found in some natural areas. There will sometimes be bridges along popular trails and paths, but on other routes you must cross on rocks or boulders, or by wading. This is obviously easier and safer when a small brook is involved than when it's a big stream or river.

Never try to cross deep or fast-flowing water unless you've had special instruction, and are in the company of others who know how to safely accomplish this. Proceed with caution even when negotiating a slow, shallow stream, and consider using a long stick for additional stability. If you have to come back the same way, keep in mind that in the event of heavy rain, the waters could rise in a flash flood and leave you trapped. Plan to head back across the waterway at the first sign of a storm.

Biting Insects

Bugs can be pesky in some areas during the warmer seasons, but they seldom present a real hazard except to those who are allergic to their bites or stings. (Consult your doctor if you have experienced severe reactions to bee stings or bug bites.)

When in doubt, carry insect repellent (see Chapter 3). The prevalence of bugs will vary enormously from one locality to another, and often from one year to another. If it's cool and windy or rainy you'll see few if any of them. In hot, humid weather they sometimes flourish, but not always predictably so.

Ticks and Lyme disease have gotten plenty of press in recent years, but very few walkers contract this disease. Be on the alert when bushwhacking or following an overgrown path in grassy or bushy areas—especially in regions known to harbor ticks—in warm weather and at low elevations. If you find a tick on your body, remove it immediately, and get tested for Lyme disease if you develop a warm-weather flu. (Contrary to some media reports, for most people the disease is not serious as long as proper treatment is received promptly.) Don't let any concerns or fears lead you to curb nature walking, since the actual risks of contracting this disease while walking are remarkably low in most environments and areas.

Remember that insects are part of nature and it's necessary to share the planet with them. See if you can avoid becoming irritated, and get on with enjoying the day.

Problems with Animals and Plants

It's extremely unlikely that you'll get into trouble with wildlife. Attacks and injuries are remarkably rare. There's always a slight risk that you could stumble upon an animal up close, and it could lash out at you if it feels threatened—but animals prefer to avoid confrontations, tend to keep their distance, and will almost always hear or smell you first.

If and when you do meet with wildlife—which is usually an exciting and delightful surprise—stop, stand still, and keep quiet or speak in a soft voice. If it's a large mammal and you feel a sense of danger, retreat slowly without turning your back to the animal. It may retreat as well. Under no circumstance should you attempt to approach wildlife closely, which would put you at much greater risk.

Some plants can present minor hazards for the walker. You'll naturally want to proceed cautiously when you're among such "unfriendly" species as thorn bushes or cacti. In a dense forest, especially when bushwhacking or following a minimally maintained path, always be on the alert for low, sharp branches that could poke, cut, or scrape you.

Contact with poison ivy, poison oak, and poison sumac can leave an annoying itchy rash for weeks. Learn to identify these plants if you don't already know them. And if you want to fortify your diet with wild edibles, do so only with great caution. Eat only what you know with absolute certainty. Learn more by taking a course, reading extensively about wild plants and mushrooms, and going on "wild edible walks" with an expert.

Sunlight and Altitude Risks

As already discussed, the sun should be treated with great respect. Nevertheless, don't deprive yourself of the healthy physical benefits of exposure to full-spectrum sunlight. Use sunscreen or cover your body with clothing when appropriate.

Unless you already live at a high altitude, allow yourself time to adjust to higher elevations (above 6,000 to 8,000 feet) when walking in mountain regions where the air is thinner and your lungs have more difficulty taking in sufficient oxygen. Plan to cover less distance than usual during your initial walks. Take frequent breaks and give your body a week or two to fully acclimate to the altitude. Pushing too hard would put you at risk of altitude sickness. Stop immediately and rest if you begin to feel dizzy or nauseated.

Safe Drinking Water

When in doubt, bring drinking water from home. You may be able to find safe water at the facilities within a park, but don't count on it. And since there's always a possibility of contamination from bacteria or parasites, never drink directly from a stream, pond, lake, or other standing or running water. The only natural source of water that can be reasonably trusted is a high mountain spring, located far from civilization.

On a camping trip, or whenever sufficient water cannot be carried for an entire trip, it must ordinarily be purified by boiling or using a water filter (which is now standard equipment for backcountry camping, and available from outdoor supply stores). Contrary to advice you'll still hear widely given, do not use iodine or other purification tablets, as recent research (confirmed by the personal experience of some of us) proves this method to be unreliable.

Risks from Other Human Beings

Solitary walking can be dangerous in some areas within and around cities, and this is occasionally true as well in remote locations. If you're visiting a park or other natural area, ask a ranger or park employee (look for them at the park entrance or visitor center) whether it's considered safe to walk alone. In the vast majority of nonurban parks in the United States—where crime is thankfully low or almost nonexistent—the answer will be yes, but some exceptions exist. The risks for a lone woman are understandably somewhat greater than for a man.

Also, be aware of local hunting seasons. These typically are in the fall or winter, but vary considerably from one region to another. You'll probably want to avoid walking in those parks and forests where hunting is actively going on. If you do go into hunting territory during the season, be sure to wear a Day-Glo orange vest and/or other bright clothing, and stick to major trails and roads.

Staying Oriented in the Natural World

No one wants to contend with the consequences of getting lost. You might be able to find your way out if you're in a small park, but there are no guarantees. And being lost in a large or remote natural area unquestionably would put your life at risk. When in doubt, don't visit such places alone until you're an expert route finder. Traveling with others is always safer.

To minimize the chances of becoming disoriented, carry a compass and obtain a map for each area you visit, and learn how to use these tools (see Chapter 3 for more about map and compass). By consulting them frequently you won't get lost.

If you don't have these items along, always stick to well-marked and/or easy-to-follow paths, trails, or roads. Study any intersections you pass and pay constant attention to your route. Then, at the very least, you'll be able to retrace your way back to where you began. It's easiest when there are major visible landmarks (mountains, cliffs, lakes, rivers) to orient yourself by. Unless the route is absolutely clear, or you have a map and compass, don't take chances by trying to return a different way. No one has a built-in sense of direction, and everyone is capable of getting turned around or lost on occasion.

Some trails and paths in a park may be marked and others not. Routes are indicated in a number of ways, including wooden or metal signs at intersections, small metal or plastic markers on trees or posts, paint blazes on trees or rocks, and cairns (piles of rocks). A good map should show all important routes or trails and indicate the color of markers, if any. A guidebook should also have this information.

What if you somehow actually manage to get lost? If you're still on a path or trail you're probably not in big trouble, since you can retrace your steps to where you started. Attempt to do so very carefully, constantly seeking visual verification that you're going the right way.

You're seriously and dangerously lost if you find yourself totally off the path and don't have a clue about what direction to go in. If this ever happens to you, sit down to rest first, try to stay calm, and see if you can identify the way you came. Look closely at the ground for signs of your footprints or other indications of the route you arrived by. Proceed slowly (never hurry), keep sighting back to a large tree or landform so you have a focal point to return to, and if necessary, walk in large circles around this point in search of the trail or path you were on.

If you were with others and became separated from them, and have reason to believe they'll be searching for you, sit tight and wait. It may be easier for them to find you than vice versa. Much additional advice about how to deal with getting lost can be found in books or courses on wilderness survival, which are worth looking into if you'll be spending time in remote areas. Your best bet of all, however, is to master the use of a map and compass, so you'll never find yourself facing such a predicament.

· 7 ·

Following a Path to Wholeness

Can walking in nature help us become healthier, more balanced, fulfilled, self-realized, whole human beings? Can it help us transform our lives? It's clear that nature walks won't automatically bestow us with well-being, maturity, or peace of mind—yet it's impossible to overestimate their benefits.

Since the activity meets a whole gamut of physical, psychological, and spiritual needs, nature walking is almost certain to make a positive contribution to your life. You're likely to gain and grow from it no matter what your expectations.

At the very least, nature walking can help you get into better shape, stretch yourself in healthy ways, maybe learn to relax, as well as enjoy life more fully. It could also lead you into adventure. And it can be an effective entry to the non-human realm, a way to strengthen your connection to the natural world.

Could you be a nature walker and at the same time live a fragmented, alienated, disillusioned existence? Not likely, or not for long. While there's no proof of cause and effect, as a group most nature walkers seem to have a life-affirming, hope-filled, positive outlook.

Walking as a Spiritual Pursuit

Any reason to walk is a good one, and you certainly don't need lofty motives or ideals to benefit from it. However, some of us are aware of being drawn to nature walking for reasons that go beyond such obvious ones as interest in nature or exercise.

Whatever your spiritual or religious beliefs, it's clear that there are aspects of life and nature that lie outside of the material, the useful, the objective, and the comprehensible. Are these all part of the unknowable? Do you relate to them in some way?

One thing is certain: for those of us who are so disposed, walks in nature can be wonderful opportunities for pondering the infinite and unanswerable. Some people are uncomfortable with the ambiguities, but if you have the courage to pose difficult questions and stay with them, nature walks can help facilitate deeper insights and understandings, including wisdom about how to live.

Walking and Meaning

Millions of people in our materialistic culture are understandably starved for meaning and purpose, and apparently don't know how or where to find them. While meaning may be discovered in different places, one of the deepest, most important sources for many of us is nature.

When we spend time in the wilds, our place in the universe may seem like less of a mystery. And although our own personal life purpose isn't always easily determined, nature offers us the opportunity to unearth vital clues.

For the unfortunate many among us who feel confused, unconnected, or lost in life, a regular practice of walking in nature can help us begin to discover or regain a sense of direction. It can open us to living in a more meaningful and purposeful way, and lead us to undertake appropriate actions.

Walking and Wonder

A sense of wonder, which is usually alive and well in childhood, tends to be dimmed or suppressed by the time we've become adults. Living in a hectic and demanding world leaves more than a few of us jaded, not easily excited or surprised.

No matter how old we are, nothing offers more potential to reawaken wonder than getting close to nature and witnessing the life process in an intimate way. We may have forgotten that life is actually a most extraordinary, inspiring, wondrous phenomenon, stunning in its richness and variety and harboring an amazingly intense impulse to carry on. It's unfortunate that we take so much of life for granted, but this can change for us. Many people experience a rebirth of wonder as they spend time walking in nature.

Walking and Joy

How often do you experience joy? While there are those for whom this is a frequent and familiar feeling, for others the difficulties and disillusionments of life predominate. It could be said that the "diseases" of cynicism, discouragement, and depression have reached an epidemic stage in modern times.

Some of us even find it hard to enjoy ourselves when things are going well. It's as if we don't have permission or believe it's possible to experience real joy or bliss—perhaps we consider these emotions unrealistic or inappropriate. And taking in the news each day only seems to add the weight of the world's problems to our own. Joy feels out of place.

The natural world is one realm where positive feelings aren't endangered species. Nature walkers aren't strangers to heightened moods. The combination of exercise, fresh air, freedom of movement, splendid scenery, and peaceful relaxation appears to conspire to create feelings that may include contentment, happiness, a sense of the rightness of life, and sometimes joy.

Walking as Meditation

There's no better environment for meditation than the natural world, and walking itself can be a superb form of meditation. The positive effects are similar to those often experienced in other forms of meditation—including a deep sense of being connected and grounded.

The benefical effects will be diminished if you allow your mind to continuously churn with thoughts. You can foster the meditative qualities of walking by going slowly, gently calming your mind, and letting go of thoughts as they arise. Focus in a restful way on your breathing or on the movement of your feet.

Walking and Fulfillment

Feelings of deep satisfaction, fulfillment, and of being nourished and complete are uncommon experiences these days. Sources of fulfillment seem inaccessible to many of us, and these feelings are clearly incompatible with being rushed, overworked, worried, or stressed out.

Nature walkers frequently find life to be otherwise, since the activity offers physical, emotional, and spiritual satisfactions. It meets deep needs some of us are barely aware of. Walking puts us in our element, links us to the landscape, serves as an expression of our being, and sometimes even fills us to overflowing.

Walking and Centeredness

In a world filled with demands and distractions, it's easy to be out of touch with our own center, the core of our physical and spiritual being. Many of us don't know who we really are, deep down. Getting acquainted and becoming comfortable with our truest self may seem like an impossibility in this hyperactive world.

Long-known methods for achieving centeredness include deep relaxation, reflection, contemplation, and meditation. Yet even if we choose to engage in these practices, it's not easy to stay in balance after we return to the busy, stressful world.

When we "walk consciously" there's an interaction between thoughts and feelings, body and mind. The more we walk in nature, the more we're likely to feel at home in our body, and the more we'll get in touch with who we really are. This takes time. Eventually a deeper level of self-understanding may evolve.

Without getting too caught up in the process, try observing your thoughts, feelings, and bodily sensations as you walk. See if you find yourself starting to feel more centered and relaxed as time goes by. Try to take this feeling home with you.

Walking and Aliveness

Residing in the mental world or living in a sedentary way leaves us totally disconnected from the physical planet. By participating in physical activities we assert and accentuate our aliveness. The body gives us immediate feedback, confirming our identity as a living, breathing, vibrant creature.

Nature walking can be a virtual celebration of aliveness. When we walk in nature we come face-to-face with the rest of the living universe. We reinhabit the material world, return to a bodily existence, and can experience in the fullness of our being what it's like to be alive on this earth.

Walking and Serenity

Serenity is indeed a rare experience in today's world. How many of us regularly experience inner peace, calm, quiet, or contentment? The natural world is especially conducive to such feelings. When we walk in nature, even with many things on our mind, we may find that serenity is a very frequent companion.

Sometimes serenity arises mysteriously and unexpectedly. It often comes with a walking high during or after an extended outing. It may be experienced in the presence of beauty. It can even accompany a heightened awareness of our mortality, a realization that life and growth and death are all parts of a single process. While some people find these thoughts initially troubling, to understand that the life of which we're a part will continue on can lend a sense of hope for the future of life and the earth.

Walking and Appreciation

As we walk in nature we're likely to appreciate what we see and experience: the glories of a wild and spectacular landscape, and maybe the exciting adventures in store for us. Without forgetting the current ecological crisis, we can be thankful that some of the natural world does remain lovely and wild.

Appreciation and gratitude aren't popular sentiments in these times of often rampant cynicism and excessive self-aggrandizement. Many cultures and spiritual or religious traditions teach gratitude—and for good reason. It's healing for human beings to express thankfulness for what exists (in contrast to resenting what's wrong or what we don't have).

When we walk in nature it's ever easier to be grateful, and increasingly difficult to take the world for granted. This is not only good for us but also good for the earth, since we'll want to help protect and preserve what we most deeply appreciate, care about, and love. The world greatly needs our gratitude, as well as the positive actions that are likely to flow from it.

· 8 ·

Keeping our Planet Walkable

To some of us, nature is like a reliable old friend, a trustworthy companion who never lets us down. The natural world is a place where we can go to walk and find solace, strength, comfort, nourishment, hope—and almost anything else we need. Native peoples say the earth is our mother. For many of us, it's almost unthinkable that serious harm could come to her, and unimaginable that the world of nature could be at risk.

Yet it's no secret that the planet is in trouble. Each day's news brings disturbing evidence of new threats to human health and the deterioration of our ecosystem. The earth is practically groaning, it seems, from the weight of overpopulation, harmful pollution including toxic waste, and devastating warfare.

Worrying or obsessing about these problems is unproductive. We also still have a great deal to be thankful for, including the fact that many areas remain relatively unspoiled. But we can't walk away from the difficulties. It's vital that we all take responsibility for the future, that we do everything possible to ensure that the planet remains walkable for endless generations to come.

The Crisis

Human beings have walked the earth for hundreds of thousands of years. For most of this time our ancestors lived as a part of nature, not separate from it. While life for our predecessors wasn't always easy (although apparently not so difficult as we've sometimes been led to believe), their relationship with the environment was one of relative balance and harmony.

This has changed drastically during the past five to ten thousand years. Humanity has set itself apart from the rest of the universe, attempting to dominate nature and exploiting the resources of the earth on a staggering scale. Civilization, with all its apparent gifts and glories, has come at an enormous expense to the environment and in some respects to ourselves.

In this century we've had to face the frightening fact that human beings now have the power to destroy the earth, and are currently engaging in behavior that is rapidly pushing us in that direction. Although risks of a cataclysmic end from nuclear weapons seem to have temporarily subsided, we continue to pollute our water and air, dump toxic wastes, degrade the biosphere, and create unhealthy conditions for all forms of life. Deforestation and the destruction of other species proceeds at an accelerating pace, and millions of people now die prematurely from cancers that many believe are environmentally related. The extraordinary reality is that we're slowly decimating our own life-support system.

Most of us have difficulty acknowledging, discussing, and confronting these threats because the problems are so unpalatable. But we must somehow find the courage to act—to reverse the deterioration and create an environmentally sustainable society. Each of us must take personal responsibility for our destructive practices and work toward helping the earth in every possible way.

If you're unconvinced that we're in a real crisis—one that threatens our life-support system and the survival of humanity—read books by apolitical ecologists who examine current conditions and the planetary prognosis. Especially recommended is *The State of the Earth,* published annually by the Worldwatch Institute in Washington, D.C.

What You Can Do

On our own we can often accomplish more than we might imagine. Together we can make a huge difference. First, if you're not already a member, join and give financial support to as many national and local environmental organizations as you can afford. These organizations are dedicated to protecting individual natural areas as well as the ecosystem as a whole. They have diverse philosophies, but are all involved in important work, and need all the help they can get.

Be aware that a growing number of anti-environmental organizations, many of them financed by corporations, have sprung up in recent years. Some have names that suggest, deceptively, that they're for environmental protection, which they are not. Always study the literature of any group you aren't familiar with, and call to ask them questions before considering joining.

Second, the more informed you are, the better a friend and spokesperson for the earth you can become. Since you won't find the whole, complex story in newspapers or on television news, read magazines that focus on nature, ecology, and the environment, including those published by environmental groups. Also, try to read some books that treat these subjects in depth.

Be forewarned that along with the above-mentioned growth of anti-environmental groups—accompanied by an increase in the number of politicians and other public figures who express anti-environmental sentiments—has come a spate of books that purport to reveal the ecological crisis as a fraud and environmentalists as elitists. They distort the issues and should be read with a discerning eye.

Third, let your voice be heard. Call or write your congressperson to express your views, especially when an issue involving the environment is coming up for a vote. In recent years the anti-environmental lobby has become better organized and is vastly better financed than the conservation lobby. Your letter or call can make a real difference.

In this country we need a much more politically active, vocal citizenry who will say no to those politicians, government leaders, and executives of the multinational corporations that are willing to trade the future of this country, our children, thousands of other species, and the earth as a whole for a tidy profit.

You could also attend town, county, or community meetings where the issues are being debated, including hearings on environmental issues where public input is invited. Express your views aloud. Read about the issues in advance so you can speak with some knowledge and authority. If you're not comfortable with public speaking, find other ways to help.

Fourth, consider volunteering for a local environmental group or other organization engaged in protecting and preserving natural areas. Assist them in getting the word out about current problems and what can be done to defeat proposed exploitation of undeveloped areas. If there's no such group in your town or region, take the initiative to start one.

Minimizing Your Impact on the Earth

A vital contribution we can all make is to live in a way that doesn't harm the earth. Recycling, avoiding unnecessary waste, refraining from purchasing products we don't really need, ceasing actions that create pollution—these are all behaviors that can have a positive impact. The more of us who live and consume responsibly, the better shape the earth will be in.

Our behavior while walking in nature is also important. See the natural world as a community you belong to. It's obviously unacceptable to litter, throw cigarette butts, or leave any other sign of our presence other than footprints. No one should have to pick up after us, whether in the natural world or anywhere else. Use a plastic bag to carry any litter or garbage home with you.

Remember that vegetation is often fragile, especially at higher elevations. Try not to trample plants or flowers. If you're following a path, stay on it. If you're bushwhacking, watch where you step to avoid doing damage.

When camping out, practice it in a way that minimizes your impact on the earth. Try to leave no lasting signs of your visit. Never dig trenches around your tent, and if you're going to have a campfire, build it with extreme care. Use only dead, downed wood for firewood (never cut live trees, or even break off branches of dead standing trees). If you can't build a campfire without leaving a scar on the earth, forgo having one.

If you need to "go to the bathroom," use facilities when they're available or take care of your business responsibly. This means staying away —at least 150 feet or more—from lakes, ponds, streams, and other waterways. Solid waste should always be buried (except in those natural areas where you're required to carry out human waste in plastic bags). Always be aware of the potential impact your actions may have on the environment.

Making a More Walker-Friendly World

Having beautiful, green, and wild places to walk in should be the birthright of every person. After all, we're children of nature, members of a species that evolved as a part of the natural world. Surely we have every right, not to mention a deep need, to remain fully connected with this realm.

Some of us are fortunate to live near natural areas or in walker-friendly communities, where sidewalks, paths, and trails are convenient to reach and use. It's ideal when walkways are so accessible that you can head for town or take a nature walk without having to get into your car or a bus. Such places do exist, but unfortunately not for the majority of our population.

Most of us require transportation to get to a park or other place for nature walking, and some of us live in areas that aren't really suitable for any kind of walking. Too many urban residents endure unhealthy, unnatural, congested environs, while some suburbanites settle for sidewalk-less and artifically landscaped imitation nature, where the forests have been flattened and replaced by vast malls or golf courses.

Not enough of the natural world is visible to most us on a daily basis, which deprives us of an important source of beauty and inspiration. It also makes it easier for us to forget that we aren't the only important beings on this planet, that the natural realm is deeply deserving of our respect.

Most of us would agree that enough of the country has been paved over. Aside from protecting existing parks and preserves, we need to maintain greenbelts in regions surrounding cities and suburbs, keeping open as many walking options as possible.

Much more could be done to create new parks in developed areas, even in these times of budgetary shortfalls. Sometimes a combination of public and private funding can be used to purchase undeveloped lands or to restore a tract to a more natural condition. Contact your local parks department or environmental groups to see if any such efforts are being made. Let elected officials know if you think more should be done. Perhaps you could start a campaign to help win public support for new parks.

One critical issue that doesn't receive nearly enough attention is population growth. While many pro-development "experts" proclaim that we've got plenty of room for more, that the carrying capacity of the earth is several times what we have now, these arguments just can't be supported from an ecological standpoint.

We're already in the process of wiping out most other species, and the resource needs of so many human beings cannot possibly be met in the long run. Further population growth worldwide is certain to cause untold suffering for all species, including our own. What's necessary (and certain to be unpopular with vested interests) is to actually reduce population size in the coming decades. How this might be humanely accomplished is beyond the scope of this discussion, but at a minimum, we must all be conscious of the ecological costs of bringing more children into the world. Family planning should be universal.

The news may be troubling, and time may be running out for us if we're not willing to make the difficult choices, but thankfully there remain grounds for hope. The earth has a capacity to heal itself, to mend much of the damage that's been done, if we give it a chance. There are no easy solutions (think about the enormous load we've saddled future generations with regarding the disposal and containment of nuclear and other toxic waste). Yet most people do care about nature, value parks, and want posterity to inherit a world worth living in.

Walk in nature and you'll be reminded every time of what it is that's worth keeping, protecting, treasuring. Try to find the time, energy, and motivation to write your elected officials. Send letters to the editor of your local newspaper, join environmental groups if you don't already belong, and do whatever else you can to see that our natural areas remain protected.

At the same time, try to let go of it all every now and then, and get out there on foot to enjoy the natural splendors we're still blessed with. Appreciate the exquisite beauty, the preciousness, the unbelievable richness of it all. Sometimes human beings get off track, and sometimes they find their way back. With your help, people should be able to enjoy walking in nature for a long time to come.

Part II

WHERE TO ENJOY NATURE WALKING IN THE UNITED STATES

· 9 ·

Selection Criteria

In each of the following fifty state chapters you'll find descriptions of ten "Recommended Areas for Nature Walks," which add up to five hundred for the country. Selections were made from literally thousands of national, state, and local parks, preserves, forests, sanctuaries, and other natural areas.

How Areas Were Chosen

The areas chosen for inclusion here have easy trails suitable for nature walks and at the same time offer beautiful or outstanding natural scenery. Priority was given to those locations with the greatest number of appropriate trails as well as the wildest, most spectacular surroundings.

I've limited selections to areas with marked and easy-to-follow trails, so many outstanding natural sites throughout the country that did not meet this criterion were omitted. A small number of exceptions were made in states where marked trails are scarce; the few unmarked trails I've recommended in such areas should be easy to follow.

In some states there were literally dozens of qualified places to choose from, whereas in a handful of others it was a challenge to find ten (namely states where parks are fewer in number, smaller, and less likely to have nature or hiking trails, or in those mountainous regions where easy trails are rare).

The information in each of the descriptions of recommended areas was obtained by mail or phone directly from the parks and preserves themselves, and often supplemented from other sources. I have also paid personal visits to a number (but by no means all) of these locations over the past twenty-five years.

Some places that would clearly qualify were left out of the book at the request of park staff. Typical reasons given were that an area already receives too many visitors or is considered too small or fragile to be able to sustain much human impact.

Other parks and preserves failed to respond to repeated requests for information, and most of these have been omitted, even though some undoubtedly would be appropriate. Reasons for a lack of response probably include inadequate staff owing to severe budget cuts in recent years or, in some cases, a desire to avoid additional publicity.

Others that did respond had to be excluded because the information sent was inadequate. In some instances I've included a qualified location for which little descriptive information could be obtained (especially in states where areas with easy nature trails are few), resulting in an unusually brief listing.

How Trails Were Chosen

The final paragraph of each listing offers "Suggested Trails for Nature Walks." The choices were based on information provided in park literature, on recommendations of park staff, and in some cases on my personal trail exploration.

The trails are generally listed in order of length and difficulty, with the shortest and easiest trails first. You will find a few exceptions, however, such as when a longer trail comes especially recommended, it includes exceptionally fine scenery, or it's more easily accessible.

Descriptions of individual trails could not be provided here—impossible in a book that surveys several thousand easy and easy-moderate trails throughout the country. By taking a look at each area's suggested trails, however, you'll get an idea of what some of the options are and what to look or ask for when visiting the site. Detailed descriptions of individual trails will often be found in local guidebooks, and some parks offer booklets or other printed information about trails.

Trail Difficulty

The simplest and most widely used rating system for trails features the categories "easy," "moderate," and "strenuous." In this book, I use the ratings "easy" and "moderate," along with the in-between category "easy-moderate."

As defined here, an *easy* trail is one that may be hilly but has no elevation changes greater than 200 to 300 feet and isn't steep except perhaps for an occasional short stretch. An easy trail may include some rocks, tree roots, and other rough spots along the way, but the footing isn't rugged.

An *easy-moderate* trail will often have elevation changes of 300 to 700 feet and is sometimes rocky but still not truly rugged. A more challenging *moderate* trail can involve elevation changes up to 1,000 feet or a bit more, and may include a somewhat rugged treadway part of the way.

All ratings other than easy are given in parentheses after the name of the trail, as in (easy-moderate) or (moderate). If no rating is listed, a trail may be assumed to be easy. A *loop* (identified in parenthesis unless it's part of the trail name) indicates a circular route, so the stated length is the total amount you'll walk from start to finish. Where the word *loop* is not used, the distance given is one way. Thus you'll be walking double the stated length if you return the way you came, and even farther if you take another trail back.

Evaluating and comparing the difficulty of trails in different areas and parts of the country have presented complications. While the easy-moderate-strenuous system is relatively standard, what's actually considered easy or strenuous in one place is often judged otherwise elsewhere, meaning the definitions are far from universal. For example, a trail with an elevation change of as little as 100 feet may be rated strenuous in the flatlands, whereas in higher mountain regions a trail with a gradual 1,000 to 2,000-foot climb will sometimes be called easy!

Since there's no consistency in trail ratings from one area to another, I've often had to transpose or adjust the ratings provided by parks to fit my own categories. In some cases, where complete information about elevation changes could not be obtained, it was necessary to make educated guesses.

Although painstaking efforts have been made to provide the most accurate information possible, errors were occasionally found in ratings received from the parks, and could have slipped in at other stages of information gathering. For these and other reasons, it's wise to never place complete trust in a trail rating.

When contacting a park for a detailed trail map and/or information about where to find the trails, try to verify that a particular trail is indeed suitable for your purposes (and also that it's currently open for public use; trails are subject to closure without notice for a number of possible reasons). On the walk itself, always use your judgment and be prepared to turn back if a trail seems too difficult for you.

· 10 ·

In a Pinch

If you don't have easy access to the natural areas that are recommended in this book, should you stay at home? Of course not. Wherever you live there are almost certain to be one or more parks, preserves, or sanctuaries within a short walk, drive, or bus or train ride. Many of our greatest cities, with all their imperfections, have large and lovely parks, as do countless towns and sprawling, mall-lined suburbs. While you won't always be out of sight of buildings or free from the sounds of traffic, you'll still be enjoying an oasis and refuge of sanity and beauty. Nature is thankfully capable of thriving almost anywhere.

You'll benefit much more from a daily walk in an urban, county, suburban, or village park than an occasional trip to the most glorious or pristine places. Do visit the nation's natural treasures whenever you can. The rest of the time get to know your local parks and preserves as intimately as possible, support them in every way you can, value their scenic uniqueness, enjoy their flora and fauna, and use them to foster your nature-walking habit!

· 11 ·

A State-by-State Guide

ALABAMA

Recommended Areas for Nature Walks

LAKE GUNTERSVILLE STATE PARK 190 Campground Road, Guntersville, AL 35976; (205)571-5444. 6,200 acres. This state park is located alongside northern Alabama's Lake Guntersville, on the dammed-up Tennessee River. The park includes sandstone and limestone rock formations, small caves, creeks, and an oak-hickory forest with pine, maple, and wild azalea. Among the wildlife are white-tailed deer, fox, raccoon, bald eagle, and wild turkey. Naturalist-led walks are offered in summer.

• *Suggested Trails for Nature Walks:* 1. The 0.5-mile Nature Trail. 2. The 0.5-mile Old Still Path. 3. The 1.5-mile Cave Trail. 4. The 2.5-mile Cutchenmine Trail. 5. The 2-mile Seale's Trail. 6. The 0.8-mile Waterfall Trail (easy-moderate). 7. The 1-mile Cascade Trail (easy-moderate). 8. The 1.5-mile Loop Trail (easy-moderate). 9. The 3-mile Tom Bevill Interpretive Trail (easy-moderate loop). 10. The 2.5-mile Lickskillet Trail (easy-moderate).

WHEELER NATIONAL WILDLIFE REFUGE Route 4, Box 250, Decatur, AL 35603; (205)353-7243. 34,500 acres. Wheeler National Wildlife Refuge is on Wheeler Reservoir and the Tennessee River in northern Alabama. This is an area of hardwood bottomlands and pine uplands, with open fields and wetlands, swamps and sloughs, ponds and creeks. The refuge protects wintering migratory birds including Canada and snow goose, black duck, and canvasback, as well as owl, hawk, bald eagle, and peregrine falcon, with white-tailed deer, opossum, raccoon, bat, and alligator among the other wildlife.

• *Suggested Trails for Nature Walks:* 1. The 0.3-mile Observation Building Trail. 2. The 0.5-mile Atkeson Trail. 3. The 0.8-mile Beaverdam Boardwalk. 4. The 1.5-mile Environmental Trail. 5. The 2-mile Dancy Bottom Trail.

GULF STATE PARK 20115 State Highway 135, Gulf Shores, AL 36542; (205)948-7275. 6,000 acres. Located in southwestern Alabama alongside the Gulf of Mexico, this state park features more than 2 miles of sand beaches, three freshwater lakes, some small streams, areas of sawgrass, and stands of oak trees with saw palmetto. Wildlife includes alligator and gray fox.

• *Suggested Trails for Nature Walks:* 1. The 0.75-mile Hurricane Ridge Trail. 2. The 0.75-mile Bear Creek Trail. 3. The 0.75-mile Bobcat Branch Trail. 4. The 1.5-mile Middle Lake Trail.

TALLADEGA NATIONAL FOREST 2946 Chestnut Street, Montgomery, AL 36107; (205)832-4470. 383,841 acres. Largest of the state's four national forests, Talladega National Forest consists of two tracts in west-central and east-central Alabama. There's a designated wilderness area, the 7,490-acre Cheaha Wilderness, and terrain includes small and rugged mountains of the southern Appalachians, with vistas from rock bluffs and outcroppings. There are also lakes, streams, and a forest of longleaf,

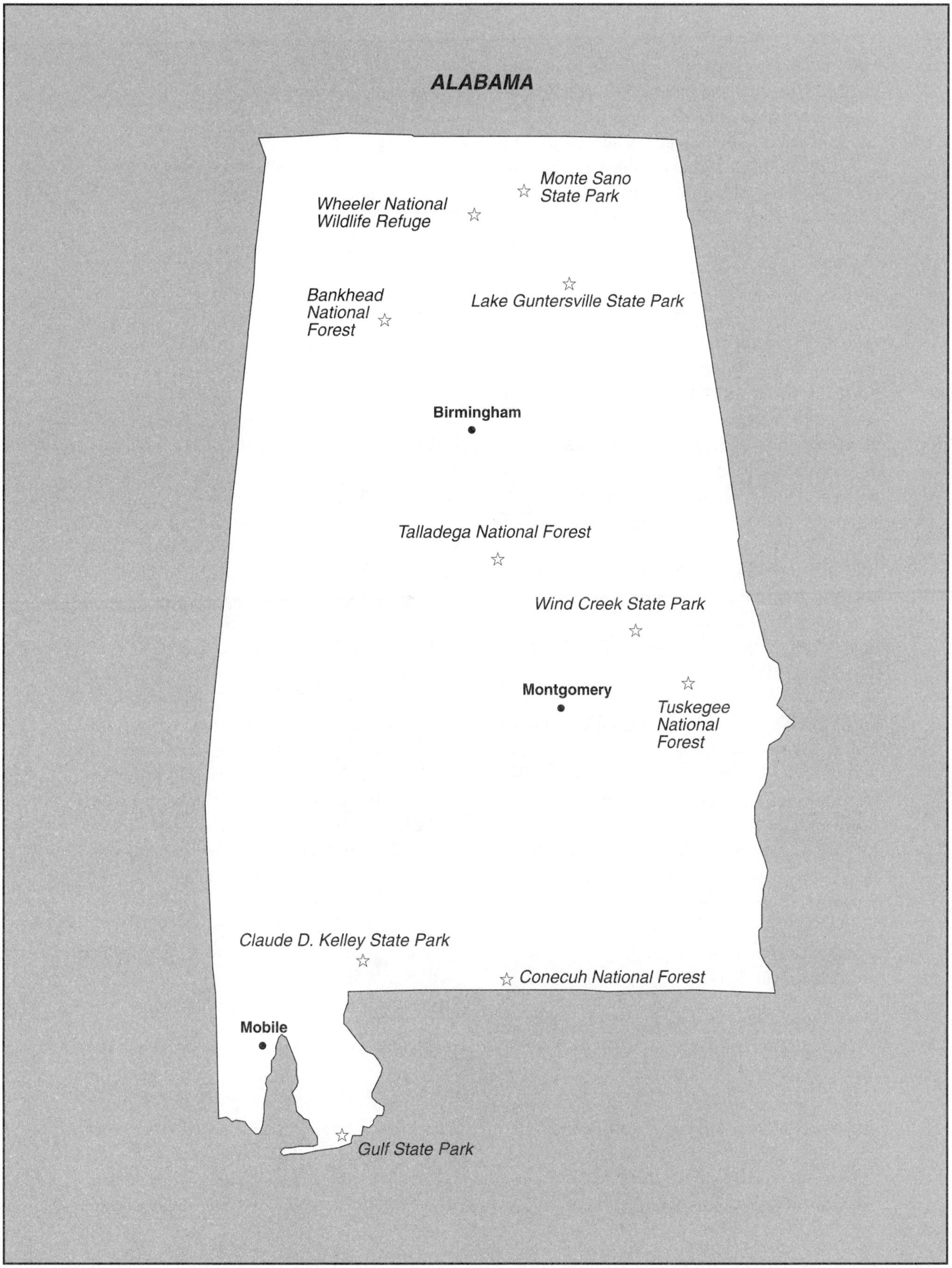

ALABAMA

Monte Sano State Park

Wheeler National Wildlife Refuge

Bankhead National Forest

Lake Guntersville State Park

Birmingham

Talladega National Forest

Wind Creek State Park

Montgomery

Tuskegee National Forest

Claude D. Kelley State Park

Conecuh National Forest

Mobile

Gulf State Park

Virginia, and loblolly pine, with chestnut oak, dogwood, redbud, and mountain laurel. White-tailed deer, bobcat, fox, opossum, beaver, hawk, and wild turkey are among the wildlife.

• *Suggested Trails for Nature Walks:* 1. The 1.5-mile Lake Chinnabee Loop Trail. 2. The 6-mile Chinnabee Silent Trail (easy-moderate). 3. The 10-mile Odum Scout Trail (easy-moderate). 4. The Nubbin Creek Trail (moderate). 5. Portions of the 100-mile Pinhota National Recreation Trail, which stretches the length of the forest, offer easy walking.

MONTE SANO STATE PARK 5105 Nolen Avenue, Huntsville, AL 35801; (205)534-3757. 2,140 acres. Situated on a small mountain in northern Alabama, Monte Sano State Park has wooded slopes with overlooks and creeks with waterfalls. The facilities include a planetarium as well as an observatory. In addition to ten trails in the park, there are eight additional trails in the adjacent Huntsville Land Trust.

• *Suggested Trails for Nature Walks:* 1. The 1.5-mile White Trail. 2. The 2-mile Blue Trail. 3. The 3.2-mile Red Trail.

CLAUDE D. KELLEY STATE PARK Route 2, Box 77, Atmore, AL 36502; (334)862-2511. 960 acres. This state park in southwestern Alabama features a 25-acre lake, streams, an abundance of ferns, and a mixed forest of pine, oak, hickory, and sweetgum. Wildlife includes white-tailed deer, armadillo, gopher tortoise, wild turkey, pileated woodpecker, owl, and red-tailed hawk.

• *Suggested Trails for Nature Walks:* 1. The 2-mile CCC Trail. 2. The 3.5-mile Gazebo Trail.

WIND CREEK STATE PARK 4325 Alabama Highway 128, Alexander City, AL 35010; (205)329-0845. 1,445 acres. Wind Creek State Park is situated on the shore of man-made, 40,000-acre Lake Martin in east-central Alabama. Included are some low ridges with rock outcroppings, small streams, wildflowers, ferns, and a forest of oak, pine, and dogwood. Among the wildlife are white-tailed deer and wild turkey. The park has a nature center, and guided walks are available.

• *Suggested Trails for Nature Walks:* 1. The 2.5-mile Campfire Trail, which consists of several loops. 2. The 5.5-mile Alabama Reunion Trail (loop).

CONECUH NATIONAL FOREST Route 5, Box 157, Andalusia, AL 36420; (205)222-2555. 83,037 acres. Situated in southern Alabama just above the Florida border, Conecuh National Forest has a number of small ponds and lakes, swamplands, and many streams, and includes the Yellow and Conecuh rivers. There are forests of longleaf pine, magnolia, dogwood, holly, and cypress, with white-tailed deer, raccoon, wild turkey, and alligator among the wildlife.

• *Suggested Trails for Nature Walks:* The 20-mile Conecuh Trail, which consists of three loops, meanders through a nearly flat area of coastal plain and passes several ponds.

TUSKEGEE NATIONAL FOREST 125 National Forest Road 949, Tuskegee, AL 36083; (205)727-2652. 11,073 acres. This national forest in eastern Alabama has rolling hills and pine ridges, hardwood bottomlands with magnolia and dogwood, many wildflowers, ponds, and major streams including Uphapee and Choctafaula creeks. Included is the 125-acre Tsinia Wildlife Viewing Area, with white-tailed deer, beaver, raccoon, quail, and wild turkey among the wildlife here.

• *Suggested Trails for Nature Walks:* The 8.6-mile Bartram National Recreation Trail (which will eventually be part of a much longer trail stretching throughout the Southeast).

BANKHEAD NATIONAL FOREST P.O. Box 278, Double Springs, AL 35553; (205)489-5111. 180,173 acres. This national forest in northwest Alabama encompasses some small mountains and valleys, sandstone cliffs and gorges, lakes and streams with waterfalls, hardwood forests, and wildlife that includes white-tailed deer and wild turkey. Of special interest are the 25,986-acre Sipsey Wilderness and the 61-mile Sipsey National Wild and Scenic River.

• *Suggested Trails for Nature Walks:* 1. Over 23 miles of interconnecting easy to moderate trails wind throughout the Sipsey Wilderness, including some trails along the Sipsey River. 2. There's a 30-mile system of horse trails in the forest, and these are open to foot travel as well.

Other Suitable Locations for Nature Walks in Alabama

Alabama has a total of twenty-four state parks, and twenty of these locations have trails. Information: Alabama Division of State Parks, P.O. Box 301452, Montgomery, AL 36130; (334)242-3333.

There are two state forests with trails: 1. Choccolocco State Forest, 1633 Joseph Springs Motorway, Anniston, AL 36201; (205)236-5709. 2. Little River State Forest, Route 2, Box 78, Atmore, AL 36502; (334)862-2411.

Several U.S. Army Corps of Engineers areas have trails. Information: Corps of Engineers, Mobile District, P.O. Box 2288, Mobile, AL 36628; (205)694-3720.

Two national wildlife refuges in Alabama include trails: 1. Bon Secour National Wildlife Refuge, P.O. Box 1650, Gulf Shores, AL 36542; (205)968-8623. 2. Eufaula National Wildlife Refuge, Route 2, Box 97B, Eufaula, AL 36027; (205)687-4065.

ALASKA

Recommended Areas for Nature Walks

TONGASS NATIONAL FOREST 16,700,000 acres. Located along the panhandle of southeast Alaska, this largest of all U.S. national forests is so huge that it has three separate headquarters: Stikine Area, P.O. Box 309, Petersburg, AK 99833, (907)772-3841 ; Ketchikan Area, Federal Building, Ketchikan, AK 99901, (907)225-3101; Chatham Area, 204 Siginaka Way, Sitka, AK 99835, (907)774-6671.

The forest has nineteen designated wilderness areas totaling 5,700,000 acres. Included are the Admiralty Island National Monument, much of which was designated the Kootznoowoo Wilderness in 1990, and the 2,300,000-acre Misty Fiords National Monument. There are areas of coastal rain forest with Sitka spruce, western hemlock, and western redcedar, muskegs (marshy areas) and bogs, alpine meadows and fiords, freshwater lakes and rivers, and streams with waterfalls.

Also here are rugged mountains and glaciated valleys, high-walled canyons and rock spires, glaciers, icefields, and snowfields, as well as thousands of islands. Wildlife includes black and grizzly bear, black-tailed deer, mountain goat, wolf, a large population of bald eagle, plus whale, sea lion, and seal offshore. Some of the trails are accessible only by boat or floatplane.

• *Suggested Trails for Nature Walks:* 1. The 1-mile Anan Creek Trail. 2. The 1.3-mile Ward Lake Nature Trail. 3. The 1-mile Hamilton Creek Trail. 4. The 2.3-mile Perserverence Lake Trail. 5. The 2.5-mile Kah Sheets Lake Trail. 6. The 4.5-mile Three Lakes Trail. 7. The 4-mile Aaron Creek Trail. 8. The 10.5-mile Petersburg Lake Trail. 9. The 10.2-mile Portage Mountain Loop Trail. 10. The 2.5-mile Colp Lake Trail (easy-moderate).

CHUGACH NATIONAL FOREST 3301 C Street, Suite 300, Anchorage, AK 99503; (907)271-2500. 5,600,000 acres. The second largest national forest in the United States, Chugach is situated along the south-central coast of Alaska, southeast of Anchorage. Within its boundaries are Prince William Sound, with sizable islands and 3,500 miles of coastline, the Kenai Peninsula and Kenai Mountains, the Chugach Mountains, and the 700,000-acre Copper River Delta.

There are high mountain ridges and valleys, with large glaciers and lakes, rivers and streams, saltwater bays and wetlands, alpine meadows, and spruce forests. Wildlife includes moose, grizzly and black bear, caribou, black-tailed deer, Dall sheep, mountain goat, wolf, wolverine, and bald eagle. Most of the forest's trails are on the Kenai Peninsula.

• *Suggested Trails for Nature Walks:* 1. The 0.5-mile Willawaw National Recreation Trail. 2. The 1-mile Byron Glacier Trail. 3. The 2-mile Grayling Lake Trail. 4. The 2.1-mile McKinley Lake Trail. 5. The 6.5-mile Crescent Creek Trail. 6. The 5.1-mile Guil Rock Trail. 7. The 3.5-mile Winner Creek Gorge Trail. 8. The 16-mile Resur-

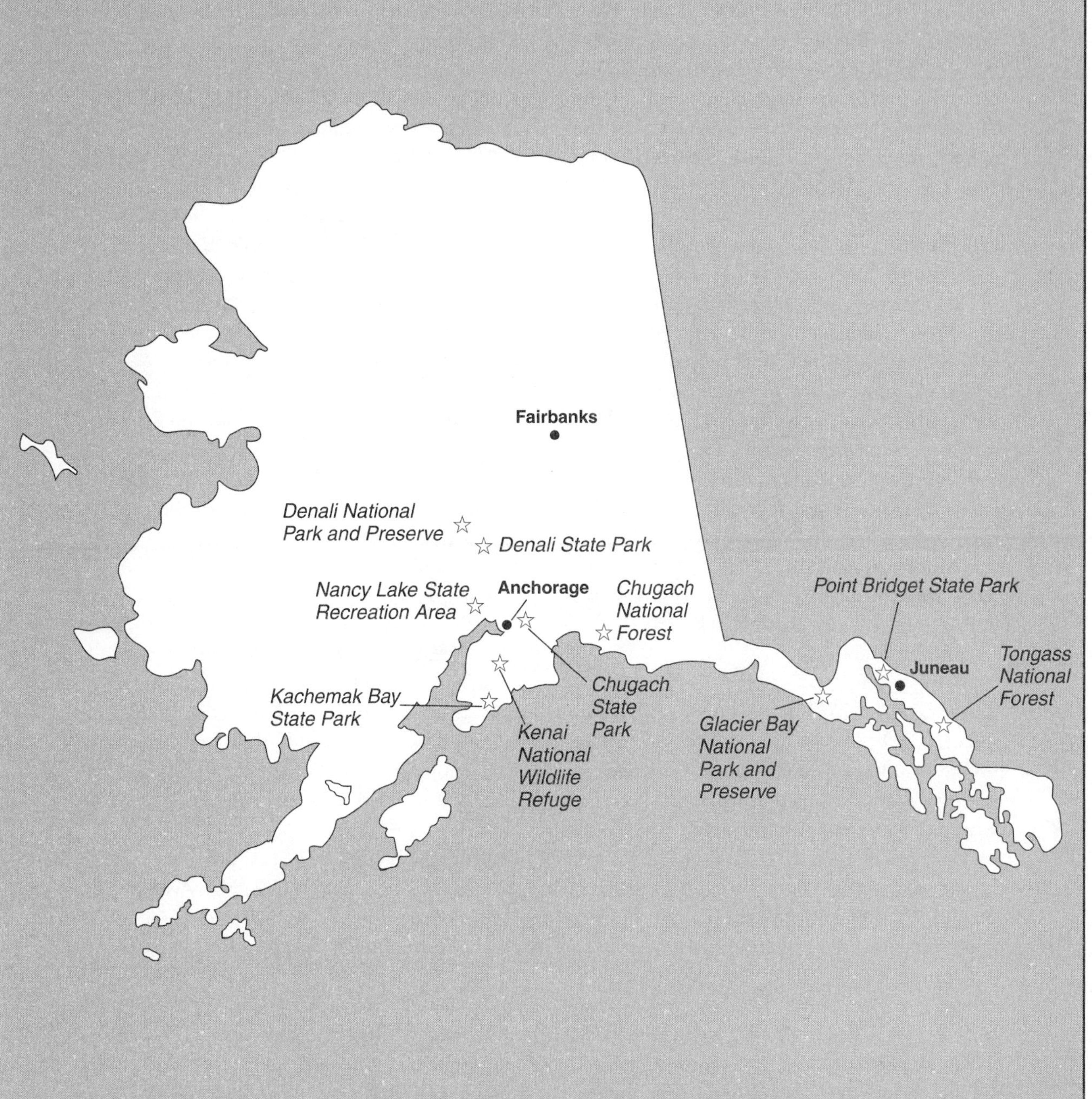
ALASKA
Fairbanks
Denali National Park and Preserve
Denali State Park
Nancy Lake State Recreation Area
Anchorage
Chugach National Forest
Point Bridget State Park
Juneau
Tongass National Forest
Chugach State Park
Kachemak Bay State Park
Kenai National Wildlife Refuge
Glacier Bay National Park and Preserve

rection River Trail. 9. The 21-mile Russian Lakes Trail. 10. The 38.5-mile Resurrection Pass Trail.

DENALI NATIONAL PARK AND PRESERVE P.O. Box 9, Denali Park, AK 99755; (907)683-2686. 6,000,000 acres. Located in the Alaska Range, in the south-central part of the state, Denali National Park is named after the highest mountain in North America, long known as Mt. McKinley (20,320 feet). While dominated by Denali, the park is also a vast wilderness of other mountains, glaciers, and perpetual snowfields.

There are dozens of rivers and creeks, sparse spruce forests along with birch and aspen at elevations up to 2,700 feet, and areas of subarctic tundra. Grizzly bear, moose, caribou, Dall sheep, wolf, lynx, wolverine, fox, and golden eagle are among the wildlife. All established trails are near the park entrance; the rest of the park is trail-less. Ranger-led walks are available.

• *Suggested Trails for Nature Walks:* 1. The 1.3-mile Morino Loop Trail. 2. The 1.3-mile Taiga Loop Trail. 3. The 1.5-mile Horseshoe Lake Trail. 4. The 2.3-mile Rock Creek Trail. 5. The 1.8-mile Roadside Trail.

GLACIER BAY NATIONAL PARK AND PRESERVE P.O. Box 140, Gustavus, AK 99826; (907)697-2230. 3,280,000 acres. Situated in southeast Alaska, this national park and preserve occupies an area that was completely covered by glaciers as recently as 200 years ago. It includes the Fairweather and Takhinsha mountain ranges, with 15,320-foot Mt. Fairweather the highest point. Access is only by air or boat.

There are many glaciers, icefields, fiords with icebergs, rocky cliffs, beaches, rivers and streams, lakes and ponds, spruce-hemlock forests, thickets of alder, and alpine meadows. Wildlife includes grizzly and black bear, moose, wolf, coyote, and bald eagle, as well as several species of whale, porpoise, and seal. Guided walks are offered by ranger-naturalists. All established trails are in Bartlett Cove, near the Glacier Bay Lodge.

• *Suggested Trails for Nature Walks:* 1. The 1-mile Forest Trail. 2. The 2-mile Bartlett River Trail. 3. The 3-mile Bartlett Lake Trail. 4. The shoreline beach of Bartlett Cove is suitable for walking.

KENAI NATIONAL WILDLIFE REFUGE P.O. Box 2139, Soldotna, AK 99669; (907)262-7021. 1,970,000 acres. This national wildlife refuge is located southwest of Anchorage on the Kenai Peninsula, adjacent to Chugach National Forest as well as Kenai Fjords National Park. The landscape here includes the Kenai Mountains with elevations over 6,000 feet, glaciers, and narrow valleys, with nine river systems, many lakes, and extensive wetlands.

Approximately 1,350,000 acres of the refuge are designated as wilderness, and unlike most wildlife refuges in Alaska or elsewhere, there are many miles of established trails. Among the wildlife are moose, Dall sheep, caribou, black and grizzly bear, mountain goat, wolf, lynx, coyote, and trumpeter swan.

• *Suggested Trails for Nature Walks:* 1. The 1-mile Silver Lake Trail. 2. The 1.4-mile Hidden Creek Trail. 3. The 1.3-mile Drake-Skookum Trail. 4. The 7-mile Seven Lakes Trail. 5. The 1-mile Bear Mountain Trail (moderate). 6. The 2.6-mile Skilak Lookout Trail (moderate). 7. The 6.3-mile Kenai River Trail (moderate). 8. The 20.8-mile Funny River Trail (moderate).

POINT BRIDGET STATE PARK c/o Southeast Area Office, 400 Willoughby Avenue, 3rd Floor, Juneau, AK 99801; (907)465-4563. 2,850 acres. Point Bridget State Park is situated on Berners Bay and the Lynn Canal, 40 miles north of Juneau. It's an area of low mountains and cliffs, rocky shoreline and beaches, meadows and streams, old-growth rain forest with Sitka spruce, as well as pine and cedar forest. Wildlife includes black bear, porcupine, beaver, Canada goose, and bald eagle, with humpback whale, harbor seal, and sea lion offshore.

• *Suggested Trails for Nature Walks:* 1. The 0.5-mile Raleigh Trail. 2. The 1-mile North Bridget

Cove Trail. 3. The 1.2-mile McMurchie Cat Road. 4. The 3.5-mile Point Bridget Trail. 5. The 2.1-mile Cedar Lake Trail. 6. The 2.5-mile Trappers Trail.

DENALI STATE PARK HC 32, Box 6706, Wasilla, AK 99687; (907)495-6273. 324,240 acres. Located 100 miles north of Anchorage and next to Denali National Park, this state park includes low ridges and hills at the foot of the Alaska Range, among them Kesugi and Curry ridges. Also here are the Chulitna and Tokositna rivers, along with many streams, alpine meadows and tundra, and forests of white spruce and paper birch, as well as alder and willow, cottonwood and poplar. Wildlife includes grizzly and black bear, moose, caribou, wolf, coyote, lynx, red fox, trumpeter swan, and arctic tern.

• *Suggested Trails for Nature Walks:* 1. The 1.2-mile Chulitna Confluence Trail. 2. The 4.8-mile Byers Lake Loop Trail. 3. The 15.2-mile Troublesome Creek Trail (moderate).

KACHEMAK BAY STATE PARK Division of Parks and Outdoor Recreation, P.O. Box 107001, Anchorage, AK 99510; (907)762-2617. 250,000 acres. Situated on Kachemak Bay next to Kenai National Wildlife Refuge and Kenai Fjords National Park, this large state park has mountains and rock formations, glaciers and snowfields, as well as rivers, streams, lakes, and bogs. The vegetation includes alpine tundra, open meadows, and spruce forests along with alder and cottonwood. Whale, seal, and sea otter are found offshore, with bald eagle and puffin among the bird life. Access to the park is by boat or plane.

• *Suggested Trails for Nature Walks:* 1. The 3.5-mile Grewingk Glacier Trail. 2. The 2-mile Wosnesenski Trail (easy-moderate). 3. The 2.5-mile China Poot Lake Trail (easy-moderate). 4. The 1-mile Saddle Trail (moderate).

CHUGACH STATE PARK HC 52, Box 8999, Indian, AK 99540; (907)345-5014. 495,000 acres. Located next to lands of Chugach National Forest in south-central Alaska, this large state park has steep mountain ridges and cirques, wide valleys with mountain lakes and streams, glaciers and icefields, coastal forests, and alpine tundra. Elevations range from sea level to 8,000 feet. Wildlife includes grizzly and black bear, moose, Dall sheep, wolf, mountain goat, hawk, eagle, and whale offshore.

• *Suggested Trails for Nature Walks:* 1. The 2.5-mile Rabbit and McHugh Lakes Trail. 2. The 9-mile Old Johnson Trail. 3. The 6.5-mile Williwaw Lakes Trail (easy-moderate). 4. The 11-mile Powerline Trail (moderate). 5. The 22-mile Arctic to Indian Traverse (moderate).

NANCY LAKE STATE RECREATION AREA HC 32, Box 6706, Wasilla, AK 99687; (907)745-3975. 22,685 acres. Nancy Lake State Recreation Area lies in the Susitna River Valley of south-central Alaska, north of Anchorage. It's a relatively flat area with low hills and dozens of lakes and ponds, several of them large, as well as muskeg swamps, bogs, and streams. There are wildflowers, brushy areas, and forests of spruce, aspen, and birch, along with cranberry, currant, and blueberry bushes. Among the wildlife are moose, black bear, beaver, loon, and arctic tern.

• *Suggested Trails for Nature Walks:* 1. The 1-mile Tulik Trail (loop). 2. The 3-mile Red Shirt Lake Trail.

Other Suitable Locations for Nature Walks in Alaska

Alaska has over 100 state parks, state recreation sites, and state recreation areas. A number of these locations have trails. Information: Division of Parks & Outdoor Recreation, 3601 C Street, Suite 1200, Anchorage, AK 99503; (907)762-2617.

There are fifteen national parks and preserves in the state, and most of them are enormous and remote. Although walking is feasible in some areas, established trails are few. Information: Alaska Regional Office, National Park Service,

2525 Gambell Street, Room 107, Anchorage, AK 99503; (907)271-2643.

Most of the sixteen national wildlife refuges in Alaska are likewise huge, remote, and without trails, although open to walking. Information: U.S. Fish and Wildlife Service, 1011 East Tudor Road, Anchorage, AK 99503; (907) 786-3487.

A few Bureau of Land Management–administered areas in the state have trails. Information: BLM Alaska State Office, 222 West 7th Avenue, Anchorage, AK 99513; (907)271-5555.

ARIZONA

Recommended Areas for Nature Walks

GRAND CANYON NATIONAL PARK P.O. Box 129, Grand Canyon, AZ 86023; (520)638-7888. 1,218,375 acres. One of the best-known and most spectacular natural areas in the country, this national park in northwest Arizona encompasses the eroded Grand Canyon of the Colorado River, which is a mile deep, up to 18 miles wide, and 277 miles long. Vistas from the canyon rims are world famous.

There are spruce-fir forests with ponderosa pine and aspen on the north rim, and Lower Sonoran Desert vegetation below, including cacti and yucca. Among the wildlife are mule deer, desert bighorn sheep, mountain lion, bobcat, coyote, fox, bat, great horned owl, American kestrel, and red-tailed hawk. Only rim trails offer easy walks; trails that descend into the canyon involve a steep uphill return. Guided walks are available.

• *Suggested Trails for Nature Walks:* 1. The 0.5-mile Cape Royal Trail (North Rim). 2. The 1-mile Cliff Springs Trail (North Rim). 3. The short Bright Angel Point Trail (North Rim). 4. The 1.5-mile Transept Trail (North Rim). 5. The 5-mile Wildforss Trail (North Rim). 6. The 5-mile Uncle Jim Trail (North Rim). 7. The 8.5-mile South Rim Trail; a 3.5-mile stretch is paved and called the South Rim Nature Trail. 8. The 12-mile Ken Patrick Trail (North Rim/moderate).

SAGUARO NATIONAL PARK 3693 South Old Spanish Trail, Tucson, AZ 85730, (602)883-6366 (Saguaro West); (602)296-8576 (Saguaro East). 83,651 acres. Consisting of two units in the Sonoran Desert's Rincon and Tucson mountains, east and west of Tucson, this park protects extensive stands of saguaro cactus. It was recently promoted from national monument to national park status.

Nearly 60,000 acres of the park consist of designated wilderness. There are desert grasslands, pine-oak woodlands, mixed conifer forests higher up, and many kinds of cacti, including cholla and prickly pear, with mesquite and ocotillo. Wildlife includes coyote, javelina, fox, and red-tailed hawk.

• *Suggested Trails for Nature Walks:* 1. The 0.3-mile Desert Ecology Trail (loop). 2. The 0.3-mile Signal Hill Petroglyph Trail (loop). 3. The 0.5-mile Desert Discovery Nature Trail (loop). 4. The 0.8-mile Valley View Overlook Trail. 5. The 1-mile Freeman Homestead Nature Trail (loop). 6. The 2.5-mile Cactus Forest Trail (inside Loop Drive). 7. The first 1.2 miles of the Loma Verde Trail (easy-moderate). 8. The 1.4-mile Garwood Trail (easy-moderate). 9. The 2-mile Squeeze Pen Trail (easy-moderate). 10. The 3.6-mile Carrillo Trail (easy-moderate).

COCONINO NATIONAL FOREST 2323 East Greenlaw Lane, Flagstaff, AZ 86004; (602)527-3600. 1,821,495 acres. Coconino National Forest in north-central Arizona features a high-desert plateau with deep canyons, high red-rock cliffs, many streams and lakes, and the volcanic San Francisco Peaks, including

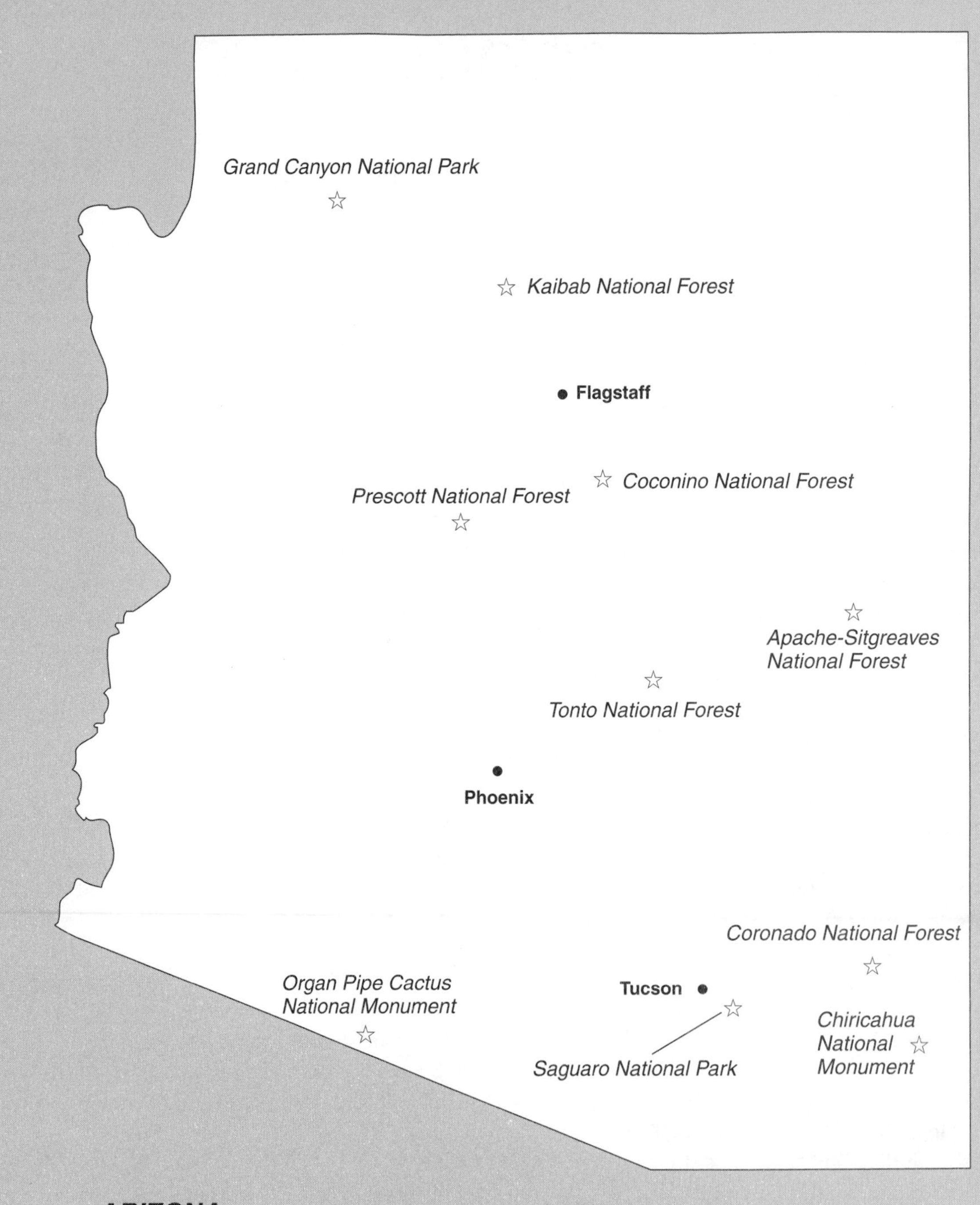
Grand Canyon National Park
Kaibab National Forest
Flagstaff
Coconino National Forest
Prescott National Forest
Apache-Sitgreaves
National Forest
Tonto National Forest
Phoenix
Coronado National Forest
Organ Pipe Cactus
National Monument
Tucson
Chiricahua
National
Monument
Saguaro National Park
ARIZONA

hundreds of cinder cones, craters, and lava caves. Elevations vary from 3,500 to 12,633 feet on Humphreys Peak.

The Mogollon Rim cuts across the southern part of the forest, and ten designated wilderness areas total 160,000 acres. Among the wildlife are elk, pronghorn, mule and white-tailed deer, black bear, mountain lion, eagle, and osprey. Vegetation ranges from desert grasslands, with cholla and cactus, to pinyon-juniper woodlands and ponderosa pine, fir, and spruce forests at higher elevations, plus bristlecone pine and alpine tundra on the peaks.

• *Suggested Trails for Nature Walks:* 1. The 1-mile Sandys Canyon Trail. 2. The 1.1-mile Fay Canyon Trail. 3. The 2.4-mile Slate Mountain Trail. 4. The 2-mile Fatmans Loop Trail. 5. The 2.2-mile Rocky Ridge Trail. 6. The 3-mile Brins Mesa Trail. 7. The 2.2-mile Long Canyon Trail. 8. The 4-mile Sunset Trail. 9. The 3.5-mile Schultz Creek Trail. 10. The 4.7-mile Little Elden Trail.

PRESCOTT NATIONAL FOREST 344 South Cortez Street, Prescott, AZ 86303; (602)771-4700. 1,250,613 acres. This national forest in central Arizona encompasses mountainous terrain with canyons and mesas, and there are eight wilderness areas totaling 104,000 acres. Vegetation includes ponderosa pine forests, areas of pinyon-juniper, grasslands, and Upper Sonoran Desert cactus. Also here are a number of lakes, streams, and the Verde National Wild and Scenic River. Among the wildlife are mule and white-tailed deer, pronghorn, elk, black bear, mountain lion, javelina, coyote, fox, and bald eagle.

• *Suggested Trails for Nature Walks:* 1. The Mingus Mountain Nature Trail. 2. The Beasley Flat Nature Trail. 3. The Lynx Creek Ruin Trail. 4. The Lynx Lake Trail (loop). 5. The 1-mile Brown Springs Trail. 6. The 1.5-mile Groom Creek Nature Trail (loop). 7. The 3.2-mile Upper Pasture Trail. 8. The 4.9-mile Granite Recreation Trail. 9. The 10-mile Old Military Trail. 10. The 3-mile Woodchute Trail (easy-moderate).

APACHE-SITGREAVES NATIONAL FOREST 309 South Mountain Avenue, P.O. Box 640, Springerville, AZ 85938; (602)333-4301. 2,003,525 acres. Apache-Sitgreaves National Forest is located on the Mogollon Rim in the Upper Sonoran desert of east-central Arizona. Elevations range from 3,500 to 11,500 feet, and there are over 200,000 acres of designated wilderness. It's a place of high ridges and canyons, streams and high lakes, spruce and fir forests, pinyon-juniper, yucca and prickly pear, mountain meadows, and alpine tundra. Elk, pronghorn, mule deer, black bear, mountain lion, bobcat, fox, and bald eagle are among the wildlife.

• *Suggested Trails for Nature Walks:* 1. The 0.75-mile Blue Vista Nature Trail. 2. The 1-mile Butler Canyon Nature Trail. 3. The 1-mile Mogollon Rim Nature Trail (loop). 4. The 4.2-mile Paradise Trail. 5. The 3-mile South Fork Trail. 6. The 4-mile Mogollon Rim Trail. 7. The 5-mile Tige Rim Trail. 8. The 2-mile Bear Canyon Lake Trail (moderate). 9. The 13.5-mile East Eagle Trail (moderate). 10. The 12.5-mile Painted Bluff Trail (moderate).

KAIBAB NATIONAL FOREST 800 South 6th Street, Williams, AZ 86046; (602)635-8200. 1,557,274 acres. Kaibab National Forest consists of three tracts of land in northern Arizona, both north and south of Grand Canyon National Park. It includes extensive areas of plateau, with canyons, colored cliffs, some mountains, and a section of the Mogollon Rim escarpment. The highest point is 10,418-foot Kendrick Peak.

Four designated wilderness areas total over 115,000 acres. There are lakes and creeks, alpine meadows and grasslands with pinyon-juniper, and forests of spruce, ponderosa pine, aspen, oak, and fir. Wildlife includes pronghorn, elk, mule deer, black bear, bison, mountain lion, coyote, and bobcat.

• *Suggested Trails for Nature Walks:* 1. The 0.5-mile Ten-X Trail. 2. The 0.75-mile Ponderosa Nature Trail (loop). 3. The 2-mile Keyhole Sink Trail. 4. The 1.8-mile Dogtown Lake Trail. 5.

The 6-mile Saddle Mountain Trail. 6. The 21.5-mile Snake Gulch-Kanab Creek Trail. 7. The 11-mile Sycamore Rim Trail (easy-moderate). 8. The 17-mile Ranger Trail (easy-moderate). 9. Segments of the Arizona Trail (easy-moderate), which runs the length of the state.

CHIRICAHUA NATIONAL MONUMENT Dos Cabezas Route, Box 6500, Willcox, AZ 85643; (602)824-3560. 12,000 acres. This national monument occupies the northwest corner of the Chiricahua Mountains, in southeastern Arizona, amid lands of Coronado National Forest. It preserves a striking landscape of sculpted rock formations, spires, pinnacles, columns, and balanced rocks, with ridges, canyons, and several streams. Vegetation includes chaparral and cactus, a variety of wildflowers, and stands of ponderosa, Apache, and Chihuahua pine, with Douglas fir, oak, juniper, aspen, and cypress. White-tailed deer, javelina, and quail are among the wildlife.

• *Suggested Trails for Nature Walks:* 1. The 0.2-mile Campground to Silver Spur Meadow Trail. 2. The 0.2-mile Visitor Center to Silver Spur Meadow Trail. 3. The 0.5-mile Bonita Creek Trail. 4. The 0.5-mile Massai Point Nature Trail. 5. The 1.2-mile Faraway Ranch Historic Trail. 6. The 0.5-mile Inspiration Point Trail (easy-moderate). 7. The 0.8-mile Hailstone Trail (easy-moderate). 8. The 1.1-mile Upper Rhyolite Trail (easy-moderate). 9. The 9-mile Sugarloaf Mountain Trail (easy-moderate).

ORGAN PIPE CACTUS NATIONAL MONUMENT Route 1, Box 100, Ajo, AZ 85321; (602)387-6849. 330,000 acres. Located in the Sonoran Desert of southwestern Arizona, along the Mexican border, this national monument protects twenty-six species of cacti—including organ pipe cactus, saguaro, prickly pear, and cholla—as well as juniper and rosewood. It's an area of mountains and valleys, canyons and plains. Wildlife includes bighorn sheep, coyote, javelina, jackrabbit, and red-tailed hawk. Guided nature walks are scheduled.

• *Suggested Trails for Nature Walks:* 1. The 1.2-mile Desert View Nature Trail (loop). 2. The 1-mile Campground Perimeter Trail. 3. The 1.3-mile Palo Verde Trail. 4. The 2.3-mile Victoria Mine Trail (easy-moderate). 5. The 4.1-mile Estes Canyon-Bull Pasture Trail (moderate).

CORONADO NATIONAL FOREST Federal Building, 300 West Congress, Tuczon, AZ 85701; (602)670-4552. 1,780,196 acres. Consisting of twelve units of land in southeast Arizona, this national forest features a number of rocky, rugged mountain ranges, with 10,720-foot Mt. Graham the highest point. There are also mesas, scenic canyons with high cliffs and rock formations, grassy hills and meadows, streams, and a few lakes. Forests are of ponderosa pine and fir, with oak, juniper, and aspen. Yucca and cactus are among the lower desert vegetation, and wildlife includes white-tailed deer, black bear, mountain lion, and peregrine falcon.

• *Suggested Trails for Nature Walks:* 1. The 0.4-mile Stronghold Trail. 2. The 0.8-mile Bog Springs Trail. 3. The Madera Canyon Nature Trail. 4. The lower part of the 4.6-mile Silver Peak Trail. 5. The 1.3-mile Marshall Gulch Trail (moderate). 6. The 3.8-mile Aspen Trail (moderate). 7. The 8.1-mile Super Trail (moderate). 8. The 5.6-mile Cunningham Loop Trail (moderate). 9. The 5.9-mile Grant Hill Loop Trail (moderate).

TONTO NATIONAL FOREST 2324 East McDowell Road, Phoenix, AZ 85006; (602)225-5200. 2,874,900 acres. Located in central Arizona, northeast of Phoenix, Tonto National Forest occupies a landscape of rough mountains, steep canyons, sandstone rock formations, mesas, and Sonoran Desert foothills. Elevations range from 1,300 to 7,903 feet (Mazatzal Peak). There are seven designated wilderness areas.

Included is a section of the Mogollon Rim, which stands 1,000 feet above surrounding lands. There are many streams and lakes, as well as several major rivers, ponderosa pine forests, and grasslands, with juniper, saguaro, and mesquite. Deer, bear, mountain lion, javelina, and wild turkey are among the wildlife.

• *Suggested Trails for Nature Walks:* 1. The 3-mile Half Moon Trail. 2. The 1.8-mile Hieroglyphic Trail (easy-moderate). 3. The 1.8-mile Pigeon Trail. 4. The 2-mile Woodbury Trail (easy-moderate). 5. The 3-mile Pine Creek Loop Trail (easy-moderate). 6. The 3.8-mile East Mountain Trail (easy-moderate). 7. The 4.4-mile Saddle Mountain Trail (easy-moderate). 8. The 4.2-mile Grapevine Trail (easy-moderate). 9. The 7.6-mile Rim Trail (easy-moderate). 10. The 10.1-mile Cave Creek Trail (easy-moderate).

Other Suitable Locations for Nature Walks in Arizona

Arizona has twenty-six state parks, and all but a few of them feature trails. Information: Arizona State Parks, 1300 West Washington, Phoenix, AZ 85007; (602)542-4174.

Petrified Forest National Park has several short trails. Information: Petrified Forest National Park, AZ 86028; (602)524-6228.

There are four national wildlife refuges in the state with trails. Information: U.S. Fish and Wildlife Service, P.O. Box 1306, Albuquerque, NM 87103.

Some Bureau of Land Management areas in Arizona have trails. Information: BLM, Arizona State Office. 3707 North 7th Street, Phoenix, AZ 85014; (602)650-0528.

Several of the Nature Conservancy's eight Arizona preserves feature trails. Information: The Nature Conservancy, Arizona Chapter, 300 East University Boulevard, Suite 230, Tucson, AZ 85705; (602)622-3861.

There are short trails in Wupatki, Sunset Crater Volcano, and Walnut Canyon national monuments. Information: Flagstaff Area National Monuments, 2717 North Steves Boulevard, Suite #3, Flagstaff, AZ 86004; (520)556-7134.

ARKANSAS

Recommended Areas for Nature Walks

OUACHITA NATIONAL FOREST P.O. Box 1270, Hot Springs, AR 71902; (501)321-5202. 1,600,000 acres. Stretching from central Arkansas to southeastern Oklahoma, Ouachita National Forest encompasses rugged mountain ridges and valleys with rock formations and outcroppings, bluffs and caves, lakes and rivers, creeks and waterfalls. Included is the 26,445-acre Winding Stair National Recreation Area. Highest elevation is 2,681-foot Rich Mountain.

There are six wilderness areas that total 65,000 acres and also seven so-called scenic areas. Vegetation consists of shrubs, grassy areas, and a forest of pine and hardwoods including oak, hickory, maple, gum, sycamore, and some old beech trees, along with dogwood and redbud. Among the wildlife are white-tailed deer, black bear, wild turkey, wading birds, and waterfowl.

• *Suggested Trails for Nature Walks:* 1. The 0.4-mile Trees of the Forest Trail. 2. The 0.5-mile Friendship Loop Trail. 3. The 0.5-mile Little Missouri Trail. 4. The 0.8-mile Serendipity Interpretive Trail (loop). 5. The 1-mile Briar Patch Loop Trail. 6. The 3.1-mile Shady Lake Trail (loop). 7. The 2-mile Lake Sylvia Wildlife Loop (easy-moderate). 8. The 4-mile Charlton Trail (moderate).

OZARK NATIONAL FOREST P.O. Box 1008, Russellville, AR 72811; (501)968-2354. 1,300,000 acres. Consisting of six tracts of land in northwestern Arkansas, this national forest features high bluffs, ridges, and mountains—the highest being 2,823-foot Mt. Magazine—along with rock formations, outcroppings, and caves including Blanchard Springs Caverns, which features some short underground trails.

Within the forest boundaries are five designated wilderness areas adding up to 65,826 acres. There are lakes, many streams with waterfalls, open grasslands, wildflowers, and forests of hardwoods and pine, with oak-hickory and beech, ash and gum, plus redbud and dogwood. Among the wildlife are white-tailed deer, black bear, wild turkey, and waterfowl.

• *Suggested Trails for Nature Walks:* 1. The 0.2-mile Blanchard Springs Interpretive Trail. 2. The 0.3-mile Koen Interpretive Trail. 3. The 1-mile Pedestal Rocks Trail. 4. The 2-mile Spring Lake Trail (loop). 5. The 3-mile Cove Lake Trail (loop). 6. The 1.1-mile Alum Cove Natural Bridge Trail (easy-moderate). 7. The 3-mile Horsehead Lake Trail (easy-moderate loop).

BUFFALO NATIONAL RIVER P.O. Box 1173, Harrison, AR 72602; (501)741-5443. This corridor of land protects 135 miles of the Buffalo River, which connects two units of Ozark National Forest in the Ozarks of northwestern Arkansas. Some of the terrain is rugged and steep, with multicolored limestone bluffs up to 440 feet high, rock formations, caves, and streams with waterfalls. There are three designated wilderness areas totaling 36,000 acres, and a hardwood forest of hickory and oak, willow

ARKANSAS
Buffalo National River
Devil's Den State Park
Ozark National Forest
Mt. Nebo State Park
Village Creek State Park
Petit Jean State Park
Pinnacle Mountain State Park
Ouachita National Forest
Little Rock
Queen Wilhelmina State Park
White Oak Lake State Park

and cottonwood. Wildlife includes elk, black bear, white-tailed deer, bobcat, raccoon, skunk, and armadillo. Ranger-led walks are available during the summer.

• *Suggested Trails for Nature Walks:* 1. The 0.5-mile Overlook Trail. 2. The 0.3-mile Morning Star Loop Trail. 3. The 1.1-mile Amphitheater Trail. 4. The 1.2-mile River Overloop Trail (loop). 5. The 1.3-mile Mill Creek Trail (loop). 6. The 2-mile Ozark to Pruitt Trail. 7. The 2.1-mile Lost Valley Trail (loop). 8. The 2.2-mile Rush Hiking Trail.

DEVIL'S DEN STATE PARK 11333 West Arkansas Highway 74, West Fork, AR 72774; (501)761-3325. 2,000 acres. Devil's Den State Park is located in the rocky Lee Creek Valley of the Boston Mountains, next to Ozark National Forest lands in northwest Arkansas. The park features sandstone caves and crevices, some old-growth woodlands, a major mountain stream, and an 8-acre lake. Naturalist-guided walks are available.

• *Suggested Trails for Nature Walks:* 1. The 1-mile Lee Creek Trail (loop). 2. The 1-mile Lake Trail. 3. The 1.5-mile Devil's Den Trail (loop). 4. The 3-mile Yellow Rock Trail (loop). 5. The 13.6-mile Butterfield Hiking Trail (moderate), which continues on into Ozark National Forest.

PINNACLE MOUNTAIN STATE PARK 11901 Pinnacle Valley Road, Roland, AR 72135; (501)868-5806. 1,770 acres. Located next to the Arkansas River in the Ouachita Mountains of central Arkansas, near Little Rock, this park features 1,011-foot Pinnacle Mountain, which has fine views from the top. The hilly park includes the Little and Big Maumelle rivers, a couple of small ponds, pine and hardwood trees, and a bottomland forest with 500-year-old baldcypress trees. There's also a 60-acre arboretum, and naturalist-led walks are available.

• *Suggested Trails for Nature Walks:* 1. The 0.5-mile Kingfisher Trail (loop). 2. The 0.8-mile Arkansas Trail, in the Arboretum. 3. The 1.3-mile Base Trail. 4. The 2-mile Rocky Valley Trail (loop). 5. Two miles of the 225-mile Ouachita Trail, which begins here and continues west through Arkansas into Oklahoma.

PETIT JEAN STATE PARK Route 3, Box 340, Morrilton, AR 72110; (501)727-5441. 3,471 acres. This state park is perched on Petit Jean Mountain in west-central Arkansas, between the Ouachita and Ozark mountain ranges. It's a place of hills and ravines, cliffs and rock formations, enormous boulders and rock shelters, hardwood forests with pine and sycamore, and a lake. Streams and waterfalls include Cedar Creek and 90-foot Cedar Falls in Little Cedar Creek Canyon. Nature walks are available here in summer.

• *Suggested Trails for Nature Walks:* 1. The 0.3-mile Rock House Cave Trail. 2. The 0.3-mile Bear Cave Trail (loop). 3. The 1-mile Canyon Trail. 4. The 1.3-mile Cedar Creek Trail (loop). 5. The 2-mile Cedar Falls Trail. 6. The 4.5-mile Seven Hollows Trail (loop). 7. The 12-mile Bay Scout Trail (easy-moderate).

VILLAGE CREEK STATE PARK 201 CR 754, Wynne, AR 72396; (501)238-9406. 7,000 acres. Located on rugged Crowley's Ridge in east-central Arkansas, Village Creek State Park encompasses a wide valley that includes Village Creek and other streams, two man-made lakes with beaches, many wildflowers in season, and mixed hardwood forests with maple and beech, yellow poplar, and butternut. White-tailed deer and wild turkey are among the wildlife. Guided nature walks are offered in the summer.

• *Suggested Trails for Nature Walks:* 1. The 0.3-mile Arboretum Trail. 2. The 0.5-mile Big Ben Nature Trail. 3. The 1.1-mile Austell Trail. 4. The 2.8-mile Lake Dunn Trail. 5. The 2.2-mile Military Road Trail (easy-moderate).

MT. NEBO STATE PARK Route 3, Box 374, Dardanelle, AR 72834; (501)229-3655. Situated alongside Ozark National Forest lands in west-central Arkansas, this state park is on flat-topped 1,800-foot Mt. Nebo, which overlooks 34,000-

acre Lake Dardanelle and the Arkansas River. Included are cliffs and overhangs with panoramas, a small lake, springs, wildflowers, and an oak-hickory forest with maple, gum, dogwood, and redbud. Among the wildlife are white-tailed deer, raccoon, woodchuck, opossum, hawk, and vulture. Guided walks are available in summer.

• *Suggested Trails for Nature Walks:* 1. The 4-mile Bench Trail. 2. The 3.5-mile Rim Trail from the Visitor Center to the waterfall (other portions are challenging). 3. The 1-mile Summit Park Self-Guided Trail (easy-moderate).

WHITE OAK LAKE STATE PARK Route 2, Box 28, Bluff City, AR 71722; (501)685-2748. 725 acres. This state park is on the Gulf Coastal Plain of southwestern Arkansas, alongside 2,765-acre and man-made White Oak Lake. Terrain here consists of rolling hills and ridges with marshlands and streams, sandy pine barrens, and woodlands of oak and hickory, beech and gum, dogwood and holly. Wildflowers include orchid and jack-in-the-pulpit. Among the wildlife are white-tailed deer, fox, beaver, raccoon, rabbit, and armadillo, along with great blue heron, osprey, vulture, and bald eagle. Guided walks are available in summer.

• *Suggested Trails for Nature Walks:* 1. The 0.3-mile Spring Branch Trail (loop). 2. The 2-mile Beech Ridge Trail. 3. The 7-mile Coastal Plain Trail.

QUEEN WILHELMINA STATE PARK HC-07, Box 53A, Mena, AR 71953; (501)394-2863. Queen Wilhelmina State Park is on 2,681-foot Rich Mountain in the Ouachita Range of western Arkansas. The rugged terrain includes steep slopes and rocky bluffs with panoramic views, along with springs and a mixed hardwood forest. The 225-mile Ouachita National Recreation Trail passes through the park, and guided nature walks are available.

• *Suggested Trails for Nature Walks:* 1. The 0.5-mile Spring Trail. 2. The 0.7-mile Reservoir Trail (easy-moderate). 3. The 1-mile Lover's Leap Trail (easy-moderate). 4. The Ouachita Trail from the campground to the Pioneer Cemetery (easy-moderate 1.3 miles).

Other Suitable Locations for Nature Walks in Arkansas

Arkansas has forty-eight state parks, thirty-eight of which have foot trails. Information: Arkansas State Parks, One Capitol Mall, Little Rock, AR 72201; (501)682-1191.

There are a few trails in Hot Springs National Park, P.O. Box 1860, Hot Springs, AR 71902; (501)623-1433.

Trails are available at two national wildlife refuges in Arkansas: 1. Felsenthal National Wildlife Refuge, P.O. Box 1157, Crossett, AR 71635; (501)364-3167. 2. Holla Bend National Wildlife Refuge, Route 1, P.O. Box 59, Dardanelle, AR 72834; (501)229-4300.

A number of U.S. Army Corps of Engineers areas in the state have trails. Information: Corps of Engineers, Little Rock District, P.O. Box 867, Little Rock, AR 72203, (501)324-5673; or Corps of Engineers, Vicksburg District, 2101 North Frontage Road, Vicksburg, MS 39180, (601)631-5286.

CALIFORNIA

Recommended Areas for Nature Walks

YOSEMITE NATIONAL PARK P.O. Box 577, Yosemite, CA 95389; (209)372-0200. 748,542 acres. World-famous Yosemite in the east-central Sierras is a place of majestic mountains and deep valleys, including the celebrated (and overvisited) Yosemite Valley, with its enormous vertical-walled cliffs, domes, rock formations, and meadows. Here as well are many rivers, creeks, and high, thundering waterfalls—among them 2,425-foot Yosemite Falls, 2,000-foot Sentinel Falls, and 1,612-foot Ribbon Falls.

Also of special interest are Tuolumne Meadows, an expanse of subalpine meadow, and the Mariposa Grove of giant sequoias. Elsewhere the park features forests of red and Douglas fir, lodgepole and ponderosa pine, mountain hemlock, and incense cedar. Wildlife includes black bear, mule deer, mountain lion, coyote, wolverine, raccoon, and marmot. Ranger-led walks are available.

• *Suggested Trails for Nature Walks:* 1. The 0.3-mile Bridalveil Fall Trail. 2. The 0.8-mile Lower Yosemite Fall Trail. 3. The 3.5-mile Wawona Meadow Loop. 4. The John Muir Trail through Lyell Canyon (8 miles). 5. The 5-mile Mirror Lake Trail (loop). 6. The 2.5-mile Wapama Falls Trail (easy-moderate). 7. The 5.2-mile Rancheria Falls Trail (easy-moderate). 8. The 2.4-mile Elizabeth Lake Trail (moderate). 9. The 6-mile Alder Creek Trail (moderate). 10. The 6.9-mile Mariposa Grove of Sequoias Loop (moderate).

SEQUOIA AND KINGS CANYON NATIONAL PARKS Three Rivers, CA 93271; (209)565-3134. 864,118 acres. Situated in the Sierras of east-central California, these two adjacent and jointly administered national parks are best known as the home of seventy-five groves of giant sequoias—including the 275-foot, 1,385-ton. 2,300-year-old General Sherman Tree, said to be the largest living thing on earth.

The parks also feature lofty peaks, among them 14,494-foot Mt. Whitney, highest in the lower 48 states—as well as deep river canyons including 6,000-foot-deep Kern Canyon and Kings Canyon, which reaches a depth of 8,200 feet outside the park. There are alpine lakes and meadows, mixed conifer forests, and foothills with oak and chaparral. Mule deer, black bear, mountain lion, bobcat, fox, coyote, wolverine, beaver, raccoon, and jackrabbit are among the wildlife. Guided walks are available.

• *Suggested Trails for Nature Walks:* 1. The 0.3-mile General Grant Tree Trail. 2. The 0.7-mile Trail for All People. 3. The 1-mile Hazelwood Nature Trail (loop). 4. The 1-mile Big Stump Basin Trail (loop). 5. The 1-mile Zumwalt Meadow Trail (loop). 6. The 1.3-mile North Grove Loop. 7. The 1.5-mile Sequoia Lake Overlook/Dead Giant Loop. 8. The 1.7-mile Tokopah Falls Trail. 9. The 2-mile Congress Trail (loop). 10. The 4-mile Mist Falls Trail (easy-moderate).

CALIFORNIA
Redwood National Park
Lassen Volcanic National Park
Mendocino National Forest
Tahoe National Forest
Sacramento
Point Reyes National Seashore
San Francisco
Yosemite National Park
Sequoia and Kings Canyon National Parks
Death Valley National Park
Los Padres National Forest
Los Angeles
Joshua Tree National Park

DEATH VALLEY NATIONAL PARK Death Valley, CA 92328; (619)786-2331. 3,367,000 acres. Located in the Mojave Desert of south-central California, the former Death Valley National Monument is now one of our newest national parks, established in 1994. The size was increased by 1,300,000 acres, making this the largest national park in the lower 48 states. Highest point is 11,049-foot Telescope Peak, with 94 percent of the park consisting of designated wilderness.

The scenery here consists of mountains and valleys, canyons and rock formations, badlands and 700-foot dunes, streams and waterfalls. Vegetation includes creosote bush and mesquite at lower elevations, joshua tree forests, pinyon-juniper, as well as limber pine and bristlecone pine higher up. Among the wildlife are desert bighorn sheep, mule deer, wild horse and burro, mountain lion, bobcat, coyote, and gray fox. Ranger-conducted walks are offered from October through April.

• *Suggested Trails for Nature Walks:* 1. The 0.3-mile Salt Creek Nature Trail. 2. The 0.3-mile Little Hebe Crater Trail. 3. The 0.4-mile Windy Point Trail. 4. The 0.4-mile Tie Canyon Trail. 5. The 1-mile Golden Canyon Trail. 6. The 1-mile Desolation Canyon Trail. 7. The 1-mile Keane Wonder Springs Trail. 8. The 1.5-mile Titus Canyon Narrows Trail. 9. The 2-mile Mosaic Canyon Trail. 10. The 1-mile Natural Bridge Canyon Trail (easy-moderate).

REDWOOD NATIONAL PARK 1111 Second Street, Crescent City, CA 95531; (800)423-6101. 106,000 acres. This national park in the Coast Range of northwest California preserves an area of old-growth redwoods—which are the tallest trees in the world, reaching as high as 367 feet and as much as 2,000 years old. Adjacent to the national park are three state parks that feature more redwoods.

There are also forests of Douglas fir, hemlock, and oak, along with prairies, beaches, streams, rivers, and steep rugged cliffs along the coast. Elevations range from sea level to 3,100 feet. Wildlife includes Roosevelt elk, black bear, black-tailed deer, mountain lion, bobcat, gray fox, kestrel, and red-tailed hawk, as well as whale, dolphin, seal, and sea lion offshore.

• *Suggested Trails for Nature Walks:* 1. The 0.8-mile Lost Man Creek Trail. 2. The 1-mile Lady Bird Johnson Grove Trail (loop). 3. The 1-mile False Klamath Cove Trail. 4. The 3.5-mile Crescent Beach Trail. 5. Segments of the Coastal Trail, which runs the length of the park. 6. The 1-mile Yurok Loop Trail (easy-moderate). 7. The 1.2-mile Hidden Beach Trail (easy-moderate). 8. The 0.6-mile Enderts Beach Trail (moderate). 9. The 4.3-mile Rellim Ridge Trail (moderate). 10. The 8.2-mile Redwood Creek Trail (moderate).

LASSEN VOLCANIC NATIONAL PARK P.O. Box 100, Mineral, CA 96063; (916)595-4444. 106,372 acres. Created to protect an active volcanic area in the Cascades of northern California, this national park is dominated by 10,457-foot Lassen Peak, which erupted earlier this century. In the region are craters, cinder cones, lava pinnacles, steaming vents, and hot springs.

Among other features there are glaciated canyons, streams, a number of lakes, meadows, wildflowers, alpine tundra, and forests of mountain hemlock, lodgepole and ponderosa pine, red fir and cedar. Wildlife includes black-tailed deer, black bear, mountain lion, coyote, porcupine, marmot, peregrine falcon, and sharp-shinned hawk. Naturalist-led walks are offered in summer.

• *Suggested Trails for Nature Walks:* 1. The 1-mile Lily Pond Nature Trail. 2. The 1.5-mile Boiling Springs Lake Trail. 3. The 1.6-mile Manzanita Lake Trail (loop). 4. The 2.3-mile Mill Creek Falls Trail. 5. The 1.5-mile Bumpass Hell Trail (easy-moderate). 6. The 4-mile Echo and Twin Lakes Trail (easy-moderate). 7. The 1.5-mile Kings Creek Falls Trail (moderate). 8. The 2-mile Cinder Cone Trail (moderate). 9. The 2-mile Mt. Harkness Trail (moderate).

JOSHUA TREE NATIONAL PARK 74485 National Park Drive, Twentynine Palms, CA 92277; (619)367-7511. 792,000 acres. Located in the Colorado and Mojave deserts of southern California, this is one of the nation's newest national parks (1994), with 234,000 acres added to the former Joshua Tree National Monument. Elevations range from 1,000 to 5,814 feet on Quail Mountain. There are ten mountains over 5,000 feet, and 630,800 acres of designated wilderness.

Amid the rugged mountains, canyons, and hills here are rock formations and massive boulders, Native American petroglyphs, and five fan palm oases, with varied desert vegetation including joshua tree, creosote bush, ocotillo, and cholla cactus. Among the wildlife are desert bighorn sheep, coyote, fox, bobcat, jackrabbit, roadrunner, burrowing owl, and golden eagle.

• *Suggested Trails for Nature Walks:* 1. The 0.3-mile Arch Rock Trail (loop). 2. The 0.4-mile Cap Rock Trail (loop). 3. The 0.5-mile Oasis of Mara Trail (loop). 4. The 0.6-mile Indian Cave Trail (loop). 5. The 1-mile Cottonwood Springs Trail. 6. The 1.7-mile Skull Rock Trail (loop). 7. The 1.1-mile Barker Dam Trail (loop). 8. The 1-mile Hidden Valley Trail (easy-moderate loop). 9. The 1.3-mile High View Trail (easy-moderate loop). 10. The 8-mile Boy Scout Trail (easy-moderate).

POINT REYES NATIONAL SEASHORE Point Reyes, CA 94956; (415)663-1092. 65,303 acres. This national seashore occupies a peninsula on the Pacific coast just north of San Francisco, with rocky shoreline, beaches and bays, steep cliffs and shelves, mountains and valleys. Highest point is 1,407-foot Mt. Wittenberg on Inverness Ridge. Included within the boundaries is the 32,000-acre Philip Burton Wilderness Area.

The region features meadows, marshes, brushlands, and forests of Douglas fir, pine, oak, maple, willow, and alder, with rhododendron and huckleberry. Among the wildlife are deer, tule elk, mountain lion, bobcat, egret, heron, owl, brown pelican, osprey, and peregrine falcon, along with gray whale, seal, and sea lion offshore.

• *Suggested Trails for Nature Walks:* 1. The 0.6-mile Earthquake Trail (loop). 2. The 0.6-mile Chimney Rock Trail. 3. The 0.6-mile Kehoe Beach Trail. 4. The 0.7-mile Woodpecker Nature Trail (loop). 5. The 1-mile Kule Loklo Trail (loop). 6. The 1.5-mile Abbots Lagoon Trail. 7. The 2-mile Muddy Hollow Trail. 8. The 3-mile Tomales Point Trail. 9. The 4.1-mile Bear Valley Trail to Arch Rock. 10. The 5-mile Coast-Laguna Loop.

TAHOE NATIONAL FOREST P.O. Box 6003, Nevada City, CA 95959; (916)265-4531. 811,740 acres. Situated in the central Sierras, northeast of Sacramento, Tahoe National Forest is characterized by high peaks and rugged ridges, valleys and foothills, steep canyons with rivers and streams, as well as many lakes and ponds. Elevations range from 1,500 feet to 9,400 feet.

There are open meadows with wildflowers, shrubs, and forests of mixed conifers, including ponderosa, lodgepole, and jeffrey pine, white and Douglas fir, old-growth sequoia, and incense cedar, as well as maple, black oak, madrone, willow, California yew, and dogwood. Among the wildlife are mule deer, black bear, mountain lion, bobcat, coyote, red fox, porcupine, raccoon, and skunk, along with great horned owl, goshawk, and golden eagle.

• *Suggested Trails for Nature Walks:* 1. The 0.5-mile Big Trees Interpretive Trail. 2. The 0.5-mile Glacier Meadow Loop Trail. 3. The 0.8-mile Rock Creek Nature Trail (loop). 4. The 0.8-mile Sand Pond Interpretive Trail. 5. The 1.5-mile Forest View Trail (loop). 6. The 2-mile Summit Lake Trail. 7. The 2.5-mile Wild Plum Loop Trail. 8. The 3.9-mile McGuire Trail. 9. The 7-mile Bullards Bar Trail. 10. The 7.6-mile American River Trail.

MENDOCINO NATIONAL FOREST 825 North Humboldt Avenue, Willows, CA 95988; (916)934-3316. 876,236 acres. Located a bit inland from the coast of northern California, Mendocino National Forest occupies varied terrain ranging from rolling hills and valleys to steep, rugged mountains and deep canyon gorges. Elevations range from 1,000 to over 8,000 feet, and there are many lakes, rivers, and streams with waterfalls. Two designated wilderness areas total 111,676 acres.

Much of the region is forested with mixed conifers, including ponderosa and sugar pine, white and Douglas fir, hemlock and cedar, as well as oak and cottonwood. There are mountain meadows, grassy glades, and areas of chaparral and manzanita. Wildlife includes mule and black-tailed deer, black bear, coyote, mountain lion, fox, bobcat, and raccoon, along with grouse, quail, wild turkey, owl, bald and golden eagle, osprey, and red-tailed hawk,

• *Suggested Trails for Nature Walks:* 1. The 0.3-mile Letts Lake Trail. 2. The 0.5-mile Letts Lake Lakeside Trail (loop). 3. The 0.5-mile Sunset Campground Trail. 4. The 1-mile Chico Tree Comanche Trail (loop). 5. The 1.5-mile Lake Red Bluff Recreation Area Trail. 6. The 3-mile Lake Pillsbury Pack Saddle Trail. 7. The 4-mile Lake Shore Trail.

LOS PADRES NATIONAL FOREST 6144 Calle Real, Goleta, CA 93177; (805)683-6711. 1,724,000 acres. Made up of two separate tracts along the coast of south-central California, and stretching from Los Angeles to Big Sur, this national forest features mountains and ridges with rock formations, canyons, streams, waterfalls, several hot springs, desert badlands, and a segment of the Big Sur Coast, including some beaches. Highest point is 8,831-foot Mt. Pinos, and ten designated wilderness areas total 823,000 acres.

Vegetation consists of woodlands and chaparral, brushlands and grasslands, meadows and subalpine plants, as well as forests of ponderosa pine and oak, white and Douglas fir, cedar and bristlecone fir. Among the wildlife are mule and black-tailed deer, black bear, mountain lion, bobcat, gray fox, coyote, and raccoon, along with seabirds, red-tailed hawk, and golden eagle.

• *Suggested Trails for Nature Walks:* 1. The 0.5-mile Pino Alto Interpretive Trail (loop). 2. The 0.5-mile Wheeler Gorge Nature Trail (loop). 3. The 1.5-mile Murietta Trail. 4. The 1.6-mile Potrero John Trail. 5. The first 1.5 miles of the East Fork Trail. 6. The first 2 miles of the 5.6-mile Lion Canyon Trail. 7. The first 3 miles of the 8.7-mile Gene Marshall-Piedra Blanca Trail. 8. The 2.6-mile Big Falls Trail (easy-moderate). 9. The 8-mile Middle Sespe Trail (easy-moderate). 10. The 17.5-mile Sespe River Trail (easy-moderate).

Other Suitable Locations for Nature Walks in California

California has no fewer than 275 state parks, and many of these locations have nature or hiking trails. Information: California State Parks Public Affairs, P.O. Box 942896, Sacramento, CA 94296; (916)653-6995.

There are eighteen national forests in the state, all of which feature trail networks. Information: U.S. Forest Service, 630 Sansome Street, San Francisco, CA 94111; (415)705-2874.

The Nature Conservancy owns and manages a number of preserves in the state with trails. Information: The Nature Conservancy of California, 201 Mission Street, 4th Floor, San Francisco, CA 94105; (415)777-0487.

Many trails are found in areas managed by the Bureau of Land Management. Information: BLM, California State Office, 2800 Cottage Way, Sacramento, CA 95825; (916)978-4754.

There are ten national wildlife refuges in the state with trails. Information: U.S. Fish and Wildlife Service, 911 Northeast 11th Avenue, Eastside Federal Complex, Portland, OR 97232.

Channel Islands National Park, which is accessible by boat, has trails. Information:

Channel Islands National Park, 1901 Spinnaker Drive, Ventura, CA 93001; (805)658-5730.

Two national monuments in California feature trails: 1. Pinnacles National Monument, Paicines, CA 95043; (408)389-4485. 2. Lava Beds National Monument, P.O. Box 867, Tulelake, CA 96134; (916)667-2282.

There are trails at three national recreation areas in the state: 1. Whiskeytown-Shasta-Trinity National Recreation Area, P.O. Box 188, Whiskeytown, CA 96095; (916)241-6584. 2. Golden Gate National Recreation Area, Fort Mason, San Francisco, CA 94123; (415)556-0560. 3. Santa Monica Mountains National Recreation Area, 30401 Agoura Road, Agoura Hills, CA 91301; (818)597-9192.

A number of U.S. Army Corps of Engineers areas have trails. Information: Corps of Engineers, Sacramento District, 1325 J Street, Sacramento, CA 95814; (916)557-5281 / Corps of Engineers, Los Angeles District, P.O. Box 2711, Los Angeles, CA 90053; (213)894-5635.

COLORADO

Recommended Areas for Nature Walks

ROCKY MOUNTAIN NATIONAL PARK Estes Park, CO 80517; (970)586-1206. 265,000 acres. Located in north-central Colorado's Front Range, as well as on the Continental Divide, this national park features dramatic Rocky Mountain scenery—with dozens of snow-covered peaks, small glaciers, canyons, cliffs, steep slopes, broad valleys, flower-filled mountain meadows, and areas of alpine tundra. Highest elevation is 14,255-foot Longs Peak.

There are many lakes, rivers, streams, and waterfalls amid forests of Douglas fir, ponderosa and lodgepole pine, spruce, aspen, and juniper. Wildlife includes elk, black bear, bighorn sheep, mule deer, moose, mountain lion, coyote, bobcat, fox, wolverine, and raccoon, along with grouse, great blue heron, loon, hawk, and eagle. Ranger-led walks are available.

• *Suggested Trails for Nature Walks:* 1. The 0.3-mile Adams Falls Trail. 2. The 0.3-mile Copeland Falls Trail. 3. The 0.5-mile Nymph Lake Trail. 4. The 0.5-mile Sprague Lake Trail. 5. The 0.6-mile Alberta Falls Trail. 6. The 0.6-mile Bear Lake Trail (loop). 7. The 1.7-mile Trail to the Pool. 8. The 1.1-mile Dream Lake Trail (easy-moderate). 9. The 2.3-mile Cub Lake Trail (easy-moderate). 10. The 3.5-mile Cascade Falls Trail (easy-moderate).

ARAPAHO AND ROOSEVELT NATIONAL FORESTS 1311 South College, Fort Collins, CO 80524; (303)498-2770. 1,300,000 acres. These two jointly administered national forests surround Rocky Mountain National Park in north-central Colorado. Included are the Front Range of the Rockies and the Continental Divide, with rugged peaks over 14,000 feet, alpine tundra, glacial cirques, canyons, plateaus, and foothills. Highest peak is 14,258-foot Mt. Evans.

There are seven designated wilderness areas. Also here are the Cache la Poudre National Wild and Scenic River and the 36,000-acre Arapaho National Recreation Area, with five large lakes. The forests are of lodgepole and ponderosa pine, aspen, Douglas fir, and juniper. Among the wildlife are mule deer, moose, pronghorn, black bear, Rocky Mountain goat, elk, bighorn sheep, mountain lion, coyote, fox, and snowshoe hare.

• *Suggested Trails for Nature Walks:* 1. The 0.5-mile Neota Creek Trail. 2. The 1-mile Lady Moon Trail. 3. The 1-mile Foothills Nature Trail. 4. The 1-mile Chians Lake Trail. 5. The 1.2-mile Jean Luning Trail. 6. The 1-mile Rainbow Lakes Trail. 7. The 3.5-mile Trap Park Trail. 8. The 3.9-mile Mount Margaret Trail. 9. The 1.5-mile Molly Lake Trail. 10. The 3.7-mile North Lone Pine Trail.

PIKE AND SAN ISABEL NATIONAL FORESTS 1920 Valley Drive, Pueblo, CO 81008; (719)545-8737. 2,344,524 acres. Situated in central and southern Colorado, jointly administered Pike and San Isabel national forests encompass several imposing mountain ranges,

COLORADO

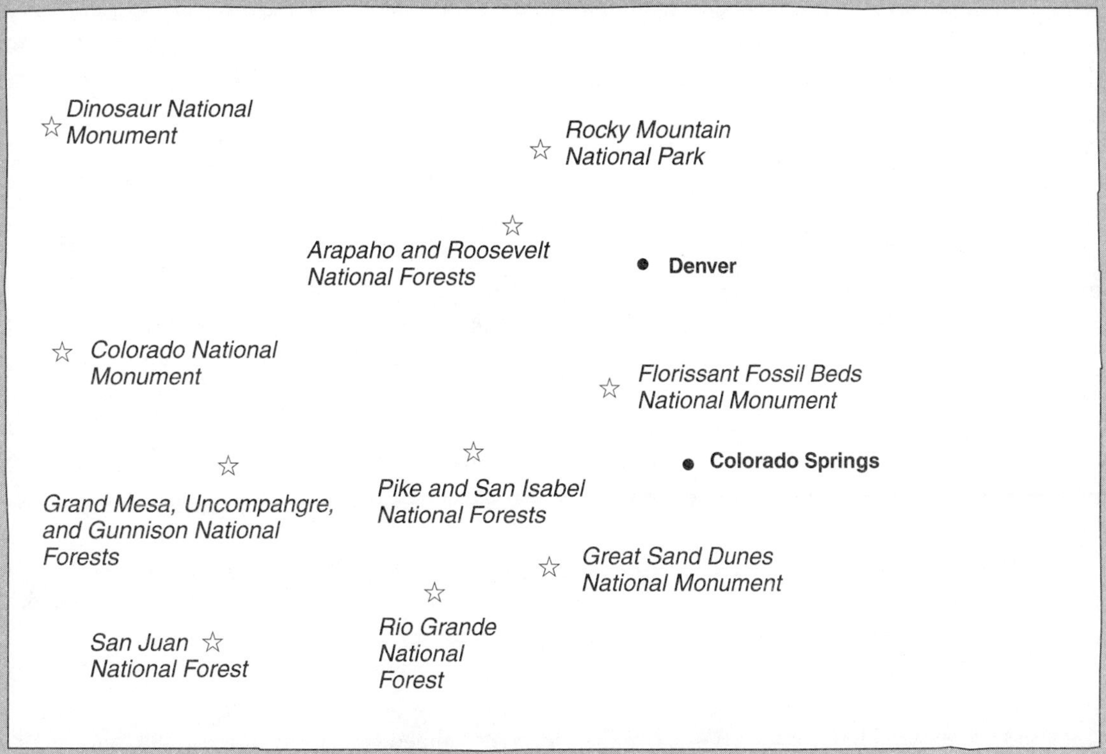

Dinosaur National Monument
Rocky Mountain National Park
Arapaho and Roosevelt National Forests
Denver
Colorado National Monument
Florissant Fossil Beds National Monument
Colorado Springs
Grand Mesa, Uncompahgre, and Gunnison National Forests
Pike and San Isabel National Forests
Great Sand Dunes National Monument
San Juan National Forest
Rio Grande National Forest

among them the Sangre de Cristo Mountains and the Spanish Peaks, with lands along the Continental Divide. There are twenty-two mountains over 14,000 feet, among them Colorado's highest peak, 14,433-foot Mt. Elbert, along with popular Pike's Peak (14,110 feet).

Included are rock outcroppings and talus slopes, canyons and plains, with many lakes and streams. Vegetation varies from desert varieties to alpine tundra and bristlecone pine, with aspen, lodgepole pine, and spruce forests in between. There are five designated wilderness areas, and the Windy Ridge Bristlecone Pine Scenic Area protects a stand of ancient trees. Elk, deer, pronghorn, black bear, bighorn sheep, mountain goat, mountain lion, coyote, bobcat, and wild turkey are among the wildlife.

• *Suggested Trails for Nature Walks:* 1. The 1.5-mile Jefferson Lake Trail. 2. The 1.5-mile Puma Point Trail. 3. The 3.8-mile Garfield Trail. 4. The 4-mile Turkey Creek Trail. 5. The 6.6-mile Middle Creek Trail. 6. The 5.5-mile Burning Bear Trail. 7. The 11.6-mile Rampart Reservoir Trail. 8. The first 3 miles of the 6.5-mile Rolling Creek Trail. 9. The 3-mile Meridian Trail (moderate). 10. The 7-mile Waldo Canyon Loop Trail (moderate).

GRAND MESA, UNCOMPAHGRE AND GUNNISON NATIONAL FORESTS 2250 Highway 50, Delta, CO 81416; (303)874-7691. 2,953,000 acres. These three jointly administered national forests in western and southwestern Colorado are home to many lofty, jagged peaks, deep canyons and gorges, high plateaus, and mesas—including 10,000-foot Grand Mesa, said to be the world's largest. Six mountains are over 14,000 feet and 120 are over 13,000 feet elevation.

There are also hundreds of lakes and ponds, streams, and rivers, along with mountain meadows, wildflowers, alpine plants, shrubs, and forests of subalpine fir and Englemann spruce, lodgepole and ponderosa pine, Douglas fir, and aspen. Eight designated wilderness areas total 828,900 acres. Among the wildlife are elk, deer, moose, black bear, bighorn sheep, coyote, fox, raccoon, skunk, marmot, turkey vulture, and golden eagle.

• *Suggested Trails for Nature Walks:* 1. The 0.5-mile Land O'Lakes Trail. 2. The 0.5-mile Beaver Ponds Trail. 3. The 0.5-mile Discovery Trail (loop). 4. The 1.5-mile Mesa Lakes Shore Trail. 5. The 1.5-mile Wilson Meadows Trail. 6. The 2.2-mile Costo Lake Trail. 7. The 5.5-mile Alder Creek Trail. 8. The 4.2-mile Ward Lake Trail. 9. The 5-mile Gold Creek Trail. 10. The 3.5-mile West Fork Trail.

SAN JUAN NATIONAL FOREST 701 Camino del Rio, Room 301, Durango, CO 81301; (303)247-4874. 1,861,000 acres. Located in southwestern Colorado, San Juan National Forest features high mountains along the Continental Divide with alpine scenery, canyons, lakes and rivers, streams and waterfalls, mountain meadows and tundra, plus forests of ponderosa pine, Douglas fir, spruce, aspen, and oak.

Elevations range from 6,400 feet to 14,246 feet, and there are three designated wilderness areas totaling 355,000 acres. Wildlife includes elk, mule deer, bighorn sheep, black bear, mountain goat, mountain lion, coyote, red fox, raccoon, and jackrabbit, along with snowy egret, blue-winged teal, great horned owl, bald eagle, and peregrine falcon.

• *Suggested Trails for Nature Walks:* 1. The 0.6-mile Animas Overlook Trail. 2. The 0.5-mile Lost Lake Trail. 3. The 0.6-mile Treasure Falls Trail. 4. The 1-mile Big Al Trail. 5. The 1-mile Can Do Trail. 6. The 1-mile Wallace Lake Trail. 7. The 1.5-mile Forebay Lake Trail. 8. The 1.5-mile Potato Lake Trail. 9. The 3-mile Fourmile Falls Trail. 10. The 4-mile Purgatory Trail (easy-moderate).

RIO GRANDE NATIONAL FOREST 1803 West Highway 160, Monte Vista, CO 81144; (719)852-5941. 1,851,792 acres. Situated in the Rockies of south-central Colorado, this national forest features the rugged terrain of high mountain peaks and knobs, some surpassing 14,000 feet, with cliffs and canyons, rock pinnacles and natural arches, ridges and plateaus, hills and talus slopes—along with many lakes, ponds, streams, and rivers, including the Rio Grande River in Box Canyon.

Three designated wilderness areas total 281,000 acres. There are alpine meadows with wildflowers and forests of ponderosa pine, Englemann spruce, and Douglas fir, including old-growth stands, as well as aspen and alder. Among the birds and other wildlife are sandhill crane, great horned owl, red-tailed hawk, golden eagle, elk, bighorn sheep, mule deer, black bear, mountain lion, bobcat, coyote, porcupine, beaver, and snowshoe hare.

• *Suggested Trails for Nature Walks:* 1. The 1-mile Timber Lake Trail. 2. The 1.5-mile Spectacle Lake Trail. 3. The 1.9-mile Three Forks Trail. 4. The 2-mile No Name Lake Trail. 5. The 2.5-mile Chama River Trail. 6. The first 2.5 miles of the 3.5-mile West Pole Creek Trail. 7. The first 3 miles of the 4.8-mile West Ute Lake Trail. 8. The 6.5-mile Adams Fork Trail (easy-moderate). 9. The 9.9-mile Squaw Creek Trail (easy-moderate). 10. The 12.1-mile Ute Creek Trail (easy-moderate).

DINOSAUR NATIONAL MONUMENT 4545 Highway 40, Dinosaur, CO 81610; (303)374-2216. 210,000 acres. Located in northwestern Colorado and extending into Utah, this national monument protects an area where thousands of dinosaur bone fossils have been found. It's a place of desert basin and plateau, rugged mountains and canyons, sandstone cliffs with petroglyphs (Indian "rock art").

Also here are creeks, the Green and Yampa rivers, and such vegetation as sagebrush and saltbush, boxelder and cottonwood trees by the river, and forests of juniper, pinyon pine, and Douglas fir higher up. Mule deer, bighorn sheep, prairie dog, river otter, and peregrine falcon are among the wildlife.

• *Suggested Trails for Nature Walks:* 1. The 0.3-mile Hog and Box Canyons Trail. 2. The 0.3-mile Cold Desert Trail. 3. The 0.3-mile Plug Hat Nature Trail. 4. The 1.5-mile Gates of Lodore Trail. 5. The 2-mile Desert Voices Nature Trail (loop). 6. The 2-mile Harpers Corner Trail. 7. The 8-mile Ruple Point Trail (easy-moderate). 8. The 8-mile Jones Hole Trail (easy-moderate).

COLORADO NATIONAL MONUMENT Fruita, CO 81521; (303)858-3617. 20,000 acres. Occupying the Colorado Plateau, near the Colorado River in the west-central part of the state, Colorado National Monument is notable for its vertical-walled canyons and huge rock formations, including spires and pedestals, domes, and arches. This is a desert landscape with intermittent streams, juniper and pinyon pine trees, yucca and cactus, mountain mahogany and sagebrush, and cottonwood in the canyons. Among the wildlife are mule deer, bighorn sheep, mountain lion, coyote, fox, prairie dog, desert cottontail, red-tailed hawk, and golden eagle.

• *Suggested Trails for Nature Walks:* 1. The 0.3-mile Window Rock Trail (loop). 2. The 0.5-mile Canyon Rim Trail. 3. The 0.5-mile Ottos Trail. 4. The 0.5-mile Coke Ovens Trail. 5. The 0.8-mile Devils Kitchen Trail. 6. The 1-mile Alcove Nature Trail. 7. The 2.3-mile Serpents Trail (moderate). 8. The 4-mile Old Gordon Trail (moderate).

FLORISSANT FOSSIL BEDS NATIONAL MONUMENT P.O. Box 185, Florissant, CO 80816; (719)748-3253. 5,998 acres. This national monument is in the Rockies of central Colorado, near Pike's Peak, at an elevation of 8,500 feet. It's on the site of an ancient lake, with extensive beds of fossil plants, animals, and insects from the Oligocene epoch, including petrified redwood and sequoia stumps. Terrain consists of rolling hills with rock outcroppings and formations, ponds, wetlands, wildflowers, and forests of spruce and pine, fir and aspen. Wildlife includes elk, deer, pronghorn, mountain lion, coyote, porcupine, and golden eagle.

• *Suggested Trails for Nature Walks:* 1. The 0.5-mile Walk Through Time Trail (loop). 2. The 1-mile Petrified Forest Loop. 3. The 2-mile Cave Trail. 4. The 1.2-mile Hans Loop (easy-moderate). 5. The 2-mile Shootin' Star Trail (easy-moderate). 6. The 2.1-mile Sawmill Trail (easy-moderate). 7. The 4-mile Hornbek Wildlife Loop (easy-moderate).

GREAT SAND DUNES NATIONAL MONUMENT 11500 Highway 150, Mosca, CO 81146; (719)378-2312. 38,659 acres. Great Sand Dunes National Monument is situated in south-central Colorado's San Luis Valley, next to the Sangre de Cristo Mountains and Rio Grande National Forest. It features 700-foot-high dunes, along with small canyons, several creeks, grasslands of Indian ricegrass, blowout grass, and prairie sunflower, as well as pinyon-juniper woodlands and ponderosa pine forests, with aspen and cottonwood. Among the wildlife are elk, mule deer, mountain lion, black bear, coyote, bobcat, rabbit, kangaroo rat, magpie, and raven.

• *Suggested Trails for Nature Walks:* 1. The 0.5-mile Montville Nature Trail (loop). 2. The 0.8-mile Pinyon Flats Trail. 3. The 0.8-mile Escape Dunes/Ghost Forest Trail. 4. The 1-mile Wellington Ditch Trail. 5. Several other short trails are found near the visitor center and campground. 6. The 5.5-mile Little Medano Creek Trail (easy-moderate).

Other Suitable Locations for Nature Walks in Colorado

Colorado has forty state parks, and thirty of these locations have nature or hiking trails. Information: Colorado State Parks, 1313 Sherman Street, #618, Denver, CO 80203; (303)866-3437.

There are two additional national forests in the state with trails: 1 Routt National Forest, 29587 West U.S. 40, Steamboat Springs, CO 80487; (303)879-1722. 2. White River National Forest, P.O. Box 948, Glenwood Springs, CO 81602; (303)945-2521.

Trails are found in three other Colorado areas administered by the National Park Service: 1. Black Canyon of the Gunnison National Monument, 2233 East Main, Suite A, Montrose, CO 81401; (970)249-7036. 2. Curecanti National Recreation Area, 102 Elk Creek, Gunnison, CO 81230; (303)641-2337. 3. Mesa Verde National Park, Mesa Verde, CO 81330; (303)529-4461.

Some Bureau of Land Management areas in the state have trails. Information: BLM, Colorado State Office, 2850 Youngfield Street, Lakewood, CO 80215; (303)239-3600.

Two national wildlife refuges in Colorado have trails. Information: U.S. Fish and Wildlife Refuge, Box 25486, Denver Federal Center, Denver, CO 80225.

Several U.S. Army Corps of Engineers lakes in the state feature trails. Information: Corps of Engineers, Omaha District, 215 North 17th Street, Omaha, NE 68102; (402)221-4137.

CONNECTICUT

Recommended Areas for Nature Walks

WHITE MEMORIAL FOUNDATION AND CONSERVATION CENTER P.O. Box 368, Litchfield, CT 06759; (203)567-0857. 4,000 acres. The White Memorial Foundation and Conservation Center is located near Litchfield in the foothills of the Berkshires, in northwestern Connecticut. Included here are four designated natural areas totaling 200 acres, along with Bantam Lake and the Bantam River, marshes and swamps, as well as a number of ponds. There are also open fields, wildflowers, and hilly woodlands with shrubs and mixed hardwoods, plus spruce, pine, hemlock, and mountain laurel. Wildlife includes white-tailed deer, bobcat, fox, raccoon, beaver, owl, and hawk.

• *Suggested Trails for Nature Walks:* 1. The 0.8-mile Interpretive Trail. 2. The 0.5-mile Butternut Brook Trail. 3. The 1-mile Lake Trail. 4. The 1.1-mile Pine Island Trail. 5. The 1.6-mile Little Pond Trail. 6. The 0.6-mile Heron Pond Trail. 7. The 0.6-mile Fawn Pond Trail. 8. The 1-mile Plunge Pool Trail. 9. The 2.8-mile Beaver Pond Trail. 10. A 6.2-mile segment of the Mattatuck Trail.

SHARON AUDUBON CENTER Route 4, Sharon, CT 06069; (203)364-0520. 684 acres. This Audubon Society center and sanctuary in northwestern Connecticut features wildflower and herb gardens, 30-acre Ford Pond and Bog Meadow Pond, and Herrick Brook, with marshes and swamps, open fields, and brushy areas, as well as a forest of hemlock, pine, and hardwoods, including oak and birch. Among the wildlife are white-tailed deer, coyote, bobcat, red fox, beaver, cottontail, mink, and ruffed grouse.

• *Suggested Trails for Nature Walks:* 1. The 0.3-mile Lucy Harvey Trail. 2. The 1-mile Fern Trail. 3. The 1-mile Hazelnut Trail. 4. The 1.6-mile Hendrickson Bog Meadow Trail. 5. The 2.4-mile Woodchuck Trail. 6. The 0.8-mile Hal Borland Trail (easy-moderate). 7. The 1.6-mile Ford Trail (easy-moderate).

DEVIL'S DEN PRESERVE P.O. Box 1162, Weston, CT 06883; (203)226-4991. 1,720 acres. Owned by the Nature Conservancy, this preserve in southwestern Connecticut includes the Saugatuck Wildlife Refuge along the Saugatuck River. It's an area of small, rugged ridges with rock outcroppings, ravines, streams, swamps, marshes, a mill pond, and a mixed hardwood forest with oak, birch, maple, hemlock, and pine, as well as mountain laurel and white azalea. Wildlife includes white-tailed deer, bobcat, coyote, and red fox, along with pileated woodpecker, wood duck, ruffed grouse, and great horned owl. Guided walks are available.

• *Suggested Trails for Nature Walks:* 1. The 1.1-mile Godfrey Pond Loop. 2. The 2.8-mile loop through Ambler Gorge. 3. The 3.3-mile loop past Portable Sawmill. 4. The 5.6-mile circuit around the preserve.

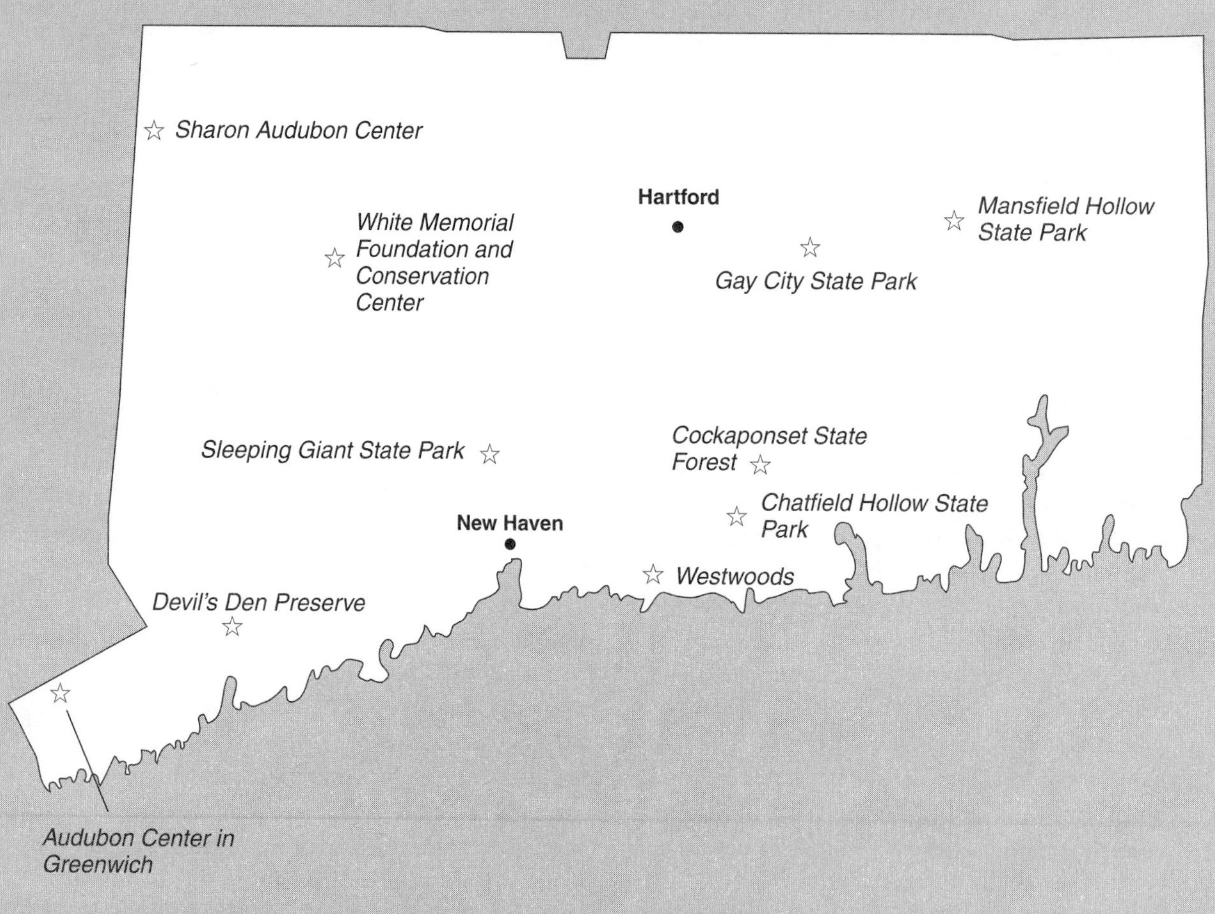
CONNECTICUT
Sharon Audubon Center
Hartford
White Memorial Foundation and Conservation Center
Mansfield Hollow State Park
Gay City State Park
Sleeping Giant State Park
Cockaponset State Forest
Chatfield Hollow State Park
New Haven
Westwoods
Devil's Den Preserve
Audubon Center in Greenwich

GAY CITY STATE PARK c/o Connecticut Office of State Parks and Recreation, 79 Elm Street, Hartford, CT 06106; (203)566-2304. 1,569 acres. Situated next to Meshomasic State Forest in central Connecticut, Gay City State Park includes the remains of an eighteenth-century mill village with old stone foundations. Terrain is hilly and the park includes rock formations, open fields, woodlands, streams, a swamp, a pond, and the Blackledge River.

• *Suggested Trails for Nature Walks:* 1. The 0.4-mile Partridge Trail. 2. The 0.8-mile Bolton Trail. 3. The 1-mile Daley Road Trail. 4. The 0.8-mile Crossover Trail. 5. The 0.3-mile Bridge Trail (easy-moderate). 6. The 0.6-mile Possum Trail (easy-moderate). 7. The 0.8-mile French Trail (easy-moderate). 8. The 1.5-mile Brimstone Trail (easy-moderate). 9. The 2.3-mile Gay City Road Trail (easy-moderate). 10. The 2.7-mile South Trail (easy-moderate).

AUDUBON CENTER IN GREENWICH 613 Riversville Road, Greenwich, CT 06831; (203)869-5272. 280 acres. Located in the southwest corner of the state, this Audubon Society property includes an environmental center. Terrain consists of low wooded ridges with meadows and old pastures, streams and swamps, ponds, and man-made Mead Lake. The Byram River runs the length of the center's lands. There are also wildflowers, ferns, shrubs, and a forest of oak, maple, beech, hemlock, ash, and dogwood. Guided walks are available. A mile away is the 127-acre Audubon Fairchild Garden, another sanctuary with several miles of trails.

• *Suggested Trails for Nature Walks:* 1. The 0.8-mile Discovery Trail. 2. The 1.3-mile Lake Trail. 3. The 2.8-mile Loop around the Center.

CHATFIELD HOLLOW STATE PARK c/o Connecticut Office of State Parks and Recreation, 79 Elm Street, Hartford, CT 06106; (203)566-2304. 356 acres. Chatfield Hollow State Park is in a wooded hollow in south-central Connecticut, adjacent to Cockaponset State Forest lands. The park features hills and streams, rock ledges and caves, man-made and 7-acre Schreeder Pond, mosses and wildflowers, dogwood and mountain laurel, and a forest of white pine, cedar, oak, hickory, birch, and beech.

• *Suggested Trails for Nature Walks:* 1. The 0.5-mile Nature Trail. 2. The 0.8-mile Covered Bridge Trail. 3. The 1.5-mile West Crest Trail (easy-moderate). 4. The 1.5-mile Lookout Trail (easy-moderate loop). 5. The 2-mile Chimney Trail (easy-moderate loop). 6. The 2-mile Ridge Trail (easy-moderate). 7. The 2.5-mile Deep Woods Trail (easy-moderate). 8. The 2.5-mile East Woods Trail (easy-moderate loop).

COCKAPONSET STATE FOREST c/o Connecticut Office of State Parks and Recreation, 79 Elm Street, Hartford, CT 06106; (203)566-2304. 15,652 acres. Located on the western side of the Connecticut River valley, in the south-central part of the state, this is Connecticut's second largest state forest. It's characterized by low ridges with rock ledges and outcroppings, streams and ponds, marshes and swamps, and several reservoirs. Among the trees here are oak, beech, hickory, birch, maple, and cedar, with dogwood, azalea, and mountain laurel. Wildlife includes white-tailed deer, raccoon, rabbit, and grouse.

• *Suggested Trails for Nature Trails:* 1. The 0.5-mile Old Forest Trail. 2. The 1.4-mile Wildwood Trail. 3. The 2.9-mile Pattaconk Trail. 4. The 7.5-mile Cockaponset Trail (easy-moderate).

SLEEPING GIANT STATE PARK c/o Connecticut Office of State Parks and Recreation, 79 Elm Street, Hartford, CT 06106; (203)566-2304. 1,439 acres. Lying north of New Haven, in the south-central part of Connecticut, Sleeping Giant State Park features small, rugged volcanic mountains that can be seen to form the shape of a sleeping man. Highest point is 739-foot Mt. Carmel, which has an observation tower. There are rocky crags and outcroppings, low ridges and cliffs, streams and waterfalls, swamps and the Mill River, shrubs and wildflowers, as well as mixed woodlands with white pine, hemlock, red oak, and mountain laurel.

• *Suggested Trails for Nature Walks:* 1. The 0.7-mile Diamond Trail. 2. The 1.5-mile Nature Trail. 3. The 1.1-mile Hexagon Trail (easy-moderate). 4. The 1.1-mile Triangle Trail (easy-moderate). 5. The 1.9-mile Circle Trail (easy-moderate). 6. The 2.2-mile Yellow Trail (easy-moderate). 7. The 2.4-mile Orange Trail (easy-moderate). 8. The 3.2-mile Violet Trail (easy-moderate). 9. The 1.6-mile Tower Path (easy-moderate). 10. The 1.6-mile Square Trail (easy-moderate).

MANSFIELD HOLLOW STATE PARK c/o Connecticut Office of State Parks and Recreation, 79 Elm Street, Hartford, CT 06106; (203)566-2304. 2,328 acres. This northeastern Connecticut state park is situated near the confluence of the Natchaug, Fenton, and Mount Hope rivers. It includes the Fenton River, 500-acre Naubesatuck Lake, which was created by damming the Natchaug River, as well as marshes and swamps, hills and bluffs, open fields, ferns, and a forest of mixed hardwoods with pine.

• *Suggested Trails for Nature Walks:* 1. The 4.5-mile Naubesatuck Lake Trail, which loops around the upper part of the lake. 2. Several other easy trails wind alongside and east of the lower portion of the lake.

WESTWOODS c/o Guilford Land Conservation Trust, Westwoods Trail Committee, P.O. Box 200, Guilford, CT 06437. 2,000 acres. Located in Guilford, in south-central Connecticut, the area known as Westwoods features low ridges with cliffs and ledges, granite outcroppings and boulders, caves and crevices, as well as marshes, swamps, streams, a pond, and a brackish lake. Vegetation includes ferns, sedges, shrubs, mosses, and wildflowers, amid a hemlock forest with oak, hickory, maple, and mountain laurel.

• *Suggested Trails for Nature Walks:* Westwoods has a network of over 40 miles of easy to moderate trails. Easiest are the Green Nature Trail (loop), the Violet-Circle Trail, and the several east-west trails, which are marked with rectangles.

Other Suitable Locations for Nature Walks in Connecticut

Connecticut has fifty-two state parks and nine state forests, and the majority of these locations have appropriate trails. Information: Connecticut Office of State Parks and Recreation, 79 Elm Street, Hartford, CT 06106; (203)566-2304.

The Nature Conservancy manages over seventy preserves in the state, and many of the larger areas have trails. Information: The Nature Conservancy, Connecticut Chapter, 55 High Street, Middletown, CT 06457; (203)344-0716.

There are trails at several Connecticut lakes administered by the U.S. Army Corps of Engineers. Information: Corps of Engineers, New England District, 424 Trapelo Road, Waltham, MA 02254; (617)647-8107.

DELAWARE

Recommended Areas for Nature Walks

BRANDYWINE CREEK STATE PARK P.O. Box 3782, Wilmington, DE 19807; (302)577-3534. 850 acres. This state park is in the Brandywine Valley north of Wilmington, at the northern tip of the state. It's an area of rolling hills with streams and marshes, open meadows, the Brandywine River, and woodlands with pine as well as a stand of 190-year-old tulip trees. Wildlife includes white-tailed deer, hawk, and bog turtle. The park has a nature center, and guided walks are available in the summer.

- *Suggested Trails for Nature Walks:* 1. The 0.8-mile Tulip Tree Trail. 2. The 0.5-mile Marsh Trail. 3. The 1-mile Old Field Trail. 4. The 1.8-mile Indian Springs Trail. 5. The 1.9-mile Hidden Pond Trail. 6. The 1.6-mile Horseshoe Trail. 7. The 1.7-mile Long Wall Trail. 8. The 2-mile Rocky Run Trail.

CAPE HENLOPEN STATE PARK 42 Cape Henlopen Drive, Lewes, DE 19958; (302)645-8983. 3,143 acres. Situated on the shore of Delaware Bay, in the southeastern part of the state, Cape Henlopen State Park has 4 miles of ocean beaches, 80-foot dunes, a saltwater lagoon, salt marshes, cranberry bogs, pine forests, and some small streams. Naturalist-led walks are offered here in the summer.

- *Suggested Trails for Nature Walks:* 1. The 0.6-mile Seaside Nature Trail. 2. The 1.2-mile Pinelands Nature Trail. 3. The 0.5-mile Salt Marsh Spur Trail. 4. The 1.8-mile Beach Loop Trail. 5. The 3.1-mile Dune Overlook Trail.

WHITE CLAY CREEK STATE PARK 425 Wedgewood Road, Newark, DE 19711; (302)731-1310. 707 acres. Located in the northwest corner of the state, this state park is adjacent to the White Clay Creek Preserve, which extends into Pennsylvania. There are hills and valleys with rock outcroppings and vistas, wetlands and grasses, streams including White Clay Creek, two small ponds, and woodlands of oak and tulip tree, hickory, and beech. Naturalist-led walks are available during summer months.

- *Suggested Trails for Nature Walks:* 1. The 2-mile Millstone Trail. 2. The 3-mile Whitetail Trail. 3. The 5-mile Twin Valley Trail.

LUMS POND STATE PARK 1068 Howell School Road, Bear, DE 19701; (302)368-6989. 1,757 acres. Lums Pond State Park lies just north of the Chesapeake and Delaware Canal, in northwestern Delaware. Here are woodlands with oak and poplar, open fields and brushlands, creeks and wetlands, with a 200-acre freshwater pond. White-tailed deer, fox, and beaver are among the wildlife. The park has a nature center, and guided walks are available in summer.

- *Suggested Trails for Nature Walks:* 1. The 0.5-mile Measured Walking Trail. 2. The 1-mile Measured Walking Trail. 3. The 7.5-mile Swamp Forest Trail.

TRAP POND STATE PARK RD 2, Box 331, Laurel, DE 19956; (302)875-5753. 966 acres.

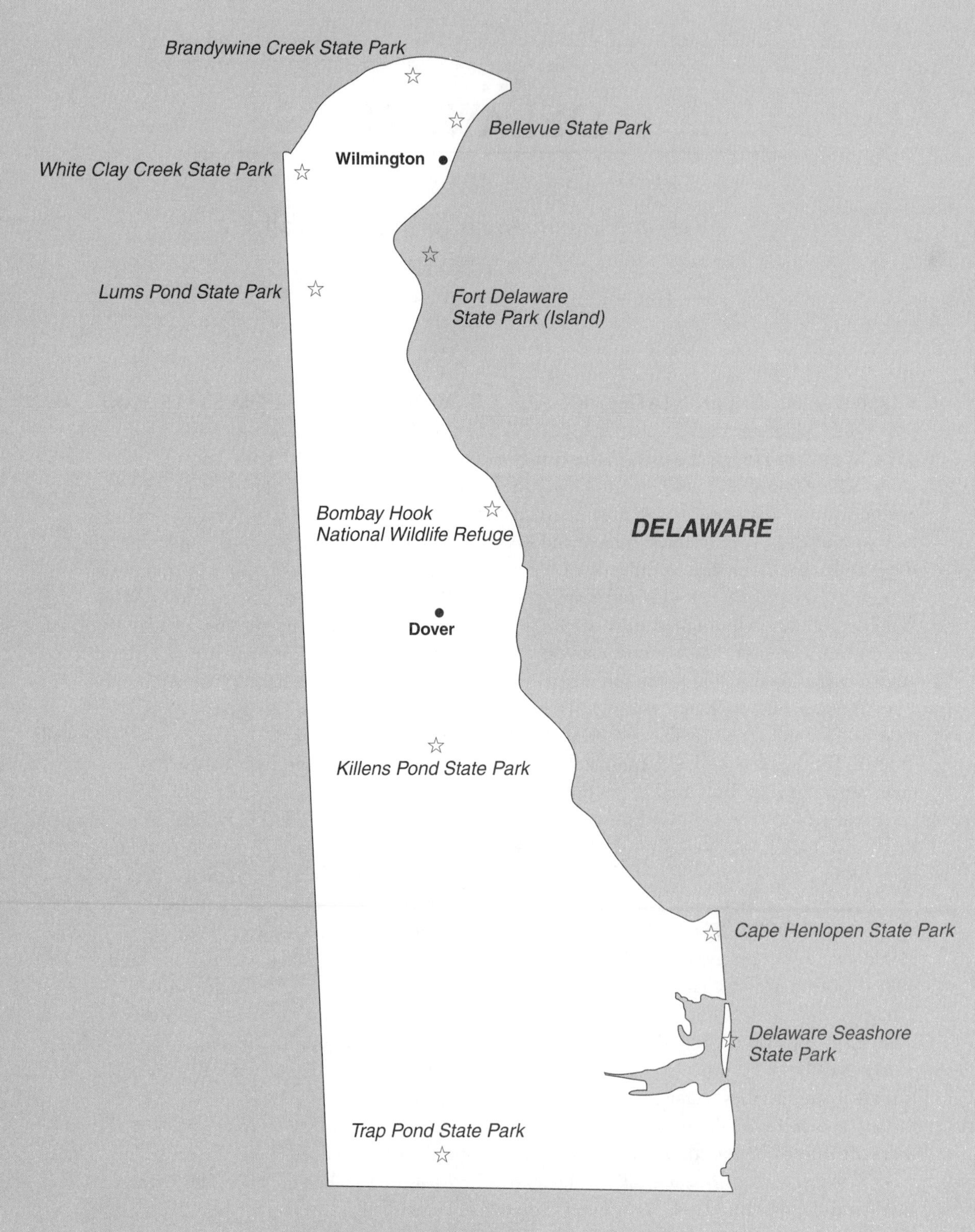

Brandywine Creek State Park
Bellevue State Park
White Clay Creek State Park
Wilmington
Lums Pond State Park
Fort Delaware
State Park (Island)
Bombay Hook
National Wildlife Refuge
DELAWARE
Dover
Killens Pond State Park
Cape Henlopen State Park
Delaware Seashore
State Park
Trap Pond State Park

This southern Delaware state park is named for the 90-acre pond that forms the park's focal point. There are also streams and wetlands, including a baldcypress swamp, and some loblolly pine trees. Among the wildlife are white-tailed deer, bald eagle, and pileated woodpecker. Guided walks are offered in summer.

• *Suggested Trails for Nature Walks:* 1. The 0.8-mile Island Trail. 2. The 1.5-mile Cypress Point Trail. 3. The 5-mile Boundary Trail.

KILLENS POND STATE PARK 5025 Killenspond Road, Felton, DE 19943; (302)284-4526. 878 acres. Situated in the central part of the state, this park features Killens Pond, which is a 66-acre mill pond, along with a segment of the Murderkill River. Terrain is relatively flat with some gentle slopes, and there are open fields as well as woodlands with oak and hickory, maple and pine, holly and cedar. Wildlife includes white-tailed deer, raccoon, and river otter.

• *Suggested Trails for Nature Walks:* 1. The short Ice Storm Trail. 2. The 3.2-mile Pondside Nature Trail.

DELAWARE SEASHORE STATE PARK Inlet 850, Rehoboth Beach, DE 19971; (302)227-2800. 2,018 acres. Delaware Seashore State Park is on a barrier island off the Atlantic coast of southeastern Delaware. Included are 6 miles of shoreline with beaches, bay islands, salt marshes, and woodlands. White-tailed deer, fox, and pelican are among the wildlife.

• *Suggested Trails for Nature Walks:* 1. The 1.5-mile Burton's Island Nature Trail. 2. Other walks are possible along the shoreline beaches.

FORT DELAWARE STATE PARK P.O. Box 170, Delaware City, DE 19706; (302)834-7941 / Port Penn Interpretive Center (302)834-0431. Located on Pea Patch Island in the Delaware River, and accessible by ferry, this northern Delaware state park preserves a Civil War era fortress that once held confederate prisoners. It's also a place of open fields, woodlands, streams, and marshes, with wading birds as well as white-tailed deer and muskrat. Four miles away is the Port Penn Interpretive Center and Museum, which features additional marshlands.

• *Suggested Trails for Nature Walks:* 1. The 0.8-mile Prison Camp Nature Trail. 2. The 1.5-mile Port Penn Wetland Trail.

BOMBAY HOOK NATIONAL WILDLIFE REFUGE RD 1, Box 147, Smyrna, DE 19977; (302)653-9345. 15,978 acres. Situated alongside the Delaware River, in the east-central part of the state, this national wildlife refuge protects migratory birds including the bald eagle, as well as other wildlife such as white-tailed deer, red fox, opossum, and beaver. The area consists of tidal salt marshes and swamps, freshwater pools, creeks and rivers, meadows and forests, with sweetgum, maple, and wild cherry trees.

• *Suggested Trails for Nature Walks:* 1. The 0.5-mile Boardwalk Trail. 2. The 0.5-mile Parson Point Trail. 3. The Bear Swamp Trail (loop). 4. Two short trails lead to observation towers.

BELLEVUE STATE PARK 800 Carr Road, Wilmington, DE 19809; (302)577-3390. 271 acres. Located near the Delaware River in the northern part of the state, Bellevue State Park is on lands that were previously part of a large estate. While it still includes a number of buildings and some recreational facilities, there are also woodlands, fields, and a pond. Guided walks are available.

• *Suggested Trails for Nature Walks:* A number of trails suitable for walking wind throughout the park. Some are for foot travel alone and others are open to horseback riding or cycling.

Other Suitable Locations for Nature Walks in Delaware

There are trails in Prime Hook National Wildlife Refuge, Route 3, Box 195, Milton, DE 19968; (302)684-8419.

Some trails are also available in Blackbird State Forest, 502 Blackbird Forest Road, Smyrna, DE 19977; (302)653-6505.

FLORIDA

Recommended Areas for Nature Walks

EVERGLADES NATIONAL PARK P.O. Box 279, Homestead, FL 33030; (305)242-7700. 1,400,800 acres. Situated at the southern tip of Florida and designated an International Biosphere Reserve, this is one of our most endangered national parks, owing to the diversion of water by canals and levees north of the park.

Everglades terrain is relatively flat, with tropical vegetation, hardwood "hammocks" (little islands), mangrove swamps, marshes, freshwater ponds, lakes, and creeks. There are also pinelands, areas of coastal prairie, and dozens of keys (islands). Wildlife includes alligator, crocodile, Florida panther, and manatee, along with great blue heron, wood stork, ibis, roseate spoonbill, brown pelican, osprey, black vulture, and southern bald eagle. Bug repellant is mandatory owing to the mosquito population. Naturalist-led walks are available.

• *Suggested Trails for Nature Walks:* 1. The 0.5-mile Eco Pond Trail (loop). 2. The 1-mile Guy Bradley Trail. 3. The 1.6-mile Bear Lake Trail. 4. The 1.6-mile Snake Bight Trail. 5. The 1.8-mile Christian Point Trail. 6. The 2-mile Bayshore Loop. 7. The 2.6-mile Rowdy Bend Trail. 8. The 7.5-mile Coastal Prairie Trail. 9. A network of trails in the Long Pine Key Area.

APALACHICOLA NATIONAL FOREST 325 John Knox Road, Suite F-100, Tallahassee, FL 32303; (904)942-9300. 557,000 acres. This northwestern Florida national forest encompasses an area of sandhills with wiregrass, steep-walled sinkholes and caves, ponds, and wetlands, as well as longleaf pine forests with oak and hickory, beech and ash, dogwood and magnolia. Two designed wilderness areas total 32,620 acres, and wildlife includes white-tailed deer, red-shouldered hawk, and wild turkey.

• *Suggested Trails for Nature Walks:* 1. The 0.5-mile Crossover Trail. 2. The 2.3-mile Gumswamp Trail. 3. The 3.1-mile Sinkhole Trail. 4. The 4-mile Trail of Lakes. 5. The 4.5-mile Wright Lake Trail. 6. A 65-mile section of the 1,300-mile Florida Trail, which crosses the forest.

OCALA NATIONAL FOREST 325 John Knox Road, Suite F-100; Tallahassee, FL 32303; (904)942-9300. 367,000 acres. Located in the north-central part of the state, Ocala National Forest occupies an area of flatwoods consisting of forests of longleaf pine, hardwood swamps with cypress and gum, live oak hammocks, and grassy prairies. There are many wild lakes and ponds, some major streams, and four designated wilderness areas that total 26,580 acres.

• *Suggested Trails for Nature Walks:* 1. The 1.8-mile Lake Eaton Loop Trail. 2. The 2.2-mile Lake Eaton Sinkhole Trail. 3. The 2.1-mile Salt Springs Trail. 4. The 5.9-mile St. Francis Trail. 5. The 67-mile Ocala Trail, which is a segment of the Florida Trail.

WITHLACOOCHEE STATE FOREST 15019 Broad Street, Brooksville, FL 34601; (904)754-6777. 128,471 acres. This state forest

FLORIDA
Osceola National Forest
Apalachicola National Forest
Jacksonville
O'Leno State Park
Paynes Prairie State Preserve
Merritt Island National Wildlife Refuge
Ocala National Forest
Orlando
Withlacoochee State Forest
Tosohatchee State Reserve
Big Cypress National Preserve
Miami
Everglades National Park

consists of four large and separate tracts in west-central Florida, north of Tampa. Included on these lands are sandy hills and ravines, limestone rocks, hardwood hammocks, prairies, ponds, and cypress swamps, as well as the Withlacoochee and Little Withlachoochee rivers. Common trees are slash, longleaf, and loblolly pine, baldcypress and pond cypress, cabbage palm, oak, maple, hickory, and gum. Among the wildlife are deer, bobcat, fox, raccoon, opossum, alligator, armadillo, red-tailed hawk, and bald eagle.

• *Suggested Trails for Nature Walks:* 1. The 2-mile McKethan Lake Nature Trail. 2. The 2.5-mile Colonel Robins Nature Trail, which consists of two loops. 3. The 31.3-mile Croom Trail, made up of several loops. 4. The 31.5-mile Richloam Trail (loop), which includes the 6.6-mile Green Swamp Connector Trail. 5. The 46.1-mile Citrus Trail, consisting of four loops.

PAYNES PRAIRIE STATE PRESERVE Route 2, Box 41, Micanopy, FL 32667; (904)466-3397. 21,000 acres. Paynes Prairie State Preserve is near Gainesville in northern Florida. Occupying a limestone basin, it includes Lake Wauberg, Alachua Lake, and Chacala Pond, as well as marshes and swamps, prairie wetlands with streams, and pine forests. Among the wildlife are alligator, otter, hawk, and sandhill crane. Ranger-led walks are available.

• *Suggested Trails for Nature Walks:* 1. The 1.3-mile La Chua Trail. 2. The 1.5-mile Bolen Bluff Trail. 3. The 4.1-mile Cone's Dike Trail. 4. The 6.5-mile Chacala Trail, which consists of several loops. 5. The 17-mile Gainesville-Hawthorne State Trail.

MERRITT ISLAND NATIONAL WILDLIFE REFUGE P.O. Box 6504, Titusville, FL 32782; (407)867-0667. 92,000 acres. This national wildlife refuge is located on a barrier island shared with Canaveral National Seashore and the Kennedy Space Center, along Florida's central Atlantic coast. The refuge encompasses ridges and marshes, saltwater estuaries, sandy beaches, portions of the Indian and Banana rivers, Mosquito Lagoon, with subtropical live oak forests, pine flatwoods, and hardwood hammocks. Wildlife includes alligator and armadillo, as well as manatee and loggerhead sea turtle, with brown pelican, wood stork, great blue heron, red-tailed hawk, and bald eagle.

• *Suggested Trails for Nature Walks:* 1. The 0.5-mile Oak Hammock Trail. 2. The 2-mile Palm Hammock Trail. 3. The 5-mile Cruickshank Trail. 4. There are also four short nature trails on Canaveral National Seashore lands directly to the north.

BIG CYPRESS NATIONAL PRESERVE HCR 61, Box 11, Ochopee, FL 33943; (813)695-4111. 729,000 acres. Occupying the region northwest of Everglades National Park in southwest Florida, Big Cypress National Preserve protects a large area of wet prairies and marshes, hardwood hammocks (islands of trees) and slash pine, with vast numbers of baldcypress trees. Wildlife includes alligator, black bear, deer, Florida panther, and bald eagle. During the rainy season portions of the trails are under water. January through April is the best time to walk here.

• *Suggested Trails for Nature Walks:* 1. The short Tree Snail Hammock Nature Trail. 2. Some 42.8 miles of the 1,300-mile Florida Trail are located here, including two loops.

OSCEOLA NATIONAL FOREST U.S. Highway 90, P.O. Box 70, Olustee, FL 32072; (904)752-2577. 157,000 acres. Osceola National Forest in northern Florida is characterized by flatwoods and ridges with longleaf and slash pine, creeks, and cypress swamps, and includes the 13,640-acre Big Gum Swamp Wilderness Area.

• *Suggested Trails for Nature Walks:* 1. The 1.5-mile Olustee Battlefield Trail. 2. A 20-mile segment of the Florida Trail. 3. A new 5-mile wilderness trail is expected to be open by 1997.

O'LENO STATE PARK Route 2, Box 1010, High Springs, FL 32643; (904)454-1853. 6,000 acres. This northern Florida state park includes a portion of the Santa Fe River, which flows underground for about 3 miles. In the area are swamps and sinkholes, sandhills and limestone outcroppings, pine forests and hardwood hammocks, with wildlife that includes white-tailed deer, bobcat, otter, wild turkey, and alligator.

• *Suggested Trails for Nature Walks:* 1. The 0.5-mile Limestone Trail. 2. The 1-mile Santa Fe River Trail. 3. The 3.5-mile Pareners Branch Loop. 4. The 6.5-mile Sweet Water Trail.

TOSOHATCHEE STATE RESERVE 3365 Taylor Creek Road, Christmas, FL 32709; (407)568-5893. 28,000 acres. Located alongside a 19-mile stretch of the St. Johns River in central Florida, Tosohatchee State Reserve includes creeks, swamps, and marshes, as well as pine flatwoods and hammocks, with some virgin slash pine, virgin cypress, and a range of wildflowers. Among the wildlife are white-tailed deer, Florida panther, bobcat, gray fox, wild turkey, hawk, and bald eagle.

• *Suggested Trails for Nature Walks:* 1. The Tosohatchee Recreational Trail, which consists of a series of loops—totaling over 25 miles—in the northern part of the reserve. 2. An additional trail extends through the southern region.

Other Suitable Locations for Nature Walks in Florida

Florida has 110 state parks and other recreational sites, and the vast majority of these have nature or hiking trails. Information: Division of Recreation and Parks, MS 535, 3900 Commonwealth Boulevard, Tallahassee, FL 32399; (904)488-9872.

There are nine national wildlife refuges in the state with trails. Information: U.S. Fish and Wildlife Service, 1875 Century Boulevard, Atlanta, GA 30345.

Several state forests have trails. Information: Division of Forestry, 3125 Conner Boulevard, Tallahassee, FL 32399; (904)488-4274.

Some of Florida's twenty-one Nature Conservancy preserves feature trails that are open to the public. Information: The Nature Conservancy, Florida Chapter, 2699 Lee Road, Suite 500, Winter Park, FL 32789; (407)628-5887.

Portions of the 1,300-mile Florida Trail, which is still in the process of being developed, are appropriate for nature walks. Information: Florida Trail Association, P.O. Box 13708, Gainesville, FL 32604; (904)378-8823.

Trails are available at some U.S. Army Corps of Engineers areas in the state. Information: Corps of Engineers, Jacksonville District, P.O. Box 4970, Jacksonville, FL 32232; (904)791-2215.

GEORGIA

Recommended Areas for Nature Walks

CHATTAHOOCHEE NATIONAL FOREST 508 Oak St. NW, Gainesville, GA 30501; (404)536-0541. 750,000 acres. Stretching across the rugged mountain region of northern Georgia, Chattahoochee National Forest includes the highest point in the state, 4,784-foot Brasstown Bald. There are also lakes and streams with waterfalls; the Chattooga Wild and Scenic River is one of several rivers.

The region is forested with hardwoods as well as hemlock and pine, dogwood and sourwood, rhododendron, and mountain laurel. Among the wildlife are black bear, white-tailed deer, wild boar, bobcat, fox, and beaver, along with belted kingfisher, pileated woodpecker, grouse, and wild turkey.

• *Suggested Trails for Nature Walks:* 1. The 0.3-mile Helton Creek Trail. 2. The 0.4-mile Horse Trough Trail. 3. The 0.5-mile Lakeshore Trail. 4. The 0.6-mile Songbird Trail. 5. The 0.7-mile Byron H. Reece Trail. 6. The 1-mile Coleman River Trail. 7. The 1.2-mile Lake Chatuge Trail (loop). 8. The 1.6-mile Bear Creek Trail. 9. The 2.7-mile South Fork Trail. 10. The 4.6-mile Lake Russell Trail (loop).

OCONEE NATIONAL FOREST 349 Forsyth Street, Monticello, GA 31064; (706)468-2244. 113,000 acres. Located in the rolling hills of north-central Georgia, with some flat areas, this national forest is probably best known for the Oconee River and the massive man-made Lake Oconee. The forest is one of piney woods and hardwoods, including shortleaf and loblolly pine, oak, and hickory, as well as dogwood and sweetgum. There are also streams with small waterfalls. Wildlife includes white-tailed deer, black bear, raccoon, opossum, skunk, rabbit, and wild turkey.

• *Suggested Trails for Nature Walks:* 1. The 0.3-mile Indian Mounds Trail. 2. The 0.3-mile Boarding House Trail. 3. The 1-mile Burgess Mountain Trail. 4. The 1-mile Falling Creek Trail. 5. The 1.8-mile Twin Bridges Trail. 6. The 2.5-mile Wise Creek Trail. 7. The 2.8-mile Ocmulgee River Trail. 8. The 4.1-mile Kinnard Creek Trail.

OKEFENOKEE NATIONAL WILDLIFE REFUGE Route 2, Box 338, Folkston, GA 31537; (912)496-3331. This national wildlife refuge in southeastern Georgia protects the enormous freshwater Okefenokee Swamp. More than 353,000 acres of the refuge consist of designated wilderness. The refuge includes the Suwannee River, a canal, many lakes, islands, areas of prairie, wildflowers, and a forest of cypress, sweetgum, magnolia, and pine trees. Among the wildlife are white-tailed deer, black bear, alligator, and raccoon, along with egret, crane, ibis, heron, wood stork, red-cockaded woodpecker, osprey, red-tailed hawk, and bald eagle.

• *Suggested Trails for Nature Walks:* 1. The 0.2-mile Peckerwood Trail (loop). 2. The 0.5-mile Chesser Island Trail (loop). 3. The 0.5-mile Deerstand Trail. 4. The 0.6-mile Canal Digger's

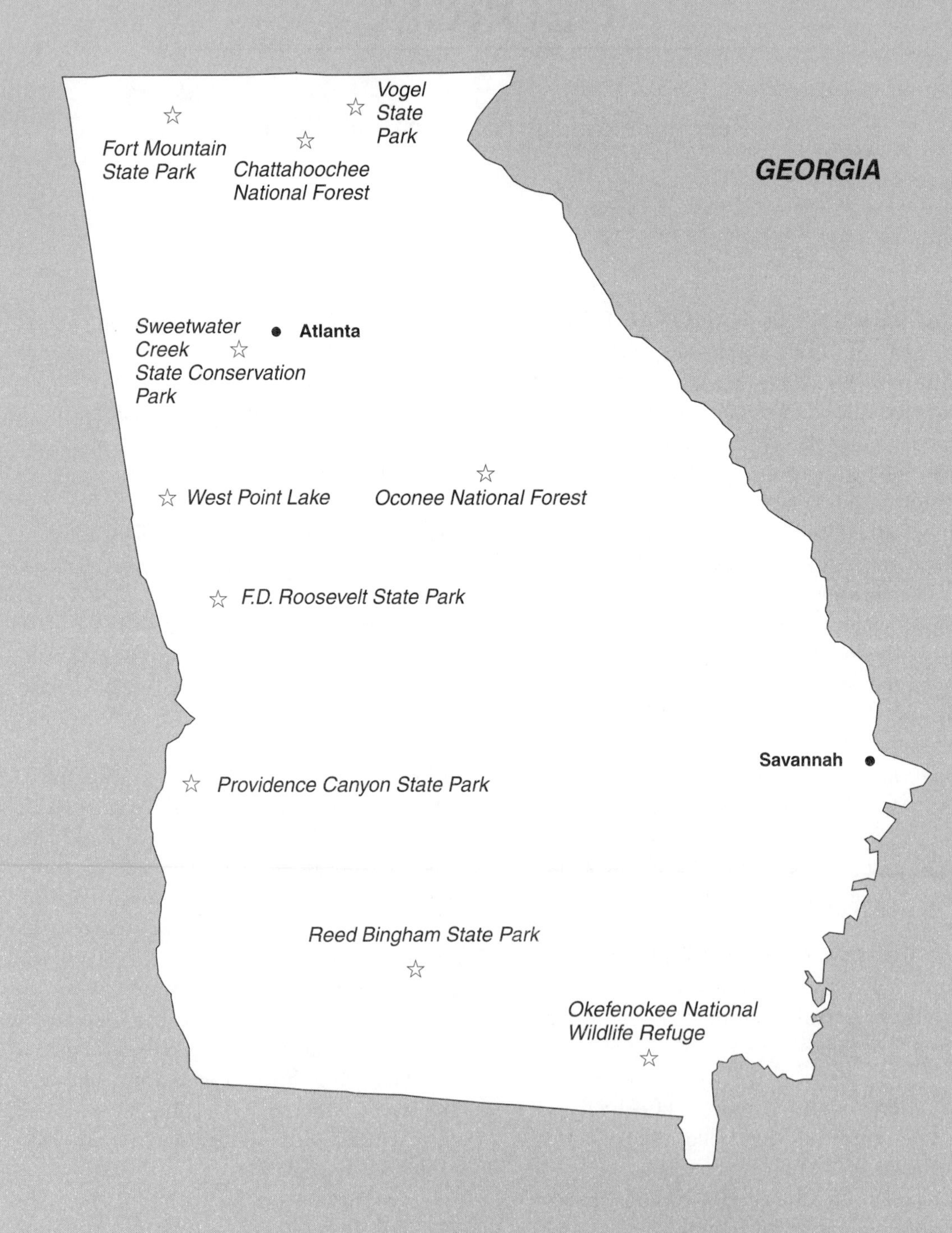
GEORGIA
Vogel State Park
Fort Mountain State Park
Chattahoochee National Forest
Sweetwater Creek State Conservation Park
Atlanta
West Point Lake
Oconee National Forest
F.D. Roosevelt State Park
Savannah
Providence Canyon State Park
Reed Bingham State Park
Okefenokee National Wildlife Refuge

Trail (loop). 5. The 0.8-mile Boardwalk to Tower. 6. Within the refuge are 2 additional miles of foot trails.

WEST POINT LAKE 500 Resource Management Drive, West Point, GA 31833; (404)645-2937. A man-made lake managed by the U.S. Army Corps of Engineers, 25,900-acre West Point Lake is on west Georgia's Chattahoochee River, along the Georgia-Alabama border. It has 525 miles of shoreline and includes a 10,000-acre wildlife management area, in a region of small hills with rock outcroppings, fields, many creeks, as well as pine and hardwood forests. The lake is recreation-oriented, featuring twenty-six day-use parks and four county parks. White-tailed deer, bobcat, raccoon, beaver, skunk, mink, songbirds, quail, wild turkey, osprey, and bald eagle are among the wildlife.

• *Suggested Trails for Nature Walks:* 1. The 0.4-mile Amity Campground Interpretive Trail. 2. The 0.5-mile Amity Campground Nature Trail. 3. The 0.4-mile Earl Cook Trail. 4. The 0.5-mile Ringer Trail. 5. The 0.7-mile R. Shaefer Heard Trail. 6. The 0.9-mile Whitetail Ridge Campground Trail. 7. State Line Campground Trails (1 mile). 8. The 1.2-mile Long Cane Trail. 9. Rocky Point Trails (1.3 miles). 10. Holiday Campground Trails (1.9 miles).

FORT MOUNTAIN STATE PARK 181 Fort Mountain Park Road, Chatsworth, GA 30705; (706)695-2621. 1,932 acres. This state park lies within the boundaries of Chattahoochee National Forest in northern Georgia's Cohutta Range. The park preserves Fort Mountain, which includes a mysterious 855-foot-long prehistoric stone wall on top. There are vistas, steep cliffs, ravines, and a 17-acre lake. The forest is one of pine and hardwoods, with maple, oak, gum, and poplar, plus rhododendron and mountain laurel.

• *Suggested Trails for Nature Walks:* 1. The 0.7-mile Big Rock Nature Trail. 2. The 1.2-mile Lake Loop Trail. 3. The 1.8-mile Old Fort Trail. 4. The 2.3-mile Gold Mine Creek Trail.

REED BINGHAM STATE PARK Box 394B-1, Route 2, Adel, GA 31620; (912)896-3551. 1,620 acres. Reed Bingham State Park in south Georgia features a 375-acre lake and a 3-mile stretch of the Little River. There are flatwoods and sandhills, cypress swamps and bogs, old fields and a freshwater pond, with longleaf and slash pine, oak, maple, hickory, and dogwood. The wildlife here includes white-tailed deer.

• *Suggested Trails for Nature Walks:* 1. The 0.5-mile Gopher Tortoise Nature Trail. 2. The 0.6-mile Birdwalk Trail. 3. The 0.9-mile Upland Loop Trail. 4. The 0.9-mile Little River Trail.

F.D. ROOSEVELT STATE PARK P.O. Box 2970, Highway 190 East, Pine Mountain, GA 31822; (706)663-4858. 10,000 acres. Located on west-central Georgia's Pine Mountain, and featuring Lake Delano, this state park includes a landscape of hills, bluffs, rock outcroppings, streams, and waterfalls, as well as woodlands, ferns, and wildflowers, with dogwood, azalea, mountain laurel, and rhododendron.

• *Suggested Trails for Nature Walks:* 1. The 1-mile Delano Trail (loop). 2. The 1.5-mile Swimming Pool Trail. 3. The 3.2-mile Mountain Creek Loop. 4. The 23-mile Pine Mountain Trail (easy-moderate), which includes the 6-mile Wolfden Loop and the 4.3-mile Dowdell's Knob Loop.

SWEETWATER CREEK STATE CONSERVATION PARK P.O. Box 816, Lithia Springs, GA 30057; (770)732-5871. 1,986 acres. Sweetwater Creek State Conservation Park is located west of Atlanta in the northwestern part of the state. It features hilly terrain with low ridges, rock outcroppings, streams including Sweetwater Creek, waterfalls, ruins of a nineteenth-century textile mill, meadows, and woodlands, with mountain laurel, wild azalea, and wildflowers and ferns.

• *Suggested Trails for Nature Walks:* 1. The 1-mile Red History Trail. 2. The 2-mile Blue Nature Trail. 3. The 4-mile White Trail. 4. Several miles of other trails wind east of Sweetwater Creek.

VOGEL STATE PARK 7485 Vogel State Park Road, Blairsville, GA 30512. 238 acres. This little state park is perched in the southern Appalachians of northern Georgia, amid the rugged lands of Chattahoochee National Forest. There are steep ridges, small streams, wildflowers in season, a mixed hardwood forest with many species of trees, and a lake.

• *Suggested Trails for Nature Walks:* 1. The 1-mile Byron Reece Nature Trail. 2. The 1-mile Trahlyta Lake Trail. 3. The 4-mile Bear Hair Gap Trail loop (easy-moderate). 4. The 0.2-mile Overlook Trail (easy-moderate).

PROVIDENCE CANYON STATE PARK Route 1, Box 158, Lumpkin, GA 31815; (912)838-6202. 1,108 acres. Situated in the southwestern part of the state, Providence Canyon is often referred to as Georgia's "Little Grand Canyon"—featuring sixteen small, eroded, colorful canyons up to 150 feet deep, along with a creek. There are rolling hills and valleys with open fields, shrubs, and forests of loblolly and longleaf pine, white and blackjack oak, hickory, dogwood, rhododendron, and wild azalea.

• *Suggested Trails for Nature Walks:* 1. The 3-mile White Blaze Trail (easy-moderate loop). 2. The 7-mile Red Blaze Trail (easy-moderate loop).

Other Suitable Locations for Nature Walks in Georgia

Georgia has fifty-nine state parks and state historic sites, and fifty of these locations have nature or hiking trails. Information: Georgia State Parks, 205 Butler Street, Southeast, Atlanta, GA 30334; (404)656-3530.

There's a network of trails at Cumberland Island National Seashore, which is accessible by ferry. Information: Cumberland Island National Seashore, P.O. Box 806, St. Marys, GA 31558; (912)882-4335.

The state has eight national wildlife refuges with trails. Information: U.S. Fish and Wildlife Service, 1875 Century Boulevard, Atlanta, GA 30345.

Several U.S. Army Corps of Engineers lakes in Georgia have trails. Information. Corps of Engineers, Savannah District, P.O. Box 889, Savannah, GA 31402, (912)944-5997; or Corps of Engineers, Mobile District, P.O. Box 2288, Mobile, AL 36628, (205)694-3720.

HAWAII

Recommended Areas for Nature Walks

HAWAII VOLCANOES NATIONAL PARK Hawaii Volcanoes National Park, HI 96718; (808)967-7311. 229,117 acres. Located on the island of Hawaii, this national park features Kilauea and Mauna Loa, two active volcanoes with continuing lava flows. Elevations range from sea level to almost 14,000 feet. Mauna Loa is said to be the most massive mountain on the planet, rising 30,000 feet from the ocean floor.

The landscape consists of craters, cinder cones, and lava tubes, along with rain forest and plant life that includes koa, pa'iniu, hapu'u, pukiawe, and coconut palm. Among the wildlife are feral cat, nene (Hawaiian goose), common mynah, pueo (Hawaiian owl), and kolea (lesser golden plover). Marine life includes humpback whale, 'ea (hawksbill sea turtle), and porpoise. Guided nature walks are offered in summer.

- *Suggested Trails for Nature Walks:* 1. The 0.3-mile Halema'uma'u Crater Overlook Trail. 2. The 0.3-mile Lava Tube Trail (loop). 3. The 0.5-mile Devastation Trail. 4. The 1-mile Kipuka Puaulu Trail (loop). 5. The 1.2-mile Bird Park Trail. 6. The 1.3-mile Iliahi Loop. 7. The 1.3-mile Pu'u Huluhulu Trail. 8. The 11-mile Crater Rim Trail. 9. The 4-mile Kilauea Iki Trail (easy-moderate loop). 10. The 3.3-mile Halema'uma'u Trail (moderate).

HALEAKALA NATIONAL PARK P.O. Box 369, Makawao, Maui, HI 96768; (808)572-7749. 28,665 acres. This national park on the island of Maui includes 10,000-foot and currently inactive Haleakala Crater, with lava flows and ash, cinder cones and vents, as well as the Kipahulu Valley to the east, with grasslands, 8,000 acres of rain forest, and coastal cliffs, plus streams with waterfalls and pools. Common plants include silversword, ti, ginger, guava, mango, kukui, koa, and bamboo, with lesser golden plover, i'iwi, nene, 'amakihi, and 'apapane among the park's birds. Ranger-led walks are available during the summer.

- *Suggested Trails for Nature Walks:* 1. The 0.3-mile Hosmer Grove Nature Trail. 2. The 0.3-mile Leleiwi Overlook Trail. 3. The 0.5-mile White Hill Trail. 4. The 0.5-mile Kuloa Point Loop Trail. 5. The first 0.7 mile of the Sliding Sands Trail. 6. The first 1.1-mile of the Halemauu Trail (easy-moderate). 7. The 2-mile Pipiwai Trail (easy-moderate).

ROUND TOP-TANTALUS FOREST RESERVE Division of Forestry and Wildlife, 1151 Punchbowl Street, Room 325, Honolulu, HI 96813; (808)587-0166. Located northeast of Honolulu on the island of Oahu, Round Top-Tantalus Forest Reserve features ridges and valleys, cliffs and rock formations, small streams and tropical rain forest, with ferns, passion fruit, guava, ginger, and hibiscus, as well as eucalyptus, bamboo, and paperbark pine.

- *Suggested Trails for Nature Walks:* 1. The 0.3-mile Tantalus Arboretum Trail. 2. The 0.5-mile Ualakaa Trail. 3. The 0.8-mile Pauoa Flats Trail.

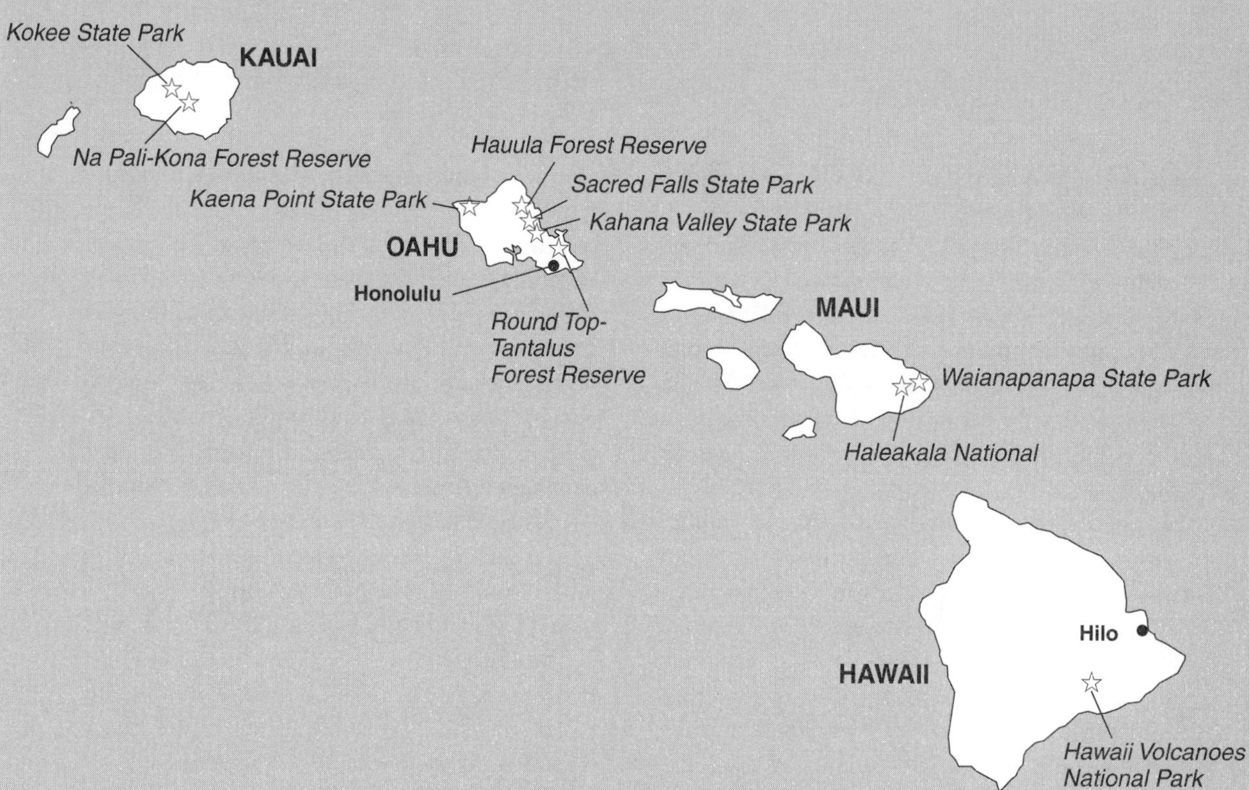
HAWAII
Kokee State Park
KAUAI
Na Pali-Kona Forest Reserve
Hauula Forest Reserve
Sacred Falls State Park
Kaena Point State Park
Kahana Valley State Park
OAHU
Honolulu
Round Top-
Tantalus
Forest Reserve
MAUI
Waianapanapa State Park
Haleakala National
Hilo
HAWAII
Hawaii Volcanoes
National Park

4. The 0.8-mile Judd Trail. 5. The 0.8-mile Moleka Trail. 6. The 1.1-mile Makiki Valley Trail. 7. The 0.7-mile Maunalaha Trail (easy-moderate). 8. The 0.7-mile Kanealole Trail (easy-moderate). 9. The 0.8-mile Puu Ohia Trail (easy-moderate). 10. The 3.4-mile Manoa Cliff Trail (easy-moderate).

KOKEE STATE PARK c/o Division of Forestry, 3060 Eiwa Street, Lihue, HI 96766; (808)241-3444. 4,345 acres. Kokee State Park is on the west-central part of the island of Kauai, next to Waimea Canyon State Park, in a mountainous area at an elevation of 4,000 feet. The park includes ridges, cliffs along the rim of Waimea Canyon, streams, as well as rain forest with koa, ohia lehua, sugi pine, oak, and redwood, along with hala, ginger, and kukui. Among the birds are apapane, amakihi, i'iwi, and lesser golden plover.

• *Suggested Trails for Nature Walks:* 1. The 0.4-mile Black Pipe Trail. 2. The 0.4-mile Waininiua Trail. 3. The 0.8-mile Kumuwela Trail. 4. The 1.2-mile Halemanu-Kokee Trail. 5. The 2-mile Puu Kaohelo-Berry Flat Trails. 6. The 2-mile Kaluapuhi Trail. 7. The 1.4-mile Canyon Trail (easy-moderate).

NA PALI-KONA FOREST RESERVE c/o Hawaii Division of Forestry and Wildlife, 3060 Eiwa Street, Room 306, Lihue, Kauai, HI 96766; (808)241-3433. Na Pali-Kona Forest Reserve is located next to Kokee State Park on the northwestern part of the island of Kauai. The reserve encompasses rugged terrain including high cliffs and bluffs, with views into Waimea and Poomau canyons. It features Kawaikoi Stream and other streams, waterfalls, bogs, huge Alakai Swamp, and areas of rain forest, with some redwood and sugi trees.

• *Suggested Trails for Nature Walks:* 1. The 0.3-mile Poomau Canyon Lookout Trail. 2. The 1.8-mile Kawaikoi Stream Trail. 3. The 3.5-mile Alakai Swamp Trail. 4. The 3.8-mile Pihea Trail (moderate).

KAHANA VALLEY STATE PARK c/o Division of State Parks, P.O. Box 621, Honolulu, HI 96809; (808)587-0300. 5,229 acres. This state park is on the northeast coast of Oahu, 26 miles north of Honolulu. It includes the Koolau Mountains and the forested Kahana Valley, with Kahana Bay, which has a beach, as well as Kahana and Kawa streams with pools. Elevations range from sea level to 2,670 feet. There are archeological sites, pasturelands, and tropical rain forest with hau and hala trees, bamboo and guava. Lesser golden plover, night heron, and Hawaiian coot are among the birds here.

• *Suggested Trails for Nature Walks:* 1. The 1.2-mile Kapa'ele'ele Ko'a and Keaniani Lookout Trail (loop). 2. The 2.5-mile Nakea Trail (loop).

SACRED FALLS STATE PARK c/o Division of State Parks, P.O. Box 621, Honolulu, HI 96809; (808)587-0300. 1,374 acres. Situated on the northeast coast of the island of Oahu, 30 miles north of Honolulu, this state park features Kaluanui Stream and 80-foot-high Sacred Falls, which has a pool beneath it, in a steep, narrow, boulder-filled canyon. Vegetation includes ferns, grassy areas, stands of Christmas berry, and mountain apple trees.

• *Suggested Trails for Nature Walks:* The 2.3-mile Sacred Falls Trail.

WAIANAPANAPA STATE PARK c/o Division of State Parks, 54 South High Street, Wailuku, HI 96793; (808)243-5354. 122 acres. Located near the eastern end of the island of Maui, Waianapanapa State Park encompasses an area of volcanic coastline with low lava cliffs and other rugged terrain. There are old foundations, caves, a stone arch, small beaches including one with black sand, sea stacks and blowholes, grassy areas, groves of hala with 3- to 6-foot leaves, and colonies of seabirds.

• *Suggested Trails for Nature Walks:* The 3-mile Hana-Waianapanapa Coastal Trail, which follows an ancient path.

KAENA POINT STATE PARK c/o Division of State Parks, P.O. Box 621, Honolulu, HI 96809; (808)548-7455. 779 acres. This state park is at the western tip of the island of Oahu, with the outermost part of the point protected as the 12-acre Ka'ena Point Natural Area Reserve. There are dunes and volcanic rock, sea cliffs and boulder slopes, small stone arches and a large sea cave called Kaneana, as well as Kaluakauila Stream and a sizable sandy beach. The area is sparsely vegetated with shrubs and native wildflowers. Among the wildlife are humpback whale, monk seal, porpoise, sea turtle, and seabirds including Laysan albatross and wedge-tailed shearwater.

• *Suggested Trails for Nature Walks:* The 2.7-mile Kaena Point Trail, which follows a dirt road.

HAUULA FOREST RESERVE Division of Forestry and Wildlife, 1151 Punchbowl Street, Room 325, Honolulu, HI 96813; (808)587-0166. Hauula Forest Reserve is just inland from the northeast coast of Oahu, near Hauula. It's a place of mountains and ridges with deep gulches, intermittent streams and an occasional waterfall, grassy areas as well as rain forest, wildflowers and ferns, with hala, Christmas berry, akia, alahee, lama, and Norfolk pine trees.

• *Suggested Trails for Nature Walks:* 1. The 2.5-mile Maakua Ridge Trail (easy-moderate loop). 2. The 2.5-mile Hauula Loop Trail (easy-moderate). 3. The 3-mile Maakua Gulch Trail (moderate).

Other Suitable Locations for Nature Walks in Hawaii

Hawaii has sixty-six state parks, and a number of these locations feature nature or hiking trails. Information: Division of State Parks, P.O. Box 621, Honolulu, HI 96809; (808)548-7455.

There's a system of state forest reserves, and some of these areas have established trails. Information: Division of Forestry and Wildlife, 1151 Punchbowl Street, Honolulu, HI 96813; (808)548-8850.

The state also has a system of nineteen natural area reserves, and a few of these locations have trails. Information: DLNR Natural Area Reserves System, 1151 Punchbowl Street, #325, Honolulu, HI 96813; (808)587-0166.

Two national wildlife refuges in Hawaii have trails. Information: Hanalei and Kilauea Point National Wildlife Refuges, P.O. Box 87, Kilauea, Kauai, HI 96754.

IDAHO

Recommended Areas for Nature Walks

SAWTOOTH NATIONAL FOREST 2647 Kimberly Road East, Twin Falls, ID 83301; (208)737-3200. 2,100,000 acres. Consisting of several units in south-central Idaho and one in Utah, this national forest features the 756,000-acre Sawtooth National Recreation Area and a number of notable mountain ranges, including the jagged Sawtooth Mountains, with dozens of peaks over 10,000 feet. Highest point is 12,076-foot Hyndman Peak. There are 1,100 lakes, more than 3,000 miles of streams, and the famous Salmon River.

Vegetation ranges from alpine wildflowers to desert plant life, with sagebrush slopes and forests of lodgepole pine, Douglas fir, Englemann spruce, cottonwood, and aspen. Wildlife includes mule deer, pronghorn, elk, black bear, mountain goat, mountain lion, gray wolf, fox, coyote, sandhill crane, and golden eagle. Guided nature walks are available during summer in the Sawtooth National Recreation Area.

• *Suggested Trails for Nature Walks:* 1. The 0.7-mile Lilly Lake Trail. 2. The 1-mile Eagle Trail. 3. The 1.5-mile Phantom Falls Trail. 4. The 2.2-mile Fishhook Creek Trail. 5. The 2.2-mile Mill Lake Trail. 6. The 1.7-mile 4th of July Trail. 7. The 2-mile Baker Lake Trail. 8. The 2-mile Norton Lake Trail (moderate). 9. The 5-mile Prairie Lakes Trail (moderate). 10. The 5-mile Sawtooth Lake Trail (moderate).

IDAHO PANHANDLE NATIONAL FORESTS 3815 Schreiber Way, Coeur d'Alene, ID 83814; (208)765-7223. 2,479,245 acres. Consisting of three national forests in northern Idaho that were combined in 1973—Coeur d'Alene National Forest, Kaniksu National Forest, and St. Joe National Forest—this is a region of rugged mountains, ridges, and valleys with rivers, streams, lakes, and ponds.

There are meadows with wildflowers, alpine plants, and forests of Douglas fir and hemlock, lodgepole and ponderosa pine, Englemann spruce and western redcedar, white pine and western larch, with dogwood and huckleberry. Among the wildlife are moose, elk, caribou, mule and white-tailed deer, black and grizzly bear, mountain lion, coyote, and mountain goat, as well as ruffed grouse, green-winged teal, nighthawk, and bald eagle.

• *Suggested Trails for Nature Walks:* 1. The 0.5-mile Hobo Cedar Grove Trail (loop). 2. The 0.5-mile Caribou Lake Trail. 3. The 1-mile Big Loop Trail. 4. The 2-mile Robinson Lake Interpretive Trail (loop). 5. The 2-mile Water, Woods, and Wildlife Interpretive Trail. 6. The 2.1-mile Mineral Point Trail. 7. The 5-mile Upper Priest Lake Trail. 8. The 6.9-mile Upper Priest River Trail. 9. The 7.6-mile Lakeshore Trail. 10. The 9-mile Beach Trail.

CLEARWATER NATIONAL FOREST 12730 Highway 12, Orofino, ID 83544; (208)476-4541. 1,831,370 acres. Located in north-central Idaho, Clearwater National Forest encompasses lofty, rugged mountains and

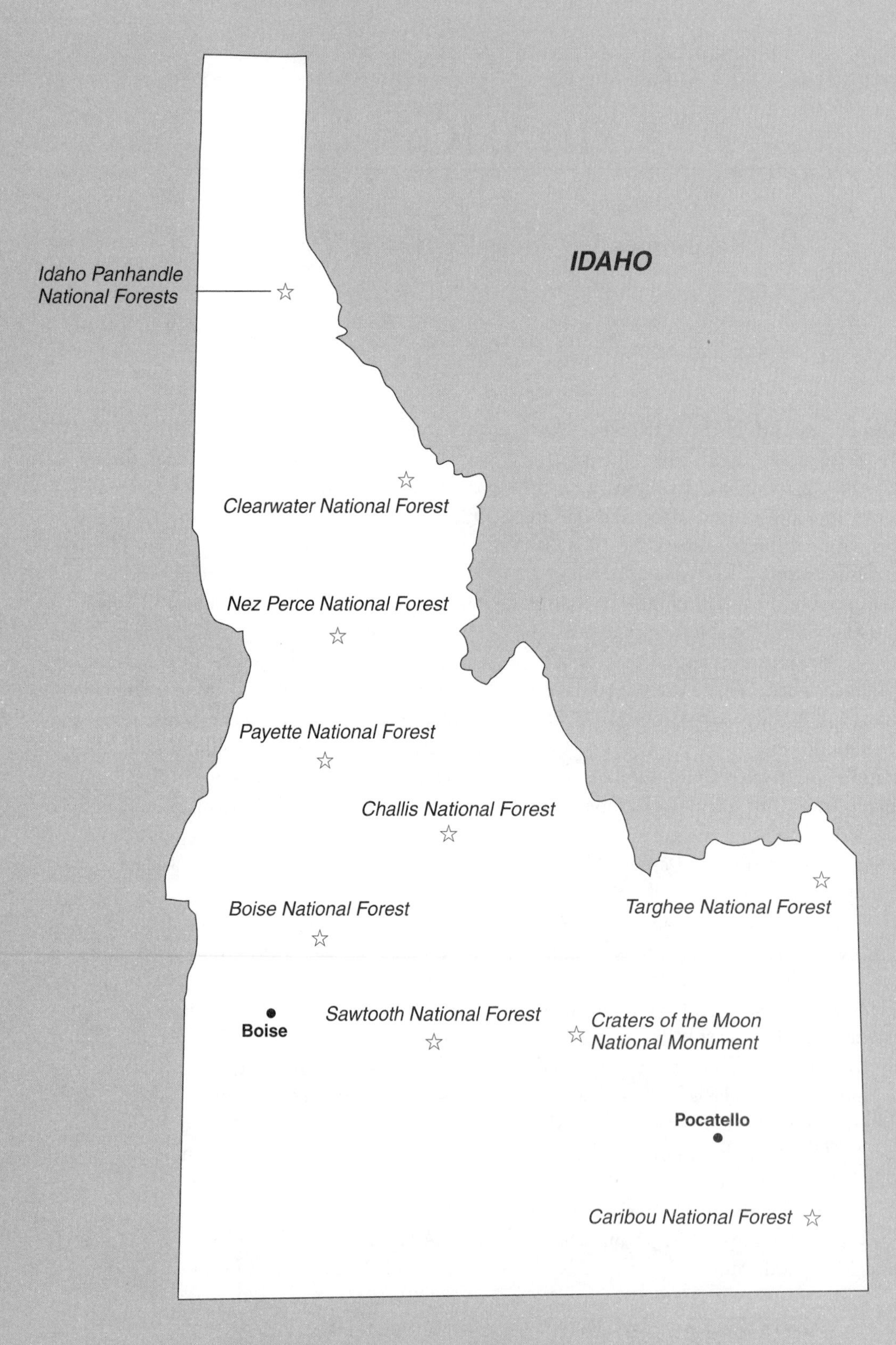
IDAHO
Idaho Panhandle
National Forests
Clearwater National Forest
Nez Perce National Forest
Payette National Forest
Challis National Forest
Boise National Forest
Targhee National Forest
Boise
Sawtooth National Forest
Craters of the Moon
National Monument
Pocatello
Caribou National Forest

ridges, including part of the Bitterroot Range, with rocky cliffs, buttes, deep canyons, mountain meadows, many lakes, hundreds of streams, and three national wild and scenic rivers.

The forest features western redcedar, lodgepole and ponderosa pine, subalpine and Douglas fir, western hemlock, Englemann spruce, and western larch trees. Wildlife includes elk, black bear, white-tailed and mule deer, moose, mountain lion, mountain goat, bobcat, coyote, and snowshoe hare, along with great horned owl, sharp-shinned hawk, bald eagle, and osprey.

• *Suggested Trails for Nature Walks:* 1. The 0.5-mile Major Fenn National Recreation Trail. 2. The 1-mile East Fork Meadow Creek North Trail. 3. The 1-mile Elk Creek Falls Access Trail. 4. The 1.7-mile Bald Mountain Lake Trail. 5. The 2-mile Flat Mountain Trail. 6. The 2-mile Lochsa River Access Trail. 7. The 4.6-mile Austin Creek Trail. 8. The 11.5-mile Kelly Creek Trail. 9. The 12.8-mile Weitas Creek Trail.

TARGHEE NATIONAL FOREST P.O. Box 208, St. Anthony, ID 83445; (208)624-3151. 1,800,000 acres. Situated in southeastern Idaho and including lands bordering on Wyoming's Yellowstone and Grand Teton national parks, this national forest is a place of high mountains, canyons, steep cliffs, deep valleys, foothills, lakes, creeks, and waterfalls. Two wilderness areas total 134,166 acres.

There are areas of desert with sagebrush, meadows, wildflowers, some alpine tundra, and forests of lodgepole pine, Englemann spruce, Douglas fir, and aspen. Among the wildlife are mule and white-tailed deer, elk, moose, black bear, pronghorn, mountain goat, bighorn sheep, and mountain lion, as well as blue grouse, white-faced ibis, sandhill crane, and trumpeter swan.

• *Suggested Trails for Nature Walks:* 1. The 1.1-mile Van Noy Canyon Trail. 2. The 2-mile Scott Canyon Trail. 3. The 2-mile Hawley Gulch Trail. 4. The 2-mile Coffee Pot Rapids Trail. 5. The 3-mile Box Canyon Trail. 6. The 4.2-mile South Fork Pass Creek Trail. 7. The 5-mile Big Elk Creek Trail. 8. The 4-mile Bear Creek Trail. 9. The 8-mile Moose Creek Trail. 10. The 7-mile South Leigh Creek Trail.

PAYETTE NATIONAL FOREST P.O. Box 1026, McCall, ID 83638; (208)634-8151. 2,300,000 acres. Payette National Forest in west-central Idaho features high peaks and deep canyons, rock outcroppings and domes, with 18,000 miles of streams, hundreds of lakes, as well as the Snake and Salmon rivers. Elevations range from 1,500 to over 9,500 feet.

Within the forest are 784,000 acres of the Frank Church–River of No Return Wilderness, and 24,000 acres of the Hells Canyon Wilderness. There are also grasslands, meadows, and dense stands of ponderosa pine, subalpine and Douglas fir, Englemann spruce, western larch, and aspen. Wildlife includes mule deer, elk, black bear, moose, bighorn sheep, mountain goat, gray wolf, bald eagle, and peregrine falcon.

• *Suggested Trails for Nature Walks:* 1. The 0.5-mile Ant Butte Trail. 2. The 0.5-mile Short Trail. 3. The 1.7-mile Lava Lake Trail. 4. The 2.8-mile Hidden Lake Trail. 5. The 4.1-mile Upper Hazard Lake Trail. 6. The 4.2-mile Clayburn Trail. 7. The 5.6-mile Elk Lake Trail. 8. The 6.4-mile Vance Creek Trail. 9. The 7.3-mile French Creek Trail. 10. The 8.5-mile Little French Creek Trail.

CHALLIS NATIONAL FOREST HC 63 Box 1671, Highway 93 North, Challis, ID 83226; (208)879-2285. 2,581,200 acres. Consisting of two huge tracts of land in the east-central part of the state, Challis National Forest stretches across several ranges of lofty, rugged mountains. It includes Idaho's highest point, 12,662-foot Borah Peak, as well as nearly 800,000 acres of the 2,300,000-acre Frank Church–River of No Return Wilderness.

Within the region are canyons, the Salmon River, many alpine lakes, streams, some tundra, meadows, sagebrush, and forests of lodgepole pine and Douglas fir. Among the wildlife are mule deer, moose, elk, pronghorn, black bear, bighorn sheep, mountain goat, bobcat, coyote, fox, beaver, and wolverine, plus spotted sandpiper, ring-necked pheasant, kestrel, and bald eagle.

• *Suggested Trails for Nature Walks:* 1. The 2-mile Big Fall Creek Trail. 2. The 2-mile Wildhorse Trail. 3. The 2-mile Bear Canyon Trail. 4. The 2-mile Red Rock Trail. 5. The 2-mile Smithie Meadows Trail. 6. The 3-mile Tool Box Trail. 7. The 4-mile Hunter Creek Trail. 8. The 4-mile Bear Creek Trail. 9. The 4-mile Miller Canyon Trail. 10. The 7-mile Summit Creek Trail (easy-moderate).

CRATERS OF THE MOON NATIONAL MONUMENT Arco, ID 83213; (208)527-3257. 53,120 acres. This national monument in south-central Idaho features a lunarlike landscape with lava flows and tubes (caves), cinder and spatter cones, crags and other volcanic formations. There's a 43,243-acre designated wilderness area, and vegetation includes sagebrush, rabbitbrush, and bitterbrush, with wildflowers as well as limber pine trees. Pronghorn, mule deer, mountain lion, bobcat, coyote, red fox, porcupine, badger, rabbit, and marmot are among the wildlife, along with mourning dove, great horned owl, raven, and prairie falcon.

• *Suggested Trails for Nature Walks:* 1. The 0.3-mile North Crater Flow Trail (loop). 2. The 0.5-mile Davil's Orchard Trail (loop). 3. The 0.5-mile Big Craters Trail (easy-moderate). 4. The 1-mile Caves Trail (easy-moderate). 5. The 1.5-mile Tree Molds Trail (easy-moderate). 6. The 2-mile Wilderness Trail to Echo Crater (easy-moderate).

BOISE NATIONAL FOREST 1750 Front Street, Boise, ID 83702; (208)364-4100. 2,265,000 acres. Boise National Forest in west-central Idaho is characterized by steep, jagged granite mountains, canyons and valleys, lakes and marshes, rivers and creeks, meadows and grassy areas, with wildflowers and sagebrush, ponderosa and lodgepole pine, Englemann spruce and Douglas fir.

Included within the forest are 331,600 acres of the 2,300,000-acre Frank Church–River of No Return Wilderness and over a half million acres of old-growth trees. Among the wildlife are elk, mule deer, black bear, bighorn sheep, mountain goat, gray wolf, bobcat, and river otter, while the bird life includes cinnamon teal, blue grouse, bald eagle, and prairie falcon.

• *Suggested Trails for Nature Walks:* 1. The first 4 miles of the 7-mile Browns Creek Trail. 2. The first 4 miles of the 10.2-mile Bear River Trail. 3. The 4.2-mile Bear Valley Creek Trail. 4. The 4.5-mile Burnt Log Trail. 5. The first 2 miles of the 3.5-mile Eagle Creek Trail (easy-moderate). 6. The 2.7-mile Flint Creek Trail (easy-moderate). 7. The 5-mile Black Warrior Trail (easy-moderate). 8. The 5-mile Johnson Creek Trail (easy-moderate). 9. The 8-mile Wilson Creek Trail (easy-moderate). 10. The 10-mile Cottonwood Creek Trail (easy-moderate).

NEZ PERCE NATIONAL FOREST Route 2, Box 475, Grangeville, ID 83530; (208)983-1950. 2,200,000 acres. This north-central Idaho national forest features mountain ridges and deep canyons, including the 7,000-foot-deep Hells Canyon in the 652,000-acre Hells Canyon National Recreation Area, which is shared with Oregon's Wallowa-Whitman National Forest. Almost a million acres of Nez Perce consists of designated wilderness.

There are five national wild and scenic rivers, many alpine lakes and streams, meadows and brushlands, as well as a forest of ponderosa and lodgepole pine, Douglas and subalpine fir, Englemann spruce and western larch, grand fir and Pacific yew. Wildlife includes mule and white-tailed deer, elk, moose, black bear, bighorn sheep, mountain lion, coyote, fox, and bald eagle.

• *Suggested Trails for Nature Walks:* 1. The 2.2-mile Tenmile Creek Trail. 2. The 0.5-mile Lost Lake Trail. 3. The first 3.7 miles of the 7.7-mile

Newsome Creek Trail. 4. The first 2 miles of the 3.6-mile Umatilla Creek Trail (easy-moderate). 5. The first 2 miles of the 4.4-mile Kirks Fork Trail (easy-moderate). 6. The 2.3-mile Flatiron Ridge Trail (easy-moderate). 7. The 3.7-mile Lick Creek Trail (easy-moderate). 8. The 4-mile Limber Luke Trail (easy-moderate). 9. The 2.9-mile Twentymile Creek Trail (moderate). 10. The 3.9-mile Driveway Extension Trail (moderate).

CARIBOU NATIONAL FOREST Federal Building, Room 172, 250 South 4th Avenue, Pocatello, ID 83201; (208)236-6700. 1,087,916 acres. Caribou National Forest in the southeastern part of the state encompasses several mountain ranges, with canyons, some caves, and a number of streams. It includes the 47,658-acre Curlew National Grassland, and highest point is 9,963-foot Meade Peak.

There are meadows, areas of sagebrush, and forests of lodgepole pine and Douglas fir, with aspen and Englemann spruce, plus juniper, chokecherry, bitterbrush, and rabbitbrush. Elk, mule deer, moose, bear, coyote, red fox, red-tailed hawk, and golden eagle are among the wildlife.

• *Suggested Trails for Nature Walks:* 1. The Cherry Springs Nature Trail (loop). 2. The 0.5-mile Big Springs Nature Trail (loop). 3. The 0.5-mile Scout Mountain Nature Trail (loop). 4. The 2-mile Gibson Jack Creek Trail (easy-moderate). 5. The 6.6-mile West Fork of Mink Creek Trail (easy-moderate). 6. The 3-mile Walker Creek Trail (moderate). 7. The 8-mile Indian Mill Trail (moderate). 8. The 9-mile South Fork of Mink Creek Trail (moderate). 9. The 12-mile Oxford Trail (moderate). 10. The 12-mile Wright's Creek National Recreation Trail (moderate).

Other Suitable Locations for Nature Walks in Idaho

Idaho has twenty-two state parks, and seventeen of these locations feature trails. Information: Idaho Department of Parks and Recreation, P.O. Box 83720, Boise, ID 83720; (208)334-4199.

There's an additional national forest in the state with a network of trails: Salmon National Forest, P.O. Box 729, Salmon, ID 83467; (208)756-2215.

Trails are found at a number of Bureau of Land Management areas in the state. Information: BLM, Idaho State Office, 3380 Americana Terrace, Boise, ID 83706; (208)384-3000.

Three national wildlife refuges in the state have trails. Information: U.S. Fish and Wildlife Service, 911 Northeast 11th Avenue, Eastside Federal Complex, Portland, OR 97232.

The Nature Conservancy manages thirteen preserves in Idaho, and some of these areas have trails. Information: The Nature Conservancy of Idaho, P.O. Box 165, Sun Valley, ID 83353; (208)726-3007.

ILLINOIS

Recommended Areas for Nature Walks

SHAWNEE NATIONAL FOREST 901 South Commercial Street, Harrisburg, IL 62946; (618)253-7114. 270,000 acres. Situated between the Mississippi and Ohio rivers in the rugged Shawnee Hills of southern Illinois, this national forest is the largest natural area in the state. Some of the terrain is rough, with sandstone bluffs, cliffs, and rock outcroppings offering vistas.

There are many lakes and ponds, streams and waterfalls, cypress swamps and other wetlands, as well as ravines, mixed hardwood forests, prairies, ferns, and abundant wildflowers, with oak, maple, beech, gum, and dogwood among the more common trees. Wildlife includes white-tailed deer, fox, bobcat, raccoon, muskrat, skunk, rabbit, mink, bat, quail, and wild turkey.

• *Suggested Trails for Nature Walks:* 1. The 0.5-mile Pomona Natural Bridge Trail. 2. The 0.8-mile Rim Rock Trail. 3. The 0.8-mile Inspiration Point Trail. 4. The 3-mile Cave Hill Trail. 5. The 8-mile Cedar Lake Trail. 6. The 5-mile High Knob Trail (easy-moderate), consisting of several loops. 7. The 7-mile Beaver Trail (easy-moderate). 8. The 8-mile Garden of the Gods Trail System (easy-moderate). 9. The 15-mile Kinkaid Lake Trail (easy-moderate). 10. Portions of the 146-mile River to River Trail, which traverses the forest.

FERNE CLYFFE STATE PARK P.O. Box 10, Goreville, IL 62939; (618)995-2411. 1,100 acres. This park is in the Shawnee Hills of southern Illinois, next to Shawnee National Forest. Here are woodlands with rock formations, caves, bluffs offering views, a 16-acre lake, a 100-foot waterfall, and many ferns. There are also forests of oak and hickory, maple and sweetgum, with redbud and dogwood.

• *Suggested Trails for Nature Walks:* 1. The 1-mile Big Rocky Hollow Trail. 2. The 1-mile Ferne Clyffe Trail. 3. The 1-mile Hawks' Cave Trail. 4. The 0.8-mile Waterfall Trail. 5. The 1-mile Blackjack Oak Trail. 6. The 1-mile Round Bluff Nature Preserve Trail. 7. The 5-mile Happy Hollow Trail (moderate).

CASTLE ROCK STATE PARK RR 2, Oregon, IL 61061; (815)732-7329. 2,000 acres. Castle Rock State Park is perched alongside the Rock River in northern Illinois. Terrain consists of rolling hills with some steep ravines and rock formations, including Castle Rock, a large sandstone butte. There are forests and remnants of prairie, with 710 acres of the park designated an Illinois Nature Preserve.

• *Suggested Trails for Nature Walks:* 1. The 0.3-mile River Bluff Trail. 2. The 1-mile Wildlife Viewing Trail. 3. The 0.5-mile Fox Trail. 4. The 1-mile Forest Ridge Trail. 5. The 1-mile Oak Ridge Trail. 6. The 1-mile Lookout Trail. 7. The 2-mile Heather Valley Trail.

WHITE PINES FOREST STATE PARK 6712 West Pines Road, Mt. Morris, IL 61054; (815)946-3717. 385 acres. Located in Rock

ILLINOIS
White Pines Forest State Park
Castle Rock State Park
Chicago
Gooselake Prairie
State Park
Sand Ridge State Forest
Weldon Springs State
Recreation Area
Decatur
Beall Woods Conservation
Area and Nature Preserve
Giant City State Park
Ferne Clyffe State Park
Shawnee National Forest
Cache River State
Natural Area

River Valley, in the northern part of the state, this park features two major streams: Pine and Spring creeks. There's a forest of white pine, with low vine-covered limestone bluffs, wildflowers in season, and wildlife that includes small mammals as well as migratory birds.

• *Suggested Trails for Nature Walks:* 1. The 0.4-mile Razor Back Trail. 2. The 0.5-mile Look Out Trail. 3. The 0.6-mile Red Squirrel Trail. 4. The 0.7-mile Whispering Pine Trail loop. 5. The 0.8-mile Gray Squirrel Trail loop. 6. The 0.8-mile Sunset Trail loop. 7. The 1.4-mile Sleepy Hollow Trail loop.

SAND RIDGE STATE FOREST P.O. Box 111, Forest City, IL 61532; (309)597-2212. 7,500 acres. This is Illinois' largest state forest, a place of gently sloping terrain and flatlands with 100-foot forested dunes and sandy soil. Common trees include oak, hickory, and pine. There are also prairie grasslands, as well as some desert vegetation such as prickly pear cactus. White-tailed deer, coyote, gray fox, and raccoon are among the wildlife.

• *Suggested Trails for Nature Walks:* 1. The 2-mile Brown Loop. 2. The 2.2-mile Green Loop. 3. The 1.6-mile White Loop. 4. The 4.5-mile Orange Loop. 5. The 7.5-mile Blue Loop. 6. The 9.5-mile Red Loop. 7. The 17-mile Yellow Loop.

BEALL WOODS CONSERVATION AREA AND NATURE PRESERVE RR 2, Mount Carmel, IL 62863; (618)298-2442. 635 acres. Situated on the Wabash River in southeastern Illinois, this is a hilly area with small rocky cliffs, two large creeks, a lake, and virgin woodlands of oak, ash, and sweetgum. A 270-acre portion of the area is designated an Illinois Nature Preserve. Wildlife includes white-tailed deer, red fox, and raccoon.

• *Suggested Trails for Nature Walks:* 1. The 1.2-mile White Oak Trail. 2. The 1.5-mile Tulip Tree Trail. 3. The 1.5-mile Sweet Gum Trail. 4. The 1.8-mile Ridgeway Trail. 5. The 2.5-mile Schneck Trail.

GIANT CITY STATE PARK 336 South Church Road, Makanda, IL 62958; (618)457-4836. 3,694 acres. Located amid the lands of Shawnee National Forest in southern Illinois, and including the 110-acre Fern Rocks Nature Preserve, Giant City State Park has hilly terrain with sandstone bluffs and canyons, huge rock formations, and caves. There are also several small ponds, streams, and a lake, with vegetation including prairie grasses and forests of white and red oak, hickory, maple, and dogwood. Among the wildlife are white-tailed deer, coyote, fox, and wild turkey.

• *Suggested Trails for Nature Walks:* 1. The 0.3-mile Post Oak Nature Trail. 2. The 0.3-mile Devil's Standtable Nature Trail. 3. The 1-mile Giant City Nature Trail. 4. The 0.8-mile Indian Creek Shelter Nature Trail. 5. The 2-mile Trillium Trail. 6. The 16-mile Red Creek Hiking Trail (moderate).

WELDON SPRINGS STATE RECREATION AREA RR 2, Box 87, Clinton, IL 61727; (217)935-2644. 442 acres. Weldon Springs State Recreation Area in central Illinois features numerous natural springs and creeks, and includes a 29-acre lake with 2 miles of shoreline. There's oak-hickory forest with maple and walnut, sweetgum and sycamore, and a bit of tallgrass prairie. White-tailed deer, fox, coyote, beaver, and hawk are among the wildlife.

• *Suggested Trails for Nature Walks:* 1. The 1-mile Salt Creek Trail. 2. The 2-mile Lakeside Nature Trail. 3. The 1-mile Beaver Dam Trail. 4. The 3-mile Whitetail Trail.

GOOSELAKE PRAIRIE STATE PARK 5010 North Jugtown Road, Morris, IL 60450; (815)942-2899. 2,537 acres. Adjacent to 2,000-acre Heidecke Lake and near the confluence of the Illinois, Des Plaines, and Kankakee rivers in northeastern Illinois, this park protects the largest area of prairie remaining in the state—made up of Indian grass, switch grass, big bluestem, and cordgrass, which can surpass 8 feet. There are also marshes and ponds, as well as wildflowers in season. Among the wildlife are deer, coyote, red fox, beaver, and cottontail rabbit.

• *Suggested Trails for Nature Walks:* 1. The 1-mile Tall Grass Nature Trail. 2. The 0.5-mile Marsh Loop Trail. 3. The 2-mile Sagashka Trail. 4. The 2.6-mile Prairie View Trail.

CACHE RIVER STATE NATURAL AREA Route 2, Box 2, Belknap, IL 62908; (618)634-9678. 8,214 acres. Situated near the southern tip of the state, Cache River State Natural Area consists of two separate units along branches of the Cache River. There are wetlands including swamps and ponds, with baldcypress and tupelo trees, as well as flatwoods and ridges with oak and hickory, sweetgum and tulip tree, ash and spicebush. Also here are grassy "barrens"—sandstone bluffs—and such wildlife as white-tailed deer, red and gray fox, coyote, beaver, muskrat, rabbit, and bat, along with heron, egret, osprey, and turkey vulture. Within the area's boundaries are three designated nature preserves.

• *Suggested Trails for Nature Walks:* 1. The 1-mile Lookout Point Trail. 2. The 1.5-mile Heron Pond Trail. 3. The 6.5-mile Little Black Slough Trail (easy-moderate).

Other Suitable Locations for Nature Walks in Illinois

Illinois has sixty-seven state parks, seventeen state fish and wildlife areas, twenty-one state conservation areas, and four state forests. Most of these areas feature nature and hiking trails. Information: Illinois Department of Conservation, 524 South Second Street, Springfield, IL 62701; (217)782-7454.

There's a system of 236 state nature preserves of varying sizes, and some of them have trails. Information: Illinois Nature Preserves Commission, Lincoln Tower Plaza, 524 South Second Street, Springfield, IL 62701; (217) 785-8686.

Eight national wildlife refuges in the state have trails. Information: U.S. Fish and Wildlife Service, 1 Federal Drive, Federal Building, Fort Snelling, MN 55111.

Trails are found at several U.S. Army Corps of Engineers areas in Illinois. Information: Corps of Engineers, St. Louis District, 1222 Spruce Street, St. Louis, MO 63103; (314) 331-8622.

INDIANA

Recommended Areas for Nature Walks

HOOSIER NATIONAL FOREST 811 Constitution Avenue, Bedford, IN 47421; (812)275-5987. 187,812 acres. This national forest consists of two large tracts in the hills of southern Indiana, including an area along the Ohio River. Of special interest are the 13,000-acre Charles C. Deam Wilderness and the Pioneer Mothers Memorial Forest, an 88-acre area of virgin forest.

Amid the rolling terrain and small ridges are ravines and rock shelters, sinkholes and caves, high bluffs and sandy beaches, with a number of lakes, ponds, streams, and waterfalls. There are hardwood forests with pine, cedar, redbud, dogwood, mountain laurel, and prairie grasses. Among the wildlife are white-tailed deer, beaver, hawk, bald eagle, and turkey vulture.

• *Suggested Trails for Nature Walks:* 1. The 1-mile Twin Oaks Interpretive Trail. 2. The 1-mile Celina Interpretive Trail. 3. The 1-mile Pioneer Mothers Trail. 4. The 1-mile German Ridge Lake Trail. 5. The 2-mile Hemlock Cliffs Trail. 6. The 3-mile Saddle Lake Trail. 7. The 5-mile Morgan Ridge East Trail. 8. The 6-mile Lick Creek Trail. 9. The 10-mile Youngs Creek Trail loop. 10. The 12.2-mile Two Lakes National Recreation Loop Trail.

INDIANA DUNES NATIONAL LAKESHORE 1100 North Mineral Springs Road, Porter, IN 46304; (219)926-7561. Located in the northwest corner of the state, Indiana Dunes National Lakeshore consists of sandy beaches and dunes, marshes and bogs, ponds and ravines. There are grasses, shrubs, mosses, and wildflowers, including pink lady's-slipper and yellow fringed orchid, sundew and pitcher plants, plus blueberries and cranberries. Some of the area is forested with conifers as well as oak, tamarack, cottonwood, tulip tree, and dogwood. White-tailed deer, red fox, and cottontail rabbit are among the wildlife. Ranger-led nature walks are available.

• *Suggested Trails for Nature Walks:* 1. The 0.5-mile Calumet Dune Trail. 2. The 0.6-mile Miller Woods Trail (loop). 3. The 1-mile Dune Succession Trail Loop. 4. The 1.2-mile West Beach Trail Loop. 5. The 1.5-mile Long Lake Trail Loop. 6. The 1.4-mile Bailly/Chellberg Trail (loop). 7. The 3-mile Little Calumet River Trail. 8. The 6-mile Ly-Co-Ki-We Trail, which is made up of several loops.

BROWN COUNTY STATE PARK P.O. Box 608, Nashville, IN 47448; (812)988-6406. 16,000 acres. Situated in the south-central part of the state, this is the largest of Indiana's state parks. There's hilly, forested terrain here with ravines, creeks, and two small lakes. Among the trees are oak, hickory, maple, beech, and sassafras, and wildlife includes white-tailed deer, raccoon, and wild turkey. Within the park boundaries are the Ogle Hollow Nature Preserve and a nature center.

• *Suggested Trails for Nature Walks:* 1. The 1.3-mile Trail #1. 2. The 1.3-mile Trail #6. 3. The

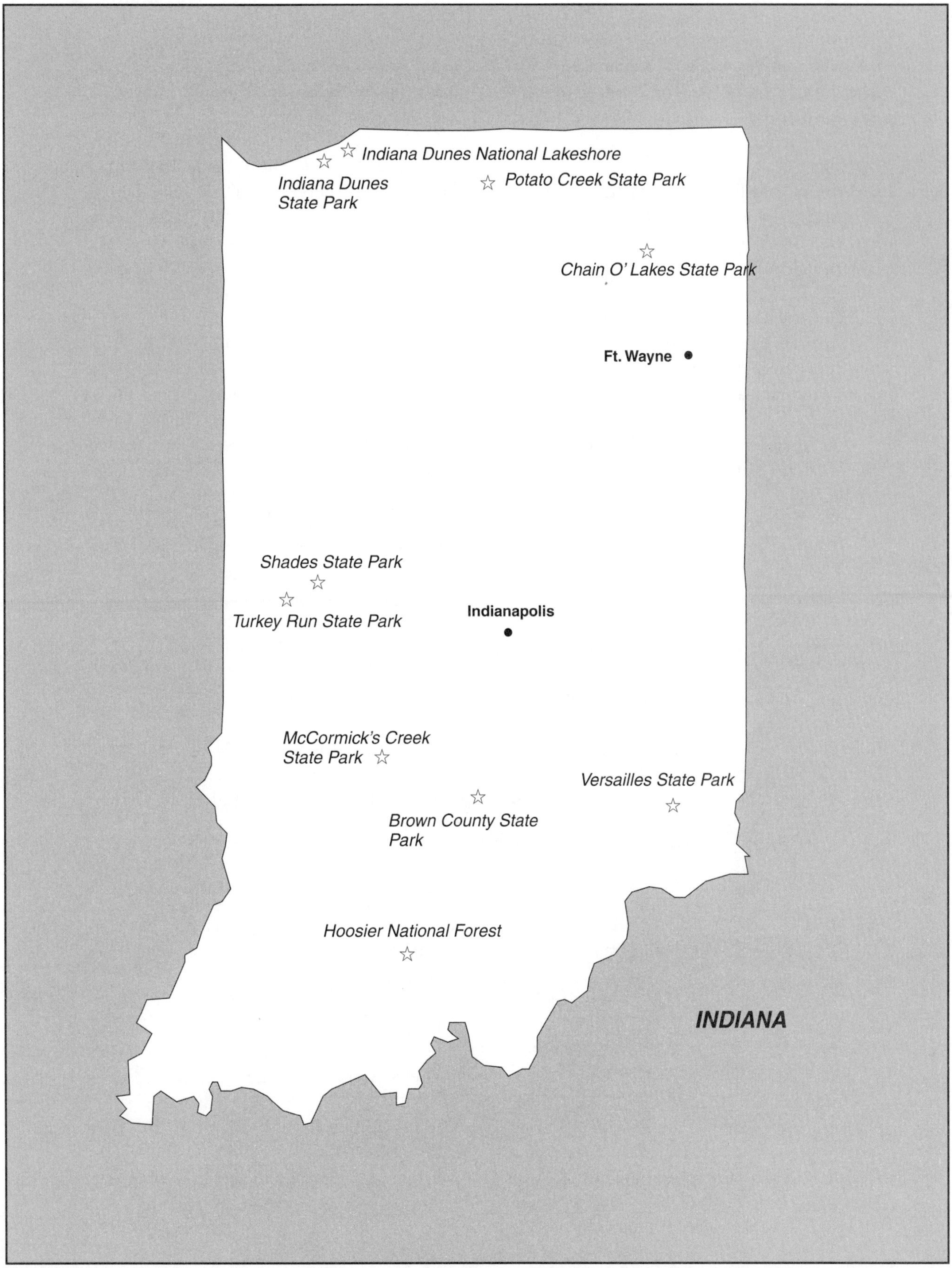

Indiana Dunes National Lakeshore
Indiana Dunes State Park
Potato Creek State Park
Chain O' Lakes State Park
Ft. Wayne
Shades State Park
Turkey Run State Park
Indianapolis
McCormick's Creek State Park
Versailles State Park
Brown County State Park
Hoosier National Forest
INDIANA

0.8-mile Trail #3. 4. The 1.3-mile Trail #4. 5. The 1.5-mile Trail #7. 6. The 2-mile Trail #2. 7. The 3.5-mile Trail #8. 8. The 10.8-mile Trail #5 (easy-moderate).

CHAIN O' LAKES STATE PARK 2355 East 75 South, Albion, IN 46701; (219)636-2654. 2,678 acres. Chain O' Lakes State Park in northeastern Indiana features a series of eleven small "kettle lakes" created during the last ice age. Eight of the lakes are connected by channels. Elsewhere are open fields, swamps, marshes, and forests of pine and locust. The park has a nature center, and naturalist-led walks are available in summer.

• *Suggested Trails for Nature Walks:* 1. The 0.5-mile Trail #3. 2. The 0.5-mile Trail #9. 3. The 1-mile Trail #7. 4. The 1.3-mile Trail #5. 5. The 1.3-mile Trail #8. 6. The 0.5-mile Trail #2. 7. The 0.8-mile Trail #1. 8. The 1-mile Trail #4. 9. The 1.5-mile Trail #6.

McCORMICK'S CREEK STATE PARK Route 5, Box 282, Spencer, IN 47460; (812)829-2235. 1,852 acres. Located in south-central Indiana, this state park has hilly terrain with small ravines and canyons, cliffs and limestone sinkholes, and a 100-foot-long cave. McCormick's Creek, Little Branch, and the White River flow through the area, which is forested with beech, maple, sycamore, and pine. Included within the park is the Wolf Cave Nature Preserve, along with a nature center.

• *Suggested Trails for Nature Walks:* 1. The 1.3-mile Trail #6. 2. The 1.5-mile Trail #9. 3. The 1.9-mile Trail #4. 4. The 2-mile Trail #2. 5. The 2.3-mile Trail #1. 6. The 2.7-mile Trail #7. 7. The 3-mile Trail #5. 8. The 2-mile Trail #3 (easy-moderate).

TURKEY RUN STATE PARK Route 1, Box 164, Marshall, IN 47859; (317)597-2635. 2,382 acres. Turkey Run State Park in western Indiana has several streams including Sugar Creek, small steep-walled sandstone gorges and canyons with cliffs, along with forests of walnut and sycamore, with some virgin hemlock. The park includes the Rocky Hollow Falls Canyon Nature Preserve.

• *Suggested Trails for Nature Walks:* 1. The 0.5-mile Trail #6. 2. The 0.7-mile Trail #5. 3. The 0.7-mile Trail #7. 4. The 1.4-mile Trail #10. 5. The 1.5-mile Trail #8. 6. The 1-mile Trail #2 (easy-moderate). 7. The 2-mile Trail #4 (easy-moderate). 8. The 3-mile Trail #1 (easy-moderate). 9. The 1-mile Trail #9 (moderate). 10. The 1.7-mile Trail #3 (moderate).

INDIANA DUNES STATE PARK 1600 North 25 East, Chesterton, IN 46304; (219)926-1952. 2,182 acres. Occupying the northwest corner of Indiana, adjacent to Indiana Dunes National Lakeshore, this state park includes over 3 miles of shoreline on Lake Michigan, a nature center, and the 1,530-acre Dunes Nature Preserve. There are beaches, high sand dunes, marshes, wildflowers, ferns, and forests of white pine and black oak.

• *Suggested Trails for Nature Walks:* 1. The 0.3-mile Trail #2. 2. The 0.8-mile Trail #3. 3. The 0.8-mile Trail #4. 4. The 1.1-mile Trail #7. 5. The 3.8-mile Trail #9. 6. The 5.5-mile Trail #10. 7. The 1.5-mile Trail #8.

POTATO CREEK STATE PARK 25601 State Road 4, North Liberty, IN 46554; (219)656-8186. 3,840 acres. This state park in northern Indiana features Potato Creek and 327-acre Worster Lake, which has a beach, along with hilly woodlands, open fields, wetlands, a pond, wildflowers, and small areas of prairie and savanna. White-tailed deer, fox, and hawk are among the wildlife. Included is the Swamp Rose Nature Preserve, and there's a nature center.

• *Suggested Trails for Nature Walks:* 1. The 1-mile Trail #3. 2. The 2-mile Trail #2. 3. The 2.5-mile Trail #1. 4. The 1.5-mile Trail #4, which has just been extended another 1 to 2 miles.

VERSAILLES STATE PARK Box 205, Versailles, IN 47042; (812)689-6424. 5,905 acres. Situated in southeastern Indiana, Versailles State Park preserves an area of wooded hills and ravines with limestone outcroppings and sinkholes, as well as Fallen Timber Creek, Laughery Creek, and man-made Versailles Lake. Common trees include oak and maple, hickory and beech, walnut and poplar. There's a nature center, and naturalist-led walks are available in summer.

• *Suggested Trails for Nature Walks:* 1. The 1.5-mile Trail #3. 2. The 2.3-mile Trail #1. 3. The 2.8-mile Trail #2.

SHADES STATE PARK Route 1, Box 72, Waveland, IN 47989; (317)435-2810. 3,082 acres. Shades State Park is noted for its 200-foot sandstone cliffs, with lookouts and deep ravines, alongside Sugar and Indian creeks. Included in the park is the Pine Hills Nature Preserve. There are springs, waterfalls, a pond, and forests of oak, hemlock, and white pine, with beech and tulip tree.

• *Suggested Trails for Nature Walks:* 1. The 0.5-mile Trail #6. 2. The 0.5-mile Trail #9. 3. The 1.5-mile Trail #10. 4. The 2.5-mile Back Pack Trail. 5. The 0.8-mile Trail #1 (easy-moderate). 6. The 0.6-mile Trail #4 (easy-moderate). 7. The 0.8-mile Trail #5 (easy-moderate). 8. The 0.9-mile Trail #7 (moderate). 9. The 0.8-mile Trail #8 (moderate). 10. The 1.3-mile Trail #2 (moderate).

Other Suitable Locations for Nature Walks in Indiana

Indiana has twenty-one state parks, nine state reservoirs, and fourteen state forests. All have trails for walking or hiking. Information: Department of Natural Resources, 402 West Washington Street, Room W256, Indianapolis, IN 46204; (317)232-4020.

There's a system of twelve state nature preserves, and most of these have at least short trails. Information: Division of Nature Preserves, 402 West Washington Street, Room 267, Indianapolis, IN 46204; (317)232-4052.

A number of U.S. Army Corps of Engineers areas in Indiana feature trails. Information: Corps of Engineers, Louisville District, P.O. Box 59, Louisville, KY 40201; (502)582-6292.

IOWA

Recommended Areas for Nature Walks

EFFIGY MOUNDS NATIONAL MONUMENT 151 Highway 76, Harpers Ferry, IA 52146; (319)873-3491. 1,481 acres. Located on the western banks of the Upper Mississippi River, in the northeast corner of the state, this national monument protects an area of ceremonial mounds constructed by Woodland Indians up to 2,500 years ago. Some of the mounds take the shape of wild animals.

It's an area of 300-foot bluffs and limestone outcroppings overlooking the Mississippi, along with the Yellow River, several ponds, marshlands, tallgrass prairie, and hardwood forest with oak and maple, hickory and aspen, as well as black walnut and basswood, honey locust and cottonwood. Wildlife includes white-tailed deer, coyote, red fox, beaver, raccoon, and otter, along with wild turkey, ruffed grouse, great blue heron, red-shouldered hawk, and bald eagle. All trails involve an initial 300 to 400-foot climb and are easy the rest of the way.

• *Suggested Trails for Nature Walks:* 1. The 2-mile Fire Point Trail (loop). 2. The 2-mile Trail to Marching Bear Group. 3. The 2-mile Trail to Compound Mound. 4. The 3.5-mile Trail to Hanging Rock.

DE SOTO NATIONAL WILDLIFE REFUGE Route 1, Box 114, Missouri Valley, IA 51555; (712)642-4121. 7,823 acres. This national wildlife refuge is on the Missouri River floodplain in western Iowa, near the Nebraska border, and includes lands on both sides of the river. Within the refuge is De Soto Lake, a large oxbow lake, as well as wetlands, grasslands, and woodlands. The refuge protects migratory waterfowl including 400,000 snow and blue geese, along with shorebirds, bald eagles, and such mammals as white-tailed deer, coyote, opossum, raccoon, beaver, and muskrat.

• *Suggested Trails for Nature Walks:* 1. The 0.4-mile Bertrand Trail. 2. The 0.8-mile Cottonwood Trail. 3. The 0.8-mile Wood Duck Pond Trail. 4. The 0.8-mile Missouri Meander Trail.

WAUBONSIE STATE PARK RR 2, Box 66, Hamburg, IA 51640; (712)382-2786. 1,247 acres. Occupying the southwest corner of the state, Waubonsie State Park includes hills and valleys, steep ridges and overlooks, and some badlands-like terrain. There are forested areas along with shrubs, wildflowers, and yucca.

• *Suggested Trails for Nature Walks:* 1. The 0.2-mile Entrance Trail. 2. The 0.2-mile Overlook Trail. 3. The 0.5-mile Ridge Trail. 4. The 0.7-mile Mincer Nature Trail. 5. The 0.9-mile Sunset Ridge Interpretive Trail. 6. The 0.7-mile Picnic Area Trail. 7. The 0.9-mile Valley Trail. 8. There are several miles of steeper multiuse trails in the northern part of the park.

INDIAN CREEK NATURE CENTER 6665 Otis Road, SE, Cedar Rapids, IA 52403; (319)362-0664. 140 acres. This nature center is located alongside east-central Iowa's Indian Creek and the Cedar River, on the outskirts of

IOWA

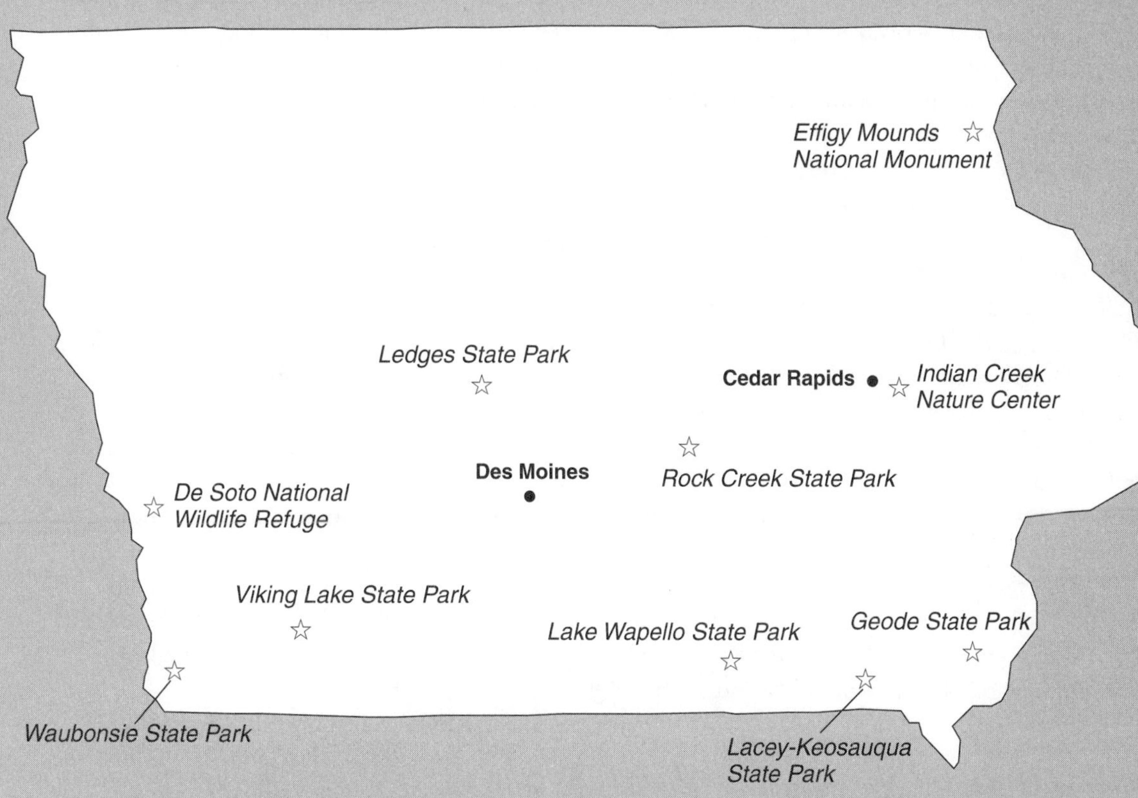
Effigy Mounds
National Monument
Ledges State Park
Cedar Rapids
Indian Creek
Nature Center
Rock Creek State Park
Des Moines
De Soto National
Wildlife Refuge
Viking Lake State Park
Lake Wapello State Park
Geode State Park
Waubonsie State Park
Lacey-Keosauqua
State Park

Cedar Rapids. It's an area of hills and ravines, prairie grasslands and meadows, and hardwood and conifer forests with maple, oak, hickory, sycamore, white pine, willow, and cottonwood, as well as wildflowers. White-tailed deer, beaver, and owl are among the wildlife. Naturalist-led walks are available.

• *Suggested Trails for Nature Walks:* 1. The 0.3-mile Eloise Schultz Memorial Trail (loop). 2. The 0.3-mile Green Footpath. 3. The 0.8-mile Blue Footpath. 4. The 1.1-mile Red Path. 5. The 2-mile Landforms Loop. 6. The 7.5-mile Sac and Fox National Recreation Trail.

LEDGES STATE PARK 1519 250th Street, Madrid, IA 50156; (515)432-1852. 1,200 acres. Overlooking the Des Moines River in central Iowa, Ledges State Park is named for the 300-million-year-old and 75-foot-high sandstone outcroppings that overlook Pease Creek. Terrain is hilly and sometimes steep, with wildflowers, shrubs, and woodlands of maple, ash, and cottonwood.

• *Suggested Trails for Nature Walks:* 1. The 3-mile Prairie Trail. 2. The 4-mile Lost Lake Nature Trail. 3. The 5-mile Reindeer Ridge Trail (easy-moderate). 4. The 5-mile Old Indian Trail (easy-moderate).

VIKING LAKE STATE PARK RR 1, Box 191, Stanton, IA 51573; (712)829-2235. 1,000 acres. This southwestern Iowa state park features 150-acre, man-made Viking Lake, with many bays, a sandy beach, and over 4 miles of shoreline. There are hills and valleys with prairie grasses, shrubs, and wildflowers including wild rose, black-eyed Susan, and yellow violet, along with forests of bur oak and basswood, black cherry and shagbark hickory, cottonwood and black willow, osage orange and eastern redcedar. Among the wildlife are white-tailed deer, coyote, red fox, beaver, raccoon, pheasant, great horned owl, and red-tailed hawk.

• *Suggested Trails for Nature Walks:* 1. The 0.5-mile Whitetail Trail. 2. The 1-mile Bur Oak Nature Trail. 3. Several miles of multiuse trails occupy one side of the lake.

LAKE WAPELLO STATE PARK RR 1, Box 81, Drakesville, IA 52552; (515)722-3371. 1,150 acres. Located in southeastern Iowa, this state park is centered on 289-acre Lake Wapello. There are hills and knolls, hollows and gullies, with marshes, a couple of ponds, PeeDee Creek, woodlands, and prairie that includes 10-foot-high big bluestem grasses.

• *Suggested Trails for Nature Walks:* 1. The 0.8-mile PeeDee Creek Nature Trail (loop). 2. A grassy 7-mile trail, accessible at several points, encircles the lake.

ROCK CREEK STATE PARK 5627 Rock Creek East, Kellogg, IA 50135; (515)236-3722. 1,697 acres. Situated in central Iowa, this state park is centered on Rock Creek Lake, a 602-acre man-made lake with a beach and 15 miles of shoreline. Wildlife here includes white-tailed deer as well as mallard, bluebill, and teal.

• *Suggested Trails for Nature Walks:* 1. The 0.5-mile Nature Trail. 2. The grassy 10-mile Multi-Use Trail, which encircles part of the lake.

LACEY-KEOSAUQUA STATE PARK P.O. Box 398, Keosauqua, IA 52565; (319)293-3502. 1,653 acres. Lacey-Keosauqua State Park is on the Des Moines River in southeastern Iowa, next to state forest lands. Terrain here is hilly with bluffs and valleys, forests and shrubs, a 30-acre lake with a beach, and nineteen ancient Indian burial mounds. Wildlife includes white-tailed deer, red fox, raccoon, and opossum.

• *Suggested Trails for Nature Walks:* Fifteen miles of unnamed trails wind throughout the park, including alongside the river, with steep spots along some trails.

GEODE STATE PARK 3249 Racine Avenue, Danville, IA 52623; (319)392-4601. 1,640 acres. Located in the southeast corner of the state and named after the crystal-filled stones found in the area, this state park features 186-acre, man-made Lake Geode, with a beach, there's a segment of the Skunk River here.

• *Suggested Trails for Nature Walks:* There's a 7-mile network of trails around the lake, including a short nature trail.

Other Suitable Locations for Nature Walks in Iowa

Iowa has a total of seventy-four state parks, state forests, and state recreation areas, and the vast majority of these sites feature trails for walking and hiking. Information: Iowa Department of Natural Resources, Wallace State Office Building, 900 East Grand Avenue, Des Moines, IA 50319; (515)281-6157.

There are three national wildlife refuges in the state that have trails. Information: U.S. Fish and Wildlife Service, 1 Federal Drive, Federal Building, Fort Snelling, MN 55111.

Several lakes in Iowa that are managed by the U.S. Army Corps of Engineers have trails. Information: Corps of Engineers, Rock Island District, P.O. Box 2004, Rock Island, IL 61204; (309)788-6361; or Corps of Engineers, Kansas City District, 601 East 12th Street, 716 Federal Building, Kansas City, MO 64106; (816)426-6816.

KANSAS

Recommended Areas for Nature Walks

CLINTON LAKE U.S. Army Corps of Engineers, Clinton Lake Project Office, Route 1, Box 120-G, Lawrence, KS 66044; (913)843-7665. This 7,000-acre reservoir in east-central Kansas is on lands administered by the Army Corps of Engineers. Adjacent to the lake is the 1,425-acre Clinton State Park and Wildlife Area. It's a place of hills and bluffs, open fields and forests, with oak, hickory, walnut, sycamore, cedar, and sumac trees. Wildlife includes white-tailed deer, gray fox, coyote, beaver, and cottontail rabbit, along with quail, mourning dove, teal, mallard, snow goose, and bald eagle.

• *Suggested Trails for Nature Walks:* 1. The 0.7-mile Backwoods Nature Trail. 2. The 4.5-mile George Latham Trail, on the west shore. 3. The 12-mile Clinton Hiking and Biking Trail, which consists of two trails on the north shore. 4. There's a 50-mile network of hiking and horseback trails on the south shore.

TORONTO STATE PARK AND WILDLIFE AREA RR 1, Box 44, Toronto, KS 66777; (316)637-2213. 1,075 acres. Toronto State Park and Wildlife Area consists of four separate tracts of land around the 2,800-acre Toronto Reservoir, in the Verdigris River Valley of southeastern Kansas. Terrain consists of rolling hills with tallgrass prairie, oak savanna, and marshlands. Among the wildlife are white-tailed deer, coyote, raccoon, wild turkey, prairie chicken, and bald eagle.

• *Suggested Trails for Nature Walks:* 1. The 0.5-mile Interpretive Trail (loop). 2. The 1-mile Blackjack Trail (loop). 3. The 1.1-mile Woodson Cove Overlook Trail (loop). 4. The 4-mile Toronto Point Trail (loop).

ELK CITY STATE PARK P.O. Box 945, Independence, KS 67301; (316)331-6295. 857 acres. This southeastern Kansas state park is situated alongside 3,510-acre Elk City Reservoir and the Elk River, near the 12,446-acre Elk City Wildlife Area. There are rolling hills with some steep slopes, limestone bluffs and rock formations, streams, prairie grasslands, and oak-hickory woodlands with birch, ash, walnut, and pecan trees. Wildlife includes deer, bobcat, fox, coyote, and wild turkey.

• *Suggested Trails for Nature Walks:* 1. The 1-mile Green Thumb Nature Trail (loop). 2. The Post Oak Self-Guided Nature Trail. 3. The 1.3-mile South Squaw Trail. 4. The 2.5-mile Table Mound Trail (moderate). 5. The 15-mile Elk River Hiking Trail (moderate), which is on nearby reservoir lands.

SAND HILLS STATE PARK 4207 East 56th Street, Hutchinson, KS 67502; (316)663-5272. 1,123 acres. Located in central Kansas, Sand Hills State Park is a place of woodlands and prairie grasslands, wetlands and sand dunes, with two seasonal ponds. Trees here include cottonwood, boxelder, elm, ash, and dogwood. White-tailed deer and wild turkey are among the wildlife.

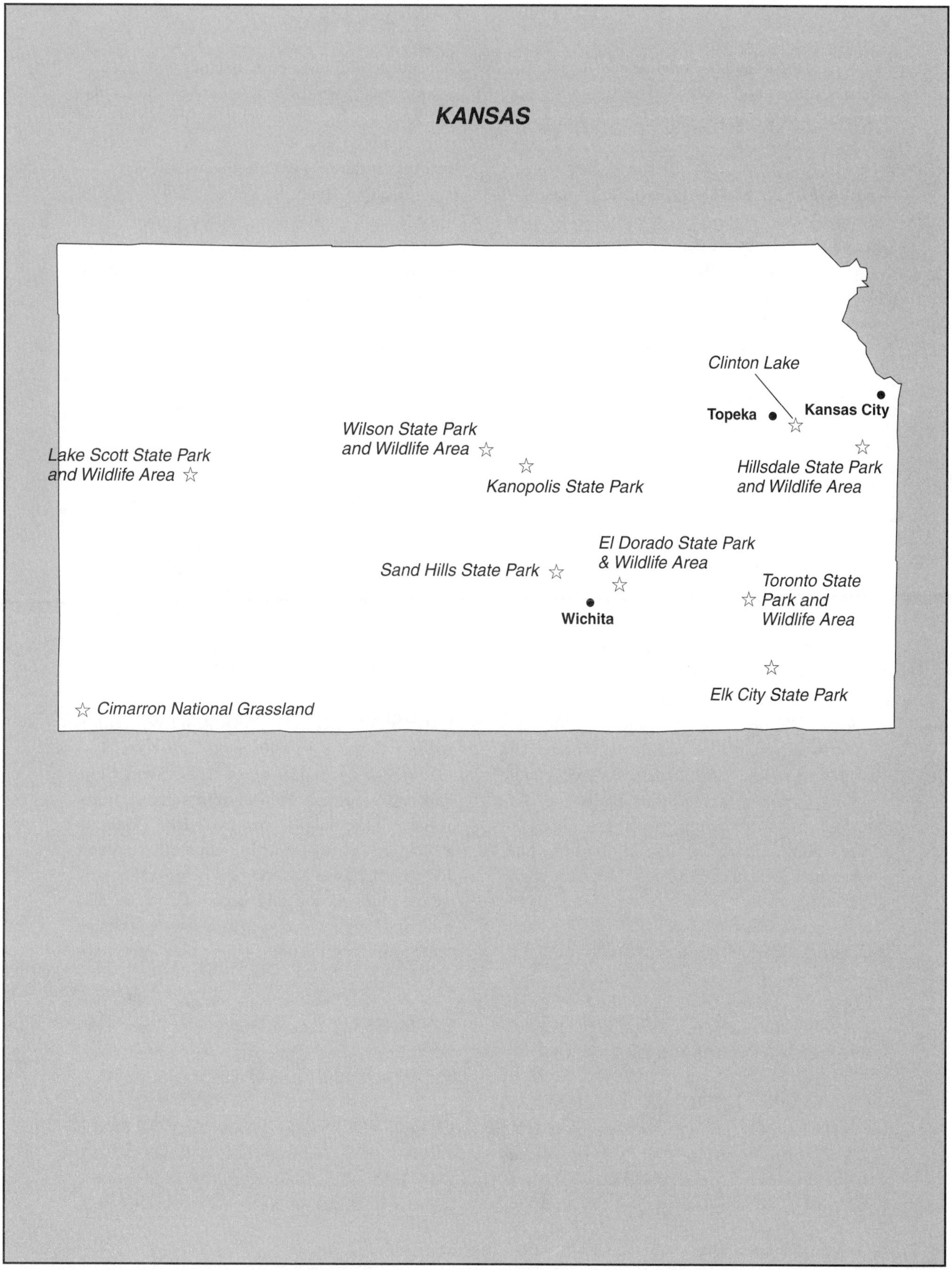

KANSAS

Clinton Lake
Topeka
Kansas City
Wilson State Park and Wildlife Area
Lake Scott State Park and Wildlife Area
Kanopolis State Park
Hillsdale State Park and Wildlife Area
El Dorado State Park & Wildlife Area
Sand Hills State Park
Toronto State Park and Wildlife Area
Wichita
Elk City State Park
Cimarron National Grassland

• *Suggested Trails for Nature Walks:* 1. The 0.6-mile Cottonwood Trail. 2. The 0.9-mile Dune Trail. 3. The 1.8-mile Prairie Trail (loop). 4. The 1.5-mile Pond Trail.

KANOPOLIS STATE PARK 200 Horsethief Road, Marquette, KS 67464; (913)546-2565. 1,585 acres. This state park in central Kansas is on the shore of Kanopolis Lake, a 3,000-acre reservoir. Terrain is hilly with some bluffs, colored sandstone canyons, rock formations, caves, and a number of creeks. Vegetation includes mixed grass prairie with redcedar, sumac, and yucca. Mule and white-tailed deer, coyote, fox, and prairie dog are among the wildlife. Naturalist-guided walks are available in summer.

• *Suggested Trails for Nature Walks:* 1. The 1.5-mile Buffalo Tracks Canyon Nature Trail. 2. The 5.5-mile Prairie Loop. 3. The 6-mile Horsethief Loop.

WILSON STATE PARK AND WILDLIFE AREA RR 1, Box 181, Sylvan Grove, KS 67481; (913)658-2465. 927 acres. Consisting of two tracts of land along the south shore of 9,000-acre Wilson Reservoir, in north-central Kansas, Wilson State Park and Wildlife Area features mixed prairie grasslands, shrubs and wildflowers, elm and hackberry trees, amid rolling terrain with sandstone bluffs and rock formations. Surrounding the lake is an 8,000-acre wildlife area. Among the wildlife are white-tailed and mule deer, coyote, rabbit, waterfowl, and wild turkey.

• *Suggested Trails for Nature Walks:* 1. The 1-mile Dakota Trail, which consists of two loops. 2. The 0.8-mile Bur Oak Nature Trail, on U.S. Army Corps of Engineers lands across the lake. 3. The 3-mile Rocktown Hiking Trail (loop), in the 305-acre Rocktown Natural Area across the lake.

CIMARRON NATIONAL GRASSLAND P.O. Box J, 242 Highway 56 East, Elkhart, KS 67950; (316)697-4621. 108,175 acres. Located in the southwest corner of Kansas, Cimarron National Grassland is an area of flat to rolling hills consisting of open grasslands with cottonwood groves, willow and tamarack, the Cimarron River—which is dry most of the year—and some man-made ponds. Deer, elk, pronghorn, and wild turkey are among the wildlife.

• *Suggested Trails for Nature Walks:* 1. The Turkey Trail, consisting of several miles of loops near the Cimarron River. 2. The 19-mile Companion Trail, which follows near and alongside the historic Sante Fe Trail.

HILLSDALE STATE PARK AND WILDLIFE AREA 26001 West 225th Street, Paola, KS 66071; (913)783-4507. 2,830 acres. This state park is located on lands that surround 4,500-acre Hillsdale Reservoir in eastern Kansas. The park has two beaches, streams, rock formations, tallgrass prairie with wildflowers, shrubs, and mixed hardwood forests of oak, walnut, and hickory. Among the wildlife are white-tailed deer, coyote, bobcat, raccoon, and rabbit, as well as quail, shorebirds, and waterfowl.

• *Suggested Trails for Nature Walks:* 1. The 2-mile Hidden Spring Nature Trail. 2. The park has an additional 30 miles of undeveloped trails.

LAKE SCOTT STATE PARK AND WILDLIFE AREA Route 1, Box 50, Scott City, KS 67871; (316)872-2061. 1,120 acres. Lake Scott State Park and Wildlife Area in western Kansas features 100-acre Lake Scott, a man-made lake located in a hilly area of prairie with bluffs, little canyons, and woodlands of ash and hackberry, walnut and willow, cottonwood and cedar. There are also some Indian pueblo ruins dating back to the late 1600s. Wildlife includes white-tailed deer, bobcat, beaver, and wild turkey.

• *Suggested Trails for Nature Walks:* 1. The 0.3-mile Big Spring Nature Trail. 2. The 7-mile Lake Scott Bridal Trail, which is open to foot travel and encircles the lake and park.

EL DORADO STATE PARK AND WILDLIFE AREA RR 3, Box 29A, El Dorado, KS 67042; (316)321-7180. 3,800 acres. Situated on the 8,000-acre El Dorado Reservoir in the Flint Hills of south-central Kansas, this state park includes some rocky shoreline, hills and low ridges, tall-grass prairie with wildflowers, shrubs, and woodlands of oak and walnut, hackberry and coffeetree, pawpaw and dogwood. Among the wildlife are white-tailed deer, raccoon, rabbit, wild turkey, prairie chicken, and waterfowl.

• *Suggested Trails for Nature Walks:* 1. The 1-mile Teter Nature Trail (loop). 2. The 12-mile Boulder Bluff Trail.

Other Suitable Locations for Nature Walks in Kansas

Kansas has twenty-four state parks, and twenty-two of these have at least short trails. There are trails as well at some state fishing lakes. Information: Kansas Department of Wildlife and Parks, RR 2, Box 54A, Pratt, KS 67124; (316)672-5911.

The U.S. Army Corps of Engineers has trails at a number of reservoirs in the state. Information: Corps of Engineers, Tulsa District, P.O. Box 61, Tulsa, OK 74121, (918)581-7349; or Corps of Engineers, Kansas City District, 716 Federal Building, 601 E. 12th Street, Kansas City, MO 64106; (816)426-6816.

There are nature trails in a number of county and city parks in Kansas. Information: Kansas Travel and Tourism, 700 Southwest Harrison, Suite 1300, Topeka, KS 66603; (800)2-KANSAS.

KENTUCKY

Recommended Areas for Nature Walks

DANIEL BOONE NATIONAL FOREST 1700 Bypass Road, Winchester, KY 40391; (606)745-3100. 683,000 acres. This national forest comprises two large tracts in the mountains of eastern and southeastern Kentucky. Of special interest is the 26,000-acre Red River Gorge Geological Area, which has over eighty natural arches and bridges, as well as two designated wilderness areas—the 13,300-acre Clifty Wilderness and the 4,791-acre Beaver Creek Wilderness.

Some of the terrain is rugged, with rimrock cliffs, rock houses and formations, steep slopes and canyon gorges, valleys with streams and waterfalls, several rivers, and two large man-made lakes. The forest consists of hardwoods and pine, with rhododendron and mountain laurel. Wildlife includes white-tailed deer, red fox, raccoon, muskrat, ruffed grouse, wild turkey, and bald eagle.

• *Suggested Trails for Nature Walks:* 1. The 0.9-mile Wintergreen Trail. 2. The 1.2-mile Clear Creek Lake Trail. 3. The 1.3-mile Rockcastle Narrows West Trail. 4. The 2.2-mile Craigs Creek Trail. 5. The 2.4-mile Flatwoods Trail. 6. The 2.5-mile Cave Run Lakeshore Trail. 7. The 3.5-mile Big Limestone Trail. 8. The 4.2-mile Lakeside South Trail. 9. The 2.1-mile Auxier Ridge Trail (easy-moderate). 10. The 4.2-mile Laurel Creek Trail (easy-moderate).

LAND BETWEEN THE LAKES NATIONAL RECREATION AREA 100 Van Morgan Drive, Golden Pond, KY 42211; (502)924-5602. 170,000 acres. Stretching between two long man-made lakes in southwestern Kentucky, with a portion in Tennessee, Land Between the Lakes National Recreation Area includes 300 miles of shoreline and 200 miles of trails. Terrain consists of rolling hills with open fields and meadows, forests, streams, small lakes, and dozens of bays. White-tailed deer, bison, elk, coyote, beaver, bald eagle, osprey, and wild turkey are among the wildlife. Guided walks are available.

• *Suggested Trails for Nature Walks:* 1. The 1-mile Woodland Walk. 2. The 2.2-mile Hematite Lake Trail. 3. The 4.5-mile Honker Lake Trail. 4. The 14-mile Canal Loop Trail, consisting of several loops. 5. The 26-mile Fort Henry National Recreation Trail, which is made up of a number of loops. 6. The 65-mile North/South National Recreation Trail (easy-moderate).

BERNHEIM ARBORETUM AND RESEARCH FOREST Clermont, KY 40110; (502)955-8512. 12,000 acres. This privately owned arboretum and research forest—which is open to the public—is in north-central Kentucky, south of Louisville. The 240-acre arboretum is accompanied by a nature center and gardens, along with meadows, forests, 32-acre Lake Nevin, and several other lakes. White-tailed deer and red-tailed hawk are among the wildlife.

• *Suggested Trails for Nature Walks:* 1. The 0.3-mile Knob Top Trail. 2. The 0.4-mile Nature

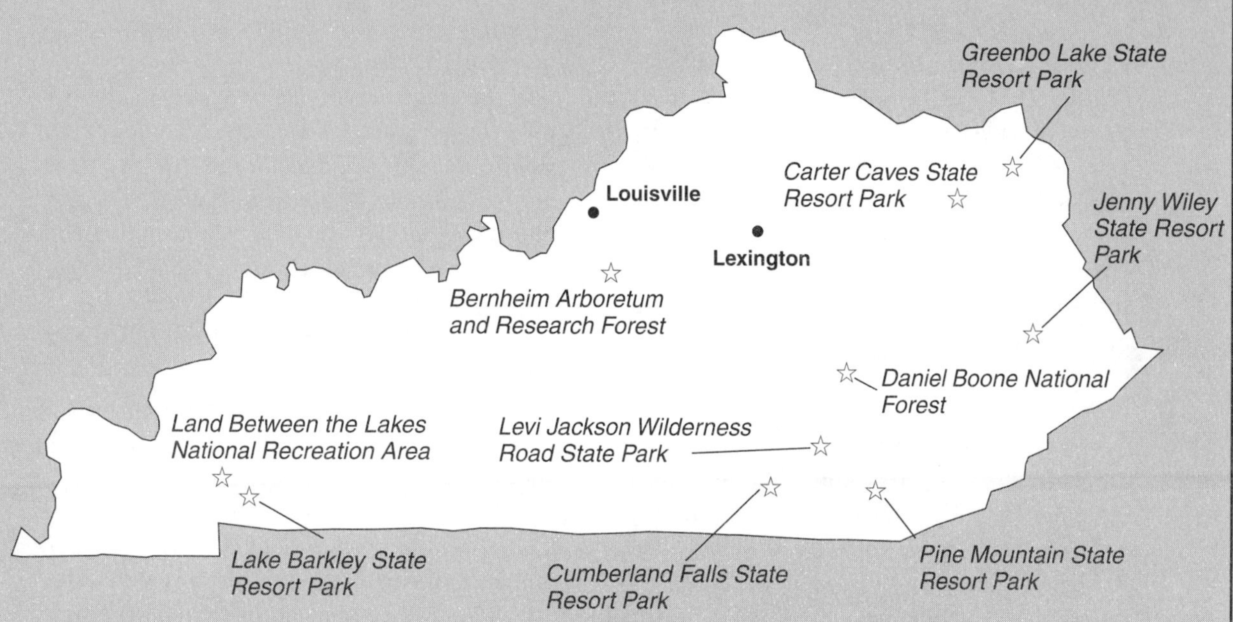
KENTUCKY
Greenbo Lake State Resort Park
Louisville
Carter Caves State Resort Park
Jenny Wiley State Resort Park
Lexington
Bernheim Arboretum and Research Forest
Daniel Boone National Forest
Land Between the Lakes National Recreation Area
Levi Jackson Wilderness Road State Park
Lake Barkley State Resort Park
Cumberland Falls State Resort Park
Pine Mountain State Resort Park

Center Trail. 3. The 0.4-mile High Point Trail. 4. The 0.5-mile Rocky Run Trail. 5. The 0.6-mile Tower Loop Trail. 6. The 0.8-mile Poplar Flat Trail (easy-moderate). 7. The 0.9-mile Jackson Hollow Trail (easy-moderate). 8. The 1.2-mile Cull Hollow Trail (easy-moderate). 9. The 1.5-mile Iron Ore Hill Trail (easy-moderate).

CUMBERLAND FALLS STATE RESORT PARK 7351 Highway 90, Corbin, KY 40701; (606)528-4121. 1,657 acres. Cumberland Falls State Resort Park in southeastern Kentucky is surrounded by lands of Daniel Boone National Forest, and includes a 1,294-acre nature preserve. Of interest are the Cumberland River with a 68-foot-high, 125-foot-wide waterfall, high sandstone cliffs, bluffs, and rock houses, several streams, tall hemlocks, and many wildflowers.

• *Suggested Trails for Nature Walks:* 1. The 1-mile Trail #4. 2. The 1-mile Trail #6. 3. The 0.5-mile Trail #7. 4. The 1.3-mile Trail #12. 5. The 1.5-mile Trail #10. 6. The 7-mile Trail #2. 7. The 1.5-mile Trail #9 (moderate). 8. The 2.5-mile Trail #11 (moderate).

CARTER CAVES STATE RESORT PARK Route 5, Box 1120, Olive Hill, KY 41164; (606)286-4411. 1,800 acres. This park in northeastern Kentucky features twenty caverns, one of which has an underground river and waterfall. There are also several natural bridges and arches, including a 220-foot-long rock bridge that's the biggest in the state and another that actually supports a highway. The area is one of forested hills with high cliffs, streams including Tygart's Creek, and 40-acre Smokey Valley Lake. Naturalist-led walks are available, and cave tours offered for a fee.

• *Suggested Trails for Nature Walks:* 1. The 0.5-mile Yellow Trail (loop). 2. The 0.5-mile Natural Bridge Trail (loop). 3. The 0.7-mile Blue Trail. 4. The 3.3-mile Red Trail (loop). 5. The 7.2-mile Carter Caves Trail. 6. The 0.8-mile Cascade Trail (easy-moderate)

LAKE BARKLEY STATE RESORT PARK Box 790, Cadiz, KY 42211; (502)924-1131. 3,200 acres. Lake Barkley State Resort Park in southwestern Kentucky sits on the shore of 57,920-acre Lake Barkley, which was created by impounding the Cumberland River, and lies directly east of Land Between the Lakes. A portion of the park has been designated a Nature Preserve. The area is wooded and there's a large beach on the lake.

• *Suggested Trails for Nature Walks:* 1. The 0.8-mile Lena Madesin Phillips Memorial Trail (loop). 2. The 0.3-mile Wagon Wheel Trail. 3. The 1.3-mile Wilderness Trail. 4. The 1.8-mile Blue Springs Trail. 5. The 2-mile Cedar Grove Trail.

PINE MOUNTAIN STATE RESORT PARK 1050 State Park Road, Pineville, KY 40977; (606)337-3066. 1,519 acres. This state park is perched on the slopes of Pine Mountain in southeastern Kentucky, near Cumberland Gap National Historic Park and amid lands of 11,363-acre Kentucky Ridge State Forest. There are sandstone outcroppings, streams with waterfalls, and forests of pine, oak, hickory, maple, tulip tree, and some old-growth hemlock, as well as mountain laurel and rhododendron. Among the wildlife are black bear, bobcat, fox, raccoon, and opossum. The park has a nature center.

• *Suggested Trails for Nature Walks:* 1. The 0.4-mile Azalea Trail (loop). 2. The 0.5-mile Living Stairway Trail (loop). 3. The 0.6-mile Hemlock Garden Trail (loop). 4. The 1.4-mile Fern Garden Trail (loop). 5. The 0.5-mile Lost Trail (easy-moderate loop). 6. The 0.5-mile Chained Rock Trail (easy-moderate). 7. The 1-mile Rock Hotel Trail (easy-moderate). 8. The 1.5-mile Honeymoon Falls Trail (easy-moderate loop). 9. The 1.8-mile Laurel Cove Trail (moderate).

LEVI JACKSON WILDERNESS ROAD STATE PARK 998 Levi Jackson Mill Road, London, KY 40741; (606)878-8000. 800 acres. Levi Jackson Wilderness Road State Park in south-central Kentucky features a section of the Wilderness Road, a route used by the early pioneers. Terrain is hilly with a forest of white pine, oak, and hickory. Included are a sandstone outcropping called Frazier Knob, a lake, and a short stretch of the Little Laurel River.

• *Suggested Trails for Nature Walks:* 1. The 1.3-mile Wilderness Road National Recreation Trail. 2. The 2.3-mile Boone Trace Trail (loop). 3. The 1-mile Bridal Trail (no longer used by horses). 4. The 2.2-mile Frazier Knob Trail (easy-moderate).

GREENBO LAKE STATE RESORT PARK HC 60, Box 562, Greenup, KY 41144; (606)473-7324. 3,330 acres. Located in northeastern Kentucky near the Ohio River, this state park has forested hills, ridges, valleys, and 225-acre, man-made Greenbo Lake. There are three major streams: Pruitt Fork Creek, Claylick Creek, and Buffalo Branch. Wildlife includes white-tailed deer and grouse.

• *Suggested Trails for Nature Walks:* 1. The 1.1-mile Fern Valley Interpretive Trail. 2. Several miles of the 24-mile Michael Tygart Trail, which continues on outside the park. 3. The 7-mile Michael Tygart Loop Trail.

JENNY WILEY STATE RESORT PARK HC 66, Box 200, Prestonburg, KY 41653; (606)886-2711. 1,771 acres. Jenny Wiley State Resort Park is on 1,100-acre, man-made Dewey Lake in eastern Kentucky. Terrain is mountainous and the park is forested with pine and cedar, oak and poplar, maple and magnolia, hemlock and hickory. There are also many wildflowers in season. Wildlife includes white-tailed deer, rabbit, and wild turkey.

• *Suggested Trails for Nature Walks:* 1. The 1-mile Steve Brackett Memorial Trail. 2. The 2.5-mile Lakeshore Trail. 3. The 1.3-mile Moss Ridge Trail (moderate loop). 4. Several miles of the 163-mile Jenny Wiley Trail, which continues on to the Ohio River (moderate).

Other Suitable Locations for Nature Walks in Kentucky

Kentucky has thirty-eight state parks, and most of them have foot trails. Information: Kentucky Department of Parks, Capital Plaza Tower, 500 Mero Street, 11th Floor, Frankfort, KY 40601; (800)255-PARK.

There are trails in Cumberland Gap National Historic Park and Mammoth Cave National Park. Information: Cumberland Gap NHP, P.O. Box 1848, Middlesboro, KY 40965; (606)248-2817. Mammoth Cave National Park, Mammoth Cave, KY 42259; (502)758-2251.

Some U.S. Army Corps of Engineers lands in the state feature trails. Information: Corps of Engineers, Louisville District, P.O. Box 59, Louisville, KY 40201, (502)582-6292; Corps of Engineers, Huntington District, 502 8th Street, Huntington, WV 25701; (304)529-5607.

LOUISIANA

Recommended Areas for Nature Walks

KISATCHIE NATIONAL FOREST 2500 Shreveport Highway, Pineville, LA 71360; (318)640-7160. Consisting of eight tracts of land in western and northern Louisiana, Kisatchie National Forest has flat to hilly topography with hardwoods and pine, including old-growth stands, beech, baldcypress, and magnolia. There are also many lakes and bayous, with bluffs and sand beaches. Of special interest is the 8,700-acre Kisatchie Hills Wilderness, featuring somewhat more rugged terrain, as well as 19 miles of the Saline Bayou National Wild and Scenic River. White-tailed deer, fox, wild turkey, and alligator are among the wildlife.

• *Suggested Trails for Nature Walks:* 1. The 1.2-mile Stuart Lake Interpretive Trail. 2. The 1.3-mile Dogwood Trail (loop). 3. The 1.6-mile Fullerton Lake Trail (loop). 4. The 2-mile Lamotte Creek Trail. 5. The 2-mile Wild Azalea Spur Trail. 6. The 3-mile Valentine Trail (loop). 7. The 7.6-mile Sugar Cane National Recreation Trail. 8. The 10-mile Lakeshore Trail. 9. The 10-mile Whiskey Chitto Trail. 10. The 31-mile Wild Azalea National Recreation Trail.

CATAHOULA NATIONAL WILDLIFE REFUGE P.O. Drawer Z, Rhinehart, LA 71363; (318)992-5261. 5,309 acres. This national wildlife refuge sits on the northeast shore of 26,000-acre and man-made Catahoula Lake, in east-central Louisiana. It's an area of bottomland hardwood forests with cypress, water elm, water oak, and water hickory, plus upland oak and pecan. There are also swamps, marshes, and bayous, with 1,200-acre Duck Lake and the French Fork Little River. Among the wildlife are white-tailed deer, bobcat, beaver, and alligator, along with tens of thousands of wintering waterfowl including heron and egret.

• *Suggested Trails for Nature Walks:* 1. The 1-mile Water Hickory Wildlife Trail. 2. The 3-mile Hiking Trail.

LOUISIANA STATE ARBORETUM Route 3, Box 494, Ville Platte, LA 70586; (318)363-2403. 600 acres. Situated next to Chicot State Park in central Louisiana, this state arboretum includes a climax forest of beech, magnolia, oak, and ash, along with a wide range of other vegetation native to Louisiana. Terrain is flat to hilly and occasionally steep, with some ravines and creeks. Wildlife includes white-tailed deer, fox, opossum, and wild turkey.

• *Suggested Trails for Nature Walks:* Several interconnecting nature trails totaling 2.5 miles wind through the arboretum.

LAKE FAUSSE POINTE STATE PARK 5400 Levee Road, St. Martinville, LA 70582; (318) 229-4764. 6,000 acres. This state park is located on an island in huge Lake Fausse Pointe, alongside the Atchafalaya Basin, which is an extensive area of wetlands. The park has woodlands,

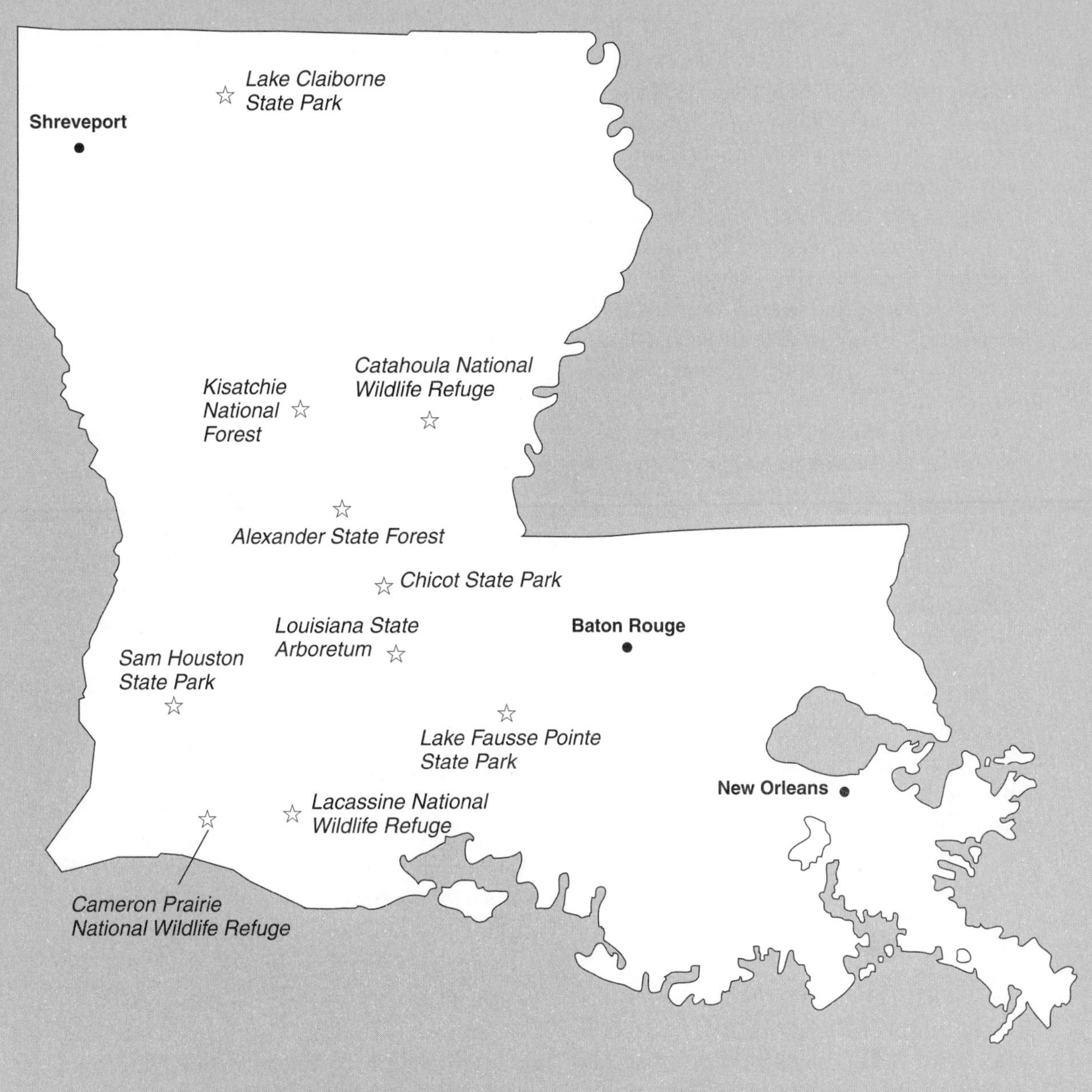

LOUISIANA
Lake Claiborne
State Park
Shreveport
Kisatchie
National
Forest
Catahoula National
Wildlife Refuge
Alexander State Forest
Chicot State Park
Louisiana State
Arboretum
Baton Rouge
Sam Houston
State Park
Lake Fausse Pointe
State Park
New Orleans
Lacassine National
Wildlife Refuge
Cameron Prairie
National Wildlife Refuge

swamps, and many waterways including bayous and canals.

• *Suggested Trails for Nature Walks:* 1. The 0.8-mile Trail A. 2. The 1.6-mile Trail B.

LACASSINE NATIONAL WILDLIFE REFUGE 209 Nature Road, Lake Arthur, LA 70549; (318)774-5923. 32,970 acres. Lacassine National Wildlife Refuge in southwestern Louisiana consists primarily of marshlands with some man-made lakes, bayous, and canals. There's a 3,345-acre designated wilderness area. The refuge attracts hundreds of thousands of migrating and wintering waterfowl, among them snow goose, ring-necked duck, and green-winged teal. Other wildlife includes alligator, armadillo, white-tailed deer, coyote, raccoon, otter, and mink.

• *Suggested Trails for Nature Walks:* There are 30 miles of levees and service roads throughout the refuge that are closed to vehicles and open to foot travel.

ALEXANDER STATE FOREST P.O. Box 298, Woodworth, LA 71485; (318)445-4511. 7,750 acres. Located south of Alexandria, in central Louisiana, Alexander State Forest features Indian Creek and 2,250-acre Indian Creek Lake. It's an area of low hills with loblolly, longleaf, and slash pine, as well as bottomland hardwoods including oak and sycamore, maple and ash, sweetgum and dogwood.

• *Suggested Trails for Nature Walks:* The 2.5-mile Indian Creek Trail (loop).

SAM HOUSTON STATE PARK 101 Sutherland Road, Lake Charles, LA 70611; (318)855-2665. 1,068 acres. This southwestern Louisiana state park is located at the confluence of three rivers: the Houston, the Calcasieu, and the Indian Bayou. There are several lagoons, streams, and dense forests, with white-tailed deer among the wildlife.

• *Suggested Trails for Nature Walks:* 1. The Hiking Trail. 2. The Old Stage Coach Trail.

LAKE CLAIBORNE STATE PARK P.O. Box 246, Homer, LA 71040; (318)927-2976. 620 acres. This state park in northern Louisiana is located on 6,400-acre Lake Claiborne, a man-made lake created by damming the Bayou D'Arbonne. Here are rolling hills with woodlands consisting of tall hardwoods and pine trees, plus ferns and mosses. There's a swimming beach on the lake.

• *Suggested Trails for Nature Walks:* 1. The 1-mile Lake Claiborne Trail. 2. There's a secondary trail as well as an undeveloped nature trail; these connect with the Lake Claiborne Trail, forming two loops.

CAMERON PRAIRIE NATIONAL WILDLIFE REFUGE 1428 Highway 27, Bell City, LA 70630; (318)598-2216. 24,548 acres. Made up of two separate units in the southwest corner of the state, Cameron Prairie National Wildlife Refuge has extensive freshwater and saltwater marshes, old fields and coastal prairie, several lakes and ponds, and bayous and canals. Wildlife includes white-tailed deer and alligator, as well as songbirds and wintering waterfowl such as snow goose and Canada goose, green-winged teal, ring-necked duck, white ibis, and egret.

• *Suggested Trails for Nature Walks:* There's a loop trail that's several miles long, and many additional miles of dikes and levees here are open to foot travel.

CHICOT STATE PARK Route 3, Box 494, Ville Platte, LA 70586; (318)363-2403. 6,000 acres. Located in the central part of the state, Chicot State Park features rolling hills, woodlands, bottomland hardwoods, and a 2,000-acre reservoir known as Lake Chicot.

• *Suggested Trails for Nature Walks:* An 8-mile trail parallels the western shore of the lake, and some short spur trails lead to the lakeshore.

Other Suitable Locations for Nature Walks in Louisiana

Louisiana has fifteen state parks, and eight of these locations have suitable trails. Information: Louisiana Office of State Parks, P.O. Box 44426, Baton Rouge, LA 70804; (504)342-8111.

Eight national wildlife refuges in the state feature trails. Information: U.S. Fish and Wildlife Service, 1875 Century Boulevard, Atlanta, GA 30345.

There are trails in some Louisiana areas administered by the U.S. Army Corps of Engineers. Information: Corps of Engineers, Vicksburg District, 2101 North Frontage Road, Vicksburg, MS 39180; (601)631-5286.

MAINE

Recommended Areas for Nature Walks

ACADIA NATIONAL PARK P.O. Box 177, Bar Harbor, ME 04609; (207)288-3338. 35,000 acres. Occupying a substantial portion of Mount Desert Island, on Maine's southeastern coast, Acadia National Park features a scenic array of small mountains, cliffs, valleys, and rocky shoreline, with numerous bays, some islands offshore, and several inland lakes, ponds, and streams. Highest elevation is 1,530-foot Cadillac Mountain.

Much of the park is conifer-forested with spruce, pine, and hemlock, along with maple, beech, birch, and aspen, and there are wildflowers and ferns in season. Wildlife includes white-tailed deer, fox, raccoon, porcupine, beaver, eagle, osprey, and pergrine falcon, in addition to seal and porpoise offshore. Naturalist-led walks are available.

• *Suggested Trails for Nature Walks:* 1. The 0.7-mile Wonderland Trail. 2. The 1-mile Jordan Pond Nature Trail (loop). 3. The 1.3-mile Ship Harbor Nature Trail. 4. The 1.4-mile Great Head Loop Trail. 5. The 1.8-mile Ocean Trail. 6. The 3.3-mile Jordan Pond Shore Trail. 7. The 4-mile Hadlock Pond Carriage Road Loop. 8. An additional 39 miles of easy carriage paths are suitable for walking. 9. The 1.8-mile Gorham Mountain Trail (moderate). 10. The 2.6-mile Bear Brook Trail (moderate).

CAMDEN HILLS STATE PARK HCR 60, Box 3110, Camden, ME 04843; (207)236-3109. 5,500 acres. Camden Hills State Park is in the Megunticook Mountains above Penobscot Bay, along the central coast of Maine, with elevations to 1,380 feet. The park features rocky coastline, streams, low ridges, rock outcroppings and ledges with ocean views, and steep bluffs and cliffs, as well as a forest of maple and beech, oak and ash, spruce and fir, hemlock and pine.

• *Suggested Trails for Nature Walks:* 1. The 0.3-mile Shoreline Trail. 2. The 0.5-mile Carriage Trail. 3. The 1.5-mile Nature Trail. 4. The 1.9-mile Cameron Mountain Trail. 5. The 2-mile Snowmobile Trail. 6. The 0.5-mile Bald Rock Trail (easy-moderate). 7. The 1.5-mile Sky Blue Trail (easy-moderate). 8. The 3-mile Ski Shelter Trail (easy-moderate). 9. The 2.6-mile Maiden Cliff Trail (moderate loop).

WELLS NATIONAL ESTUARINE RESEARCH RESERVE 342 Laudholm Farm Road, Wells, ME 04090; (207)646-1555. 1,950 acres. Wells Reserve on the southern coast of Maine includes creeks and several tidal rivers, salt marshes and red maple swamps, dunes and sandy barrier beaches, open fields with wildflowers, and upland forests of oak and pine. Among the wildlife are white-tailed deer, red fox, muskrat, and river otter, along with piping plover, least tern, snowy egret, osprey, and bald eagle.

• *Suggested Trails for Nature Walks:* 1. The 0.9-mile Webhannet Overlook Loop. 2. The 1.3-mile Salt Marsh Loop. 3. The 1.4-mile Barrier Beach Walk. 4. The 1.8-mile Little River Loop. 5. The 1.6-mile Salt Hay Loop.

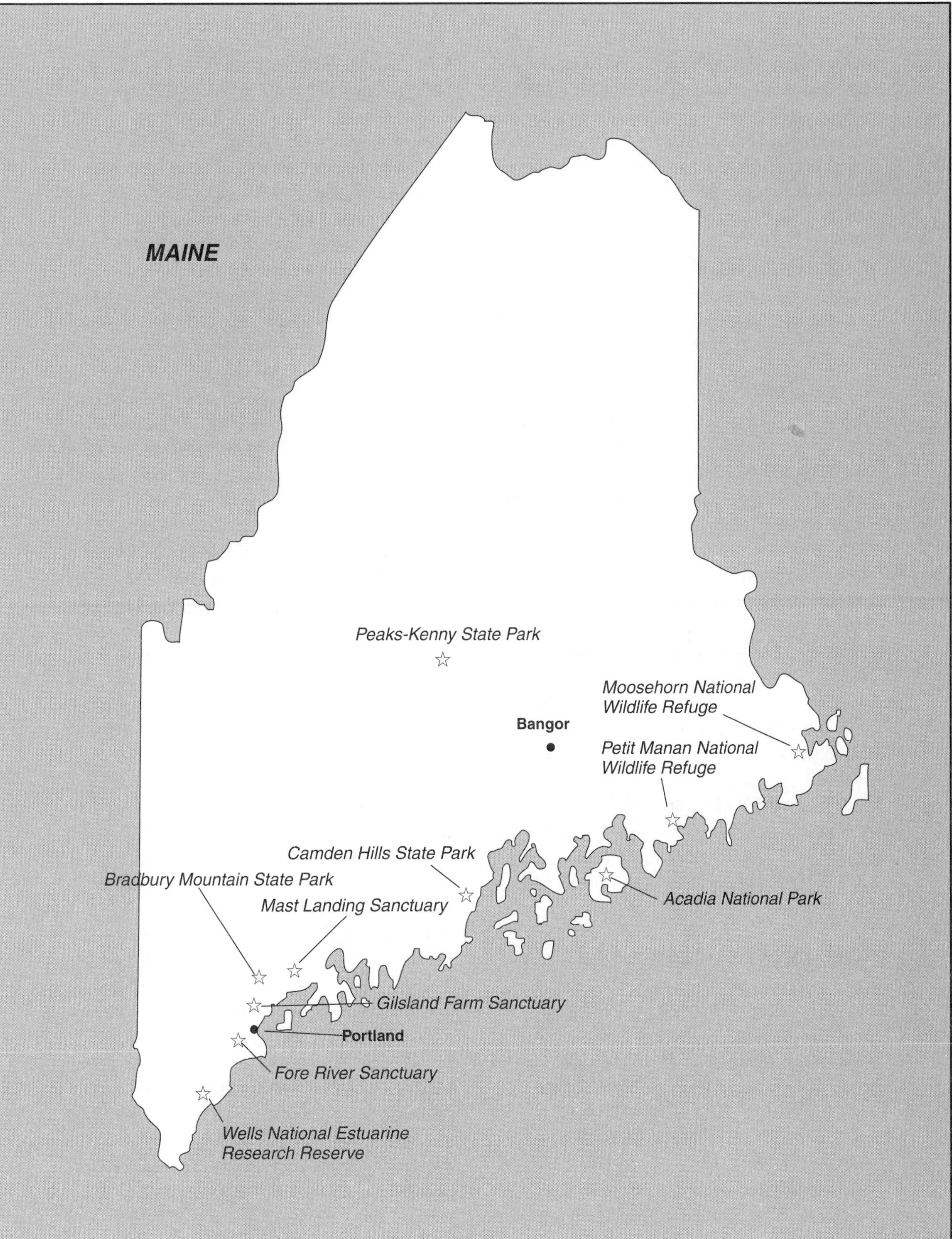
MAINE
Peaks-Kenny State Park
Moosehorn National Wildlife Refuge
Bangor
Petit Manan National Wildlife Refuge
Camden Hills State Park
Bradbury Mountain State Park
Acadia National Park
Mast Landing Sanctuary
Gilsland Farm Sanctuary
Portland
Fore River Sanctuary
Wells National Estuarine Research Reserve

BRADBURY MOUNTAIN STATE PARK 528 Hallowell Road, Pownal, ME 04069; (207)688-4712. 440 acres. Overlooking Casco Bay near the southern coast of Maine, this state park features little 485-foot Bradbury Mountain, with a forest of maple, ash, and hemlock, as well as wildflowers and mushrooms in season. Wildlife in the park includes moose, white-tailed deer, fox, raccoon, skunk, wild turkey, great horned owl, eagle, and hawk.

• *Suggested Trails for Nature Walks:* 1. The 0.2-mile Bluff Trail. 2. The 0.2-mile Summit Trail. 3. The 1-mile Northern Loop Trail. 4. The 1-mile Tote Road Trail. 5. The 1.5-mile Boundary Trail. 6. The 2-mile Knights Woods Loop Trail.

MAST LANDING SANCTUARY c/o Maine Audubon Society, Gilsland Farm Sanctuary, P.O. Box 6009, Falmouth, ME 04105; (207)781-2330. 140 acres. This Maine Audubon Society sanctuary is on the Harraseeket River in Freeport, in the southern part of the state. It includes Mill Stream, a mixed forest of hardwoods and conifers, a hemlock ravine, maple swamps, as well as old fields and apple orchards. White-tailed deer, red fox, fisher, raccoon, porcupine, snowshoe hare, great blue heron, and broad-winged hawk are among the wildlife.

• *Suggested Trails for Nature Walks:* 1. The 0.3-mile Mill Stream Trail. 2. The 0.3-mile Bench Loop Trail. 3. The 0.4-mile Estuary Trail. 4. The 0.5-mile Orchard and Deer Run Trails. 5. The 1.6-mile Loop Trail.

PEAKS-KENNY STATE PARK Route 1, Box 10, Dover-Foxcroft, ME 04426; (207)564-2003. 840 acres. Peaks-Kenny State Park is on 10-mile-long, 6,000-acre Sebec Lake in central Maine, with some rocky shoreline and a sandy beach. It's a place of hilly terrain with streams and a forest of hardwoods, fir, and spruce.

• *Suggested Trails for Nature Walks:* 1. The 0.5-mile Loop Trail. 2. The 0.7-mile Cove Trail. 3. The 2.5-mile Brown's Point Trail. 4. The 2.3-mile Birch Mountain Ledge Trail (moderate).

GILSLAND FARM SANCTUARY P.O. Box 6009, Falmouth, ME 04105; (207)781-2330. 60 acres. Situated on the Presumpscot River estuary along Maine's southern coast, near Portland, this sanctuary is the headquarters of the Maine Audubon Society, and has gardens as well as an environmental center. Terrain is gently hilly with bluffs along the river, salt marshes and mudflats, meadows and shrublands, and woodlands of red oak, red maple, hemlock, white pine, aspen, birch, and ash. Bird life includes migratory waterfowl and shorebirds. Guided walks are available.

• *Suggested Trails for Nature Walks:* 1. The 0.6-mile Pond Meadow Trail (loop). 2. The 0.7-mile West Meadow Trail (loop). 3. The 1.2-mile North Meadow Trail (loop). 4. There are several short spur trails.

MOOSEHORN NATIONAL WILDLIFE REFUGE P.O. Box 1077, Calais, ME 04619; (207)454-3521. 24,446 acres. Consisting of two units in the easternmost part of the state, Moosehorn National Wildlife Refuge has hilly terrain with ledges, a number of small lakes and ponds, fields, and wetlands including bogs, marshes, and streams. There are also forests of maple and beech, birch and aspen, pine and spruce, with 7,660 acres of designated wilderness. Among the wildlife here are American woodcock, ruffed grouse, osprey, bald eagle, loon, Canada goose, and other waterfowl, along with white-tailed deer, moose, black bear, bobcat, river otter, and beaver.

• *Suggested Trails for Nature Walks:* 1. The 0.3-mile Bird Walk. 2. The 0.4-mile Woodcock Trail. 3. The 1.2-mile Animals and their Habitats Trail. 4. Many miles of refuge roads that are closed to vehicles are open to foot travel.

FORE RIVER SANCTUARY c/o Maine Audubon Society, Gilsland Farm Sanctuary, P.O. Box 6009, Falmouth, ME 04105; (207)781-2330. 85 acres. Administered by the Maine Audubon Society and located in Portland, this sanctuary features the Fore River and Jewell Falls, along with salt marshes and freshwater brooks, small ponds, gentle hills and ravines, fields and grassy areas, and the old Cumberland and Oxford Canal, which was abandoned in 1870.

Vegetation includes ferns, blackberry and blueberry, juniper and honeysuckle, such wildflowers as wintergreen, trout lily, and lady's-slipper, as well as a forest of red oak and beech, white birch and aspen, hemlock and white pine. Among the wildlife are white-tailed deer, woodchuck, raccoon, skunk, river otter, and mink, along with grouse, kestrel, and red-tailed hawk.

• *Suggested Trails for Nature Walks:* There's a 2.5-mile trail system that includes a loop, as well as the old canal towpath.

PETIT MANAN NATIONAL WILDLIFE REFUGE P.O. Box 279, Milbridge, ME 04658; (207)546-2124. 3,368 acres. Located along the eastern coast of Maine, this is one of several coastal national wildlife refuges in the state. There's rugged shoreline along Petit Manan Point, plus three islands—with old fields and bogs, marshes and swamps, wildflowers, and woodlands of spruce, pine, and mixed hardwoods. Among the wildlife are white-tailed deer, coyote, bobcat, raccoon, and snowshoe hare, along with waterfowl, shorebirds, and raptors including falcon, hawk, and eagle.

• *Suggested Trails for Nature Walks:* 1. The 1.5-mile Birch Point Trail. 2. The 0.5-mile Shore Trail (easy-moderate).

Other Suitable Locations for Nature Walks in Maine

Maine has twenty-eight state parks, and fourteen of these locations have nature or hiking trails. Information: Bureau of Parks and Recreation, State House Station 22, Augusta, ME 04333; (207)287-3821.

In a category by itself is huge Baxter State Park, which features wilderness trails. Information: Baxter State Park, 64 Balsam Drive, Millenocket, ME 04462; (207)723-5140.

New Hampshire's White Mountain National Forest has a large tract of land in Maine with trails. Information: White Mountain National Forest, RFD 2, Box 2270, Bethel, ME; (207) 824-2134.

There are four national wildlife refuges in the state that have trails. Information: U.S. Fish and Wildlife Service, 300 Westgate Center Drive, Hadley, MA 01035.

The Maine Audubon Society owns fifteen sanctuaries in Maine, and most of them have nature trails. Information: Maine Audubon Society, P.O. Box 6009, Falmouth, ME 04105; (207)781-2330.

MARYLAND

Recommended Areas for Nature Walks

CHESAPEAKE AND OHIO NATIONAL HISTORICAL PARK P.O. Box 4, Sharpsburg, MD 21782; (301)739-4200. 20,780 acres. This extremely long and narrow park stretches 184 miles from Washington, D.C., to Cumberland, Maryland. It was established to protect the historic Chesapeake and Ohio (C & O) Canal, which was completed in 1850, as well as the Potomac River.

The landscape here is one of hills and mountains, rocky cliffs and bluffs, deep gorges and streams, with the Great Falls of the Potomac and Little Falls, as well as ruins of old mines. There are also wildflowers in season and forests of oak, hickory, and sycamore. Among the wildlife are white-tailed deer, red fox, raccoon, woodchuck, muskrat, cottontail, pileated woodpecker, heron, egret, and waterfowl. Ranger-led walks are available.

• *Suggested Trails for Nature Walks:* 1. The 0.3-mile Lock 16 Spur. 2. The 0.5-mile Lock 19 Loop. 3. The 0.5-mile Angler's Spur Trail. 4. The 0.6-mile Woodland Trail. 5. The 1.1-mile Berma Road. 6. The 4.2-mile Gold Mine Loop. 7. The 184.5-mile C & O Canal Towpath Trail.

CATOCTIN MOUNTAIN PARK 6602 Foxville Road, Thurmont, MD 21788; (301)663-9388. 5,768 acres. Adjacent to Cunningham Falls State Park in north-central Maryland, Catoctin Mountain Park is administered by the National Park Service and is the home of the presidential retreat Camp David. It's a place of small mountains with rock formations and outcroppings, creeks, and a hardwood forest of hickory and oak, beech and birch, poplar and hemlock—as well as wild cherry and sassafras, orchids, and wild ginger. Wildlife includes white-tailed deer, fox, woodchuck, and raccoon, along with ruffed grouse, pileated woodpecker, barred owl, and turkey vulture. Ranger-led walks are available.

• *Suggested Trails for Nature Walks:* 1. The 0.2-mile Spicebush Trail. 2. The 0.3-mile Cunningham Falls Trail. 3. The 0.4-mile Browns Farm Trail (loop). 4. The 0.5-mile Charcoal Trail (loop). 5. The 0.5-mile Renaissance Trail. 6. The 0.6-mile Whiskey Still Trail. 7. The 1-mile Hog Rock Trail (loop). 8. The 1-mile Thurmont Vista Trail (easy-moderate). 9. The 1.3-mile Deerfield Trail (easy-moderate loop). 10. The 2.8-mile Cunningham Falls Trail from Visitor Center (easy-moderate).

SENECA CREEK STATE PARK 11950 Clopper Road, Gaithersburg, MD 20878; (301)924-2127. 6,109 acres. This state park occupies a valley that includes a 12-mile stretch of Seneca Creek, near the Potomac River in west-central Maryland. It's an area of hills and low ridges with rock outcroppings, small streams, and 90-acre Clopper Lake. There are open fields, wildflowers and sagegrass, and oak-hickory forests with maple, poplar, and beech. Among the wildlife are white-tailed deer, fox, opossum, and raccoon.

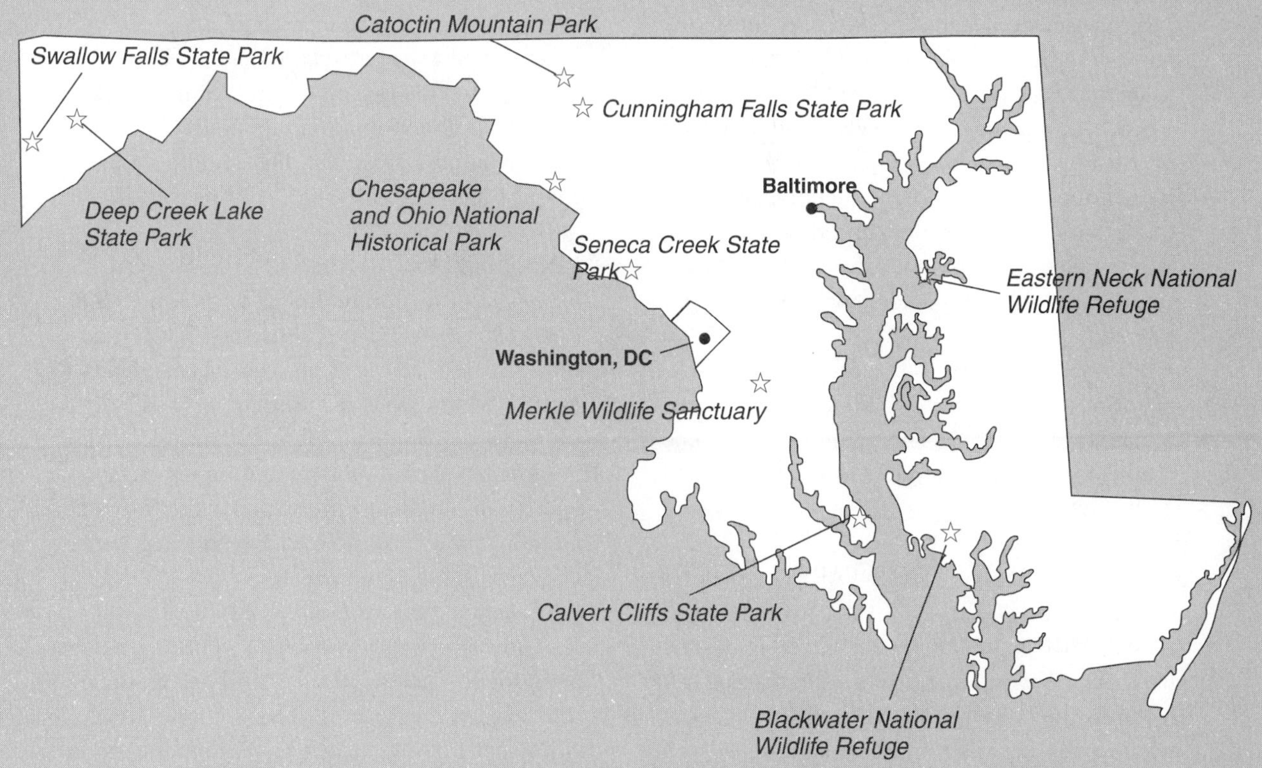
MARYLAND
Catoctin Mountain Park
Swallow Falls State Park
Cunningham Falls State Park
Baltimore
Chesapeake
and Ohio National
Historical Park
Deep Creek Lake
State Park
Seneca Creek State
Park
Eastern Neck National
Wildlife Refuge
Washington, DC
Merkle Wildlife Sanctuary
Calvert Cliffs State Park
Blackwater National
Wildlife Refuge

• *Suggested Trails for Nature Walks:* 1. The 0.3-mile Old Pond Trail. 2. The 0.8-mile Long Draught Trail. 3. The 1.3-mile Mink Hollow Trail. 4. The 3.5-mile Lake Shore Trail. 5. The 1.3-mile Great Seneca Trail (easy-moderate).

DEEP CREEK LAKE STATE PARK 898 State Park Road, Swanton, MD 21561; (301) 387-4111. 1,818 acres. Located on 3,600-acre and man-made Deep Creek Lake, near the northwestern end of Maryland, Deep Creek Lake State Park includes a mile of lakeshore with a beach, woodlands, wildflowers, and a portion of Meadow Mountain. There are hardwood forests of oak, maple, cherry, hickory, and basswood, with pine, dogwood, and rhododendron. White-tailed deer, fox, raccoon, and beaver are among the wildlife. Guided nature walks are offered.

• *Suggested Trails for Nature Walks:* 1. The 0.3-mile Snake Root Nature Trail. 2. The 2.5-mile Indian Turnip Trail. 3. The 0.5-mile Brant Mine Trail (loop). 4. The 3-mile Meadow Mountain Trail.

CALVERT CLIFFS STATE PARK c/o Point Lookout State Park, P.O. Box 48, Scotland, MD 20687; (301)872-5688. 1,313 acres. This state park on the western shore of Chesapeake Bay features the 100-foot-high Cliffs of Calvert, where extensive fossils have been found, as well as open beach along the bay. There are hills and flatlands, fields and marshes, creeks, a small pond, and an oak-hickory forest with beech, maple, ash, holly, and mountain laurel. Wildlife includes white-tailed deer, fox, muskrat, and bald eagle.

• *Suggested Trails for Nature Walks:* 1. The 1.1-mile Black Trail. 2. The 1.8-mile Red Trail. 3. The 2.6-mile White Trail. 4. The 3.6-mile Blue Trail. 5. The 3.8-mile Green Trail.

MERKLE WILDLIFE SANCTUARY 11704 Fenno Road, Upper Marlboro, MD 20772; (301)888-1410. 1,670 acres. Administered by the Maryland Department of Natural Resources, Merkle Wildlife Sanctuary is situated next to the Patuxent River in central Maryland. Terrain here is relatively flat. There are several ponds and streams, marshes and other wetlands, open fields with shrubs, and ferns and mosses, as well as forests of white oak, beech, hickory, cedar, sweetgum, maple, and sycamore, with holly, dogwood, and pawpaw. Among the wildlife are fox, raccoon, opossum, skunk, and bald eagle, along with Canada goose and barn owl.

• *Suggested Trails for Nature Walks:* 1. The 0.8-mile PawPaw Trail (loop). 2. The 1.5-mile Lookout Trail. 3. The 2-mile Mattaponi Trail. 4. The 3-mile Mounds Trail. 5. The 4-mile Poplar Springs Trail.

CUNNINGHAM FALLS STATE PARK 14039 Catoctin Hollow Road, Thurmont, MD 21788; (301)271-7574. 5,000 acres. This state park is situated next to north-central Maryland's Catoctin Mountain Park. Terrain here is hilly with rock outcroppings, 44-acre Hunting Creek Lake, streams including Big Hunting Creek, and 78-foot Cunningham Falls, which is the highest waterfall in the state. The park is forested with oak, maple, poplar, and beech.

• *Suggested Trails for Nature Walks:* 1. The 0.2-mile Cunningham Falls Trail. 2. The 0.3-mile Campground Access Trail. 3. The 0.3-mile Catoctin Furnace Trail. 4. The 0.8-mile Lower Trail. 5. The 0.8-mile Cliff Trail (easy-moderate). 6. The 2-mile Old Misery Trail (moderate).

EASTERN NECK NATIONAL WILDLIFE REFUGE 1730 Eastern Neck Road, Rock Hall, MD 21661; (410)639-7056. 2,285 acres. Located on an island off the eastern side of Chesapeake Bay, at the foot of the Chester River, this national wildlife refuge consists of tidal marsh and mudflats, grasslands and croplands, hardwood and pine forests, freshwater impoundments and creeks. Wildlife includes white-tailed deer, red fox, raccoon, beaver, muskrat, and opossum, as well as great blue heron, green-winged teal, Canada goose, tundra swan, peregrine falcon, and bald eagle.

• *Suggested Trails for Nature Walks:* 1. The 0.3-mile Tubby Cove Boardwalk Trail. 2. The 0.5-mile Nature Trail (loop). 3. The 0.5-mile Duck Inn Trail. 4. The 0.6-mile Boxes Point Trail.

SWALLOW FALLS STATE PARK 222 Herrington Lane, Oakland, MD 21550, (301)387-6938; (301)334-9180. 251 acres. Swallow Falls State Park is located within 9,248-acre Garrett State Forest and near Herrington Manor State Park at the western border of Maryland. It's on the Youghiogheny River, and features four waterfalls including 51-foot Muddy Creek Falls. There are also rock formations, a hardwood forest of oak, maple, hickory, and basswood, a 40-acre Sensitive Management Area with virgin white pine and hemlock, as well as rhododendron and ferns. White-tailed deer, raccoon, and rabbit are among the wildlife.

• *Suggested Trails for Nature Walks:* 1. The 1.3-mile Canyon Trail (loop). 2. The 5.5-mile Trail to Herrington Manor State Park.

BLACKWATER NATIONAL WILDLIFE REFUGE 2145 Key Wallace Drive, Cambridge, MD 21613; (410)228-2677. 17,121 acres. This national wildlife refuge lies near Chesapeake Bay in the southeastern part of the state. It consists predominantly of tidal marsh with freshwater ponds, swamps, creeks, and rivers, including the Blackwater and Little Blackwater rivers, as well as fields, grasses, and woodlands of loblolly pine and hardwoods. The refuge protects migratory waterfowl including Canada goose, blue-winged teal, and mallard, along with great blue heron, osprey, bald eagle, and peregrine falcon. Among the other wildlife are white-tailed and sika deer, red fox, muskrat, Delmarva fox squirrel, and otter.

• *Suggested Trails for Nature Walks:* 1. The 0.3-mile Marsh Edge Trail (loop). 2. The 0.5-mile Woods Trail, consisting of two loops. 3. The 5-mile Wildlife Drive, which is open to foot travel as well as vehicles.

Other Suitable Locations for Nature Walks in Maryland

Maryland has fifty state parks and state forests, and the vast majority of these locations have nature or hiking trails. Information: State Forest and Park Service, 580 Taylor Avenue, E-3, Annapolis, MD 21401; (410)974-3771.

Three short trails as well as beach walks are available at Assateague Island National Seashore. Information: Assateague Island National Seashore, 7206 National Seashore Lane, Berlin, MD 21811; (410)641-3030.

There are trails at the Patuxent Research Refuge, 12100 Beech Forest Road, Laurel, MD 20708; (301)497-5760.

MASSACHUSETTS

Recommended Areas for Nature Walks

CAPE COD NATIONAL SEASHORE P.O. Box 250, South Wellfleet, MA 02663; (508)349-3785. 44,000 acres. Stretching out into the ocean at the southeastern end of the state, glacially deposited Cape Cod is a place of sandy beaches and dunes, cliffs, inland ponds, salt and freshwater marshes, swamps, and hardwood forests. Forty miles of shoreline are protected by the national seashore.

Vegetation includes shrubs and grasses, as well white cedar, eastern redcedar, pitch pine, black cherry, red maple, beech, and oak trees. Among the wildlife are white-tailed deer, red fox, raccoon, woodchuck, muskrat, rabbit, quail, and piping plover and other shorebirds and waterfowl. Ranger-led walks are offered in summer.

• *Suggested Trails for Nature Walks:* 1. The 0.3-mile Buttonbush Trail. 2. The 0.5-mile Cranberry Bog Trail. 3. The 0.8-mile Small Swamp Trail (loop). 4. The 0.8-mile Pilgrim Spring Trail (loop). 5. The 1-mile Nauset Marsh Trail (loop). 6. The 1-mile Beech Forest Trail, consisting of two loops. 7. The 1.3-mile Atlantic White Cedar Swamp Trail (loop). 8. The 1.5-mile Fort Hill Trail (loop). 9. The 4-mile Great Island Trail. 10. Many options for beach walks are available.

WACHUSETT MEADOW WILDLIFE SANCTUARY 113 Goodnow Road, Princeton, MA 01541; (508)464-2712. 1,100 acres. This Massachusetts Audubon Society sanctuary is in the central part of the state, next to 1,950-acre Wachusett Mountain State Reservation. Terrain here is hilly with meadows and old fields, shrublands, a swamp, brooks, and several ponds. There's also maple and beech, alder and hickory, birch and basswood, pine and hemlock, along with pitcher plants and wildflowers. Wildlife includes white-tailed deer, fox, coyote, raccoon, porcupine, woodchuck, muskrat, river otter, and snowshoe hare.

• *Suggested Trails for Nature Walks:* 1. The 0.4-mile Rock Pasture Trail. 2. The 0.5-mile Birch Trail. 3. The 0.7-mile Fifth Pasture Loop. 4. The 1-mile West Border Trail. 5. The 1.2-mile Brown Hill Loop. 6. The 1.8-mile Pasture Trail. 7. The 1.5-mile Mountain Trail. 8. The 0.5-mile Summit Trail (easy-moderate).

ARCADIA WILDLIFE SANCTUARY 127 Combs Road, Easthampton, MA 01027; (413) 584-3009. 625 acres. Managed by the Massachusetts Audubon Society, the Arcadia Wildlife Sanctuary is in the Connecticut River Valley, in west-central Massachusetts. It borders on the Connecticut River Oxbow and features the Mill River and Wood Duck Pond, brooks and bogs, marshes and swamps, open fields and floodplain forest of hardwoods and conifers. Among the sanctuary's bird life are belted kingfisher, black-billed cuckoo, great blue heron, Canada goose, and sharp-shinned hawk. Included on the property is a nature center.

• *Suggested Trails for Nature Walks:* 1. The 0.2-mile Warbler Trail. 2. The 0.2-mile Horseshoe

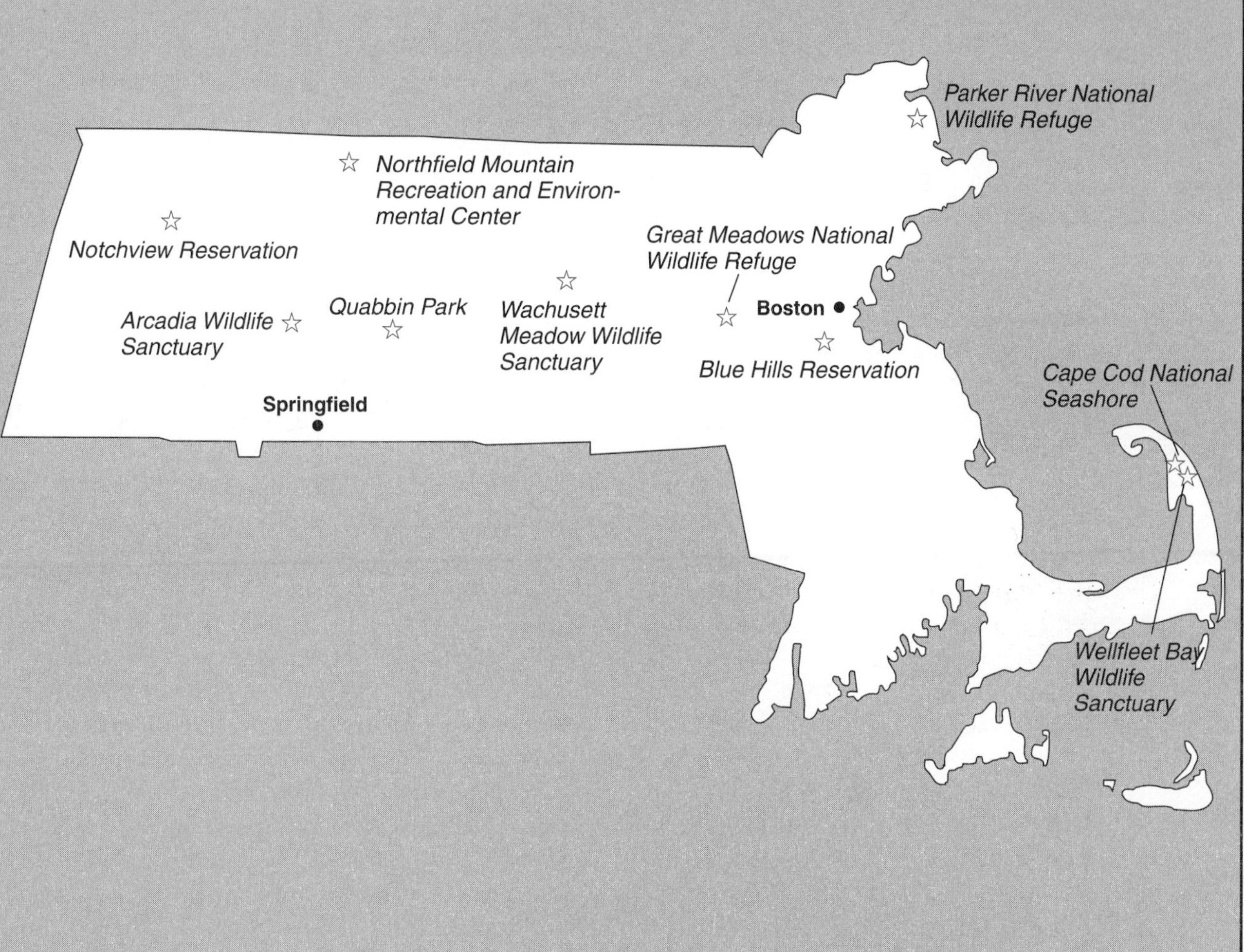
MASSACHUSETTS
Parker River National Wildlife Refuge
Northfield Mountain Recreation and Environmental Center
Notchview Reservation
Great Meadows National Wildlife Refuge
Arcadia Wildlife Sanctuary
Quabbin Park
Wachusett Meadow Wildlife Sanctuary
Boston
Blue Hills Reservation
Cape Cod National Seashore
Springfield
Wellfleet Bay Wildlife Sanctuary

Trail. 3. The 0.2-mile Woodcock Trail. 4. The 0.2-mile Fire Road. 5. The 0.3-mile Fern Trail. 6. The 0.3-mile Robert LaPalm Trail. 7. The 0.4-mile River Trail. 8. The 0.4-mile Robert Chaffee Trail. 9. The 0.4-mile Trolley Line. 10. The 0.9-mile Old Coach Road.

BLUE HILLS RESERVATION 695 Hillside Street, Milton, MA 02186; (617)698-1802. 5,800 acres. Situated just south of Boston, with elevations ranging from 259 feet to over 600 feet, this large reservation has more than 125 miles of trails. It's an area of rocky hills, including 635-foot Blue Hill, along with ponds, meadows, marshes, swamps, bogs, and oak-hickory forests with pine, hemlock, and mountain laurel. White-tailed deer, fox, and wild turkey are among the wildlife. There's an environmental center here as well, and nature walks are available.

• *Suggested Trails for Nature Walks:* 1. The 0.8-mile Houghtons Pond Loop. 2. The 2-mile Dark Hollow Loop. 3. The 2-mile Wolcott Path Loop. 4. The 3-mile Braintree Pass Path. 5. The 3.8-mile Ponkapoag Pond Loop. 6. The 6-mile Massachuseuck Trail. 7. The 1-mile Great Blue Hill Trail (moderate).

NOTCHVIEW RESERVATION 83 Old Route 9, Windsor, MA 01270; (413)298-3239. 3,000 acres. Notchview Reservation is in the Hoosac Range of western Massachusetts, next to Windsor State Forest. The terrain is hilly with several streams, open fields, and a forest of hardwoods and spruce. Highest point is 2,297-foot Judges Hill. Among the wildlife are white-tailed deer, black bear, bobcat, woodchuck, raccoon, porcupine, and beaver.

• *Suggested Trails for Nature Walks:* 1. The 1-mile Hume Brook Interpretive Trail (loop). 2. The 0.3-mile Quill Tree Trail. 3. The 0.4-mile Spruce Hill Trail. 4. The 0.5-mile Ant Hill Trail. 5. The 1.8-mile Circuit Trail (loop). 6. The 1.7-mile Whitestone Trail. 7. The 1.6-mile Mixed Wood Trail (easy-moderate loop). 8. The 1.8-mile Minor Trail (easy-moderate).

PARKER RIVER NATIONAL WILDLIFE REFUGE Northern Boulevard, Plum Island, Newburyport, MA 01950; (508)465-5753. 4,662 acres. Located on the state's northeastern coast, Parker River National Wildlife Refuge encompasses Plum Island, Broad Sound, several rivers, and many streams. There are barrier beaches with dunes, fields, salt marshes, shrublands, and pine woodlands. Among the migratory waterfowl protected here are Canada geese and ducks, plus the endangered piping plover, least tern, and other wildlife including white-tailed deer, fox, and woodchuck.

• *Suggested Trails for Nature Walks:* 1. The 0.3-mile Pines Trail. 2. The 0.8-mile Nelson Island Access Trail. 3. The 1.4-mile Hellcat Interpretive Trail. 4. The Saw-Whet Trail (forthcoming). 5. Walking is possible along six miles of beach.

WELLFLEET BAY WILDLIFE SANCTUARY P.O. Box 236, South Wellfleet, MA 02663; (508)349-2615. 1,000 acres. This Massachusetts Audubon Society sanctuary is on Cape Cod's Wellfleet Bay. It's a place of barrier beaches, freshwater and saltwater marshes, creeks, a pond, meadows, and pine woodlands, with maple, oak, cedar, spruce, and black cherry. Among the wildlife are white-tailed deer, red fox, muskrat, sandpiper, snowy egret, great blue heron, green-winged heron, great horned owl, and sharp-shinned hawk. There's a nature center, and guided walks are available.

• *Suggested Trails for Nature Walks:* 1. The 1-mile Bay View Trail/Short Loop. 2. The 1.4-mile Bay View Trail/Long Loop. 3. The 0.6-mile Silver Spring Trail (loop). 4. The 1.2-mile Try Island Trail (loop). 5. The 1.4-mile Goose Pond Trail (loop). 6. The 1.6-mile Fresh Brook Trail (loop).

QUABBIN PARK Division of Watershed Management, P.O. Box 628, Belchertown, MA 01007; (413)323-7221. This park sits at the southern end of 25,000-acre Quabbin Reservoir in central Massachusetts. It's a hilly area of hardwood and conifer forests, fields, and meadows, with wildflowers, marshes, ponds, and the Swift River. Wildlife includes white-tailed deer, fox, bobcat, coyote, and beaver, plus loon, hawk, and eagle.

• *Suggested Trails for Nature Walks:* 1. The 1-mile Rotary Vista Loop. 2. The 1.2-mile Quabbin Hill Loop Trail. 3. The 1.5-mile Beaver Pond to Tower Trail (easy-moderate). 4. The 3.6-mile Tower to Hank's Picnic Area Loop (easy-moderate).

GREAT MEADOWS NATIONAL WILDLIFE REFUGE Weir Hill Road, Sudbury, MA 01776; (617)443-4661. 3,000 acres. Consisting of two separate unit on the Sudbury and Concord rivers, 20 miles west of Boston, Great Meadow National Wildlife Refuge features freshwater marshes, streams, a pond, large man-made pools, fields, meadows, and woodlands. The refuge protects many species of migratory and resident birds, including wood duck, mallard, Canada goose, and blue-winged teal; there are also fox, raccoon, muskrat, cottontail rabbit, and white-tailed deer among the other wildlife.

• *Suggested Trails for Nature Walks:* 1. The 0.8-mile Weir Hill Trail (loop). 2. The 1.7-mile Dike Trail (loop). 3. There are several other short trails, including the Wood Duck Hollow Trail, the Black Duck Creek Trail, the Timber Trail, and the Edge Trail.

NORTHFIELD MOUNTAIN RECREATION AND ENVIRONMENTAL CENTER 99 Millers Falls Road, Northfield, MA 01360; (413)659-3713. 2,000 acres. Situated alongside and east of the Connecticut River in north-central Massachusetts, Northfield Mountain Recreation and Environmental Center is on lands that include a 300-acre reservoir and a hydroelectric power plant. Much of the area has been kept in a natural state, with streams, marshes, meadows, wildflowers, and forests of maple, oak, and pine. White-tailed deer, porcupine, and fisher are among the wildlife.

• *Suggested Trails for Nature Walks:* 1. The 1-mile Hidden Quarry Nature Trail. 2. There's a 25-mile network of other trails, many of which are used for cross-country skiing in the winter; the easiest trails run northeast of the visitor center.

Other Suitable Locations for Nature Walks in Massachusetts

Massachusetts has over 140 state parks, state forests, state recreation areas, and state reservations. The vast majority of these locations have nature or hiking trails. Information: Division of Forests and Parks, 100 Cambridge Street, Boston, MA 02202; (617)727-3180.

The Massachusetts Audubon Society owns and administers twenty-three sanctuaries in the state, most of which have trails. Information: Massachusetts Audubon Society, 208 South Great Road, Lincoln, MA 01773; (617)259-9500.

There are five national wildlife refuges in the state with trails. Information: U.S. Fish and Wildlife Service, 300 Westgate Center Drive, Hadley, MA 01035; (413)253-8200.

Trails are available at several Massachusetts areas managed by the U.S. Army Corps of Engineers. Information: Corps of Engineers, New England District, 424 Trapelo Road, Waltham, MA 02254; (617)647-8107.

MICHIGAN

Recommended Areas for Nature Walks

HURON-MANISTEE NATIONAL FORESTS 1755 South Mitchell Street, Cadillac, MI 49601; (800)821-6263. 912,000 acres. These two jointly administered national forests are located in the west-central and northeastern regions of Michigan's Lower Peninsula. Terrain here is flat to rolling, with occasional vistas. The forests consist of hardwoods along with pine and hemlock trees.

Of special interest is the 3,450-acre Nordhouse Dunes Wilderness Area alongside Lake Michigan, with sandy beaches and 140-foot dunes. There are also eight major rivers, many lakes, scores of streams, marshes, and swamps, with shrubs, mosses, ferns, and wildflowers in season. White-tailed deer, fox, coyote, loon, and eagle are among the wildlife.

• *Suggested Trails for Nature Walks:* 1. The 0.8-mile Arboretum Trail (loop). 2. The 1-mile Pines Point Trail. 3. The 1-mile Jewell Lake Trail. 4. The 1.2-mile Island Lake Nature Trail (loop). 5. The 1.4-mile Nordhouse Dunes Trail. 6. The 1.6-mile Algoma Trail. 7. The 1.9-mile Michigan Trail. 8. The 2.2-mile Nipissing Trail. 9. The 6.1-mile Reid Lake Trail, consisting of four loops. 10. The 10.5-mile Manistee River Trail.

OTTAWA NATIONAL FOREST East U.S. 2, Ironwood, MI 49938; (906)932-1330. 954,000 acres. This national forest in the western part Michigan's Upper Peninsula has over 500 lakes, seven major rivers, seventy-six waterfalls, countless streams, and areas of wetlands. There are hardwood forests of maple and birch, aspen and basswood, along with hemlock and pine. Three designated wilderness areas total 49,316 acres. It's a region of rolling hills with elevations up to 1,500 feet, cliffs, bluffs, and rock outcroppings. Wildlife includes white-tailed deer, moose, black bear, fox, beaver, snowshoe hare, skunk, otter, and mink, along with ruffed grouse, osprey, and bald eagle.

• *Suggested Trails for Nature Walks:* 1. The 0.3-mile Sandstone Falls Trail. 2. The 0.5-mile Rainbow Falls Trail. 3. The 0.5-mile Brule Lake Trail. 4. The 0.8-mile Conglomerate Falls Trail. 5. The 1-mile Cascade Falls Trail. 6. The Sylvania Visitor Center Interpretive Trail. 7. The 3-mile White Deer Lake Trail. 8. The 30-mile Sylvania Wilderness trail network. 9. The 118-mile section of the 3,200-mile North Country Trail (easy-moderate).

SLEEPING BEAR DUNES NATIONAL LAKESHORE 9922 Front Street, Hwy M-72, Empire, MI 49630; (616)326-5134. 71,000 acres. Situated in the northwestern part of the Lower Peninsula, and bordering on Lake Michigan, Sleeping Bear Dunes National Lakeshore is notable for its high sand dunes, 400-foot bluffs, and inland lakes. Included are North Manitou and South Manitou islands offshore. There are forests of maple and beech as well as conifers, with some virgin cedar on South Manitou Island. White-tailed deer and fox are among the wildlife.

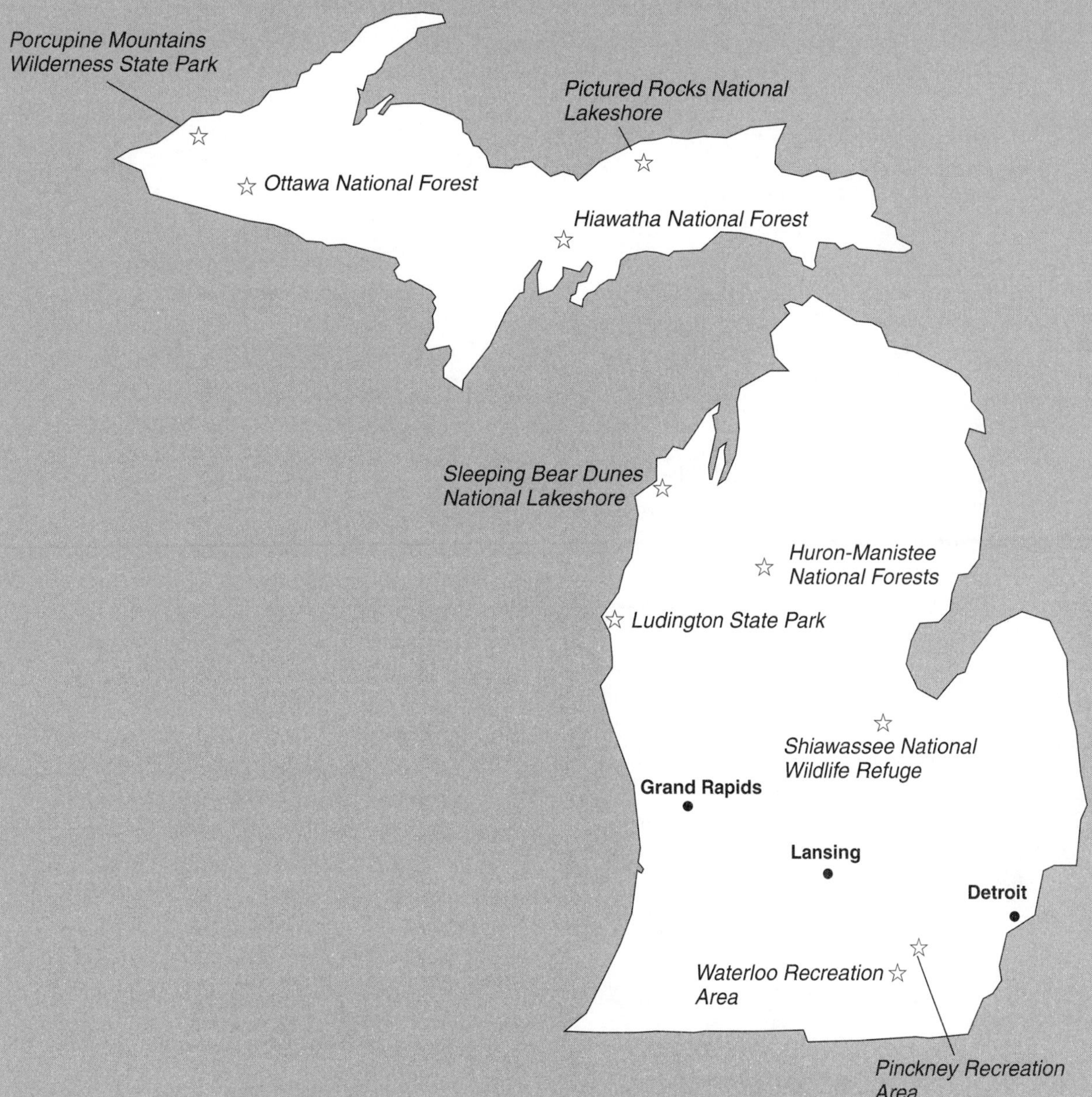
MICHIGAN
Porcupine Mountains
Wilderness State Park
Pictured Rocks National
Lakeshore
Ottawa National Forest
Hiawatha National Forest
Sleeping Bear Dunes
National Lakeshore
Huron-Manistee
National Forests
Ludington State Park
Shiawassee National
Wildlife Refuge
Grand Rapids
Lansing
Detroit
Waterloo Recreation
Area
Pinckney Recreation
Area

• *Suggested Trails for Nature Walks:* 1. The 0.8-mile Empire Bluff Trail. 2. The 1.5-mile Windy Moraine Trail (loop). 3. The 1.5-mile Cottonwood Trail (loop). 4. The 1.8-mile Dunes Trail. 5. The 2.4-mile Shauger Hill Trail (loop). 6. The 2.5-mile Old Indian Trail, consisting of 2 loops. 7. The 2.7-mile Pyramid Point Trail (loop). 8. The 2.8-mile Good Harbor Bay Trail (loop). 9. The 2.8-mile Dunes-Sleeping Bear Point Trail (loop). 10. The 14.7-mile Platte Plains Trail, which is made up of three loops.

PICTURED ROCKS NATIONAL LAKESHORE P.O. Box 40, Munising, MI 49862; (906)387-2607. 67,000 acres. This long and narrow park in Michigan's Upper Peninsula protects 40 miles of Lake Superior shoreline. It has beautiful beaches—including one that extends twelve miles—as well as sand dunes, 200-foot cliffs with rock formations, inland lakes and ponds, streams, and waterfalls. Some areas are forested with northern hardwoods and such conifers as pine, spruce and fir. Among the wildlife are moose, white-tailed deer, black bear, gray wolf, and peregrine falcon.

• *Suggested Trails for Nature Walks:* 1. The 0.5-mile Sand Point Marsh Trail. 2. The 0.5-mile Grand Sable Dunes Trail. 3. The 0.6-mile Miners Falls Trail. 4. The 0.7-mile White Pine Trail (loop). 5. The 1.5-mile Chapel Falls Trail. 6. The 2-mile White Birch Trail (loop). 7. The 2-mile Beech Forest Trail (loop). 8. The 2.5-mile Seven-mile Creek Trail. 9. The 2.7-mile Chapel Beach Trail. 10. The 5-mile Beaver Basin Loop.

PORCUPINE MOUNTAINS WILDERNESS STATE PARK 412 South Boundary Road, Ontonagon, MI 49953; (906)885-5275. 60,000 acres. Located in the Porcupine Mountains of Michigan's Upper Peninsula, this park features one of the largest wild areas in the state—with 35,000 acres of virgin forest, more than any other location in the Midwest. Much of the terrain is rocky and rugged, and elevations range from 601 feet to 1,958 feet. Forested with pine, hemlock, and maple, the park has many lakes, rivers, and streams. Wildlife includes black bear, white-tailed deer, red fox, bobcat, coyote, peregrine falcon, and bald eagle. Naturalist-led walks are available in summer.

• *Suggested Trails for Nature Walks:* 1. The 1-mile Visitor Center Nature Trail (loop). 2. The 1-mile Union Mine Trail (loop). 3. The 1-mile West River Trail (loop). 4. The first 0.5 mile of the Escarpment Trail from Lake of the Clouds parking area. 5. The first mile of the Lake Superior Trail from M-107. 6. The 2-mile Union Spring Trail. 7. The 3-mile Lily Pond Trail. 8. The 0.5-mile Summit Peak Tower Trail (easy-moderate). 9. The 11-mile Little Carp River Trail (easy-moderate).

HIAWATHA NATIONAL FOREST 2727 N. Lincoln Road, Escanaba, MI 49829; (906)786-4062. 893,348 acres. Consisting of two large tracts in the eastern and central part of Michigan's Upper Peninsula, this national forest borders on three Great Lakes. It's a forest of northern hardwoods including maple and beech, quaking aspen and white birch, plus pine, hemlock, and cedar.

There are also meadows and wildflowers, hills and sand dunes, cliffs and some small canyons—along with 418 lakes, 777 miles of rivers and streams, and major areas of wetlands. Wildlife includes white-tailed deer, black bear, timber wolf, bobcat, porcupine, and raccoon, as well as loon, great blue heron, sandhill crane, northern goshawk, and bald eagle.

• *Suggested Trails for Nature Walks:* 1. The 1-mile Horseshoe Bay Trail. 2. The 2.9-mile North Country Trail Connector. 3. The 7.3-mile Bruno's Run Trail (loop). 4. The 26-mile Pine Martin Run Trail, consisting of a number of loops. 5. The 40-mile Bay De Noc-Grand Island Trail. 6. Sections of the 3,200-mile North Country Trail (easy-moderate), which passes through the forest.

LUDINGTON STATE PARK P.O. Box 709, Ludington, MI 49431; (616)843-2423. 5,300 acres. Ludington State Park is located between Lake Michigan and huge Hamlin Lake, in the west-central part of the Lower Peninsula. It features high dunes, two beaches, hills and ravines, ferns and wildflowers, the Sable River, and a forest of hardwoods and virgin conifers including maple and beech, oak, and aspen, along with pine, hemlock, and cedar.

• *Suggested Trails for Nature Walks:* 1. The 0.4-mile Skyline Trail. 2. The 0.6-mile Eagle's Nest Trail. 3. The 0.7-mile Dune Trail. 4. The 1-mile Coast Guard Trail. 5. The 1-mile Lighthouse Trail. 6. The 1.3-mile Lost Lake Trail. 7. The 1.5-mile Beechwood Trail. 8. The 1.6-mile Sable River Trail. 9. The 1.6-mile Island Trail. 10. The 2.7-mile Logging Trail.

WATERLOO RECREATION AREA 16345 McClure Road, Chelsea, MI 48118; (313)475-8307. 22,000 acres. Situated in the wooded hills and ridges of southeastern Michigan, Waterloo Recreation Area features eleven lakes, along with marshes, bogs, old fields, and hardwood forests of oak, hickory, beech, and maple. Within the recreation area is the Gerald E. Eddy Geology Center.

• *Suggested Trails for Nature Walks:* 1. The 0.5-mile Dry Marsh Nature Trail (loop). 2. The 0.8-mile Old Field Trail (loop). 3. The 0.8-mile Bog Trail. 4. The 1-mile Woodland Nature Trail (loop). 5. The 1-mile Spring Pond Trail (loop). 6. The 1.1-mile Lowland Trail (loop). 7. The 1.3-mile Oak Woods Trail (loop). 8. The 3.6-mile Lakeview Trail (loop). 9. The 5.3-mile Hickory Hills Trail (loop). 10. The 22-mile Waterloo-Pinckney Trail, which extends to the nearby Pinckney Recreation Area.

SHIAWASSEE NATIONAL WILDLIFE REFUGE 6975 Mower Road, Saginaw, MI 48601; (517)759-1669. 9,000 acres. This national wildlife refuge occupies the Saginaw Valley, in the east-central part of Michigan's Lower Peninsula, and includes the Green Point Environmental Learning Center. No fewer than four rivers meet here to become the Saginaw River, and there are smaller streams, marshes, pools, grasslands, and bottomland hardwood forests. The refuge was established to protect Canada geese, ducks, and other migratory waterfowl, with white-tailed deer, muskrat, raccoon, and bald eagle among the other wildlife here.

• *Suggested Trails for Nature Walks:* 1. The 3.5-mile Woodland Trail, which includes a shorter 1-mile loop. 2. The 4.5-mile Ferguson Bayou Trail, which features a shorter 1.5-mile loop.

PINCKNEY RECREATION AREA 8555 Silver Hill Road, Pinckney, MI 48169; (313)426-4913. 11,000 acres. Located in the southeastern part of the state, Pinckney Recreation Area includes a chain of seven lakes, some of which have beaches, along with many smaller lakes and ponds. The forested terrain is hilly and occasionally rocky, and white-tailed deer are among the wildlife.

• *Suggested Trails for Nature Walks:* 1. The 2-mile Silver Lake Trail (loop). 2. The 5-mile Crooked Lake Trail (loop). 3. The 17-mile Potawatomi Trail (loop). 4. The 35-mile Waterloo-Pinckney Trail, which extends to the Waterloo Recreation Area.

Other Suitable Locations for Nature Walks in Michigan

Michigan has ninety-six state parks, and the vast majority of these locations feature nature or hiking trails. There are also six huge state forests with trails. Information: Parks and Recreation Division, P.O. Box 30257, Lansing, MI 48909; (517)373-9900.

Lake Superior's Isle Royale National Park, accessible by a long ferry ride, has 166 miles of trails. Information: Isle Royale National Park, Houghton, MI 49931; (906)482-0984.

There are trails at three national wildlife refuges in the state. Information: U.S. Fish and Wildlife Service, 1 Federal Drive, Federal Building, Fort Snelling, MN 55111.

The Nature Conservancy owns thirty-seven preserves in the state, and some of these have nature trails. Information: The Nature Conservancy, Michigan Chapter, 2840 East Grand River Avenue #5, East Lansing, MI 48823; (517)332-1741.

MINNESOTA

Recommended Areas for Nature Walks

SUPERIOR NATIONAL FOREST P.O. Box 338, Duluth, MN 55801; (218)720-5324. 3,000,000 acres. Located along the Canadian border in northeastern Minnesota, this enormous national forest is best known as the home of the famous 1-million-acre Boundary Waters Canoe Area Wilderness. Much of the terrain is hilly with ridges and little mountains, ledges and rocky bluffs.

The highest point is 2,301-foot Eagle Mountain. There are over 2,000 lakes and 2,300 miles of streams, as well as swamps and bogs with pitcher plants, orchids, other wildflowers, and a forest of northern hardwoods and conifers including spruce, fir, and pine. Among the wildlife are white-tailed deer, black bear, moose, timber wolf, fox, grouse, loon, and eagle.

• *Suggested Trails for Nature Walks:* 1. 0.5-mile Onion River Trail. 2. The 1-mile White Pine Interpretive Trail. 3. The 1-mile Fenske Lake Trail. 4. The 1-mile Kawishiwi Trail. 5. The 1-mile McDougal Lake Trail. 6. The 2-mile Cascade River Trail. 7. The 2-mile North Dark River Trail. 8. The 2.5-mile Flathorn Lake Trail. 9. The 2.5-mile Divide Lake Trail. 10. The 3-mile Pfeiffer Lake Trail (loop).

CHIPPEWA NATIONAL FOREST Route 3, Box 244, Cass Lake, MN 56633; (218)335-8600. Hilly Chippewa National Forest in north-central Minnesota features over 700 lakes, many creeks, rivers including the Mississippi, other wetlands, mixed hardwood forests, and such wildflowers as pink lady's-slipper, trillium, and marsh marigold, along with blueberries, raspberries, and cranberries.

Of special interest is the relatively remote Suomi Hills Recreation Area. Among the more common trees in the forest are oak, ash, maple, birch, and aspen, plus cedar, balsam fir, spruce, and some some old-growth red and white pine. Wildlife includes white-tailed deer, black bear, coyote, timber wolf, raccoon, beaver, and river otter, as well as grouse, woodcock, owl, great blue heron, loon, osprey, hawk, and bald eagle.

• *Suggested Trails for Nature Walks:* 1. The 0.5-mile Turtle Mound Trail. 2. The 0.5-mile Lost Forty Trail. 3. The 1-mile Lake Erin Trail. 4. The 1-mile Camp Radibeau CCC Trail. 5. The 2-mile Norway Beach Trail. 6. The 2-mile Sugar Lake Trail. 7. The 3-mile Carter Lake Trail. 8. The 3-mile Skeeter Lake Trail. 9. The 6-mile Shingobee National Recreation Trail. 10. The 6-mile Webster Lake Trail.

ITASCA STATE PARK Lake Itasca, MN 56460; (218)266-3654. 32,690 acres. This state park in northwestern Minnesota encompasses the headwaters of the Mississippi River, along with 25 miles of the St. Croix River, 7 miles of the Kettle River, huge Lake Itasca, and dozens of smaller lakes and ponds. A 2,000-acre wilderness sanctuary protects an area of virgin forest. There are also meadows and streams, marshes and bogs, and hardwood forests with aspen, maple and basswood, as well as spruce and pine.

MINNESOTA

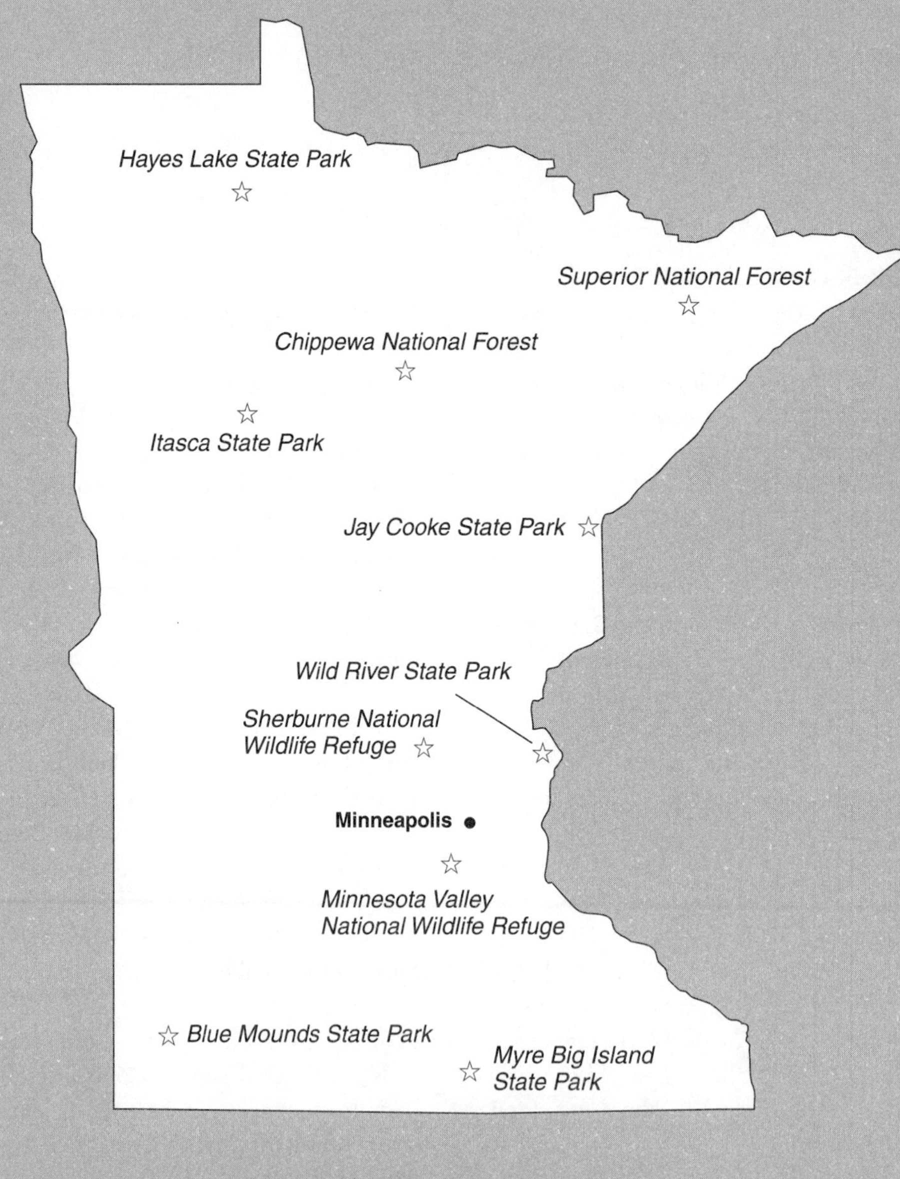
Hayes Lake State Park
Superior National Forest
Chippewa National Forest
Itasca State Park
Jay Cooke State Park
Wild River State Park
Sherburne National
Wildlife Refuge
Minneapolis
Minnesota Valley
National Wildlife Refuge
Blue Mounds State Park
Myre Big Island
State Park

Wildlife includes white-tailed deer, black bear, porcupine, coyote, beaver, loon, osprey, and bald eagle. Naturalist-led walks are offered in summer.

• *Suggested Trails for Nature Walks:* 1. The 0.5-mile Mary Lake Trail. 2. The 0.5-mile Bohall Trail. 3. The 1.2-mile Red Pine Trail. 4. The 1.1-mile Schoolcraft Trail. 5. The 2-mile Brower Trail. 6. The 2-mile Dr. Robert's Trail. 7. The 2.4-mile Ozawindib Trail. 8. The 2.7-mile DeSoto Trail. 9. The 3.1-mile Deer Park Trail. 10. The 3.8-mile Nicollet Trail.

WILD RIVER STATE PARK 39755 Park Trail, Center City, MN 55012; (612)583-2125. 6,803 acres. Wild River State Park lies alongside the St. Croix River in eastern Minnesota. Amid the nearly level terrain—with some hills and low ridges—are streams, marshes, swamps, meadows, prairie remnants, wildflowers, and oak forests with maple, basswood, and pine trees. White-tailed deer, great blue heron, barred owl, northern harrier, osprey, and bald eagle are among the wildlife. Naturalist-led walks are available.

• *Suggested Trails for Nature Walks:* 1. The 1-mile Mitigwaki Loop. 2. The 1-mile Old Logging Trail. 3. The 1.5-mile River Trail. 4. The 1.5-mile River Terrace Loop. 5. The 2-mile Amador Prairie Loop. 6. The 2-mile Pioneer Loop. 7. The 3-mile Deer Creek Loop (easy-moderate). 8. The 3-mile Goose Creek Loop (easy-moderate). 9. The 5-mile Sunrise Loop (easy-moderate). 10. The 10-mile Sunrise Trail (easy-moderate).

JAY COOKE STATE PARK 500 East Highway 210, Carlton, MN 55718; (218)384-4610. 8,818 acres. Located near Duluth, on the Wisconsin border, Jay Cooke State Park includes some steep, rugged terrain with rock formations, streams, and the St. Louis River, which bisects the park. There are hardwood forests of maple, birch, and basswood, as well as pine and hemlock. Among the wildlife are black bear, white-tailed deer, coyote, timber wolf, beaver, and great blue heron.

• *Suggested Trails for Nature Walks:* 1. The 1.5-mile Ogantz Trail. 2. The 2-mile CCC-Thomson Loop Trail. 3. The 2.5-mile White Pine-CCC Loop Trail. 4. The 2.7-mile Grand Portage Trail. 5. The 3-mile Carlton Trail. 6. The 3-mile Silver Creek Trail. 7. The 4.2-mile Triangle and Oak trails.

BLUE MOUNDS STATE PARK Route 1, Box 52, Luverne, MN 56156; (507)283-4892. 2,028 acres. Named after some large quartzite outcroppings here, this park in the southwest corner of the state features 1,500 acres of tall-grass prairie with a variety of wildflowers and grasses, including 7-foot big bluestem. Among the other vegetation are prickly pear cactus and oak trees. Also in the park are Mound Creek, two man-made lakes, and some 90-foot cliffs. Wildlife includes white-tailed deer, bison, and coyote, and naturalist-led walks are offered.

• *Suggested Trails for Nature Walks:* 1. The 0.6-mile Lower Mound Lake Trail. 2. The 0.8-mile Burr Oak Trail. 3. The 1.7-mile Upper Mound Lake Trail. 4. The 0.8-mile Upper Cliffline Trail. 5. The 0.8-mile Lower Mound Trail. 6. The 0.9-mile Upper Mound Trail. 7. The 1.1-mile Lower Cliffline Trail.

MINNESOTA VALLEY NATIONAL WILDLIFE REFUGE 4101 East 80th Street, Bloomington, MN 55425; (612)335-2323. 8,136 acres. Consisting of seven separate units, this national wildlife refuge protects wildlife and lands alongside the Minnesota River directly south of Minneapolis. There are streams including Sand Creek, bluffs, boulders, swamps, marshes, prairie grasslands, oak savannas, and hardwood forests of oak, ash, elm, maple, cottonwood, and willow. Among the wildlife are white-tailed deer, bobcat, red fox, raccoon, cottontail, and hare, plus bald eagle, great blue heron, grouse, and waterfowl.

• *Suggested Trails for Nature Walks:* 1. The 0.5-mile Bass Ponds Trail. 2. The 2-mile Black Dog Preserve Trail. 3. The 2-mile Little Prairie Loop Trail. 4. The 1.5-mile Johnson Slough Trail. 5.

The 4.5-mile Mazomani Trail. 6. The 3.5-mile State Corridor Trail.

HAYES LAKE STATE PARK HCR 4, Box 84, Roseau, MN 56751; (218)425-7504. 2,950 acres. Located next to 669,000-acre Beltrami Island State Forest, this state park in northwestern Minnesota features large Hayes Lake and the dammed-up North Fork Roseau River. Terrain is relatively level with some small ridges and valleys, bogs and muskegs, wildflowers including orchid and gentian, and forests of pine and aspen, spruce and poplar, willow and dogwood. Black bear, white-tailed deer, moose, lynx, bobcat, timber wolf, fox, raccoon, and beaver are among the wildlife.

• *Suggested Trails for Nature Walks:* 1. The 0.5-mile Pine Ridge Nature Trail. 2. The 1-mile Homestead Trail. 3. The 2-mile Bear Track Trail. 4. The 3-mile Pine Ridge Trail. 5. The 4.5-mile Moose Ridge Trail.

MYRE BIG ISLAND STATE PARK Route 3, Box 33, Albert Lea, MN 56007; (507)373-4492. 1,596 acres. This southern Minnesota state park is located southeast of Albert Lea on 2,645-acre Albert Lea Lake, and includes 118-acre Big Island. There are hills of glacial moraine, marshes, some oak savanna, prairie grasses, wildflowers, and a northern hardwood forest of maple, elm, ash, and basswood on the island. Among the wildlife are white-tailed deer, gray fox, raccoon, opossum, great horned owl, rough-legged hawk, white pelican, and numerous waterfowl. Guided walks are available.

• *Suggested Trails for Nature Walks:* 1. The 0.8-mile Big Island Short Loop. 2. The 1.1-mile Big Island Long Loop. 3. The 1.8-mile Great Marsh Trail. 4. The 5.2-mile Bur Oak Esker Trail.

SHERBURNE NATIONAL WILDLIFE REFUGE 17076 293rd Avenue, Zimmerman, MN 55398; (612)389-3323. 31,000 acres. Sherburne National Wildlife Refuge is situated in east-central Minnesota's St. Francis River Valley. The refuge features gently rolling hills with tallgrass prairie and hardwood forest, oak savanna, grasses including little and big bluestem, switch grass, and Indian grass, as well as wetlands and the St. Francis River. Wildlife includes white-tailed deer, sandhill crane, trumpeter swan, egret, loon, and bald eagle.

• *Suggested Trails for Nature Walks:* 1. The 0.5-mile Prairie Trail. 2. The 0.5-mile Woodland Trail. 3. The 3-mile Mahnomen Trail. 4. The 5-mile Blue Hill Trail, which includes a 0.3-mile spur trail to a viewpoint.

Other Suitable Locations for Nature Walks in Minnesota

Minnesota has sixty-eight state parks, and all but two feature trails. There are also fifty-six state forests, and seventeen of these areas include trails. Information: Minnesota Department of Natural Resources, 500 Lafayette Road, Box 40, St. Paul, MN 55155; (612)296-6157.

Seven national wildlife refuges in Minnesota have trails. Information: U.S. Fish and Wildlife Service, 1 Federal Drive, Federal Building, Fort Snelling, MN 55111.

The Nature Conservancy administers a number of preserves in the state, and some of them have trails. Information: The Nature Conservancy, Minnesota Chapter, 1313 Fifth Street Southeast, Suite 320, Minneapolis, MN 55414.

Voyageurs National Park has trails that are accessible only by boat. Information: Voyageurs National Park, 3131 Highway 53, International Falls, MN 56649; (218)283-9821.

Trails are found at a few U.S. Army Corps of Engineers areas along the Mississippi River. Information: Corps of Engineers, St. Paul District, 180 East Kellog Boulevard, St. Paul, MN 55101; (612)220-0325.

MISSISSIPPI

Recommended Areas for Nature Walks

DESOTO NATIONAL FOREST 100 West Capitol Street, Suite 1141, Jackson, MS 39269; (601)965-4391. 501,000 acres. Located in the southeastern part of the state and co-administered with Mississippi's five other national forests, Desoto National Forest features rolling hills and low ridges with piney woods—including slash, longleaf, and loblolly pine—as well as maple, oak, hickory, and sweetgum trees, plus palmetto, pitcher plant, and wild orchid.

The forest has two designated wilderness areas, the 5,052-acre Black Creek Wilderness and the 960-acre Leaf Wilderness. There are savannas and swamps, lakes and ponds, and dark streams colored by tannic acid. Among these is Black Creek, which has white sandbars, along with the Big Biloxi River and the Leaf River. White-tailed deer, armadillo, pileated woodpecker, and wild turkey are among the wildlife here

• *Suggested Trails for Nature Walks:* 1. The 0.8-mile Turkey Fork Trail. 2. The 22-mile Tuxachanie National Recreation Trail. 3. The 40-mile Black Creek National Recreation Trail. 4. The 22-mile Big Foot Horse Trail, which is open to foot travel and has four loops. 5. The 23-mile Long Leaf Horse Trail, consisting of two loops.

ROOSEVELT STATE PARK 2149 Highway 13 South, Morton, MS 39117; (601)732-6316. This state park in central Mississippi stands adjacent to Bienville National Forest and the Bienville Wildlife Area. Terrain includes gentle hills and slopes with woodlands, wildflowers, and 160-acre Shadow Lake, which has a sandy beach.

• *Suggested Trails for Nature Walks:* 1. The 0.3-mile Pinelane Trail. 2. The 0.3-mile Rolling Hill Trail. 3. The 0.4-mile Lakeview Trail. 4. The 0.4-mile Muscadine Trail. 5. The 0.8-mile Hollowhill Trail. 6. The 1.2-mile Beaver Dam Trail. 7. The 2-mile Civil War Hill Trail.

BIENVILLE NATIONAL FOREST 100 West Capitol Street, Suite 1141, Jackson, MS 39269; (601)965-4391. 178,000 acres. Bienville National Forest is in central Mississippi, an area of flatlands with small hills, forests of shortleaf and loblolly pine as well as hardwoods, and several lakes. Of special interest are the 189-acre Bienville Pines Scenic Area, which features old-growth pine, and the 150-acre Harrell Prairie Hill Botanical Area, a tract of prairie grasslands. Wildlife includes white-tailed deer, red-cockaded woodpecker, and wild turkey.

• *Suggested Trails for Nature Walks:* 1. The 0.5-mile Shongelo Trail. 2. The 1-mile Marathon Trail. 3. The 2-mile Bienville Pines Trail. 4. The 23-mile Shockaloe National Recreation Horse Trail, which is suitable for walks.

HOMOCHITTO NATIONAL FOREST 100 West Capitol Street, Suite 1141, Jackson, MS 39269; (601)965-4391. 189,000 acres. Encompassing terrain ranging from hilly to flat, this national forest in southwestern Mississippi

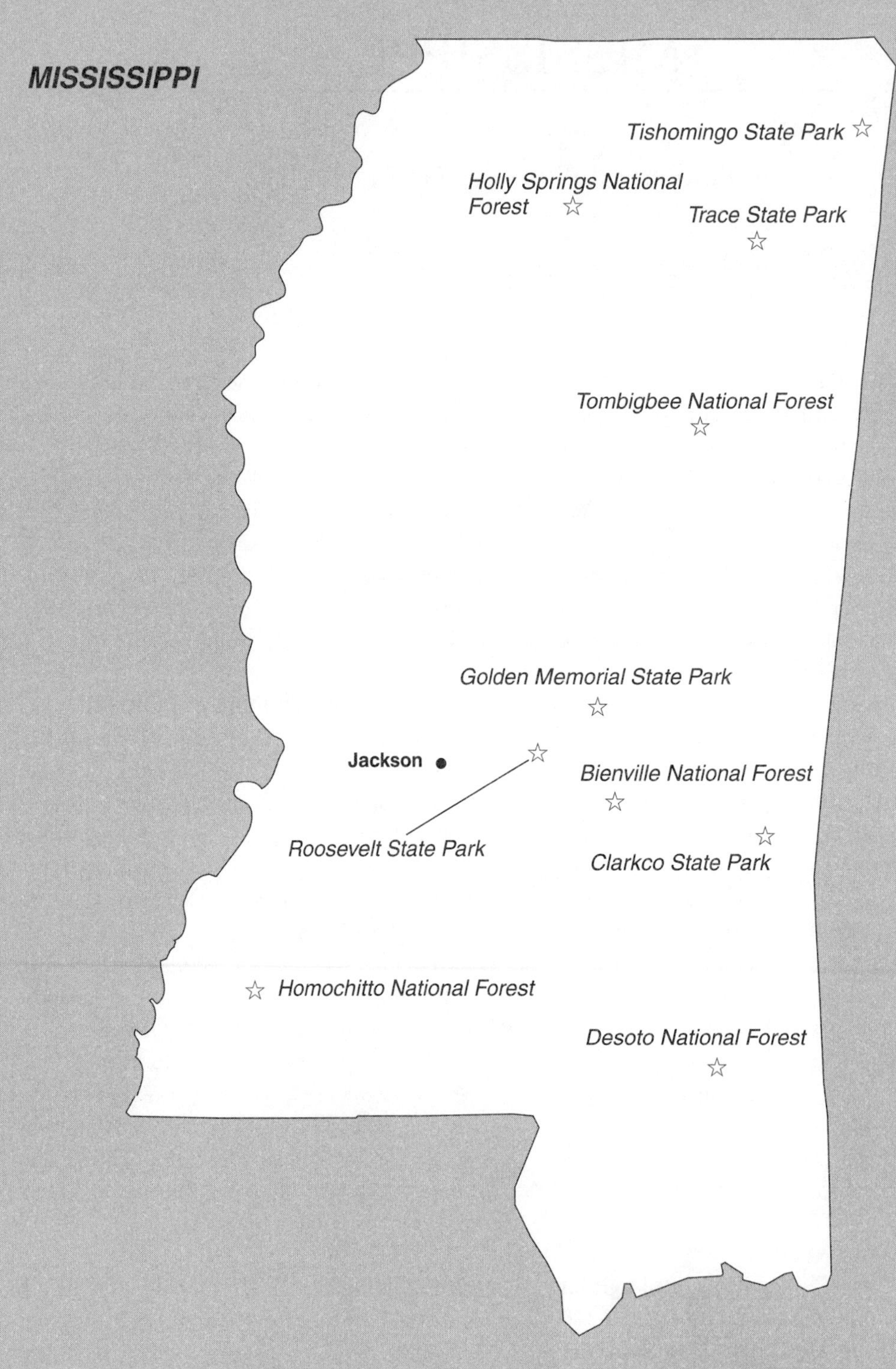
MISSISSIPPI
Tishomingo State Park
Holly Springs National Forest
Trace State Park
Tombigbee National Forest
Golden Memorial State Park
Jackson
Bienville National Forest
Roosevelt State Park
Clarkco State Park
Homochitto National Forest
Desoto National Forest

includes the Homochitto River, a few lakes, azalea and other wildflowers, as well as forests of mixed pine and hardwoods. Among the wildlife are white-tailed deer, beaver, raccoon, opossum, armadillo, alligator, and wild turkey.

• *Suggested Trails for Nature Walks:* 1. The 0.9-mile Clear Springs Lake Trail. 2. The 2.2-mile Pipes Lake Trail. 3. The 10.5-mile Clear Springs Trail (loop).

HOLLY SPRINGS NATIONAL FOREST Highway 78 East, Box 400, Holly Springs, MS 38635; (601)252-2633. 147,000 acres. Located in northern Mississippi, near Memphis, Holly Springs National Forest has mixed pine forests with hardwoods, as well as shrubs, bottomland wildflowers, over forty lakes and ponds, and an area of Native American burial mounds. White-tailed deer, woodcock, and quail are among the wildlife.

• *Suggested Trails for Nature Walks:* 1. The 1.4-mile Puskus Trail. 2. The 4.4-mile Chewalla Trail.

TOMBIGBEE NATIONAL FOREST Route 1, Box 98A, Ackerman, MS 39735; (601)285-3264. Tombigbee National Forest in northeastern Mississippi features rolling hills with a number of lakes and creeks, pine and hardwood forests, as well as ancient Indian burial mounds. Wildlife includes white-tailed deer, coyote, armadillo, owl, and wild turkey.

• *Suggested Trails for Nature Walks:* 1. The 3-mile Choctaw Lake Trail (loop). 2. The 15-mile Witch Dance Horse Trail, a loop trail which is open to foot travel.

TISHOMINGO STATE PARK P.O. Box 880, Tishomingo, MS 38873; (601)438-6914. Named after a chief of the Chickasaw Nation, and situated in the northeast corner of Mississippi, Tishomingo State Park includes hills and rocky ridges as well as small canyons, boulders, sandstone bluffs, rock formations, and crevices. A large creek flows through the area, and there's a sizable lake.

• *Suggested Trails for Nature Walks:* A 13-mile system of nature trails winds throughout the park and alongside Bear Creek, forming loops of varying lengths.

CLARKCO STATE PARK 386 Clarkco Road, Quitman, MS 39355; (601)776-6651. 815 acres. Clarkco State Park is located near the Alabama border in eastern Mississippi. It's an area of rolling hills and woodlands with 65-acre Clarkco Lake, which includes a sand beach.

• *Suggested Trails for Nature Walks:* 1. The 3.5-mile Nature Trail, which encircles the lake. 2. A 0.8-mile trail leads to the old CCC camp.

TRACE STATE PARK 2139 Faulkner Road, Belden, MS 38826; (601)489-2958. Located in northeastern Mississippi, this state park is centered on 600-acre, man-made Trace Lake. The terrain is gently rolling with creeks, a pond, wildflowers in season, and a forest of hardwoods and pine trees.

• *Suggested Trails for Nature Walks:* 1. The 1.2-mile Jason M. Stewart Nature Trail. 2. Some 25 miles of other trails wind throughout the park.

GOLDEN MEMORIAL STATE PARK Route 1, Box 8, Walnut Grove, MS 39189; (601)253-2237. The focal point of this state park in central Mississippi is 13-acre Golden Lake, which has a sand beach and is surrounded by forested hills. The park includes the second highest pine tree in the state.

• *Suggested Trails for Nature Walks:* The 4-mile Nature Trail, which encircles Golden Lake.

Other Suitable Locations for Nature Walks in Mississippi

Many of Mississippi's twenty-three state parks have short trails. Information: Department of Wildlife, Fisheries, and Parks, P.O. Box 451, Jackson, MS 39225; (601)364-2140.

There are six national wildlife refuges in the state with trails. Information: U.S. Fish and Wildlife Service, 1875 Century Boulevard, Atlanta, GA 30345.

Gulf Islands National Seashore has several short trails. Information: Gulf Islands National Seashore, 3500 Park Road, Ocean Springs, MS 39564; (601)875-9057.

Trails are available at several reservoirs administered by the U.S. Army Corps of Engineers. Information: Corps of Engineers, Vicksburg District, 2101 North Frontage Road, Vicksburg, MS 39180; (601)631-5286.

MISSOURI

Recommended Areas for Nature Walks

MARK TWAIN NATIONAL FOREST 401 Fairgrounds Road, Rolla, MO 65401; (314)364-4621. 1,500,000 acres. Situated in the Ozarks of southern Missouri, Mark Twain National Forest includes the St. Francois Mountains and other rugged terrain, with high knobs and steep bluffs, rock outcroppings, and caves. The 16,500-acre Irish Wilderness is one of seven designated wilderness areas here.

There are large rivers and creeks, with narrow and scenic gorges ("shut-ins"), waterfalls, forests of upland oak and hickory, bottomland hardwoods, cedar, and pine, along with dogwood and redbud, azalea and columbine, jack-in-the-pulpit and yellow lady's-slipper. White-tailed deer, coyote, bobcat, fox, rabbit, owl, hawk, and turkey vulture are among the wildlife.

• *Suggested Trails for Nature Walks:* 1. The 0.5-mile Woodchuck Trail. 2. The 0.5-mile Huzzah Ponds Trail (loop). 3. The 1-mile Blossom Rock Trail (loop). 4. The 1.2-mile Songbird Trail (loop). 5. The 1.3-mile Skyline Trail. 6. The 1.5-mile White Oak Trail (loop). 7. The 1.5-mile Cedar Bluff Trail (loop). 8. The 1.5-mile Pinewoods Lake Trail (loop). 9. The 1.5-mile Loggers Lake Trail (loop). 10. The 2-mile Blue Springs Trail.

LAKE OF THE OZARKS STATE PARK P.O. Box 170, Kaiser, MO 65047; (314)348-2694. 17,152 acres. Located on huge Lake of the Ozarks in the central part of the state, this is Missouri's largest state park. A 1,275-acre tract within the park has been designated the Patterson Hollow Wild Area. Terrain includes precipitous bluffs, rocky hills with vistas, ravines, and many caves. There are also open fields, wildflowers, streams, and forests of oak, hickory, and dogwood. Among the wildlife are white-tailed deer, red-tailed hawk, and turkey vulture.

• *Suggested Trails for Nature Walks:* 1. The 0.5-mile Lazy Hollow Trail. 2. The 0.5-mile Shady Ridge Trail. 3. The 1-mile Coakley Hollow Trail. 4. The 1-mile Lake View Bend Trail. 5. The 2.5-mile Fawn's Ridge Trail. 6. The 2.5-mile Grand Glaize Trail. 7. The 3-mile Rocky Top Trail. 8. The 6-mile Woodland Trail. 9. The 2-mile Squaw's Revenge Trail. 10. The 6-mile Trail of Four Winds.

CUIVRE RIVER STATE PARK Route 1, Box 25, Troy, MO 63379; (314)528-7247. 6,250 acres. Cuiver River State Park is in the Lincoln Hills of northern Missouri, with rolling and often rugged terrain that includes 120-foot limestone bluffs, sinkholes, and caves, along with Big Sugar Creek, the Cuivre River, and 50-acre Lake Lincoln. The park has two designated Wild Areas, the 1,082-acre Northwoods Wild Area and the 1,675-acre Sugar Creek Wild Area. There are forests of maple and oak, hickory and ash, dogwood and sumac, as well as some prairie grasslands; wildlife includes white-tailed deer, woodcock, and wild turkey. Naturalist-led walks are available.

MISSOURI

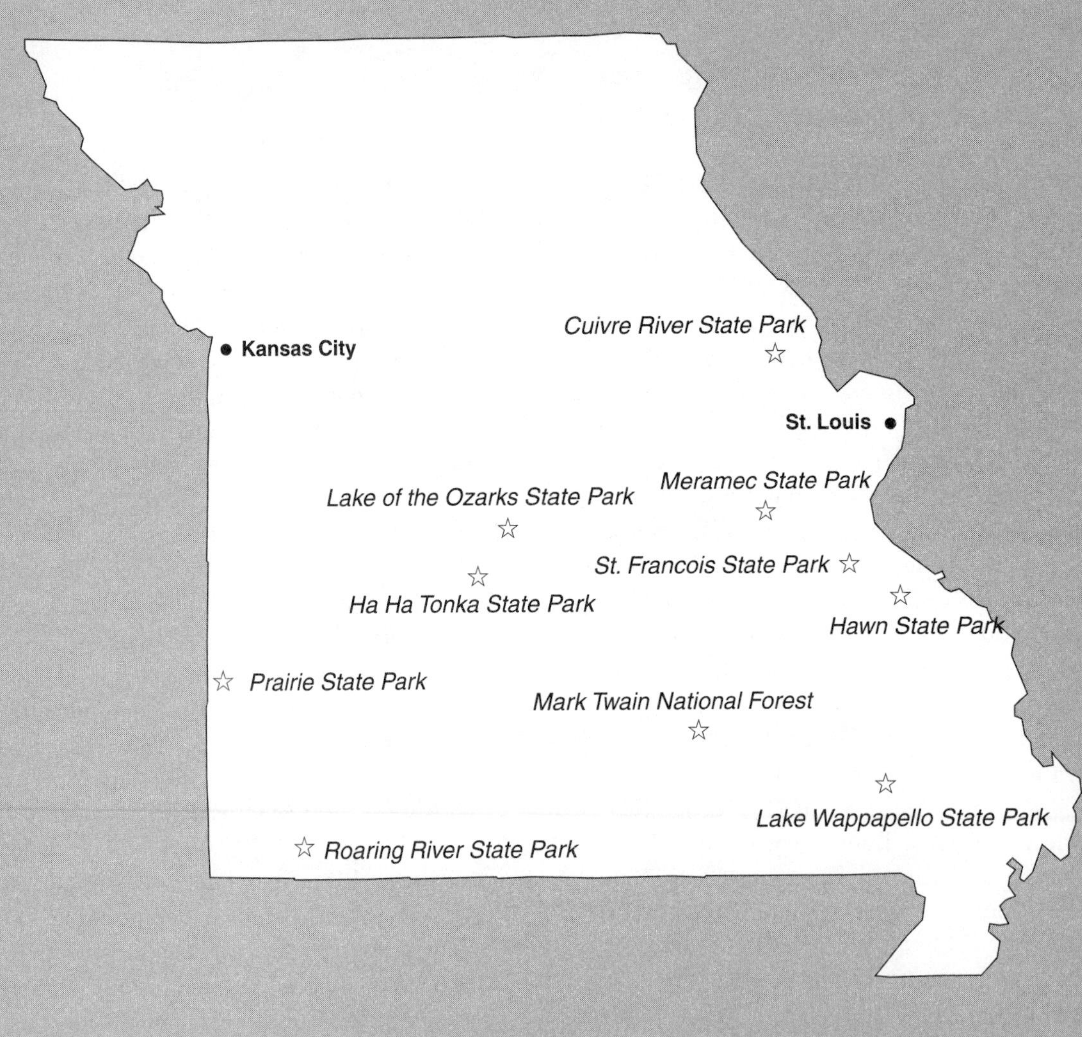
Kansas City
St. Louis
Cuivre River State Park
Meramec State Park
Lake of the Ozarks State Park
St. Francois State Park
Ha Ha Tonka State Park
Hawn State Park
Prairie State Park
Mark Twain National Forest
Lake Wappapello State Park
Roaring River State Park

• *Suggested Trails for Nature Walks:* 1. The 1-mile Hamilton Hollow Trail (loop). 2. The 1-mile Turkey Hollow Trail (loop). 3. The 1-mile Mossy Hill Trail (loop). 4. The 2-mile Frenchman's Bluff Trail (loop). 5. The 4-mile Lakeside Trail (loop). 6. The 6-mile Lone Spring Trail, consisting of two loops. 7. The 7-mile Big Sugar Creek Trail (easy-moderate loop). 8. The 8-mile Cuivre River Trail (easy-moderate loop).

PRAIRIE STATE PARK P.O. Box 97, Liberal, MO 64762; (417)843-6711. 3,542 acres. This park protects the largest area of tallgrass prairie left in the state, and includes four designated Natural Areas. It's an area of rolling hills with creeks, sandstone ledges, and many species of grasses and wildflowers. Bison, elk, coyote, prairie chicken, and sandpiper are among the wildlife.

• *Suggested Trails for Nature Walks:* 1. The 2.5-mile Drover's Trail. 2. The 1.5-mile Gayfeather Trail. 3. The 3-mile Coyote Trail.

HA HA TONKA STATE PARK Route 1, Box 658, Camdenton, MO 65020; (314)346-2986. 2,953 acres. Hilly Ha Ha Tonka State Park sits alongside one arm of the enormous Lake of the Ozarks in central Missouri. Of special interest are geological formations including natural bridges, rocky bluffs, sandstone ledges, sinkholes, and eight caves. There's a 750-acre designated Natural Area, and the stone ruins of a castle—along with Ha Ha Tonka Spring, the outlet of an underground river carrying 48 million gallons of water daily—amid a landscape of savanna with grasslands as well as semiopen forests of oak, hickory, and basswood.

• *Suggested Trails for Nature Walks:* 1. The 0.5-mile Castle Bluff Trail. 2. The 0.8-mile Turkey Pen Hollow Trail. 3. The 1.5-mile Quarry Trail (loop). 4. The 0.5-mile Dell Rim Trail (easy-moderate). 5. The 0.5-mile Colosseum Trail (easy-moderate). 6. The 1-mile Devil's Kitchen Trail (easy-moderate). 7. The 1.5-mile Spring Trail loop (easy-moderate). 8. The 0.8-mile Island Trail (moderate). 9. The 1-mile Boulder Ridge Trail (moderate loop).

LAKE WAPPAPELLO STATE PARK Williamsville, MO 63967; (314)297-3232. 1,854 acres. This state park is located on the Allison Peninsula of man-made, 8,600-acre Lake Wappapello, in southeastern Missouri. There are many miles of shoreline, with a sand beach, creeks, hills and valleys, ferns and wildflowers, as well as forests of oak, hickory, buckeye, beech, sycamore, and tulip tree. Wildlife includes white-tailed deer, beaver, wild turkey, osprey, and eagle.

• *Suggested Trails for Nature Walks:* 1. The 0.5-mile Lake View Trail (loop). 2. The 2-mile Asher Creek Trail (loop). 3. The 3.5-mile Allison Cemetery Trail (loop). 4. The 15-mile Lake Wappapello Trail (easy-moderate loop).

ROARING RIVER STATE PARK Route 2, Box 2530, Cassville, MO 65625; (417)847-2539. 3,354 acres. Situated on the Springfield Plateau of southwestern Missouri, this state park has rugged 300-foot ridges, cliffs, rock outcroppings, valleys, and deep gorges, along with the Roaring River and Roaring River Spring, which discharges 20 million gallons of water each day. There are forests of oak, hickory, and cedar, with butternut and spicebush, as well as open glades and savannas. Included is the 2,075-acre Roaring River Hills Wild Area, with a tract of virgin forest. Black bear, bobcat, armadillo, and bald eagle are among the the wildlife. The park also has a nature center, and naturalist-led walks are scheduled.

• *Suggested Trails for Nature Walks:* 1. The 0.2-mile Deer Loop Trail. 2. The 0.7-mile River Trail. 3. The 1.5-mile Devil's Kitchen Trail (loop). 4. The 1.5-mile Pibern Trail. 5. The 2.3-mile Eagle's Nest Trail (easy-moderate loop). 6. The 3.5-mile Firetower Trail (moderate).

HAWN STATE PARK Route 3, Box 3240, Sainte Genevieve, MO 63670; (314)883-3603. 3,271 acres. Hawn State Park is near the Mississippi River at the eastern edge of the St. Francois Mountains, in east-central Missouri. Pickle Creek and the River Aux Vases pass through the park, which includes the 2,080-acre Whispering Pine Wild Area. Terrain is hilly with forests of shortleaf pine, white and black oak, red maple, shagbark hickory, and dogwood. There are also sandstone bluffs, knobs, granite outcroppings, overhangs, and small canyons. Wildlife includes white-tailed deer, raccoon, owl, and wild turkey. Guided nature walks are offered here in summer.

• *Suggested Trails for Nature Walks:* 1. The 1-mile Pickle Creek Trail. 2. The 10-mile Whispering Pine Trail, which consists of a 6-mile North Loop and a 4-mile South Loop.

ST. FRANCOIS STATE PARK Box 268, Bonne Terre, MO 63628; (314)358-2173. 2,735 acres. Located in the Pine Run Hills of east-central Missouri, St. Francois State Park includes Coonville Creek and the 2,101-acre Coonville Creek Wild Area, as well as the Big River, which forms the park's southern boundary. There are ridges and hollows, dolomite bluffs and grassy glades, with forests of white and red oak, black gum, and shagbark hickory, plus sycamore, ash, black walnut, and silver maple trees along the river. Naturalist-led walks are available.

• *Suggested Trails for Nature Walks:* 1. The 0.5-mile Missouri Trail. 2. The 2.7-mile Swimming Deer Trail (loop). 3. The 3-mile Mooner's Hollow Trail (loop). 4. The 11-mile Pine Run Trail (easy-moderate), consisting of a 6.7-mile South Loop and a 4.3-mile North Loop.

MERAMEC STATE PARK Route 4, Box 4, Sullivan, MO 63080; (314)468-6072. 6,734 acres. This park on the Ozark Plateau in east-central Missouri is bisected by the Meramec Wild and Scenic River, and includes the 461-acre Meramec Upland Forest Natural Area. Terrain consists of rugged hills and high bluffs with rock outcroppings, deep hollows, beaver ponds, and over thirty caves. There are some open glades with prairie grasses and wildflowers, as well as a forest of white, black, and red oak, hickory, dogwood, black walnut, and basswood trees.

• *Suggested Trails for Nature Walks:* 1. The 0.8-mile River Trail (loop). 2. The 1.3-mile Natural Wonders Trail. 3. The 0.5-mile Walking Fern Trail. 4. The 1.8-mile Deer Hollow Trail. 5. The 1.5-mile Bluff View Trail (easy-moderate loop). 6. The 6-mile Wilderness Trail (easy-moderate loop).

Other Suitable Locations for Nature Walks in Missouri

Missouri has forty-six state parks, and many of these locations feature trails. Information: Missouri Department of Natural Resources, P.O. Box 176, Jefferson City, MO 65102; (314)751-2479.

Three national wildlife refuges in the state have trails. Information: U.S. Fish and Wildlife Service, 1 Federal Drive, Federal Building, Fort Snelling, MN 55111.

The Nature Conservancy manages forty-one preserves in Missouri, and some of them have trails. Information: The Nature Conservancy, Missouri Chapter, 2800 South Brentwood Boulevard, St. Louis, MO 63144; (314)968-1105.

There are trails in the Ozark National Scenic Riverways. Information: Ozark National Scenic Riverways, P.O. Box 490, Van Buren, MO 63965; (314)323-4236.

The U.S. Army Corps of Engineers administers a number of man-made lakes in Missouri with trails. Information: Corps of Engineers, St. Louis District, 1222 Spruce Street, St. Louis, MO 63103, (314)331-8622; Corps of Engineers, Little Rock District, P.O. Box 867, Little Rock, AR 72203, (501)324-5673; Corps of Engineers, Kansas City District, 601 East 12th Street, 716 Federal Building, Kansas City, MO 64106, (816)426-6816.

MONTANA

Recommended Areas for Nature Walks

GLACIER NATIONAL PARK West Glacier, MT 59936; (406)888-5441. 1,013,598 acres. Bordering on Canada's Waterton Lakes National Park, and constituting part of the Waterton/Glacier International Peace Park, northwest Montana's Glacier National Park features high and jagged Rocky Mountain peaks, dozens of glaciers, steep ridges, basins, and valleys with wildflowers, grasslands, alpine meadows, streams with waterfalls, and many mountain lakes. Highest elevation is 10,448-foot Mt. Cleveland.

Much of the area is forested with lodgepole pine and fir, Englemann spruce and larch, western hemlock and western redcedar. Wildlife includes elk, moose, mule and white-tailed deer, black and grizzly bear, bighorn sheep, mountain goat, wolf, mountain lion, coyote, red fox, beaver, river otter, and marmot, along with loon, great blue heron, osprey, red-shouldered hawk, and bald eagle. Ranger-led walks are available.

• *Suggested Trails for Nature Walks:* 1. The 0.3-mile Huckleberry Mountain Nature Trail. 2. The 0.3-mile Sunrift Gorge Trail. 3. The 0.7-mile Sun Point Falls Trail. 4. The 0.8-mile St. Mary Falls Trail. 5. The 1-mile Rainbow Falls Trail. 6. The 1.1-mile Rocky Point Trail. 7. The 1.8-mile Beaver Pond Trail. 8. The 1.8-mile Redrock Falls Trail. 9. The 2.4-mile Swiftcurrent Pass Trail (loop). 10. The 3.8-mile Twin Falls Trail.

KOOTENAI NATIONAL FOREST 506 U.S. Highway 2 West, Libby, MT 59926; (406)293-6211. 2,245,793 acres. Kootenai National Forest encompasses several ranges of lofty, rugged peaks, ridgetops, high basins, and cirques, as well as river valleys, rolling hills, and plains in the northwest corner of Montana. At 8,738 feet, Snowshoe Peak is the highest elevation, and the Kootenai River at 1,862 feet is the lowest. The forest has one designated wilderness area, the 94,360-acre Cabinet Mountains Wilderness.

There are many streams, over 100 lakes, two major rivers, wildflower-filled mountain meadows, areas of tundra, and forests of giant western redcedar, hemlock, spruce, white and lodgepole pine, Douglas fir, and larch. Among the wildlife are elk, mule and white-tailed deer, black and grizzly bear, moose, bighorn sheep, mountain goat, mountain lion, coyote, and bobcat, plus ruffed grouse, nighthawk, loon, great horned owl, and bald eagle.

• *Suggested Trails for Nature Walks:* 1. The 0.5-mile Big Creek Trail. 2. The 0.5-mile Fire Lakes Trail. 3. The 0.9-mile Ross Creek Interpretive Trail. 4. The 1-mile Ant Flat Nature Trail (loop). 5. The 1-mile Murphy Lake Nature Trail. 6. The 1.9-mile Hoskins Lake Trail. 7. The 2-mile Old Highway Trail. 8. The 3.4-mile Loveland Peak Trail. 9. The 4.5-mile Bighorn Trail. 10. The 1.5-mile Grouse Lake Trail (easy-moderate).

LEWIS AND CLARK NATIONAL FOREST P.O. Box 869, Great Falls, MT 59403; (406)791-7700. 1,843,397 acres. This national forest is

MONTANA

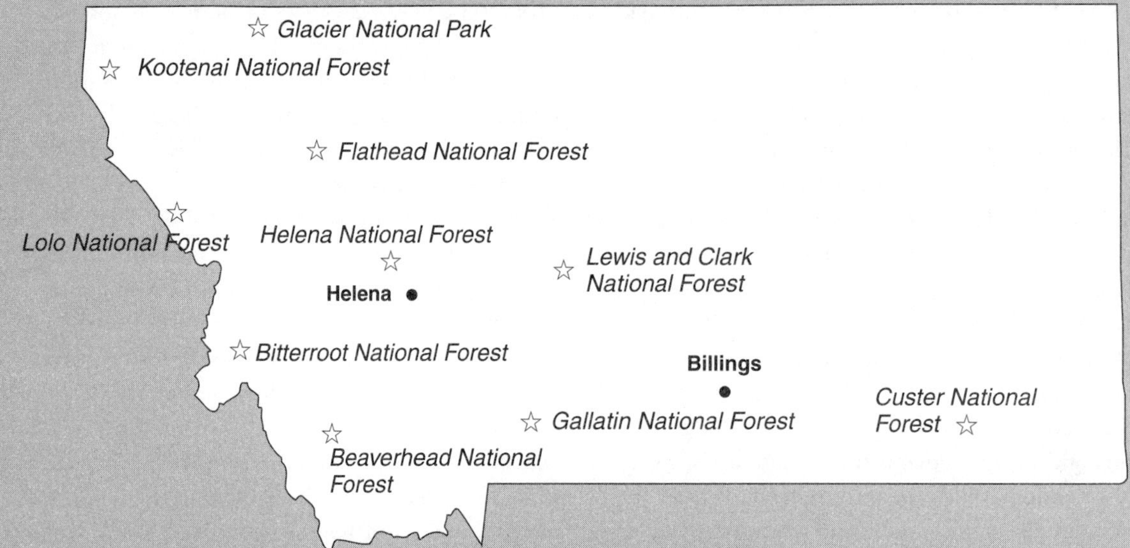
Glacier National Park
Kootenai National Forest
Flathead National Forest
Lolo National Forest
Helena National Forest
Lewis and Clark National Forest
Helena
Bitterroot National Forest
Billings
Custer National Forest
Gallatin National Forest
Beaverhead National Forest

made up of units in central and northwest Montana. It's characterized by steep, rugged peaks and ridges, deep valleys, and rolling hills, with many lakes, streams, and rivers. The forest has three designated wilderness areas, including a portion of the 1-million-acre Bob Marshall Wilderness.

There are alpine meadows, grasslands, many varieties of wildflowers, and forests of subalpine and Douglas fir, ponderosa and lodgepole pine, Englemann spruce and aspen. Wildlife includes grizzly and black bear, mule and white-tailed deer, moose, elk, pronghorn, mountain lion, bighorn sheep, mountain goat, bobcat, wolverine, beaver, marmot, grouse, and wild turkey.

• *Suggested Trails for Nature Walks:* 1. The 0.5-mile Cataract Falls Trail. 2. The 0.5-mile Memorial Falls Trail. 3. The 0.8-mile Wood Lake Trail. 4. The 0.8-mile Benchmark Trail. 5. The 1.5-mile North Fork Deep Creek Trail. 6. The 1.7-mile Crystal Lake Loop Trail. 7. The West Fork Jones Creek Trail. 8. The 5-mile Jones Creek Trail. 9. The 5-mile Circle Creek Trail. 10. The 5-mile Middle Fork Birch Creek Trail.

BEAVERHEAD NATIONAL FOREST 420 Barrett Street, Dillon, MT 59725; (406)683-3900. 2,147,000 acres. Beaverhead National Forest in southwestern Montana includes portions of the Bitterroot, Centennial, and Madison ranges, with a segment of the Continental Divide and many elevations over 11,000 feet. There are craggy granite peaks and ridges, canyons, and valleys, with many creeks and lakes as well as several major rivers.

It's also a region of open meadows and grassy areas, sagebrush hills, wildflowers including Indian paintbrush, yarrow, and lupine, and a forest of lodgepole and whitebark pine, Douglas fir, spruce, willow, and aspen, along with gooseberry and chokecherry. Among the wildlife are moose, grizzly bear, elk, deer, mountain goat, hoary marmot, and grouse.

• *Suggested Trails for Nature Walks:* 1. The 3-mile Foolhen Ridge Trail. 2. The first 3 miles of the 4.5-mile Lion Creek Trail. 3. The first 6 miles of the 7-mile Seymour Creek Trail. 4. The 7.1-mile Pintler Creek Trail. 5. The 8-mile West Fork Fishtrap Creek Trail. 6. The 8-mile David Creek Trail. 7. The 11-mile West Fork LaMarche Trail. 8. The 14-mile Pattengail Creek Trail. 9. The 3-mile Cherry Creek Trail (easy-moderate). 10. The 7-mile Blue Creek Trail (easy-moderate).

BITTERROOT NATIONAL FOREST 1801 North First Street, Hamilton, MT 59840; (406)363-7161. 1,600,000 acres. Located in the northern Rockies of west-central Montana and continuing into east-central Idaho, this national forest includes the Bitterroot and Sapphire mountain ranges, with elevations from 3,200 feet to 10,157 feet on Trapper Peak. The Bitterroot and Selway rivers are found here, and three designated wilderness areas add up to 743,800 acres.

There are many streams and lakes, grassy foothills with sage and juniper plus ponderosa pine, and higher forests of Douglas and grand fir, spruce and whitebark pine, alder and larch. Among the wildlife are elk, moose, white-tailed and mule deer, black bear, bighorn sheep, mountain goat, mountain lion, coyote, boxcat, fox, and marmot, as well as cinnamon teal, pied-billed grebe, great horned owl, pergrine falcon, and red-tailed hawk.

• *Suggested Trails for Nature Walks:* 1. 0.4-mile Centennial Grove Nature Trail (loop). 2. The 2-mile Big Creek Trail. 3. The 2.5-mile Boulder Creek Trail. 4. The 3.1-mile Lake Como North Trail. 5. The 4-mile Rock Creek Trail. 6. The 1.5-mile Blodgett Overlook Trail (easy-moderate). 7. The 2.1-mile Kent Peak Trail (easy-moderate). 8. The 2.5-mile Mill Creek Trail (easy-moderate). 9. The 2.5-mile Kootenai Creek Trail (easy-moderate). 10. The 3-mile Watchtower Creek Trail (easy-moderate).

FLATHEAD NATIONAL FOREST 1935 Third Avenue East, Kalispell, MT 59901; (406)755-5401. 2,300,000 acres. Consisting of several tracts of land in northwestern Montana,

Flathead National Forest features high, rocky, snowcapped peaks and deep glaciated canyons, precipitous cliffs and talus slopes, with elevations from 4,000 feet to more than 9,000 feet on the Continental Divide. Nearly half of the forest is designated wilderness, and includes 70 percent of the 1-million-acre Bob Marshall Wilderness.

Of special interest is the 1,000-foot-high limestone escarpment known as the Chinese Wall, along with the three forks of the Flathead National Wild and Scenic River—and the 15,349-acre Jewel Basin Hiking Area, which has many lakes. There are forests of redcedar and spruce, pine and fir, alpine and western larch. Wildlife includes elk, moose, white-tailed and mule deer, grizzly and black bear, gray wolf, coyote, mountain goat, mountain lion, bald eagle, and peregrine falcon.

• *Suggested Trails for Nature Walks:* 1. The 0.5-mile Wall Lake Trail. 2. The 1.2-mile Tally Lake Overlook Trail. 3. The 1.5-mile Finger Lake Trail. 4. The 1.5-mile Glacier Slough Trail. 5. The South Fork Trail. 6. The 1-mile Stove Pipe Canyon Trail (easy-moderate). 7. The 1.2-mile Tally Gorge Trail (easy-moderate). 8. The 1.4-mile Danny On Nature Trail (easy-moderate). 9. The 4-mile Ashley Mountain Trail (easy-moderate). 10. The 4-mile Lupine Lake Trail (moderate).

LOLO NATIONAL FOREST Building 24, Fort Missoula, MT 59801; (406)329-3814. 2,091,944 acres. This western Montana national forest includes mountain peaks and valleys, cliffs and rock outcroppings, alpine meadows and grassy areas, as well as lakes, streams, and the Bitterroot River. Of special interest is the 60,000-acre Rattlesnake National Recreation Area and Wilderness, in addition to three other designated wilderness areas.

The forest consists of lodgepole and ponderosa pine, Douglas fir, spruce, cottonwood, and larch, with some old-growth trees, and there are many shrubs and wildflowers. Among the wildlife are elk, moose, grizzly and black bear, deer, bighorn sheep, mountain goat, mountain lion, wolverine, porcupine, and beaver, as well as blue heron, osprey, bald eagle, and red-tailed hawk.

• *Suggested Trails for Nature Walks:* 1. The 0.3-mile Nature Trail. 2. The 1.8-mile Maclay Flat Interpretive Trail (loop). 3. The 2.2-mile Meadow Trail (loop). 4. The 2.4-mile Southside Ski Trail (loop). 5. The 3.4-mile Sam Braxton National Recreation Trail. 6. The 15-mile Main Rattlesnake Travel Corridor. 7. The 2.9-mile Crazy Canyon Trail (moderate). 8. The 10-mile Curry Trail System (moderate).

HELENA NATIONAL FOREST 2880 Skyway Drive, Helena, MT 59601; (406)449-5201. 976,673 acres. Helena National Forest in west-central Montana has many mountains with elevations surpassing 9,400 feet, limestone cliffs, canyons, rock formations, creeks, as well as the Missouri and Blackfoot rivers. Two designated wilderness areas total 112,000 acres.

There are also alpine meadows, wildflowers, shrubs, and a forest of subalpine and Douglas fir, lodgepole and ponderosa pine, as well as aspen. Wildlife includes elk, pronghorn, mule and white-tailed deer, moose, grizzly and black bear, bighorn sheep, wolverine, otter, snowshoe hare, and bald eagle.

• *Suggested Trails for Nature Walks:* 1. The 1-mile Maupin Creek Trail. 2. The first mile of the Larabee Gulch Trail. 3. The first 2 miles of the 3.5-mile Missouri Canyon Trail. 4. The Continental Divide Trail from MacDonald Pass to Ten Mile Picnic Ground (2.5 miles). 5. The 3-mile Blackfoot Meadows Trail. 6. The first 5 miles of the Upper Little Blackfoot Trail (easy-moderate). 7. The Refrigerator Canyon Trail (easy-moderate). 8. The East Fork McClellan Creek Trail to Casey Meadows (3 miles/moderate).

GALLATIN NATIONAL FOREST 3710 Fallon Street, Box C, Bozeman, MT 59715; (406)755-5401. 1,738,138 acres. Located in south-central Montana, Gallatin National Forest is notable for its high alpine peaks, rugged knife-edge ridges, deep canyons, limestone formations, badlands of volcanic rock, and boulder fields. There are also plateaus and open meadows, cirques and glaciated valleys, mountains streams and waterfalls, and many lakes. Included is a section of the Continental Divide.

Of special interest is the 575,000-acre Absaroka-Beartooth Wilderness, which has more than twenty-five peaks over 12,000 feet, some glaciers, 300 lakes, and 5,000 waterfalls. Common trees in the forest include lodgepole pine, Englemann spruce, Douglas fir, and limber pine; there's also a petrified forest. Among the wildlife are grizzly and black bear, moose, elk, deer, bighorn sheep, mountain goat, coyote, porcupine, and beaver.

• *Suggested Trails for Nature Walks:* 1. The 0.3-mile Hyalite Creek Interpretive Trail. 2. The 0.5-mile West Shore Interpretive Trail. 3. The first mile of the 3-mile Hidden Lake Trail. 4. The first 4 miles of the 11-mile Hidden Lake to Porcupine Trail. 5. The 0.6-mile Palisade Falls National Recreation Trail (easy-moderate). 6. The 1.2-mile History Rock Trail (easy-moderate). 7. The first 2 miles of the 5-mile East Fork Trail (easy-moderate). 8. The first 2 miles of the 12-mile Bozeman Creek to Bear Lakes Trail (easy-moderate). 9. The 2.5-mile Windy Pass Trail (moderate). 10. The 2.5-mile Golden Trout Lakes Trail (moderate).

CUSTER NATIONAL FOREST 2602 First Avenue North, P.O. Box 2556, Billings, MT 59103; (406)657-6361. 2,451,359 acres. This national forest consists of separate tracts in southern and southeastern Montana, with lands next to Wyoming's Yellowstone National Park, as well as in North Dakota and South Dakota. It includes four national grasslands, and there are also sixteen peaks over 12,000 feet, among them 12,799-foot Granite Peak, highest in the state.

In the area are glaciers, mesas, rolling hills, valleys, badlands, limestone rock formations and outcroppings, caves, hundreds of lakes, streams, waterfalls, prairie grasslands, and forests of ponderosa and lodgepole pine, Douglas fir, and Englemann spruce. Wildlife includes pronghorn, moose, mule and white-tailed deer, grizzly and black bear, bighorn sheep, and golden eagle.

• *Suggested Trails for Nature Walks:* 1. The 0.2-mile Greenough Lake Trail. 2. The 0.5-mile Wild Bill Lake National Recreation Trail. 3. Other trails at Wild Bill Lake. 4. The 2.5-mile Main Rock Creek Trail. 5. The first few miles of the Lake Fork Trail (easy-moderate). 6. The first 2.5 miles of the Basin Creek Lakes Trail (moderate).

Other Suitable Locations for Nature Walks in Montana

Montana has forty-five state parks, and fifteen of these locations feature trails. Information: Montana Parks Division, 1420 East 6th Avenue, Helena, MT 59620; (406)444-3750.

Some of the Bureau of Land Management areas in the state have trails. Information: BLM, Montana State Office, 222 North 32nd Street, Billings, MT 59107; (406)255-2888.

There are six national wildlife refuges in Montana with trails. Information: U.S. Fish and Wildlife Service, Box 25486, Denver Federal Center, Denver, CO 80225.

NEBRASKA

Recommended Areas for Nature Walks

INDIAN CAVE STATE PARK RR 1, Box 30, Shubert, NE 68437; (402)883-2575. 3,052 acres. Situated on the Missouri River in southeastern Nebraska, this hilly state park features a large sandstone cave with petroglyphs, rock outcroppings, bluffs, grasslands, wildflowers, and over 2,300 acres of forest. Common trees here include oak and hickory, cottonwood and basswood, black walnut and black cherry. Among the wildlife are white-tailed deer, red fox, coyote, opossum, raccoon, and skunk, along with great blue heron, great horned owl, and turkey vulture.

• *Suggested Trails for Nature Walks:* 1. The 0.8-mile Indian Cave Trail. 2. The 1-mile Trail #8. 3. The 1-mile Trail #4. 4. The 1-mile Trail #6. 5. The 1-mile Trail #2. 6. The 3-mile North Ridge Trail (loop). 7. The 6-mile Hardwood Trail.

NIOBRARA STATE PARK P.O. Box 226, Niobrara, NE 68760; (402)857-3373. 1,260 acres. This state park is located on the state's northeastern border, at the confluence of the Missouri and Niobrara rivers. Terrain is hilly with high bluffs and cliffs, bottomlands, and wetlands, as well as a forest of cedar, elm, ash, and hackberry trees. Wildlife includes white-tailed deer, muskrat, beaver, and mink, along with wild turkey, ring-necked pheasant, red-tailed hawk, and bald eagle.

• *Suggested Trails for Nature Walks:* 1. The 2.1-mile Niobrara Trail. 2. The 1.5-mile Cabin Ridge Trail. 3. The 2-mile Tent-Picnic Trail. 4. The 2-mile Ridge to River Trails.

CHADRON STATE PARK 15951 Highway 385, Chadron, NE 69337; (308)432-6167. 974 acres. Chadron State Park is in the Pine Ridge region of northwestern Nebraska, amid Nebraska National Forest lands. The park has hilly terrain with buttes, prairie grasslands, tall ponderosa pines, and a pond.

• *Suggested Trails for Nature Walks:* 1. The 1.8-mile Steamboat Butte Trail. 2. The 1.9-mile Blue Trail. 3. The 2.8-mile Yellow Trail. 4. The 4-mile Black Hills Overlook Trail (loop). 5. The Pine Ridge Trail, which continues on outside the park.

PONCA STATE PARK P.O. Box 688, Ponca, NE 68770; (402)755-2284. 892 acres. Overlooking the Missouri River in northeastern Nebraska, Ponca State Park features rolling hills and bluffs with shrubs, wildflowers including western wild rose, columbine, and yucca, as well as a forest of bur oak, basswood, ash, elm, and hackberry. Among the wildlife are white-tailed deer, coyote, raccoon, opossum, cottontail, whip-poor-will, bald eagle, and turkey vulture.

• *Suggested Trails for Nature Walks:* 1. The 0.5-mile Trail #2. 2. The 0.7-mile Trail #6. 3. The 1.6-mile Trail #4 (loop). 4. The 2.1-mile Trail #1. 5. The 3.4-mile Trail #7. 6. Several miles of other trails wind throughout the park.

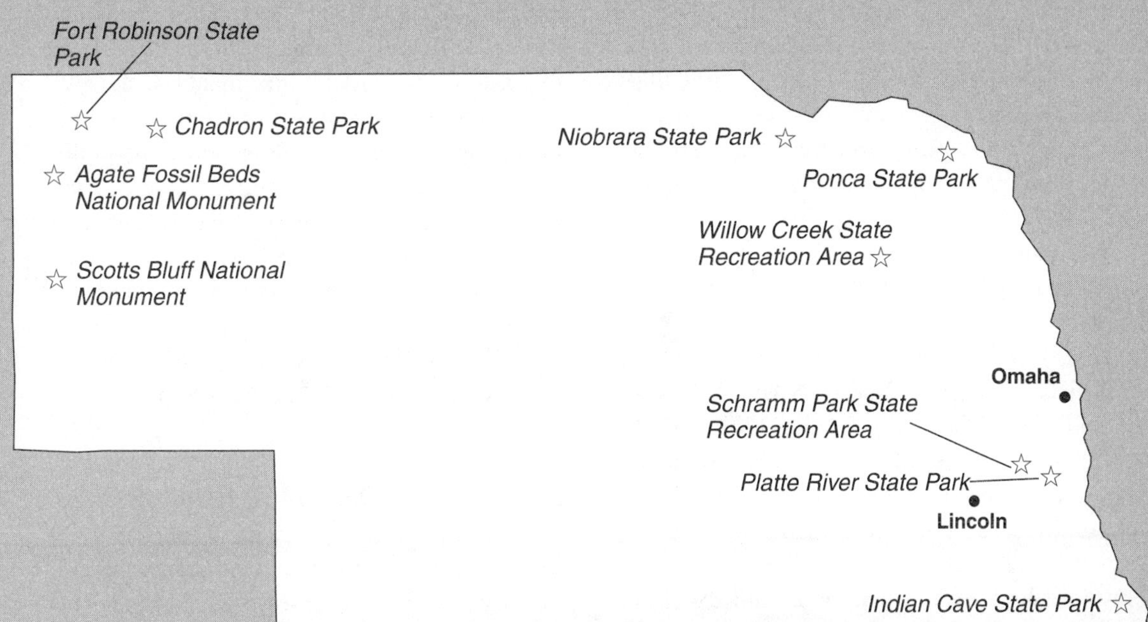
NEBRASKA
Fort Robinson State Park
Chadron State Park
Agate Fossil Beds National Monument
Scotts Bluff National Monument
Niobrara State Park
Ponca State Park
Willow Creek State Recreation Area
Omaha
Schramm Park State Recreation Area
Platte River State Park
Lincoln
Indian Cave State Park

AGATE FOSSIL BEDS NATIONAL MONUMENT P.O. Box 27, Gering, NE 69341; (308)436-4340. 2,700 acres. Agate Fossil Beds National Monument was established to protect beds of 19 million-year-old mammalian fossils, including some unusual and extinct species. Within the national monument are 200-foot hills and rock formations, the Niobrara River, areas of prairie with little bluestem and blue gamma grasses, wildflowers in season, and willow as well as cottonwood trees by the river. Mule deer, pronghorn, and coyote are among the wildlife.

• *Suggested Trails for Nature Walks:* 1. The 0.5-mile Daimonelix Trail. 2. The 1-mile Fossil Hills Trail.

SCOTTS BLUFF NATIONAL MONUMENT P.O. Box 27, Gering, NE 69341; (308)436-4340. 3,000 acres. This national monument lies directly south of the North Platte River in the Great Plains of western Nebraska. The centerpiece is Scotts Bluff, an 800-foot-high rock formation of sandstone and clay that was visible to pioneers along the historic Oregon Trail. The area also features open prairie with varied grasses and wildflowers, plus Rocky Mountain juniper and ponderosa pine trees. Wildlife includes mule and white-tailed deer, coyote, fox, badger, rabbit, and prairie dog.

• *Suggested Trails for Nature Walks:* 1. A trail leads to the remains of the Oregon Trail, which may be followed for some distance. 2. The 1.6-mile Saddle Rock Trail (easy-moderate).

PLATTE RIVER STATE PARK 14421 346th Street, Louisville, NE 68037; (402)234-2217. 418 acres. Situated next to the Platte River in eastern Nebraska, this park has hilly topography with bluffs, tallgrass prairie, and hardwood forests, and features Stone Creek, Decker Creek, and Jenny Newman Lake. Wildlife includes white-tailed deer, wild turkey, and migrating waterfowl.

• *Suggested Trails for Nature Walks:* A 10-mile network of trails extends throughout the wooded areas of the park.

SCHRAMM PARK STATE RECREATION AREA 21004 West Highway 31, Grenta, NE 68028; (402)332-3887. 331 acres. Schramm Park State Recreation Area is on the Platte River in eastern Nebraska, and includes the Ak-Sar-Ben Aquarium and Nature Center. Terrain is hilly with rock formations, woodlands, prairie grasslands, assorted wildflowers, and some man-made ponds. Among the wildlife are white-tailed deer, coyote, fox, raccoon, opossum, skunk, and rabbit, as well as ducks and geese.

• *Suggested Trails for Nature Walks:* 1. The 1.5-mile Nature Trail #1. 2. The 1.5-mile Nature Trail #2.

FORT ROBINSON STATE PARK P.O. Box 392, Crawford, NE 69339; (308)665-2900. 22,000 acres. Established to protect a historic military post, Fort Robinson State Park is next to the Nebraska National Forest lands in the Pine Ridge region of northwestern Nebraska. It's a place of hills and buttes with rock formations, lakes and ponds, Soldier Creek and the White River, prairie grasslands and ponderosa pine forests, with ash and boxelder, cottonwood and willow, as well as yucca and prickly pear cactus. Wildlife includes bison, bighorn sheep, mule and white-tailed deer, coyote, red fox, and porcupine, along with great horned owl, red-tailed hawk, and turkey vulture. There's a nature center, and guided walks are offered.

• *Suggested Trails for Nature Walks:* 1. The 1.5-mile Ice House Ponds Nature Trail. 2. Several trails wind through the northwestern part of the park.

WILLOW CREEK STATE RECREATION AREA Route 2, Box 18, Pierce, NE 68767; (402)329-4053. 1,600 acres. Located on Willow Creek in northeastern Nebraska, this state recreation area has a 700-acre reservoir, a swimming beach, woodlands, and wildlife including deer, rabbit, mourning dove, quail, pheasant, and wild turkey.

• *Suggested Trails for Nature Walks:* A 3-mile trail loops around the western part of the recreation area.

Other Suitable Locations for Nature Walks in Nebraska

Nebraska has eighty-seven state parks and state recreation areas, and some of these locations feature nature or hiking trails. Information: Nebraska Game and Parks Commission, P.O. Box 30370, Lincoln, NE 68503; (402)471-0641.

There are two national wildlife refuges and a wetland management district in Nebraska with trails. Information: U.S. Fish and Wildlife Service, Box 25486, Denver Federal Center, Denver, CO 80225.

Nebraska National Forest has a number of easy-moderate trails. Information: Nebraska National Forest, 125 North Main Street, Chadron, NE 69337; (308)432-3367.

There's a short trail in Samuel R. McKelvie National Forest. Information: Samuel R. McKelvie National Forest, Nenzel, NE 69219; (402)823-4154.

NEVADA

Recommended Areas for Nature Walks

TOIYABE NATIONAL FOREST 1200 Franklin Way, Sparks, NV 89431; (702)331-6444. 4,000,000 acres. Consisting of several large tracts in southern and central Nevada, with a portion in California, Toiyabe is the the largest national forest in the lower 48 states. It features a great diversity of scenery, vegetation, and climate, from desert to subalpine. There are lofty and rugged mountains, deep canyons and caves, open plains, streams with waterfalls, and alpine lakes—with elevations from 4,100 feet to 12,374 feet, and eight designated wilderness areas.

Of special interest is the 316,000-acre Spring Mountain National Recreation Area, an area of enormous biodiversity and scenic interest established in 1993. Vegetation includes joshua tree, pinyon pine, sagebrush, and juniper at lower elevations, ponderosa pine and fir higher up, thousands of acres of ancient bristlecone pine and hemlock, as well as subalpine tundra at highest elevations. Among the wildlife are elk, pronghorn, black bear, mule deer, bighorn sheep, wild horse, mountain lion, coyote, and bobcat.

• *Suggested Trails for Nature Walks:* 1. The 0.2-mile Bristlecone Loop. 2. The 0.2-mile Robber's Roost Trail. 3. The 1-mile Echo Cliff Loop (easy-moderate). 4. The 4-mile Charity Valley Trail (easy-moderate). 5. The first 4 miles of the 6-mile Mt. Rose Trail (easy-moderate). 6. The 5-mile Bristlecone Trail (easy-moderate). 7. The 16.5-mile East Carson River Trail (easy-moderate). 8. The 1.5-mile Mary Jane and Big Falls Trail (moderate). 9. The 2.2-mile Snodgrass Creek Trail (moderate). 10. The 3.3-mile Driveway Trail (moderate).

GREAT BASIN NATIONAL PARK Baker, NV 89311; (702)234-7331. 77,100 acres. Established in 1986, this national park in eastern Nevada encloses a small portion of the vast Great Basin, which covers most of Nevada and parts of four surrounding states. Elevations here range from 6,200 feet to 13,063 feet on Wheeler Peak. There are rugged mountains and deep valleys, salt lakes and marshes, pinnacles and limestone caves, including the large cavern known as Lehman Caves.

Vegetation ranges from sagebrush to alpine varieties, with forests of fir, pine, and spruce, pinyon-juniper woodlands, open meadows with wildflowers, and bristlecone pine trees that are almost 5,000 years old. Wildlife includes pronghorn, mule deer, bighorn sheep, mountain lion, bobcat, and golden eagle. Ranger-led nature and cave walks are available.

• *Suggested Trails for Nature Walks:* 1. The 0.3-mile Visitor Center Nature Trail. 2. The 0.8-mile Cave Tour. 3. The 3-mile Alpine Lakes Loop Trail (easy-moderate). 4. The 1-mile Lexington Arch Trail (moderate). 5. The Bristlecone Pine-Glacier Trail (moderate).

HUMBOLDT NATIONAL FOREST 976 Mountain City Highway, Elko, NV 89801; (702)738-5171. 2,500,000 acres. Humboldt

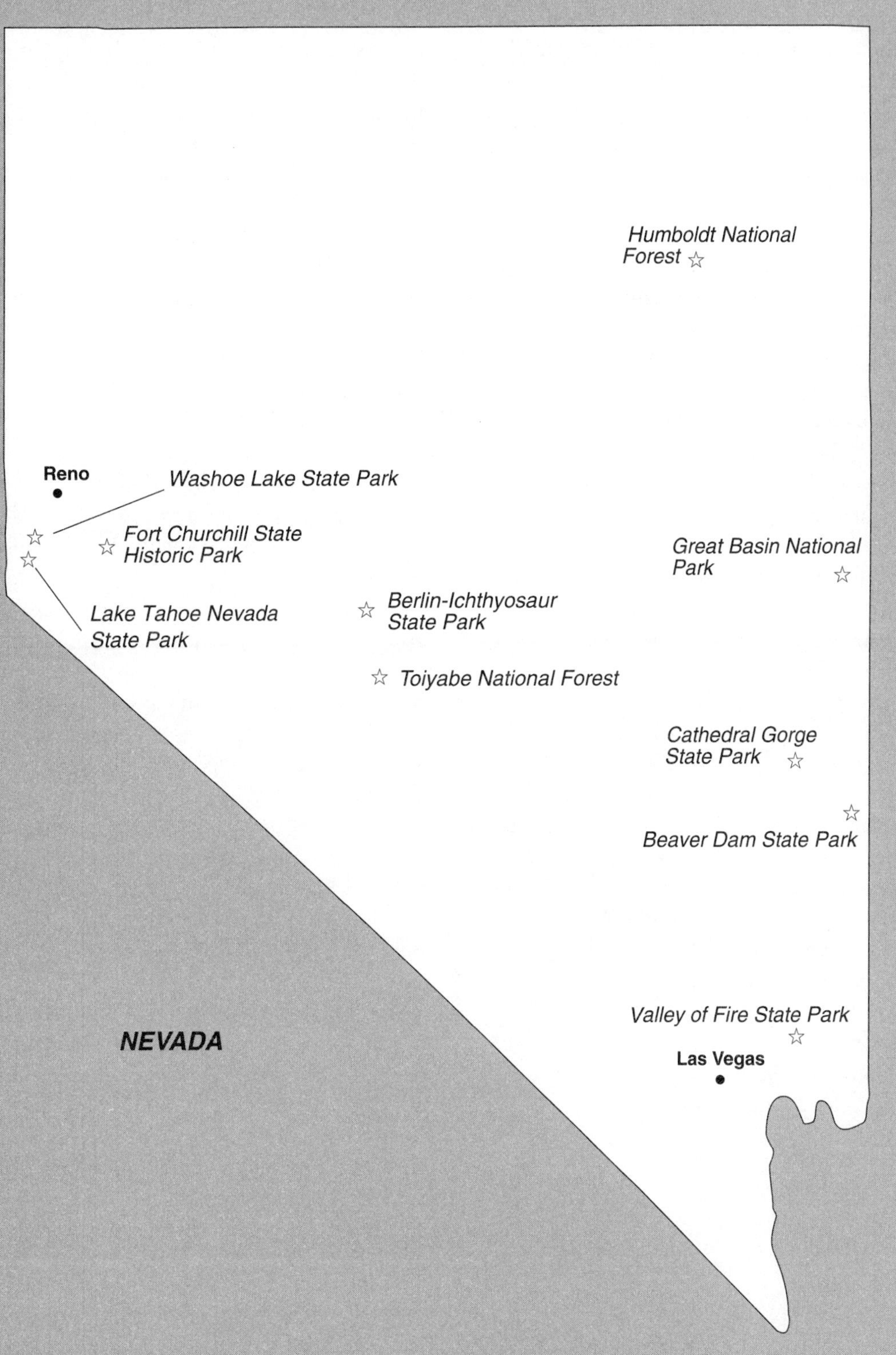
Humboldt National Forest
Reno
Washoe Lake State Park
Fort Churchill State Historic Park
Great Basin National Park
Lake Tahoe Nevada State Park
Berlin-Ichthyosaur State Park
Toiyabe National Forest
Cathedral Gorge State Park
Beaver Dam State Park
Valley of Fire State Park
NEVADA
Las Vegas

National Forest is made up of nine separate units in eastern and northern Nevada. There are several mountain ranges here, including the Ruby Mountains and the East Humboldt Mountains, with high rocky peaks, deep canyons, cirque basins, rolling hills, and plateaus, plus many streams and lakes.

Vegetation ranges from Douglas fir, spruce, limber pine, and bristlecone pine at higher elevations to sagebrush, cacti, and pinyon-juniper woodlands below, as well as aspen, willow, and cottonwood trees. Among the wildlife are mule deer, bighorn sheep, elk, wild horse, pronghorn, mountain lion, mountain goat, coyote, raccoon, beaver, badger, otter, and mink, along with great horned owl, red-tailed hawk, and golden eagle.

• *Suggested Trails for Nature Walks:* 1. The 0.5-mile Changing Canyon Trail. 2. The 1.5-mile Smith Lake Trail (easy-moderate). 3. The 4-mile Winchell Lake Trail (easy-moderate). 4. The 5-mile Greys Lake Trail (easy-moderate). 5. The 6-mile Long Canyon Trail (easy-moderate). 6. The forest has many miles of other trails.

BEAVER DAM STATE PARK P.O. Box 176, Panaca, NV 89042; (702)728-4467. 2,393 acres. Located in eastern Nevada at an elevation of 5,000 feet, Beaver Dam State Park has rugged terrain with small canyons, ravines, cliffs, streams, and a 15-acre reservoir. Vegetation includes cactus and sagebrush, willow and cottonwood trees, along with ponderosa pine and pinyon-juniper. Mule deer, mountain lion, coyote, fox, and rabbit are among the wildlife.

• *Suggested Trails for Nature Walks:* 1. The 0.5-mile Interpretive Trail. 2. The 0.5-mile Waterfall Trail. 3. The 0.3-mile Oak Knoll Trail. 4. The 1.5-mile East Shore Trail.

BERLIN-ICHTHYOSAUR STATE PARK HC 61, Box 61200, Austin, NV 89310; (702)964-2440. 1,200 acres. Situated in central Nevada, this state park was created to protect an area of 225 million-year-old Ichthyosaur fossils (an extinct marine reptile). The park also preserves the historic mining village of Berlin, now a ghost town. It's in the Shoshone Mountains at an elevation of 7,000 feet, with canyons, high desert, pinyon-juniper stands, sagebrush, and Indian paintbrush. Wildlife includes mule deer, bobcat, coyote, and jackrabbit.

• *Suggested Trails for Nature Walks:* 1. The 0.5-mile Fossil House Trail. 2. The 0.8-mile Union Canyon Trail. 3. The 0.8-mile Berlin Townsite Trail. 4. The 0.5-mile Richmond Canyon Trail (moderate). 5. The 1-mile Ames Place Trail (moderate).

VALLEY OF FIRE STATE PARK P.O. Box 515, Overton, NV 89040; (702)397-2088. 46,000 acres. Valley of Fire State Park is located next to Lake Meade National Recreation Area in the Mojave Desert of southeastern Nevada. The park features 150 million-year-old red sandstone formations, arches and pinnacles, sandy canyons and caves, petrified logs and stumps, as well as 3,000-year-old Indian petroglyphs. Vegetation includes burro and creosote bush, cholla and beavertail cactus, with spring wildflowers. Among the wildlife are fox, coyote, jackrabbit, skunk, tortoise, iguana, Gila monster, roadrunner, and red-tailed hawk.

• *Suggested Trails for Nature Walks:* 1. Two short interpretive trails lead to petrified logs. 2. The 0.3-mile Petroglyph Canyon Trail. 3. The 1.5-mile Fire Canyon/Silica Dome Trail. 4. The 3.5-mile White Domes Trail (moderate).

LAKE TAHOE NEVADA STATE PARK P.O. Box 8867, Incline Village, NV 89452; (702)831-0494. 14,000 acres. This state park stands on the northeastern shore of enormous Lake Tahoe, in the western corner of Nevada. Scenery includes sandy beaches and mountain meadows, several smaller lakes, rocky cliffs and canyons, with stands of aspen and jeffrey pine, along with manzanita.

• *Suggested Trails for Nature Walks:* 1. The 1.6-mile Spooner Lake Trail (loop). 2. The 1.5-mile trail from Hidden Beach to Tunnel Creek Station (moderate). 3. The 2.5-mile trail from Hidden Beach to Twin Lakes (moderate). 4. The 4-mile section of the Tahoe Rim Trail north of Spooner Lake (moderate). 5. The 5-mile Spooner Lake-Marlette Lake Trail (moderate).

FORT CHURCHILL STATE HISTORIC PARK Silver Springs, NV 89429; (702)577-2345. 710 acres. Located alongside the Carson River in west-central Nevada, Fort Churchill State Historic Park features the adobe ruins of a fort built in the 1860s. It's a relatively flat area characterized by sagebrush hills, desert wildflowers including rabbitbrush and Indian rice-grass, and cottonwood trees and waterfowl by the river.

• *Suggested Trails for Nature Walks:* 1. The 0.8-mile Historic Trail. 2. The 1.5-mile Nature Trail.

CATHEDRAL GORGE STATE PARK P.O. Box 176, Panaca, NV 89042; (702)728-4467. 1,600 acres. This park in southeastern Nevada includes Cathedral Gorge, with rock formations and spires, domes and terraces, cliffs and narrow canyons, grassy areas with wildflowers, sagebrush, yucca, barberry, and bitterbrush, as well as juniper trees. The park is at an elevation of 4,700 feet, and mule deer, coyote, fox, and hawk are among the wildlife.

• *Suggested Trails for Nature Walks:* 1. The 0.5-mile Nature Trail (loop). 2. The 4-mile trail which runs along a wash.

WASHOE LAKE STATE PARK 4855 East Lake Boulevard, Carson City, NV 89701; (702)885-4319. 3,000 acres. Located in western Nevada's Washoe Valley, between the Carson and Virginia ranges, this state park features 5,700-acre Washoe Lake as well as Little Washoe Lake, with a sandy beach, dunes, streams, grasses, and sagebrush. Wildlife includes mule deer, coyote, beaver, badger, muskrat, jackrabbit, and skunk, along with great blue heron, sandhill crane, white-faced ibis, and waterfowl.

• *Suggested Trails for Nature Walks:* 1. The 0.3-mile Dunes Trail. 2. The 1-mile Deadman's Creek Trail. 3. A large network of biking trails, open to foot travel, extends into the mountains east, south, and west of the park.

Other Suitable Locations for Nature Walks in Nevada

Nevada has twenty state parks and state recreation areas, and fourteen of these locations feature trails. Information: Division of State Parks, Capitol Complex, Carson City, NV 89710; (702)687-4370.

Some Bureau of Land Management areas in the state have trails. Information: Bureau of Land Management, Nevada State Office, P.O. Box 12000, Reno, NV 89520; (702)785-6500.

NEW HAMPSHIRE

Recommended Areas for Nature Walks

WHITE MOUNTAIN NATIONAL FOREST 719 Main Street, Laconia, NH 03246; (603)528-8721. 798,000 acres. Constituting much of north-central and northern New Hampshire, and extending into Maine, White Mountain National Forest features the highest and most rugged mountains of the Northeast, including 6,288-foot Mt. Washington. Famous for their unusually severe weather, these mountains offer the greatest expanse of above-treeline terrain in the eastern United States.

Five designated wilderness areas in the forest total 112,000 acres. There are steep notches and ravines, precipitous cliffs and rock formations, with alpine vegetation and wildflowers, as well as rivers, brooks, waterfalls, ponds, marshes, and bogs. Most of the region is forested with sugar maple, birch, oak, beech, red spruce, and balsam fir. Among the wildlife are moose, black bear, white-tailed deer, bobcat, red fox, raccoon, beaver, great blue heron, woodcock, and great horned owl.

• *Suggested Trails for Nature Walks:* 1. The 0.4-mile Crystal Cascade Trail. 2. The 0.4-mile Sabbaday Falls Trail. 3. The 0.5-mile Rail N' River Trail. 4. The 0.7-mile Lovequist Loop Trail. 5. The 0.8-mile Thompson Falls Trail. 6. The 1-mile Lost Pond Trail. 7. The 1.5-mile Champney Falls Trail. 8. The 1.6-mile Ammo Ravine Trail. 9. The 2-mile Tunnel Brook Trail. 10. The 2.8-mile Lincoln Woods Trail.

FRANCONIA NOTCH STATE PARK Franconia, NH 03580; (603)823-5563. 6,800 acres. This state park is in Franconia Notch, a deep, 8-mile-long mountain pass in the White Mountains, amid lands of White Mountain National Forest. Notable features are 800-foot-long Flume Gorge, with 90-foot vertical walls, and Old Man of the Mountain, which is a 40-foot rock formation. Also here are the headwaters of the Pemigewasset River, with pools and potholes.

There are several lakes, streams, waterfalls, bogs, and marshes, as well as cliffs, ravines, rock ledges, and talus slopes. The area is forested with northern hardwoods including maple, beech, and birch, plus fir, spruce, pine, and hemlock, as well as blueberry and mountain holly, mosses and ferns, shrubs and wildflowers. Among the wildlife are black bear, bobcat, fox, raccoon, porcupine, snowshoe hare, falcon, hawk, and bald eagle.

• *Suggested Trails for Nature Walks:* 1. The 0.3-mile Roaring River Nature Trail (loop). 2. The 2-mile Flume Trail (loop). 3. The Basin-Cascades Trail to Kinsman Falls (0.6 miles). 4. The 4-mile Pemi Trail. 5. The 1.5-mile Bald Mountain-Artists Bluff Trail (easy-moderate). 6. The Lonesome Lake Trail to Lonesome Lake (1.6 miles/moderate).

HARRIS CENTER FOR CONSERVATION EDUCATION 341 Kings Highway, Hancock, NH 03449; (603)525-3394. 7,000 acres.

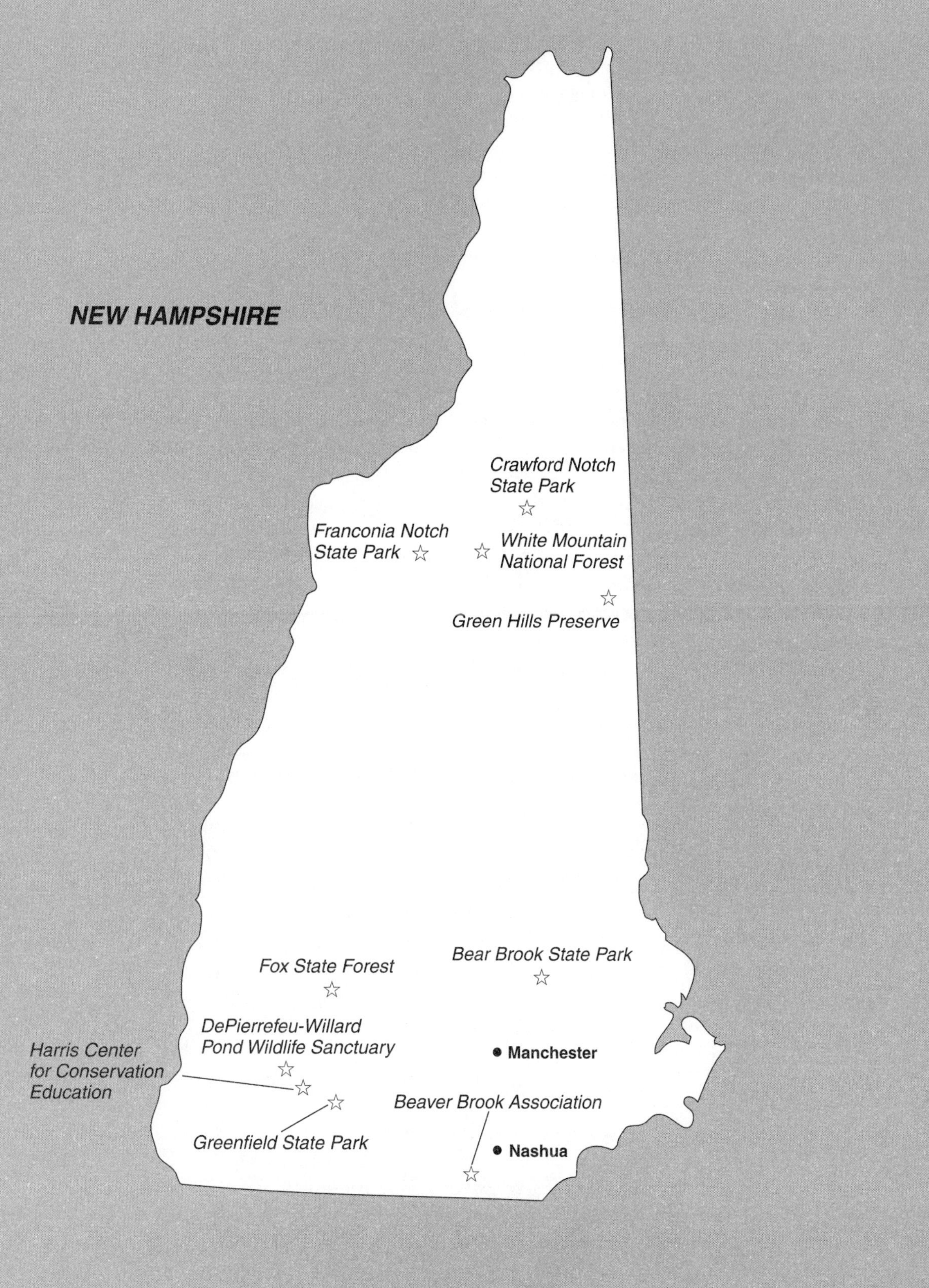
NEW HAMPSHIRE
Crawford Notch State Park
Franconia Notch State Park
White Mountain National Forest
Green Hills Preserve
Fox State Forest
Bear Brook State Park
DePierrefeu-Willard Pond Wildlife Sanctuary
Harris Center for Conservation Education
Manchester
Beaver Brook Association
Greenfield State Park
Nashua

Situated in southwestern New Hampshire, the Harris Center is an environmental center that occupies a "supersanctuary," encompassing small mountains with rocky ledges and boulders, ponds and streams, bogs and grassy areas. There are also mosses, ferns, wildflowers, and a forest of birch, moosewood, spruce, white pine, and balsam fir, along with juniper and blueberry. Wildlife includes bobcat, beaver, snowshoe hare, and grouse.

• *Suggested Trails for Nature Walks:* 1. The 0.5-mile Dandelyon Trail. 2. The 1-mile Boulder Trail Loop. 3. The Babbitt Trail (loop). 4. The 1.7-mile Channing Trail. 5. The 1.2-mile Thumbs Down Trail (easy-moderate). 6. The 1.5-mile Harriskat Trail (moderate).

CRAWFORD NOTCH STATE PARK Twin Mountain, NH 03580; (603)374-2272. 6,000 acres. This state park occupies Crawford Notch, a deep, wide, and 6-mile-long valley in the White Mountains of north-central New Hampshire. Surrounded by lands of White Mountain National Forest, it features steep mountains with open ledges and precipitous cliffs, streams with waterfalls, among them 200-foot Arethusa Falls and 100-foot Ripley Falls, as well as the Saco and Dry rivers. The area is forested with northern hardwoods including birch and maple, fir and spruce.

• *Suggested Trails for Nature Walks:* 1. The 0.5-mile Pond Loop Trail. 2. The 1-mile Sam Willey Trail (loop). 3. The 0.5-mile Ripley Falls Trail (easy-moderate). 4. The 1.3-mile Arethusa Falls Trail (moderate). 5. The 1.4-mile Mt. Willard Trail (moderate).

BEAR BROOK STATE PARK RR 1, Box 507, Allenstown, NH 03275; (603)485-9874. 10,000 acres. Located next to the Suncook River in the south-central part of the state, Bear Brook is New Hampshire's largest state park. There are streams here including Bear Brook, as well as several ponds, marshes, and bogs, low rocky ridges and hills with outcroppings, hemlock ravines, shrubs and wildflowers, and a pine and oak forest. White-tailed deer and beaver are among the wildlife, and the park has a nature center.

• *Suggested Trails for Nature Walks:* 1. The 0.3-mile Pioneer Nature Trail (loop). 2. The 0.5-mile Smith Pond Trail. 3. The 1.5-mile Beaver Pond Loop. 4. There's a network of nearly 40 miles of other trails, some of which offer easy walking.

BEAVER BROOK ASSOCIATION 117 Ridge Road, Hollis, NH 03049; (603)465-7787. 1,700 acres. Owned by the Beaver Brook Association and open to the public for recreation and other purposes, this is a tract of land on the Nissitissit River in southern New Hampshire, just north of the Massachusetts border. There are two major brooks, several ponds, marshes, swamps, meadows, and fields with wildflowers, as well as mixed forests of pine, oak, maple, ash, beech, hemlock, birch, and aspen, with some old-growth trees.

• *Suggested Trails for Nature Walks:* 1. The 0.8-mile Nesting Box Demonstration Trail (loop). 2. The 1-mile Natural History and Forestry Trail. 3. Over 25 miles of other trails and old roads here are suitable for walking.

FOX STATE FOREST P.O. Box 1175, Hillsboro, NH 03244; (603)464-3453. 1,445 acres. Fox State Forest in southern New Hampshire features hills and valleys with rock ledges, swamps and marshes, bogs and brooks, mushrooms and ferns, with a forest of conifers and hardwoods. Highest point is 1,210-foot Monroe Hill. Among the trees are old-growth hemlock, beech, and white pine, as well as fir, birch, aspen, maple, butternut, black gum, and basswood. Wildlife includes white-tailed deer, bobcat, fox, raccoon, porcupine, muskrat, beaver, otter, mink, and snowshoe hare, plus great blue heron, grouse, barred owl, and red-tailed hawk.

• *Suggested Trails for Nature Walks:* 1. The 0.5-mile Mushroom Trail (loop). 2. The 0.5-mile Tree Identification Trail (loop). 3. The 1.5-mile Mud Pond Trail. 4. Almost 20 miles of other trails wind throughout the forest.

GREEN HILLS PRESERVE P.O. Box 119, Glen, NH 03838; (603)383-9153. 2,822 acres. Established in 1990 by the Nature Conservancy, Green Hills Preserve is located just east of the Saco River in North Conway, in north-central New Hampshire. The preserve encompasses a number of small mountains and hills, including 2,369-foot Black Cap Mountain and 1,739-foot Peaked Mountain. Included are rock formations, ledges, streams, a pond, and a forest of hardwoods with pine, fir, spruce, and hemlock.

• *Suggested Trails for Nature Walks:* 1. The 1.2-mile Pudding Pond Trail. 2. The 1.3-mile Black Cap Trail (easy-moderate). 3. The 1.3-mile Peaked Mountain Trail (moderate). 4. The 0.2-mile Peaked Mountain Connector Trail.

DEPIERREFEU-WILLARD POND WILDLIFE SANCTUARY Audubon Society of New Hampshire, 3 Silk Farm Road, Concord, NH 03301; (603)224-9909. 1,000 acres. Situated in southwestern New Hampshire, this is the largest Audubon Society sanctuary in the state. It's centered on 100-acre Willard Pond and also includes Hatch Mill Pond, along with high hills, huge boulders and ledges, marshes and bogs, a brook, and woodlands with white pine, red maple, paper birch, and white ash. Among the wildlife are white-tailed deer, wood duck, hooded merganser, and common loon.

• *Suggested Trails for Nature Walks:* 1. The 0.5-mile Mill Pond Trail (loop). 2. The 0.3-mile Tudor Trail (loop). 3. The 0.3-mile Pine Point Trail. 4. The 1.3-mile Goodhue Hill Trail. 5. The 1.5-mile Bald Mountain Trail (moderate).

GREENFIELD STATE PARK P.O. Box 123, Greenfield, NH 03047; (603)547-3497. 400 acres. Greenfield State Park is located on large Otter Lake in the southwest corner of the state, with gently rolling terrain and elevations between 800 and 900 feet. There are several ponds, swamps and bogs, a sandy beach, and a conifer forest with oak, along with bunchberry, cranberry, and blueberry.

• *Suggested Trails for Nature Walks:* 1. The 2-mile Hiking Loop Trail. 2. The Scout Trail to Spruce Swamp. 3. The trail around Beaver Pond. 4. The trail along the shoreline of Otter Lake. 5. The short trails to Mud Pond.

Other Suitable Locations for Nature Walks in New Hampshire

New Hampshire has forty-two state parks, and many of them have nature or hiking trails. Information: Division of Parks and Recreation, P.O. Box 1856, Concord, NH 03302; (603)271-3254.

Trails are available at three national wildlife refuges in the state. Information: U.S. Fish and Wildlife Service, 300 Westgate Center Drive, Hadley, MA 01035.

The Audubon Society of New Hampshire manages over fifty sanctuaries and refuges in the state, and a number of them feature nature trails. Information: Audubon Society of New Hampshire, 3 Silk Farm Road, Concord, NH 03301; (603)224-9909.

The Society for the Protection of New Hampshire Forests owns sixty-five forest reservations that are open to the public. Some of the properties have trails. Information: Society for the Protection of New Hampshire Forests, 54 Portsmouth Street, Concord, NH 03301; (603)224-9945.

There are trails at some of the fifteen Nature Conservancy preserves in the state. Information: The Nature Conservancy, New Hampshire Chapter, 2½ Beacon Street, Suite 6, Concord, NH 03301; (603)224-5853.

NEW JERSEY

Recommended Areas for Nature Walks

DELAWARE WATER GAP NATIONAL RECREATION AREA Bushkill, PA 18324; (717)588-2451. 70,000 acres. Located along the northwestern border of New Jersey, with a portion in Pennsylvania, this national recreation area protects 38 miles of the Delaware River as well as adjacent lands. Best known feature is the Delaware Water Gap, a deep gap in the Kittatinny Mountains that was cut by the river. Elevations range from 300 feet to over 1,500 feet.

Within the area's boundaries is Worthington State Forest, site of some of the trails. There are steep mountain ridges with streams and many waterfalls, and a forest of eastern hardwoods with hemlock and redcedar. Wildlife includes white-tailed deer, black bear, raccoon, opossum, muskrat, beaver, river otter, hawk, and bald eagle. Short naturalist-led walks are available. See the Pennsylvania chapter for the area's trails in that state.

• *Suggested Trails for Nature Walks:* 1. The 1.1-mile Karamac Trail. 2. The 1-mile Thunder Mountain Trail. 3. The 0.4-mile Holly Springs Trail. 4. The first 2.5 miles of the 3.5-mile Dunnfield Creek Trail. 5. The 1.6-mile Sunfish Pond Fire Road Trail. 6. The 4-mile Woods Road Trail. 7. The 2.5-mile Rattlesnake Swamp Trail (easy-moderate). 8. The 2.7-mile Rockcores Trail (easy-moderate).

STOKES STATE FOREST 1 Coursen Road, Branchville, NJ 07826; (201)948-3820. 15,482 acres. Situated near the northern tip of New Jersey, southwest of High Point State Park, Stokes State Forest encompasses the ridges of the Kittatinny Mountains, with elevations from 420 to 1,653 feet on Sunrise Mountain. Included is the 525-acre Tillman Ravine Natural Area.

There are open mountain vistas, rock formations, streams, small waterfalls, and a forest of mixed hardwoods with oak, hickory, birch, beech, and maple, plus pine, cedar, and hemlock, along with rhododendron and mountain laurel. Among the wildlife are white-tailed deer, black bear, bobcat, coyote, fox, raccoon, opossum, and beaver.

• *Suggested Trails for Nature Walks:* 1. The 0.5-mile Tibbs Trail. 2. The 0.6-mile Shay Trail. 3. The 0.8-mile Steam Mill Trail. 4. The 1-mile Silver Mine Trail. 5. The 1-mile Deep Root Trail. 6. The 1-mile Lead Mine Trail. 7. The 1.4-mile Blue Mountain Trail. 8. The 1.8-mile Steffen Trail. 9. The 1.5-mile Rock Oak Trail (easy-moderate). 10. The 1.6-mile Howell Trail (easy-moderate).

HIGH POINT STATE PARK 1480 State Route 23, Sussex, NJ 07461; (201)875-4800. 14,056 acres. This state park features the highest elevation in New Jersey, 1,803-foot High Point, with vistas from a 220-foot obelisk on top. It's in the Kittatinny Mountains at the northern tip of the state, next to the New York border, and includes the 850-acre Dryden Kuser Natural Area. There are streams, three lakes, a cedar swamp, and forests of oak, hickory, maple,

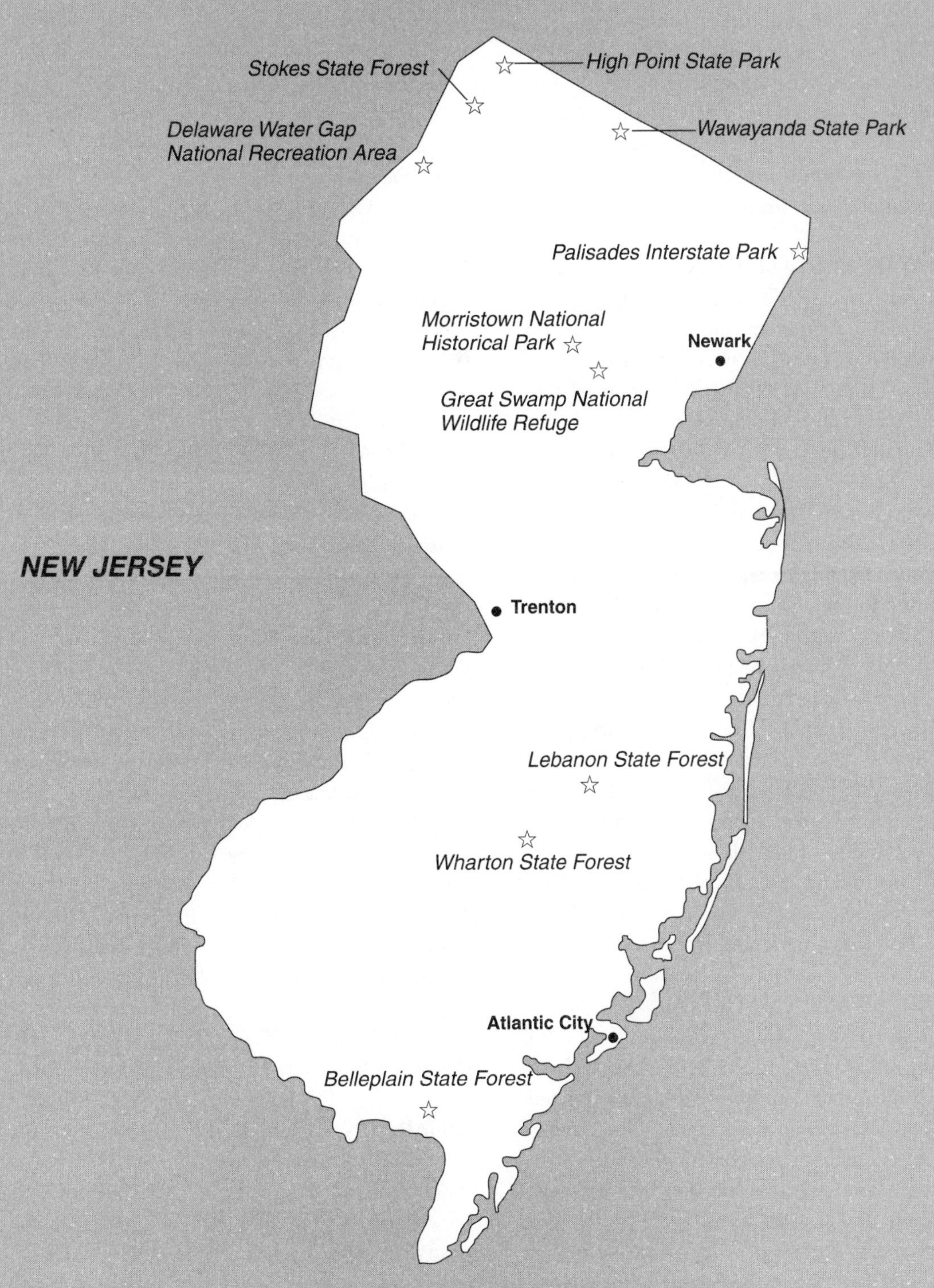
NEW JERSEY
Stokes State Forest
High Point State Park
Delaware Water Gap
National Recreation Area
Wawayanda State Park
Palisades Interstate Park
Morristown National
Historical Park
Newark
Great Swamp National
Wildlife Refuge
Trenton
Lebanon State Forest
Wharton State Forest
Atlantic City
Belleplain State Forest

birch, hemlock, spruce, and pine, along with rhododendron, blueberry, and huckleberry. Wildlife includes white-tailed deer, black bear, porcupine, beaver, and turkey vulture.

• *Suggested Trails for Nature Walks:* 1. The 0.5-mile Life Trail. 2. The 0.5-mile Old Trail. 3. The 1-mile Ayer's Trail. 4. The 1.5-mile Cedar Swamp Trail. 5. The 1.5-mile Mashipacong Trail. 6. The 4-mile Iris Trail. 7. The 0.8-mile Steenykill Trail (easy-moderate).

WAWAYANDA STATE PARK P.O. Box 198, Highland Lakes, NJ 07422; (201)853-4462. 13,000 acres. At an elevation of 1,140 feet on northern New Jersey's Wawayanda Plateau, this state park features 255-acre Wawayanda Lake, several smaller lakes and ponds, and three designated natural areas: the 2,167-acre Wawayanda Swamp Natural Area, the 1,325-acre Bearfort Mountain Natural Area, and the 339-acre Hemlock Ravine Natural Area. There are streams, wetlands including cedar swamps, and a mixed hardwood forest with oak and hemlock. White-tailed deer, beaver, barred owl, and red-shouldered hawk are among the wildlife.

• *Suggested Trails for Nature Walks:* 1. The 1.1-mile Red Dot Trail. 2. The 1.5-mile Laurel Pond Trail. 3. The 1.3-mile Cedar Swamp Trail. 4. The 0.5-mile South End Trail. 5. The 1.5-mile Banker Trail. 6. The 1.7-mile Double Pond Trail. 7. The 1.8-mile William Hoeferlin Trail. 8. The 2.4-mile Pump House Trail. 9. The 2.8-mile Iron Mountain Trail. 10. The 1.4-mile Terrace Pond South Trail (easy-moderate).

GREAT SWAMP NATIONAL WILDLIFE REFUGE RD 1, Box 152, Basking Ridge, NJ 07920; (908)647-1222. 7,200 acres. Great Swamp National Wildlife Refuge is located south of Morristown in northern New Jersey. The eastern half is a designated wilderness area, and there are extensive marshes and swamps, grasslands and brushy areas, with ponds and streams, many species of wildflowers, mountain laurel, and low hardwood-forested ridges with oak and beech.

The refuge is home to many species of waterfowl, especially Canada goose, wood duck, and mallard, along with mourning dove, turkey vulture, and American kestrel. Other wildlife includes white-tailed deer, red fox, raccoon, opossum, muskrat, river otter, and bog turtle. The trails are often wet, and some become impassible at times owing to flooding.

• *Suggested Trails for Nature Walks:* 1. The Wildlife Observation Center trails (totaling about 1 mile). 2. The 2.4-mile Blue Trail. 3. The 0.9-mile Yellow Trail. 4. The 0.5-mile Red Trail. 5. The 1.6-mile Orange Trail. 6. The 0.4-mile Silver Trail. 7. The 0.5-mile Beige Trail. 8. The 0.7-mile Green Trail. 9. The 0.7-mile White Trail.

BELLEPLAIN STATE FOREST P.O. Box 450, Woodbine, NJ 08270; (609)861-2404. 11,790 acres. Situated on the coastal plain of southern New Jersey, Belleplain State Forest features 26-acre Lake Nummy and several other lakes, as well as streams, swamps, shrubs, wildflowers, and a forest of pitch pine, oak, and white cedar, with gray birch and red maple, black gum and sweetgum, plus holly and mountain laurel, blueberry and huckleberry. Among the wildlife are white-tailed deer, fox, opossum, raccoon, muskrat, beaver, and cottontail. The forest has a nature center.

• *Suggested Trails for Nature Walks:* 1. The 0.3-mile Goosekill Trail. 2. The 0.9-mile Lake Nummy Nature Trails. 3. The 0.6-mile Meisle Trail. 4. The 0.7-mile North Shore Trail. 5. The 0.7-mile Boundary Trail. 6. The 0.9-mile Tarkiln Bogs Trail. 7. The 1.5-mile Seashore Line Trail. 8. The 1.7-mile Old Cape Trail. 9. The 2.2-mile Ponds Trail. 10. The 7.2-mile Eagle Creek Trail.

WHARTON STATE FOREST RD #9, Batsto, Hammonton, NJ 08037; (609)561-0024. 109,000 acres. Stretching across south-central New Jersey's pine barrens, this forest is the state's largest protected natural area. The sandy, nearly level terrain includes swamps and floodplains, marshes and bogs, ponds and lakes, streams and small rivers, amid a forest of pitch pine, shortleaf pine, and oak, with blueberries and huckleberries. There are two designated natural areas, as well as a nature center in historic Batsto Village. Wildlife includes white-tailed deer, gray fox, raccoon, woodchuck, otter, hawk, and turkey vulture.

• *Suggested Trails for Nature Walks:* 1. The network of nature trails in the Batso Natural Area. 2. The 28-mile segment of the 49.5-mile Batona Trail, which continues on through Lebanon State Forest and Bass River State Forest. 3. Several hundred miles of little-used sand roads offer other options for walks.

LEBANON STATE FOREST P.O. Box 215, New Lisbon, NJ 08064; (609)726-1191. 32,012 acres. Lebanon State Forest is located in the almost flat pine barrens of south-central New Jersey, a place of sandy soil, small lakes and ponds including 5-acre Pakim Pond, cedar swamps and cranberry bogs, wildflowers, ferns, pitcher plants, blueberries, mountain laurel, and forests of pitch pine and oak. Among the wildlife are green heron, owl, ruffed grouse, hawk, skunk, raccoon, fox, and white-tailed deer.

• *Suggested Trails for Nature Walks:* 1. The 9.4-mile section of the 49.5-mile Batona Trail. 2. The Red Trail to Pakim Pond. 3. The White Trail to Mt. Misery. 4. Many miles of lightly traveled sand roads are also suitable for walking.

PALISADES INTERSTATE PARK P.O. Box 155, Alpine, NJ 07620; (201)768-1360. 2,500 acres. This state park is part of a larger New York–New Jersey park system established early this century to protect the cliffs and western shoreline of the Hudson River. It features vertical cliffs of igneous rock, with high columns and talus below, as well as swamps, bogs, streams, and an oak-hickory forest of birch and maple, beech and tulip tree, with dogwood and wild azalea. Wildlife includes white-tailed deer, red fox, raccoon, opossum, and muskrat, along with ruffed grouse, pileated woodpecker, great horned owl, broad-winged hawk, and eagle.

• *Suggested Trails for Nature Walks:* 1. The 11-mile Shore Path, which runs alongside the river and offers flat as well as rough stretches. 2. The 11-mile section of the 200-mile Long Path follows along the clifftops. 3. Several shorter trails connect the two major trails, making possible loops of varying lengths.

MORRISTOWN NATIONAL HISTORICAL PARK Washington Place, Morristown, NJ 07960; (201)539-2085. 1,000 acres. Consisting of several tracts of land, this park in northern New Jersey was established to protect the historic location of the 1779–80 winter encampment of George Washington's Continental Army, which suffered through the worst winter of the century.

The hilly Jockey Hollow area southwest of Morristown includes reconstructed soldier huts and an eighteenth-century farm, as well as old fields, meadows with wildflowers, streams, and hundreds of acres of forest with oak and tulip tree, red maple and beech, black birch and dogwood. Among the wildlife are white-tailed deer, bobcat, fox, woodchuck, beaver, skunk, and mink.

• *Suggested Trails for Nature Walks:* The Jockey Hollow area has about 23 miles of well-marked and easy but hilly trails, ranging from narrow paths to wide horse trails. Additional trails are found at the other historic sites that constitute the park.

Other Suitable Locations for Nature Walks in New Jersey

New Jersey has thirty-six state parks and eleven state forests, and most of these locations feature suitable trails. Information: Division of Parks and Forestry, CN 404, Trenton, NJ 08625; (609)292-2797.

The New Jersey Audubon Society manages several sanctuaries that have trails. Information: New Jersey Audubon Society, P.O. Box 125, Franklin Lakes, NJ 07417; (201)891-1211.

There are appropriate trails at two county reservations: 1. Watchung Reservation, c/o Union County Department of Parks, 452 New Providence Road, Mountainside, NJ 07092. 2. South Mountain Reservation, c/o Essex County Environmental Center, 621 Eagle Rock Avenue, Roseland, NJ 07068.

NEW MEXICO

Recommended Areas for Nature Walks

CARSON NATIONAL FOREST P.O. Box 558, Taos, NM 87571; (505)758-6200. 1,500,000 acres. Consisting of several sizable tracts in northern New Mexico, Carson National Forest features numerous mountains as well as mesas, canyons, and talus slopes. There are lakes and streams, forests of Englemann spruce, Douglas fir, ponderosa pine, pinyon-juniper, aspen, and cottonwood, along with alpine grasses and stands of bristlecone pine.

Five designated wilderness areas total 86,193 acres. Elevations in the forest range from 6,000 to over 13,000 feet. Prominent mountains include 13,161-foot Wheeler Peak, the highest point in the state. Among the wildlife are pronghorn, elk, mule deer, black bear, bighorn sheep, mountain lion, marmot, American kestral, nighthawk, turkey vulture, and golden eagle.

• *Suggested Trails for Nature Walks:* 1. The 0.8-mile Agua Piedra Trail. 2. The 1-mile El Nogal Nature Trail. 3. The 1-mile Pot Creek Trail. 4. The 2-mile La Jara Trail. 5. The 4-mile Sawmill Park Trail. 6. The 4.7-mile East Fork Trail. 7. The 5.7-mile Columbine Canyon Trail (easy-moderate). 8. The 3.5-mile Williams Lake Trail (moderate). 9. The 4.8-mile Elliott Barker Trail (moderate).

CIBOLA NATIONAL FOREST 2113 Osuna Road NE, Suite A, Albuquerque, NM 87113; (505)761-4650. 1,653,000 acres. Cibola National Forest is made up of several tracts of land in western and central New Mexico. It's home to a number of rugged mountain ranges with elevations surpassing 11,000 feet, along with precipitous cliffs, bluffs, rock outcroppings, and canyons.

There are mountain meadows with wildflowers, forests of spruce, fir, and aspen, as well as maple and oak, ponderosa pine, and pinyon-juniper woodlands. Wildlife includes pronghorn, black bear, white-tailed and mule deer, Rocky Mountain elk, mountain lion, bobcat, and prairie dog, along with great horned owl, peregrine falcon, red-tailed hawk, and golden eagle.

• *Suggested Trails for Nature Walks:* 1. The 0.3-mile La Cueva Trail. 2. The 0.8-mile Crest Nature Trail. 3. The 0.8-mile Summit Nature Trail (loop). 4. The 0.8-mile Sandia Cave Trail. 5. The 2-mile Tramway Trail. 6. The 2-mile loop via the Crest Trail, the Crest Spur Trail, and La Luz Trail. 7. The 4.8-mile Faulty Trail (easy-moderate). 8. The 2-mile Tree Spring Trail (moderate). 9. The 2.8-mile Osha Loop Trail (moderate). 10. The 5-mile 10 K Trail (moderate).

CHACO CULTURE NATIONAL HISTORICAL PARK Route 4, Box 6500, Bloomfield, NM 87413; (505)786-7014. 34,000 acres. Located in northwestern New Mexico's San Juan Basin, at an elevation of 6,200 feet, this national historical park protects Chaco Canyon, which includes ancient Anasazi Indian pueblo ruins, petroglyphs, and prehistoric roads.

NEW MEXICO

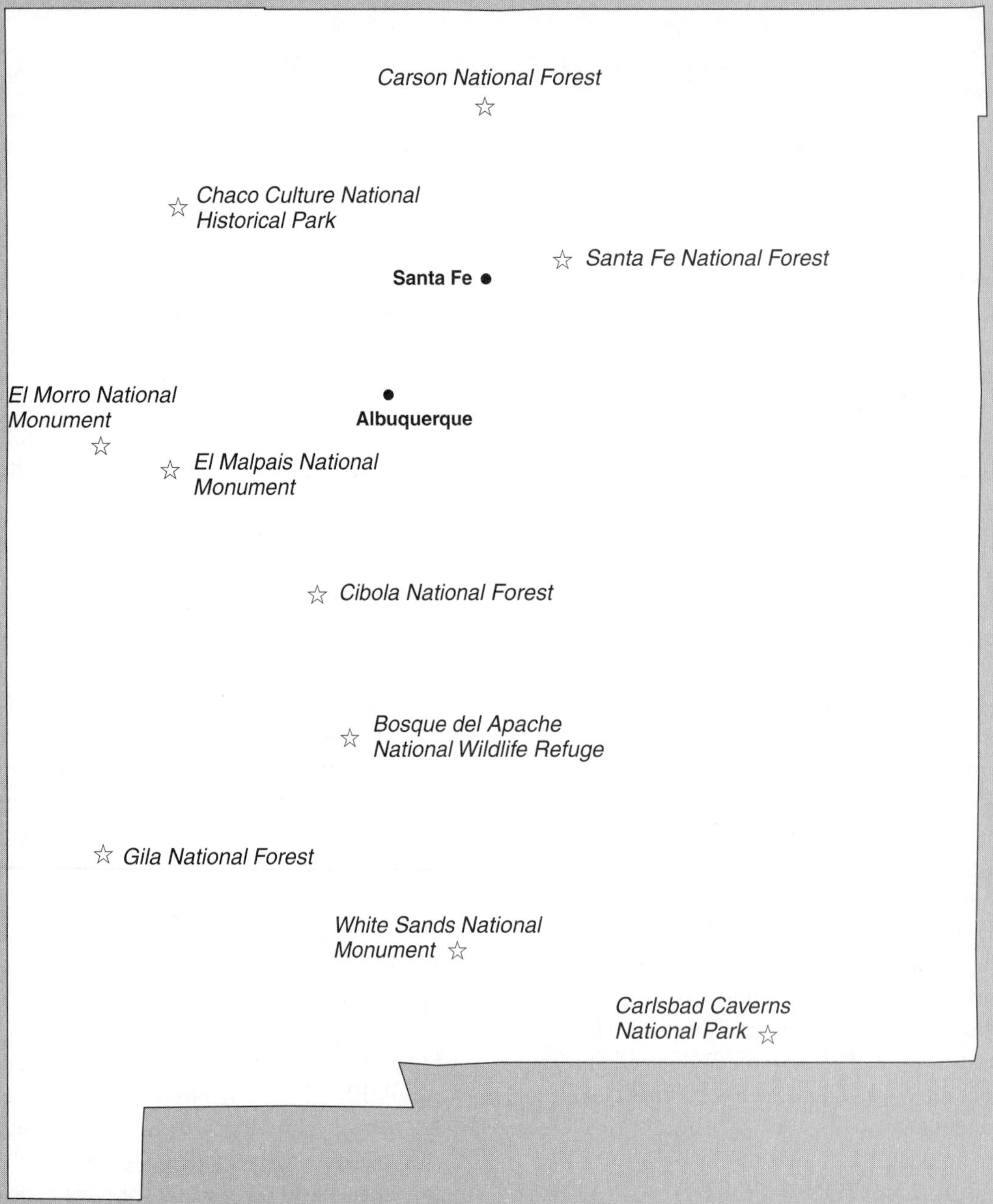

Carson National Forest

Chaco Culture National
Historical Park

Santa Fe National Forest

Santa Fe

El Morro National
Monument

Albuquerque

El Malpais National
Monument

Cibola National Forest

Bosque del Apache
National Wildlife Refuge

Gila National Forest

White Sands National
Monument

Carlsbad Caverns
National Park

There are also sandstone-topped mesas, cliffs, and talus slopes, with sagebrush, saltbush, and desert wildflowers among the vegetation. Wildlife includes coyote, bobcat, gray fox, badger, porcupine, jackrabbit, and prairie dog. A permit is required from the visitor center to use most trails.

• *Suggested Trails for Nature Walks:* 1. Eight short self-guiding trails lead through the ruins on the canyon floor. 2. The 1.5-mile Wijiji Trail. 3. The 2.2-mile Penasco Blanco Trail. 4. The 4.1-mile South Mesa Trail (loop). 5. The 4.8-mile Pueblo Alto Trail (loop).

GILA NATIONAL FOREST 3005 East Camino del Bosque, Silver City, NM 88061; (505)388-8201. 3,321,101 acres. Gila National Forest in western and southwestern New Mexico includes the rugged mountains of the Mongollon Range, with many elevations over 10,000 feet. Highest point is 10,895-foot Whitewater Baldy. There are also deep canyons, steep ridges with vistas, mesas, many streams, several rivers including the Gila River, and a few lakes.

Three designated wilderness areas in the forest total 790,000 acres. Vegetation ranges from pinyon-juniper grasslands and cactus to spruce, fir, pine, and aspen, along with alpine meadows. Among the wildlife are pronghorn, elk, mule deer, black bear, bighorn sheep, mountain lion, coyote, fox, and jackrabbit, plus snowy egret, great blue heron, osprey, and turkey vulture.

• *Suggested Trails for Nature Walks:* 1. The 2.5-mile Ft. Bayard Big Juniper Tree Trail. 2. The 5.4-mile Caledonia Trail. 3. The 1.9-mile Squaw Creek Trail (easy-moderate). 4. The 4.4-mile Rocky Point Trail (easy-moderate). 5. The 7-mile Frisco Box Trail (easy-moderate). 6. Portions of the 32-mile Gila River Trail (easy-moderate). 7. The 2.3-mile Catwalk National Recreation Trail (moderate). 8. The 4-mile Aspen Mountain Trail (moderate). 9. The 12-mile Crest Trail (moderate).

SANTA FE NATIONAL FOREST 1220 St. Francis Drive, P.O. Box 1689, Santa Fe, NM 87504; (505)988-6940. 1,587,181 acres. Consisting of lands both east and west of Santa Fe, in northern New Mexico, this national forest encompasses several mountain ranges including the Sangre de Cristo Mountains. Elevations vary from 5,300 feet in White Rock Canyon to 13,101 feet on Truchas Peak, second highest mountain in the state.

Four designated wilderness areas total 291,669 acres. Along with high peaks and steep canyons there are glacial lakes, streams, and rivers with sandstone bluffs, mountain meadows, grasslands, and forests of spruce-fir, ponderosa pine, aspen, oak, and pinyon-juniper. Wildlife includes mule deer, elk, black bear, bighorn sheep, mountain lion, blue grouse, and wild turkey.

• *Suggested Trails for Nature Walks:* 1. The 1.5-mile St. Johns-Atalaya Trail. 2. The 4-mile Borrego-Bear Wallow Loop (easy-moderate). 3. The 2.4-mile Damian Trail (easy-moderate). 4. The 3.9-mile Lucero Trail (easy-moderate). 5. The 8-mile Penas Negras Trail (easy-moderate). 6. The 10.7-mile Vacas Trail (easy-moderate). 7. The 3-mile Ponderosa Ridge-Atalaya Trail (moderate). 8. The 3.6-mile Palomas Trail (moderate). 9. The 2-mile Perchas Trail.

CARLSBAD CAVERNS NATIONAL PARK 3225 National Parks Highway, Carlsbad, NM 88220; (505)785-2232. 46,766 acres. Located in the rugged Guadalupe Mountains, in southeastern New Mexico's Chihuahuan Desert, this national park is famous for its enormous limestone caverns and caves—among them the Big Room, which is 1,800 feet long, 1,100 feet wide, and 255 feet high. There are some eighty-one caves altogether, including 29-mile-long Carlsbad Cavern.

Above ground the landscape consists of desert canyons, high plateaus, and rock formations, with elevations from 3,600 feet to 6,350 feet, and some 33,125 acres of designated wilderness. The wildlife includes a bat population of approximately 1 million, which emerges from the caves at dusk during summer. Several different ranger-guided cave walks are available.

• *Suggested Trails for Nature Walks:* 1. The 1.3-mile Red Tour (self-guided cavern walk). 2. The 3-mile Blue Tour (easy-moderate self-guided cavern walk). 3. The 1-mile Nature Trail. 4. The 1-mile North Boundary Trail (easy-moderate). 5. The 3-mile Rattlesnake Canyon Trail (easy-moderate). 6. The 3.5-mile Guano Road Trail (easy-moderate). 7. The 6-mile Yucca Canyon Trail (moderate).

BOSQUE del APACHE NATIONAL WILDLIFE REFUGE P.O. Box 1246, Socorro, NM 87801; (505)835-1828. 57,191 acres. Bosque del Apache National Wildlife Refuge is in the northern Chihuahuan Desert, 90 miles south of Albuquerque. There are three large designated wilderness areas, with wetlands including marshes and ponds, canals, and the Rio Grande River, as well as bluffs, ledges, and canyons.

Also here are fields, desert wildflowers, cottonwood and willow trees, saltbush and mesquite, prickly pear cactus and cholla. Among the birds are sandhill crane, whooping crane, snow goose, eagle, and red-tailed hawk; other wildlife includes mule deer, coyote, bobcat, fox, and porcupine.

• *Suggested Trails for Nature Walks:* 1. The 1.1-mile Bosque Trail (loop). 2. The 1.7-mile Rio Viejo Trail (loop). 3. The 1.5-mile Marsh Overlook Trail (loop). 4. The 2.2-mile Canyon Trail (easy-moderate loop).

EL MALPAIS NATIONAL MONUMENT P.O. Box 939, Grants, NM 87020; (505)287-3407. 114,000 acres. This national monument in west-central New Mexico features large areas of jagged-surfaced lava flows, with lava tubes (caves) and spatter cones, amid mountains and mesas, 500-foot sandstone bluffs and natural arches, petroglyphs and badlands scenery. Vegetation includes brushy areas with cacti, wildflowers, Douglas fir, and ponderosa pine. Among the wildlife are deer, pronghorn, bat, and wild turkey.

• *Suggested Trails for Nature Walks:* 1. The short Big Tubes Cairn Trail. 2. The 0.8-mile El Calderon Trail. 3. The 7.5-mile Zuna-Acoma Trail, which has a surface of rough lava.

EL MORRO NATIONAL MONUMENT Route 2, Box 43, Ramah, NM 87321; (505)783-4226. 1,300 acres. Situated in the western part of the state, El Morro National Monument features a 200-foot-high and steep-walled sandstone mesa with Anasazi pueblo ruins on top, as well as ancient petroglyphs and rock carvings. Vegetation includes grasslands, shrubs, and cacti, and there's an oasis beneath the cliffs.

• *Suggested Trails for Nature Walks:* 1. The 0.5-mile Inscription Rock Trail (loop). 2. The 2-mile Mesa Top Trail (loop).

WHITE SANDS NATIONAL MONUMENT P.O. Box 1086, Holloman AFB, NM 88330; (505)479-6124. 144,000 acres. This national monument is in the Tularosa Basin of the northern Chihuahuan Desert, in south-central New Mexico. Surrounded by mountains, the area is dominated by white gypsum sand dunes, and there's a dry Ice Age lake that only on occasion has water. Coyote, fox, porcupine, and rabbit are among the wildlife. The monument is within the White Sands Missile Range, and is subject to occasional closure. Ranger-led nature walks are available in summer.

• *Suggested Trails for Nature Walks:* 1. The 1-mile Big Dune Nature Trail. 2. The 2.3-mile Alkali Flat Trail.

Other Suitable Locations for Nature Walks in New Mexico

New Mexico has thirty-eight state parks, and twenty-nine of these locations feature nature or hiking trails. Information: New Mexico State Parks, P.O. Box 1147, Santa Fe, NM 87504; (505)827-7465.

Lincoln National Forest includes a network of trails. Information: Lincoln National Forest, 1101 New York Avenue, Alamogordo, NM 88310; (505)434-7200.

There are three national wildlife refuges in the state with trails. Information: U.S. Fish and Wildlife Service, P.O. Box 1306, Albuquerque, NM 87103; (505)766-3940.

Trails are available at some Bureau of Land Management areas. Information: BLM, New Mexico State Office, 1474 Rodeo Drive, Santa Fe, NM 87502; (505)438-7400.

A few U.S. Army Corps of Engineers lakes in New Mexico have trails. Information: Corps of Engineers, Albuquerque District, P.O. Box 1580, Albuquerque, NM 87103; (505)766-2724.

NEW YORK

Recommended Areas for Nature Walks

ADIRONDACK PARK c/o New York State Department of Environmental Conservation, 50 Wolf Road, Albany, NY 12233; (518)457-2500. 6,000,000 acres. Occupying a large portion of northern New York, the enormous Adirondack Park is the largest state park in the country, with 2,400,000 acres of the total consisting of protected lands designated as the Adirondack Forest Preserve. Terrain ranges from high and extremely rugged mountains in the northeast to hills and small mountains elsewhere.

Highest point is 5,344-foot Mt. Marcy. The park has a number of designated wilderness areas, with some 2,700 lakes, thousands of miles of rivers and streams, extensive marshlands, swamps, and bogs. There's a conifer and northern hardwood forest of spruce, fir, maple, beech, and birch, with rhododendron, azalea, and other wildflowers. Wildlife includes white-tailed deer, black bear, coyote, bobcat, fox, raccoon, porcupine, beaver, snowshoe hare, fisher, otter, and mink.

• *Suggested Trails for Nature Walks:* 1. The 0.4-mile Rankin Pond Trail. 2. The 0.5-mile Huntington Nature Trail. 3. The 1.1-mile Boreas River Trail. 4. The 1.1-mile Windfall Pond Trail. 5. The 1.3-mile Copperas Pond Trail. 6. The 2-mile Moore Trail. 7. The 2.8-mile Cascade Pond Trail. 8. The 4.3-mile Puffer Pond Trail. 9. The 5.4-mile Putnam Pond-Bear Pond-Rock Pond Loop. 10. The 132-mile Northville-Placid Trail.

CATSKILL PARK c/o New York State Department of Environmental Conservation, 50 Wolf Road, Albany, NY 12233; (518)457-2500. 700,000 acres. This huge state park stands between the Hudson and Delaware river valleys, in the southeastern part of the state. Over 250,000 acres are state-owned and designated the Catskill Forest Preserve, and there are several wilderness areas. Terrain is mountainous and often steep, with high ledges, rock formations, and a number of round-topped mountains.

Highest point is 4,180-foot Slide Mountain. In the park are dozens of large streams, a few lakes, and waterfalls including 260-foot Kaaterskill Falls, highest in the state. The forest is made up of mixed hardwoods and conifers, with oak, hickory, beech, maple, hemlock, spruce, and fir, as well as dogwood and rhododendron. Among the wildlife are deer, bear, coyote, fox, bobcat, porcupine, raccoon, woodchuck, beaver, snowshoe hare, and mink.

• *Suggested Trails for Nature Walks:* 1. The Escarpment Trail from North Lake to Artist's Rock (0.4 mile). 2. The 0.4-mile Kaaterskill Falls Trail. 3. The first 1.4 miles of the Trout Pond Trail. 4. The Phoenicia-East Branch Trail from Denning plus the Peekamoose-Table Trail to the Neversink River (1.6 miles). 5. The first 3 miles of the Colgate Lake Trail. 6. The Long Pond-Beaverkill Ridge Trail to Long Pond (3.6 miles). 7. The 11-mile Neversink-Hardenburgh Trail. 8. The Escarpment Trail to Inspiration Point (easy-moderate 1.9 miles). 9. The Devil's Path-Overlook-Echo Lake Trail (easy-moderate 4.5 miles).

NEW YORK
Wellesley Island State Park
Adirondack Park
Iroquois National Wildlife Refuge
Syracuse
Buffalo
Albany
Finger Lakes National Forest
Allegany State Park
Catskill Park
Mohonk Preserve
Minnewaska State Park Preserve
Ward Pound Ridge Reservation
Rockefeller State Park Preserve
New York City

MINNEWASKA STATE PARK PRESERVE P.O. Box 893, New Paltz, NY 12561; (914)255-0752. 12,000 acres. Located in the Shawangunk Mountains of southeastern New York, Minnewaska State Park features a number of rocky ridges and dramatic high cliffs, with giant boulders, talus, and deep ravines. Some elevations exceed 2,000 feet.

There are two notable lakes, along with number of streams, some high waterfalls, swamps, pitch pine barrens, and a forest of oak and birch, maple and basswood, with hemlock and mountain laurel, huckleberries and blueberries. Wildlife includes white-tailed deer, bobcat, fox, raccoon, porcupine, opossum, eagle, and hawk. A large system of carriage paths offers hilly but easy walks of any length.

• *Suggested Trails for Nature Walks:* 1. The 0.6-mile Beacon Hill Path. 2. The 0.8-mile Sunset Path. 3. The 1.9-mile Lake Minnewaska Circuit. 4. The 2.6-mile Lower Awosting Carriageway. 5. The Upper Awosting Carriageway to Lake Awosting (3.1 miles). 6. The Hamilton Point to Castle Point Carriageway (3.7 miles). 7. The Castle Point Carriageway to Awosting Beach (4.8 miles). 8. The 3.4-mile Lake Awosting Circuit. 9. The Millbrook Mountain Carriageway (3.1 miles).

MOHONK PRESERVE 1000 Mountain Rest Road, New Paltz, NY 12561; (914)255-0919. 5,500 acres. Open for public recreation, this private preserve in the Shawangunk Mountains of southeastern New York features numerous high cliffs and rock walls with talus, crevices and caves, giant boulders and rock formations. There's a forest of maple, oak, birch, pine, and hemlock, with mountain laurel and rhododendron, as well as other shrubs, ferns, mosses, and wildflowers. Among the wildlife are white-tailed deer, bobcat, black bear, fox, raccoon, porcupine, woodchuck, opossum, rabbit, grouse, hawk, and eagle.

• *Suggested Trails for Nature Walks:* A large network of old, well-marked carriage roads wind throught the preserve, offering many miles of easy walking and countless vistas.

FINGER LAKES NATIONAL FOREST Route 224, P.O. Box W, Montour Falls, NY 14865; (607)594-2750. 14,584 acres. Situated between Seneca and Cayuga lakes in New York's Finger Lakes region, Finger Lakes National Forest was established in 1983 and is administered by Vermont's Green Mountain National Forest. It's a region of low ridges and hills with ravines and streams, ponds, old pastures, shrublands, and forests. The Finger Lakes Trail, which is part of the North Country National Scenic Trail, passes through.

• *Suggested Trails for Nature Walks:* 1. The 1-mile Southslope Trail. 2. The 2.3-mile Potomac Trail. 3. The 2.5-mile Burnt Hill Trail. 4. The 4.5-mile No-Tan-Takto Trail. 5. The 1.3-mile Gorge Trail (easy-moderate). 6. A 2-mile section of the Finger Lakes Trail (easy-moderate). 7. The 12-mile Interlocken National Recreation Trail (easy-moderate).

WARD POUND RIDGE RESERVATION Box 461, Cross River, NY 10518; (914)763-3493. 4,700 acres. Ward Pound Ridge is in the southeastern corner of the state, northeast of New York City. It's a place of hilly terrain with low cliffs, rock formations, caves, deep hollows, small streams, and the Cross River. Highest point is 938 feet. Most of the area is hardwood forested and includes open fields, meadows, marshes, and hemlock ravines, and the reservation is home to 83 species of butterflies. Among the wildlife are white-tailed deer, bobcat, and river otter, along with heron, osprey, and bald eagle.

• *Suggested Trails for Nature Walks:* 1. The 1-mile Pink Trail. 2. The 2-mile Yellow Trail. 3. The 3-mile Green Trail. 4. The 4-mile Blue Trail. 5. The 4.7-mile White Trail. 6. The 5-mile Red Trail.

ALLEGANY STATE PARK Salamanca, NY 14779; (716)354-9121. 64,000 acres. Located on the Allegheny River and Allegheny Reservoir in western New York, this state park has hilly and sometimes mountainous terrain with rock outcroppings, ledges, and caves. There are streams, ponds, several lakes with sand beaches, meadows, and a forest of northern hardwoods, with oak and maple, beech and birch, hickory and tulip tree, pine and hemlock. Wildlife includes white-tailed deer, black bear, woodchuck, raccoon, porcupine, beaver, skunk, and bat. Guided nature walks are available.

• *Suggested Trails for Nature Walks:* 1. The 2-mile Red Jacket Nature Trail (loop). 2. The 2.5-mile Eastwood Meadows Trail (loop). 3. Several cross-country ski trails in the Art Roscoe Ski Touring Area offer easy walks. 4. The 0.5-mile Bear Springs Trail (easy-moderate). 5. The 3-mile Blacksnake Mountain Nature Trail (easy-moderate loop). 6. The 6.5-mile Beehunter Trail (easy-moderate).

WELLESLEY ISLAND STATE PARK Route 1, Box W437, Alexandria Bay, NY 13607; (315)482-2722. 2,636 acres. Wellesley Island State Park is on the St. Lawrence River's Alexandria Bay, in the Thousand Islands region of northwestern New York. Occupying the lands of a former farm, this hilly park includes a 600-acre nature preserve and a nature center. There are sandstone ledges and granite knobs, swamps and marshes, open fields and woodlands, wildflowers and ferns. Among the wildlife are white-tailed deer, beaver, snowshoe hare, woodcock, and grouse.

• *Suggested Trails for Nature Walks:* 1. The 0.5-mile North Loop Trail. 2. The 1.5-mile Sand Cove Loop. 3. The 2.5-mile Eel Bay Loop. 4. The 3-mile East Trail Loop. 5. The 5-mile Round the Peninsula Trail.

ROCKEFELLER STATE PARK PRESERVE P.O. Box 338, Tarrytown, NY 10591; (914)631-1470. 859 acres. Situated north of New York City, this state park is characterized by hills and low ridges with rock formations, meadows and old pastures, streams and wetlands, 24-acre Swan Lake, and the Pocantico River. There are wildflowers, mushrooms, ferns, and forests of oak, ash, tulip tree, and hemlock, with white-tailed deer among the wildlife. Most trails consist of wide carriage paths.

• *Suggested Trails for Nature Walks:* 1. The 1.3-mile Swan Lake Trail. 2. The 0.6-mile Overlook Trail. 3. The 0.6-mile Big Tree Trail. 4. The 0.8-mile Woodland Trail. 5. The 0.8-mile Witch's Spring Trail. 6. The 0.8-mile Brook Trail. 7. The 0.9-mile Ash Tree Trail. 8. The 1-mile David's Loop. 9. The 1.2-mile Pocantico River Loop. 10. The 2.1-mile 13 Bridges Trail.

IROQUOIS NATIONAL WILDLIFE REFUGE P.O. Box 517, Alabama, NY 14003; (716)948-5445. 10,818 acres. Located in western New York, with an additional 10,000 acres of state wildlife management areas on either side, the Iroquois National Wildlife Refuge protects migratory waterfowl and other birds including Canada goose, tundra swan, and many varieties of ducks. Among the mammals here are white-tailed deer, red and gray fox, raccoon, muskrat, beaver, opossum, cottontail rabbit, skunk, and mink. The refuge consists of swamps and marshes, wet meadows and pastures, shrubs and woodlands, with creeks as well as large water empoundments.

• *Suggested Trails for Nature Walks:* 1. The 1-mile Swallow Hollow Trail (loop). 2. The 1.2-mile Onondaga Trail. 3. The 1.6-mile Kanyoo Trail, which consists of two loops.

Other Suitable Locations for Nature Walks in New York

New York has 150 state parks, and many of these locations have nature or hiking trails. Information: New York State Parks, Empire State Plaza, Albany, NY 12238; (518)474-0456.

Trails are available at five national wildlife refuges in the state. Information: U.S. Fish and Wildlife Service, 300 Westgate Center Drive, Hadley, MA 01035.

There are several short trails at Fire Island National Seashore, 120 Laurel Street, Patchogue, NY 11772; (516)289-4810.

NORTH CAROLINA

Recommended Areas for Nature Walks

GREAT SMOKY MOUNTAINS NATIONAL PARK 107 Park Headquarters Road, Gatlinburg, TN 37738; (615)436-1200. 520,004 acres (275,900 acres in North Carolina). Straddling the border of North Carolina and Tennessee, this national park is named for the imposing and often misty mountains that dominate the landscape. It features one of the largest wilderness areas in the eastern United States, with an extraordinary range of flora and fauna and over 100,000 acres of virgin forest—more than any other eastern location.

This is also the most frequently visited national park in the country. Elevations range from 840 feet to 6,643 feet on Clingman's Dome, second highest mountain in the East. It has a temperate deciduous forest, with redbud and dogwood, rhododendron and mountain laurel, as well as spruce and fir trees at higher elevations. Streams and waterfalls are ubiquitous. Among the wildlife are white-tailed deer, black bear, wild boar, bobcat, mountain lion, and red fox. Naturalist-led walks are available. See the Tennessee chapter for Smokies trails in that state.

• *Suggested Trails for Nature Walks:* 1. The 0.3-mile Toms Branch Falls Trail. 2. The 0.5-mile Spruce-Fir Trail. 3. The 0.8-mile Balsam Mountain Trail. 4. The 0.8-mile Smokemont Trail. 5. The 1-mile Indian Creek Falls Trail. 6. The 1-mile Flat Creek Falls Trail. 7. The 0.8-mile Juneywhank Falls Trail (easy-moderate). 8. The 2-mile Kephart Prong Trail (moderate).

NANTAHALA NATIONAL FOREST P.O. Box 2750, Ashville, NC 28802; (704)257-4200. 516,000 acres. Stretching south from Great Smoky Mountains National Park in the southwest corner of the state, with lands alongside Tennessee and Georgia, this national forest includes many mountains, cliffs, and gorges, including 2,000-foot-deep Nantahala Gorge. There are bald mountains (treeless on top), several large lakes, and scores of streams with waterfalls, among them 250-foot Cullasaja Falls and 411-foot Whitewater Falls, said to be the highest in the eastern United States.

The forest has five designated wilderness areas. Of special interest is the 3,800-acre Joyce Kilmer Memorial Forest, which is part of the 14,900-acre Joyce Kilmer-Slickrock Wilderness and features virgin trees. Elsewhere are hardwood forests of oak, beech, and maple, with pine and hemlock, plus mountain laurel, azalea, and rhododendron. Wildlife includes white-tailed deer, black bear, fox, raccoon, hawk, and turkey vulture.

• *Suggested Trails for Nature Walks:* 1. The 0.5-mile Snowbird Nature Trail. 2. The 0.7-mile Pickens Nose Trail. 3. The 0.7-mile Lewellyn Cove Nature Trail (loop). 4. The 0.8-mile Wasilik Poplar Trail. 5. The 1-mile Whitewater Falls Trail. 6. The 1.1-mile Clifftop Nature Trail. 7. The 1.2-mile Joyce Kilmer Memorial Trail. 8. The 2.2-mile Chattooga River Trail (loop). 9. The 2.4-mile Jackrabbit Mountain Trail. 10. The 17.4-mile Tsali Trail (easy-moderate).

NORTH CAROLINA
Medoc Mountain
State Park
Pisgah National
Forest
Winston-Salem
William B. Umstead
State Park
Duke Power State Park
Raleigh
Great Smoky Mountains
National Park
Charlotte
Croatan National Forest
Uwharrie National Forest
Nantahala
National Forest
Morrow Mountain State
Park
Carolina Beach State
Park

PISGAH NATIONAL FOREST P.O. Box 2750, Ashville, NC 28802; (704)257-4200. 495,000 acres. Pisgah National Forest is situated alongside the Tennessee border in northwest North Carolina. It's an area of mountainous terrain with many "balds" (grassy-summited mountains), meadows, steep ridges, cliffs, deep gorges, streams, and waterfalls.

The forest consists of hardwoods with oak and maple, poplar and birch, pine and spruce, fir and hemlock, as well as rhododendron and mountain laurel, flame azalea, and blueberry. Three designated wilderness areas total 37,370 acres. Wildlife includes white-tailed deer, black bear, fox, bobcat, and raccoon, along with grouse, wild turkey, owl, hawk, and turkey vulture.

• *Suggested Trails for Nature Walks:* 1. The 0.6-mile Pisgah Environmental Trail. 2. The 0.7-mile Moore Cove Falls Trail. 3. The 1.5-mile Cloudland Trail. 4. The 1.6-mile Spring Creek Nature Trail. 5. The 2-mile Shut-In Creek Trail. 6. The 2.4-mile Woodruff Branch Trail. 7. The 3-mile Big Laurel Creek Trail. 8. The 3.2-mile Sam Knob Trail. 9. The 3-mile North Slope Loop Trail. 10. The 5-mile Pink Beds Loop Trail.

UWHARRIE NATIONAL FOREST Route 3, Box 470, Troy, NC 27371; (919)576-6391. 46,000 acres. Located in the Piedmont region of central North Carolina, and including one designated wilderness area, Uwharrie National Forest has a landscape of hills and small mountains with rocky ridges, streams and rivers, pine and hardwood forests, as well as ferns and wildflowers, dogwood and mountain laurel. Among the wildlife are white-tailed deer, fox, raccoon, and rabbit, along with quail, wild turkey, owl, hawk, and bald eagle.

• *Suggested Trails for Nature Walks:* 1. The 1.4-mile Hannahs Creek Trail. 2. The 2-mile Denson's Creek Nature Trail (loop). 3. The 3.2-mile Robbins Branch Trail. 4. The 3.4-mile Dutch John Trail. 5. The 5.6-mile Badin Lake Trail. 6. The 33-mile Uwharrie Trail (moderate).

CROATAN NATIONAL FOREST 141 East Fisher Avenue, New Bern, NC 28560; (919)638-5628. Croatan National Forest lies alongside the Atlantic on eastern North Carolina's coastal plain. It features forests, savannas with wildflowers, swamps, marshes, bogs, several sizable lakes, and a number of creeks and rivers, among them the White Oak, Neuse, and Newport rivers. There are four designated wilderness areas totaling 30,010 acres. Common trees include longleaf and loblolly pine, oak, and cypress, with gum and poplar. White-tailed deer, black bear, alligator, osprey, bald eagle, northern harrier, and wild turkey are among the wildlife.

• *Suggested Trails for Nature Walks:* 1. The 0.6-mile Island Creek Trail. 2. The 1-mile Hunter Creek Trail. 3. The 1.4-mile Cedar Point Tideland National Recreation Trail. 4. The 21-mile Neusiok Trail, which runs from the Neuse to the Newport River.

WILLIAM B. UMSTEAD STATE PARK Route 8, Box 130, Raleigh, NC 27612; (919)787-3033. 5,381 acres. William B. Umstead State Park is located near Raleigh in the north-central part of the state. The park features the 50-acre Piedmont Beech Natural Area and the Crabtree Natural Area, along with three man-made lakes, some streams, and forests of pine and hardwoods, with rhododendron and mountain laurel, as well as many wildflowers in season. Wildlife includes white-tailed deer, raccoon, and beaver.

• *Suggested Trails for Nature Walks:* 1. The 0.5-mile Inspiration Trail. 2. The 0.5-mile Beech Trail. 3. The 0.8-mile Pott's Branch Trail. 4. The 1-mile Oak Rock Trail. 5. The 2.2-mile Sal's Branch Trail (easy-moderate). 6. The 3-mile Loblolly Trail (easy-moderate). 7. The 4.5-mile Company Mill Trail (easy-moderate). 8. The 6.5-mile Sycamore Trail (easy-moderate).

MEDOC MOUNTAIN STATE PARK P.O. Box 400, Hollister, NC 27844; (919)445-2280. 2,300 acres. This park in east-central North Carolina is located on the remnant of an ancient mountain, but now the highest elevation here is just 325 feet. There are small ravines with some steep slopes and granite outcroppings, a couple of major streams including Little Fishing Creek, and open meadows with withflowers; as well as forests of pine and hardwoods, with sweetgum, oak, birch, alder, and mountain laurel. Among the wildlife are gray fox, opossum, river otter, red-shouldered hawk, barred owl, and wild turkey.

• *Suggested Trails for Nature Walks:* 1. The 0.8-mile Stream Loop Trail. 2. The 1.3-mile Discovery Loop Trail. 3. The 1-mile Dam Site Loop Trail. 4. The 3-mile Bluff Loop Trail. 5. The 3-mile Summit Loop Trail (easy-moderate).

MORROW MOUNTAIN STATE PARK 49104 Morrow Mountain Road, Albemarle, NC 28001; (704)982-4402. 4,640 acres. Located on the hill-size ridges of the Uwharrie Mountains in west-central North Carolina, this state park includes some steep hills with rock outcroppings, hardwood forests of oak, poplar, hickory, and beech, along with pine, mountain laurel, and azalea. There are also streams and swamps, with man-made Lake Tillary and the Yadkin, Pee Dee, and Uwharrie rivers. White-tailed deer, red-tailed hawk, and osprey are among the wildlife.

• *Suggested Trails for Nature Walks:* 1. The 0.6-mile Three Rivers Trail. 2. The 0.6-mile Quarry Trail. 3. The 0.6-mile Laurel Trail. 4. The 0.8-mile Mountain Loop Trail. 5. The 2.6-mile Rocks Trail. 6. The 3-mile Morrow Mountain Trail (easy-moderate). 7. The 4.1-mile Fall Mountain Trail (easy-moderate). 8. The 2-mile Hattaway Mountain Trail (moderate). 9. The 2.8-mile Sugarloaf Mountain Trail (moderate).

CAROLINA BEACH STATE PARK P.O. Box 475, Carolina Beach, NC 28428; (910)458-8206. 1,773 acres. Carolina Beach State Park is on Pleasure Island, between Cape Fear River and the Atlantic Ocean, in southeastern North Carolina. Terrain here is mostly flat with some sandhills and dunes, tidal marsh, swamps, savannas, and three ponds. Vegetation includes grasses and shrubs, a forest of loblolly and longleaf pine, live oak and cypress, as well as Venus flytrap and pitcher plant, orchid and water lily. Among the wildlife are alligator, gray fox, opossum, river otter, fiddler crab, brown pelican, woodpecker, and osprey.

• *Suggested Trails for Nature Walks:* 1. The 0.5-mile Fly-Trap Trail (loop). 2. The 0.8-mile Swamp Trail. 3. The 1-mile Campground Trail. 4. The 3-mile Sugarloaf Trail (loop). 5. The Snow's Cut Trail.

DUKE POWER STATE PARK 159 Inland Sea Lane, Troutman, NC 28166; (704)528-6350. 1,362 acres. This state park is situated on the northeastern shore of man-made, 32,510-acre Lake Norman in west-central North Carolina, on land donated by the Duke Power Company. There are 13 miles of shoreline, as well as a 33-acre artificial lake, streams, some pine forest with stands of oak and hickory, birch and beech, sweetgum and dogwood, plus mountain laurel. Wildlife includes white-tailed deer, gray and red fox, raccoon, muskrat, and opossum, as well as osprey, red-tailed hawk, and waterfowl.

• *Suggested Trails for Nature Walks:* 1. The 0.8-mile Alder Trail (loop). 2. The 5.4-mile Lakeshore Trail (loop).

Other Suitable Locations for Nature Walks in North Carolina

Almost all of North Carolina's thirty-five state parks and recreation areas have trails. Information: Division of Parks and Recreation, P.O. Box 27687, Raleigh, NC 27611; (919)733-PARK.

In the state are six national wildlife refuges with trails. Information: U.S. Fish and Wildlife Service, 1875 Century Boulevard, Atlanta, GA 30345.

A number of areas along the Blue Ridge Parkway in North Carolina and Virginia have trails. Information: Blue Ridge Parkway, 200 BB&T Building, One Pack Square, Asheville, NC 28801; (704)259-0779.

The Nature Conservancy manages over 100 preserves and projects in the state, some of which feature trails. Most are open to the public through guided field trips. Information: The Nature Conservancy, North Carolina Chapter, Carr Mill, Suite D-12, Carrboro, NC 27510; (919)967-7007.

There are trails at several areas managed by the U.S. Army Corps of Engineers. Information: Corps of Engineers, Wilmington District, P.O. Box 1890, Wilmington, NC 28402; (919)251-4827.

NORTH DAKOTA

Recommended Areas for Nature Walks

THEODORE ROOSEVELT NATIONAL PARK P.O. Box 7, Medora, ND 58645; (701) 623-4466. 70,416 acres. Named after our turn-of-the-century conservationist-president, who founded the Forest Service, Theodore Roosevelt National Park consists of two tracts of land in the western part of the state. It features colorful badlands, buttes, tablelands, canyons, and many petrified trees.

There are areas of prairie as well as stands of hardwoods, with elm and cottonwood, juniper and sagebrush. The Little Missouri River passes through the park, and wildlife includes bison, wild horse, elk, pronghorn, deer, mountain sheep, fox, and prairie dog. Naturalist-led walks are available in the summer.

• *Suggested Trails for Nature Walks:* 1. The 0.6-mile Ridgeline Nature Trail (loop). 2. The 0.8-mile Coal Vein Trail. 3. The 1.1-mile Squaw Creek Nature Trail. 4. The 1.6-mile Caprock Coulee Nature Trail. 5. The 3.3-mile Upper Caprock Coulee Trail. 6. The 3.7-mile Jones Creek Trail. 7. The 11-mile Buckhorn Trail (easy-moderate loop). 8. The 16-mile Achenbach Trail (easy-moderate loop). 9. The 16-mile Petrified Forest Trail (easy-moderate loop).

CROSS RANCH STATE PARK / CROSS RANCH NATURE PRESERVE HC 2, Box 152, Sanger, ND 58567; (701)794-3731. This 560-acre state park and adjacent 6,000-acre Nature Conservancy preserve lie alongside the Missouri River in central North Dakota. Terrain is hilly to flat, and the area includes prairie as well as bottomland forest. Bison, deer, hawk, and wild turkey are among the wildlife.

• *Suggested Trails for Nature Walks:* 1. The 2-mile Cross Ranch Nature Trail. 2. The 2.6-mile Matah Trail (loop). 3. The 4-mile Ma-Ak-Oti Trail (loop). 4. The 3-mile Cottonwood Trail. 5. The 2.1-mile Bison Trail. 6. The 2.3-mile Bob Levis Trail.

LITTLE MISSOURI STATE PARK c/o Cross Ranch State Park, HC 2, Box 152, Sanger, ND 58567; (701)794-3731. 5,749 acres. This wild state park is on the Little Missouri River near enormous Lake Sakakawea, in west-central North Dakota. It's a region of rugged badlands scenery with some hilly and steep terrain. Vegetation includes cactus and wild lily, and among the wildlife are bobcat, coyote, fox, and golden eagle.

• *Suggested Trails for Nature Walks:* 1. The 0.5-mile Nature Trail. 2. The Valley Way Trail (loop). 3. The 3-mile Travois Trail. 4. The 4-mile Wagon Trail. 5. The 5-mile TX Trail. 6. The 8-mile Jim Creek Trail. 7. The 2.5-mile Indian Trail (easy-moderate). 8. The 1.5-mile Eagle's Nest Trail (easy-moderate).

ICELANDIC STATE PARK 13571 Highway 5, Cavelier, ND 58220; (701)265-4561. 912 acres. Located in a wooded river valley in northeastern North Dakota, Icelandic State Park features the 200-acre Gunlogson Nature Preserve, 220-acre Lake Renwick, and the Tongue River.

NORTH DAKOTA

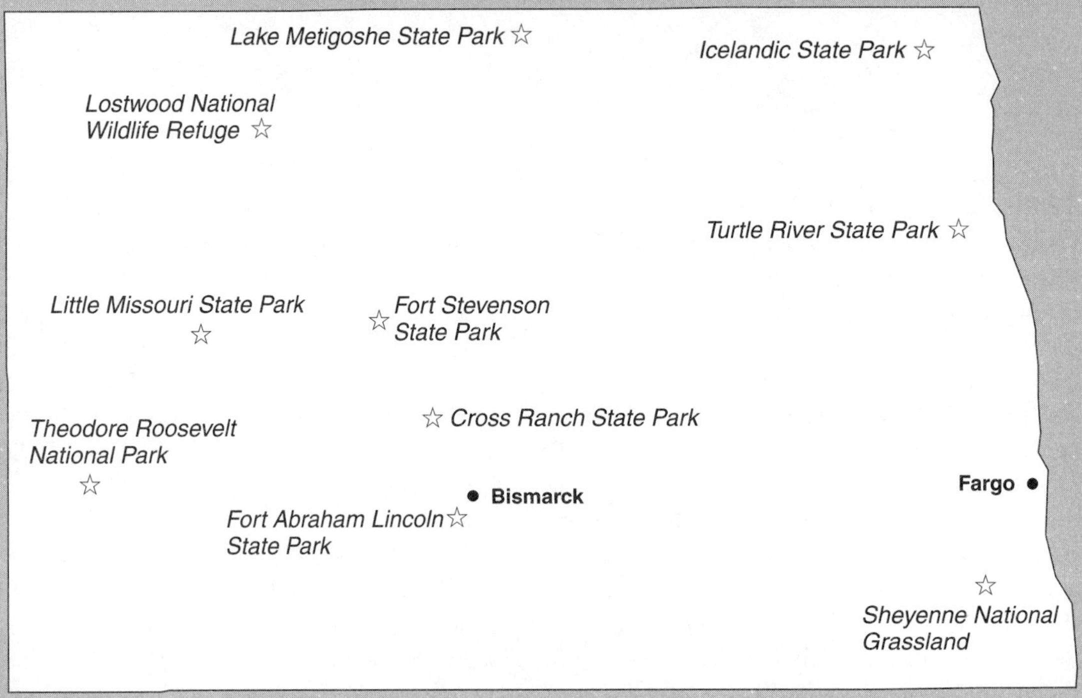

Lake Metigoshe State Park ☆
Icelandic State Park ☆
Lostwood National Wildlife Refuge ☆
Turtle River State Park ☆
Little Missouri State Park ☆
☆ Fort Stevenson State Park
☆ Cross Ranch State Park
Theodore Roosevelt National Park ☆
● **Bismarck**
Fargo ●
Fort Abraham Lincoln ☆ State Park
☆ Sheyenne National Grassland

There are also marshlands and oak woodlands with elm, ash, and boxelder, plus ferns. Wildlife includes white-tailed deer and beaver.

• *Suggested Trails for Nature Walks:* 1. The 0.8-mile Wildwood National Recreation Trail. 2. The 0.5-mile Shady Springs Trail. 3. The 1.5-mile Basswood Trail. 4. The 2-mile Settlers Trail.

TURTLE RIVER STATE PARK Route 1, Box 9A, Arvilla, ND 58214; (701)594-4445. 784 acres. Situated in eastern North Dakota, this state park has hilly woodlands of mixed hardwoods, prairie grasslands with wildflowers, wetlands, and the Turtle River, which winds throughout the park. Among the wildlife are deer, moose, raccoon, beaver, woodchuck, and skunk, along with great blue heron and migratory waterfowl.

• *Suggested Trails for Nature Walks:* 1. The 0.7-mile Centennial Accessible Trail. 2. The 0.8-mile Nature Trail. 3. In the southwest portion of the park is a network of horse trails open to foot travel.

FORT STEVENSON STATE PARK Route 1, Box 262, Garrison, ND 58540; (701)337-5576. 438 acres. Central North Dakota's Fort Stevenson State Park is on the north shore of man-made Lake Sakakawea, a 178-mile-long reservoir, which is said to be the largest in the country. The park is named after a frontier fort dating back to the late 1800s, and includes a beach and a prairie dog town.

• *Suggested Trails for Nature Walks:* 1. The 0.3-mile Nature Trail. 2. The three interconnecting Fitness and Recreation Trails that are 1, 2, and 3 miles long, respectively.

LAKE METIGOSHE STATE PARK #2 Lake Metigoshe State Park, Bottineau, ND 58318; (701)263-4651. 1,551 acres. This state park is in the Turtle Mountains of northern North Dakota, on the Canadian border. It's a hilly area with a number of lakes, sandy beaches, and marshes, as well as forests of oak and aspen, elm and birch. Wildlife includes moose, elk, white-tailed deer, coyote, beaver, raccoon, woodchuck, osprey, eagle, and loon.

• *Suggested Trails for Nature Walks:* The 3-mile Old Oak National Recreation Trail.

LOSTWOOD NATIONAL WILDLIFE REFUGE RR 2, Box 98, Kenmare, ND 58746; (701)848-2722. 26,900 acres. Lostwood National Wildlife Refuge in northwest North Dakota has rolling terrain with mixed grass prairie, brushlands, stands of trees, marshes, sloughs, and shallow lakes. An area of 5,577 acres has been designated the Lostwood Wilderness Area. The refuge is host to such birds as blue-winged teal, piping plover, sharp-tailed grouse, mallard, canvasback, and Canada goose, as well as other wildlife including deer, badger, coyote, fox, muskrat, jackrabbit, and mink.

• *Suggested Trails for Nature Walks:* A 5-mile trail loop, open only during summer months, leads past several of the lakes.

FORT ABRAHAM LINCOLN STATE PARK Route 2, Box 139, Mandan, ND 58554; (701)663-9571. 1,006 acres. Located on the Missouri and Heart rivers in south-central North Dakota, Fort Abraham State Park includes the ruins of a mid-1600s Mandan Indian village as well as a late 1800s fort where Lt. Col. George Custer was stationed. There are hills and bluffs with prairie grasslands, low brush, and stands of cottonwood and willow, oak and ash, elm and boxelder trees near the river. Among the wildlife are deer, fox, coyote, porcupine, and skunk, along with sandhill crane, sharp-tailed grouse, bald and golden eagle, red-tailed hawk, and turkey vulture. Nature walks are available in summer.

• *Suggested Trails for Nature Walks:* 1. The 0.8-mile Ridgeline Nature Trail (loop). 2. The short Mandan Indian Village Trail. 3. Around the partially reconstructed fort are self-guided interpretive trails.

SHEYENNE NATIONAL GRASSLAND P.O. Box 946, Lisbon, ND 58054; (701)683-

4342. 70,200 acres. Situated near the Sheyenne River in the southeastern part of the state, this national grassland consists of rolling hills and plains with tallgrass prairie and savanna, shrubs and wildflowers, stands of bur oak and aspen, basswood and elm, along with a few streams. Wildlife includes white-tailed deer, raccoon, jackrabbit, prairie chicken, sharp-tailed grouse, and wild turkey.

• *Suggested Trails for Nature Walks:* The North Country National Scenic Trail, which will eventually be 3,200 miles long, winds through the grassland for about 25 miles. Access is available at several road crossings.

Other Suitable Locations for Nature Walks in North Dakota

North Dakota has nineteen state parks and recreation areas, and thirteen of these locations have trails. Information: North Dakota Parks and Recreation Department, 1835 Bismarck Expressway, Bismarck, ND 58504; (701)328-5357.

All of North Dakota's three state forests have trails. Information: North Dakota Forest Service, First and Brander, Bottineau, ND 58318; (701)228-5422.

There are trails in Little Missouri National Grasslands. Information: USDA-Forest Service, 1511 East Interstate Avenue, Bismarck, ND 58501; (701)250-4443.

Six national wildlife refuges and a national game preserve in the state feature trails. Information: U.S. Fish and Wildlife Service, 1500 East Capitol Avenue, Bismarck, ND 58501; (701)250-4418.

Trails are available on some local U.S. Army Corps of Engineers lands. Information: Corps of Engineers, St. Paul District, 180 E. Kellog Boulevard, St. Paul, MN 55101, (612)220-0325; Corps of Engineers, Omaha District, 215 North 17th Street, Omaha, NE 68102, (402)221-4137.

OHIO

Recommended Areas for Nature Walks

CUYAHOGA VALLEY NATIONAL RECREATION AREA 15610 Vaughn Road, Brecksville, OH 44141; (216)650-4636. 33,000 acres. Situated in northeastern Ohio's Cuyahoga Valley, between Cleveland and Akron, this national recreation area features 22 miles of the winding Cuyahoga River. Terrain is hilly with low ridges and sandstone ledges, plateaus and ravines, areas of floodplain, freshwater ponds and marshes, and streams with waterfalls.

There are also meadows and pastures, wildflowers, as well as deciduous and conifer forests, with maple, beech, oak, hickory, sycamore, willow, tulip tree, hemlock, and pine. Among the wildlife are white-tailed deer, red fox, raccoon, beaver, ruffed grouse, and hawk. Within the area's boundaries are Brecksville and Bedford reservations, along with Virginia Kendall Park.

• *Suggested Trails for Nature Walks:* 1. The 0.5-mile Visitor Center Loop Trail. 2. The 1-mile Lake Trail (loop). 3. The 1.5-mile Oak Hill Trail (loop). 4. The 2.5-mile Cross-Country Trail (loop). 5. The 2.8-mile Tree Farm Trail (loop). 6. The 19.5-mile Ohio & Erie Towpath Trail, which extends the length of the area. 7. The 9.8-mile Bike and Hike Trail. 8. The 3.3-mile Old Carriage Trail (easy-moderate). 9. The 4.4-mile Salt Run Trail (easy-moderate loop). 10. A 9.6-mile section of the 1,200-mile Buckeye Trail (easy-moderate), which loops around the state.

WAYNE NATIONAL FOREST 811 Constitution Avenue, Bedford, IN 47421; (812)275-5987. 178,000 acres. Wayne National Forest consists of four large tracts on the Allegheny Plateau of southern and southeastern Ohio, with some lands alongside the Ohio River. It's co-administered with Hoosier National Forest, with headquarters in Indiana. The region includes wetlands, lakes and ponds, streams, and rivers, amid hilly terrain featuring ridges, rock formations, outcroppings, rock shelters, and caves.

There are also open meadows with wildflowers, white pine plantations, and forests of oak, maple, cherry, poplar, walnut, and birch, including old-growth stands—along with cedar and pine, dogwood and redbud, plus blueberries and blackberries. Among the wildlife are white-tailed deer, ruffed grouse, wood duck, great blue heron, owl, red-tailed hawk, and wild turkey.

• *Suggested Trails for Nature Walks:* 1. The 0.5-mile Whiskey Run Trail (loop). 2. The 0.8-mile Rock House Trail. 3. The 3.2-mile Lamping Homestead Trail, consisting of two loops. 4. The 5-mile Covered Bridge Trail. 5. The 8-mile Lakeshore Trail (loop). 6. The 3.4-mile Scenic River Trail (easy-moderate). 7. The 6-mile Symmes Creek Trail (easy-moderate loop). 8. The 7-mile Ohio View Trail (easy-moderate). 9. The 8-mile Morgan Sisters Trail (easy-moderate), made up of three loops. 10. The 15-mile Wildcat Hollow Trail (easy-moderate), which consists of two loops.

SALT FORK STATE PARK 14755 Cadiz Road, Lore City, OH 43755; (614)439-3521.

OHIO
Cleveland
Cuyahoga Valley National Recreation Area
Quail Hollow State Park
Beaver Creek State Park
Salt Fork State Park
Columbus
John Bryan State Park
Burr Oak State Park
Hueston Woods State Park
Wayne National Forest
Lake Hope State Park
Strouds Run State Park
Cincinnati

17,229 acres. Located in the east-central part of the state, Salt Fork is the largest of Ohio's state parks. It's in an area of rolling hills and valleys, with meadows and hardwood forest, many streams, and Salt Fork Lake, a 2,952-acre reservoir. Wildlife includes white-tailed deer, red fox, raccoon, muskrat, ruffed grouse, and wild turkey.

• *Suggested Trails for Nature Walks:* 1. The 0.7-mile Sunshine Brook Nature Trail. 2. The 0.8-mile Morgans Knob Loop Trail. 3. The 1-mile Valley Brook Loop Trail. 4. The 1-mile Hillcrest Trail. 5. The 1-mile Beach Point Loop Trail. 6. The 1-mile Pine Crest Loop Trail. 7. The 1.5-mile Deer Run Trail. 8. The 1.8-mile Stone House Loop Trail. 9. The 2-mile Gunn's Glen Trail. 10. The 2-mile Shadebush Trail.

HUESTON WOODS STATE PARK Route 1, College Corner, OH 45003; (513)523-6347. 3,596 acres. Situated in southwestern Ohio, Hueston Woods State Park is especially notable for a 200-acre stand of virgin beech and maple forest, with wildflowers and ferns, along with 625-acre Acton Lake. The park has a nature center, and guided walks are available.

• *Suggested Trails for Nature Walks:* 1. The 0.7-mile Blue Heron Trail. 2. The 0.7-mile Gallion Run Trail. 3. The 0.8-mile Sycamore Trail. 4. The 0.8-mile Sugar Bush Trail. 5. The 0.9-mile Cedar Falls Trail. 6. The 1-mile Equisetum Trail. 7. The 1.5-mile West Shore Trail. 8. The 1.5-mile Indian Mound Trail. 9. The 1.8-mile Big Woods Trail. 10. The 2.2-mile Mud Lick Trail.

JOHN BRYAN STATE PARK 3790 State Route 370, Yellow Springs, OH 45387; (513)767-1274. 755 acres. This park in western Ohio features a stretch of the Little Miami National Scenic River, with a limestone gorge, cliffs, rock formations, and small waterfalls. Common trees include maple, oak, cottonwood, and sycamore. Adjacent to the park are the Clifton Gorge Nature Preserve and the Glen Helen Nature Preserve.

• *Suggested Trails for Nature Walks:* 1. The 0.7-mile Orton Memorial Trail. 2. The 0.5-mile Horace Mann Trail. 3. The 1-mile Camp Trail. 4. The 1.2-mile Arboretum Trail. 5. The 1.2-mile South Gorge Trail. 6. The 1.3-mile John L. Rich Trail. 7. The 1.3-mile Stagecoach Trail. 8. The 2-mile North Rim Trail.

QUAIL HOLLOW STATE PARK 13340 Congress Lake Avenue, Hartville, OH 44632; (216)877-6652. 698 acres. Located in northeastern Ohio, Quail Hollow State Park has rolling hills with areas of tallgrass prairie, two ponds, marshes and swamps, peat bogs, and forests of deciduous trees as well as conifers. Wildlife includes white-tailed deer, red fox, raccoon, and beaver.

• *Suggested Trails for Nature Walks:* 1. The 0.8-mile Sedge Marsh Trail. 2. The 0.8-mile Peat Bog Trail. 3. The 1.3-mile Coniferous Forest Trail. 4. The 1.3-mile Deciduous Forest Trail. 5. The 1.5-mile Woodland Swamp Trail. 6. The 1.5-mile Meadowlands Trail. 7. The 1.5-mile Beaver Lodge Trail.

LAKE HOPE STATE PARK Zaleski, OH 45698; (614)596-5253. 3,103 acres. Surrounded by the lands of 18,200-acre Zaleski State Forest in southeastern Ohio, this state park includes some rugged topography, with deep gorges and steep ridges, a 120-acre lake, oak-hickory forest, and wildflowers. White-tailed deer, beaver, and wild turkey are among the wildlife.

• *Suggested Trails for Nature Walks:* 1. The 0.5-mile Buckeye Nature Trail. 2. The 0.5-mile Red Oak Trail. 3. The 1-mile Tulip Tree Trail. 4. The 1.5-mile Olds Hollow Nature Trail. 5. The 1.5-mile Hebron Hollow Trail. 6. The 2-mile Little Sandy Trail. 7. The 3-mile Peninsula Trail. 8. The 3.5-mile Hope Furnace Trail.

STROUDS RUN STATE PARK 11661 State Park Road, Athens, OH 45701; (614)592-2302. 2,606 acres. Strouds Run State Park is in southeastern Ohio, near Athens. Terrain is hilly and sometimes rough, with steep ravines, sandstone outcroppings, streams including Strouds Run, 161-acre Dow Lake, and some ancient Indian burial mounds. There are hardwood forests of oak and hickory, maple and beech, with tulip tree and dogwood. Among the wildlife are white-tailed deer, fox, opossum, raccoon, and wild turkey.

• *Suggested Trails for Nature Walks:* 1. The 0.5-mile Sycamore Valley Trail. 2. The 1-mile Beaver Pond Trail. 3. The 1-mile Indian Mound Trail. 4. The 1-mile Pioneer Cemetery Trail. 5. The 1.5-mile Homestead Trail. 6. The 1.5-mile Vista Point Trail. 7. The 2-mile Broken Rock Trail. 8. The 7-mile Lakeview Trail.

BURR OAK STATE PARK 12000 Burr Oak Road, Glouster, OH 45732; (614)767-3570. 2,592 acres. Adjacent to lands of Wayne National Forest and the Sunday Creek Wildlife Area, this park in southeastern Ohio is centered on 664-acre Burr Oak Lake, which was created by damming Sunday Creek. It's an area of hills, ridges, and valleys, with wildflowers and forests of oak, hickory, and other hardwoods. Wildlife includes white-tailed deer, ruffed grouse, and wild turkey.

• *Suggested Trails for Nature Walks:* 1. The 0.5-mile Chipmunk Trail. 2. The 1.5-mile Red Fox Trail. 3. The 1.5-mile Ravine Trail. 4. The 3.5-mile Lakeview Trail. 5. The 19-mile Backpack Trail (easy-moderate). 6. The 3-mile Buckeye Cave Trail (moderate).

BEAVER CREEK STATE PARK 12021 Echo Dell Road, East Liverpool, OH 43920; (216) 385-3091. 3,038 acres. This hilly park in eastern Ohio includes a steep-walled gorge with rocky cliffs and 4 miles of Little Beaver Creek, a national wild and scenic river. There are also smaller streams with waterfalls, as well as forests of hemlock, birch, and yew, with mountain laurel. White-tailed deer, black bear, red fox, raccoon, and wild turkey are among the wildlife.

• *Suggested Trails for Nature Walks:* 1. The 1-mile Fisherman's Trail. 2. The 1.5-mile Lusk Lock Trail. 3. The 1-mile Pine Ridge Trail. 4. The 2.5-mile Vondergreen Loop. 5. The 3.5-mile Dogwood Trail (moderate). 6. The 4.5-mile Vondergreen Trail (moderate).

Other Suitable Locations for Nature Walks in Ohio

Ohio has seventy-two state parks, all but eleven of which have nature and hiking trails. Information: Division of Parks & Recreation, 1952 Belcher Drive, Building C-3, Columbus, OH 43224; (614)265-7000.

There are eighteen state forests, and several of them have trails. Information: Division of Forestry, 4383 Fountain Square, Columbus, OH 43224; (614)265-6694.

Trails are available at the Ottawa National Wildlife Refuge, 14000 West State Route 2, Oak Harbor, OH 43449; (419)898-0014.

A number of areas with lakes and dams that are administered by the U.S. Army Corps of Engineers feature trails. Information: Corps of Engineers, Louisville District, P.O. Box 59, Louisville, KY 40201, (502)582-6292; Corps of Engineers, Huntington District, 502 8th Street, Huntington, WV 25701; (304)529-5607; Corps of Engineers, Pittsburgh District, 1000 Liberty Avenue, Pittsburgh, PA 15222, (412)644-4191.

Some Nature Conservancy preserves in the state have trails. Information: The Nature Conservancy, Ohio Field Office, 1504 West First Avenue, Columbus, OH 43212; (614)486-4194.

Portions of the the 1,200-mile Buckeye Trail, which loops around the state, are suitable for nature walks. Information: Buckeye Trail Association, P.O. Box 254, Worthington, OH 43085.

OKLAHOMA

Recommended Areas for Nature Walks

WICHITA MOUNTAINS WILDLIFE REFUGE Route 1, Box 448, Indiahoma, OK 73552; (405)429-3222. 59,020 acres. Located in the Wichita Mountains of southwestern Oklahoma, this national wildlife refuge includes two designated wilderness areas: the 5,000-acre Charons Garden Wilderness Area and the North Mountain Wilderness Area. Elevations range from 1,350 to 2,479 feet on Mt. Pinchot. Along with mountains and rock outcroppings there are forests of scrub oak and cedar, prairie grasslands, and a number of small lakes. Bison, Rocky Mountain elk, deer, and prairie dog are among the wildlife.

• *Suggested Trails for Nature Walks:* 1. The 0.3-mile Quanah Parker Trail. 2. The 1-mile Elk Trail (loop). 3. The 2-mile Longhorn Trail (loop). 4. The 1.5-mile Kite Trail. 5. The 1.5-mile Little Baldy Mountain Trail. 6. The 2-mile Elk Mountain Trail (easy-moderate). 7. The 8-mile Buffalo Trail (easy-moderate loop).

CHICKASAW NATIONAL RECREATION AREA P.O. Box 201, Sulphur, OK 73086; (405)622-3165. 9,500 acres. Chickasaw National Recreation Area in south-central Oklahoma features 2,350-acre Lake of the Arbuckles and Veterans Lake, along with springs and streams, hilly mixed-grass prairie, yucca and prickly pear cactus, as well as forests of oak, hickory, sycamore, pecan, walnut, and redcedar. Wildlife includes white-tailed deer, bison, coyote, bobcat, gray fox, raccoon, beaver, skunk, cottontail rabbit, and armadillo, plus roadrunner, quail, barred owl, wild turkey, and red-tailed hawk. There's a nature center, and guided walks are available.

• *Suggested Trails for Nature Walks:* 1. Several short self-guiding loop trails are located near the nature center. 2. Other short trails are on Bromide Hill, as well as near the Buffalo Pasture and overlooking Lake of the Arbuckles. 3. The 13-mile Chickasaw National Recreation Area Trail traverses the area.

MCGEE CREEK STATE PARK Route 1, Box 6-A, Farris, OK 74542; (405)889-5822. Situated in the edge of southeastern Oklahoma's Ouachita Mountains, this state park is centered on man-made McGee Creek Lake. There are several streams, including McGee Creek, and an 8,900-acre portion of the park has been designated the McGee Creek Natural Scenic Recreation Area.

• *Suggested Trails for Nature Walks:* 1. The 1-mile Nature Trail. 2. The 1.1-mile West Boundary Trail. 3. The 1.4-mile Little Bugaboo Trail. 4. The 1.6-mile Whiskey Flats Trail. 5. The 2.5-mile West Branch Trail. 6. The 1.2-mile Rocky Point Trail.

FOUNTAINHEAD STATE PARK HC 60, Box 1340, Checotah, OK 74426; (918)689-5311. 2,832 acres. East-central Oklahoma's Fountainhead State Park is on a peninsula that extends into the 102,500-acre man-made Lake

OKLAHOMA

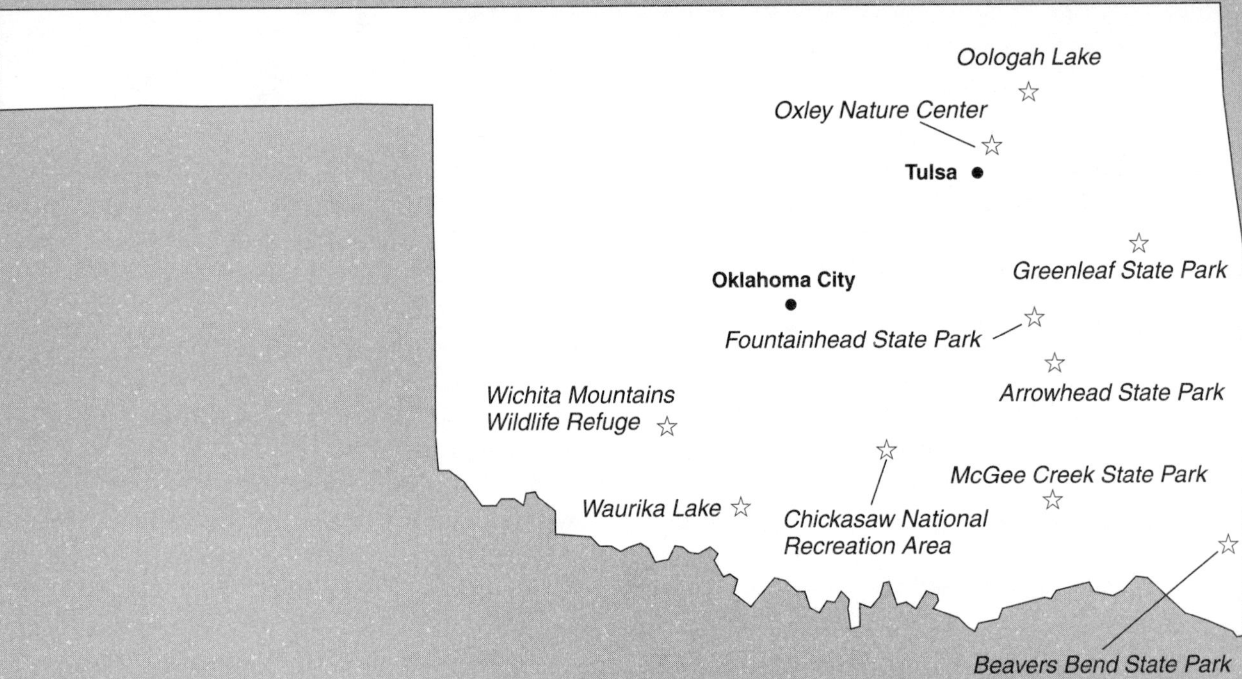
Oologah Lake
Oxley Nature Center
Tulsa
Greenleaf State Park
Oklahoma City
Fountainhead State Park
Arrowhead State Park
Wichita Mountains
Wildlife Refuge
McGee Creek State Park
Waurika Lake
Chickasaw National
Recreation Area
Beavers Bend State Park

Eufaula, the largest lake in the state. There are oak and hickory trees, with cottonwood and dogwood, and the wildlife here includes deer and wild turkey.

• *Suggested Trails for Nature Walks:* 1. The 0.3-mile Crazy Snake Interpretive Trail. 2. The 0.8-mile Arrow-Maker Interpretive Trail. 3. The 3-mile Pickens Trail.

OXLEY NATURE CENTER 5701 East 36th Street North, Tulsa, OK 74115; (918)669-6644. 800 acres. Located in Mohawk Park on the northern outskirts of Tulsa, and offering environmental education programs and courses, Oxley Nature Center is also a preserve and wildlife refuge. The area includes fields and prairie, marshes and forest, lakes and ponds, along with three streams: Bird Creek, Flat Rock Creek, and Coal Creek. Guided walks are offered.

• *Suggested Trails for Nature Walks:* 1. The 0.3-mile Blue Heron Trail. 2. The 0.3-mile Red Fox Trail. 3. The 0.4-mile Prairie Trail. 4. The 0.5-mile Flowline Trail. 5. The 0.5-mile Green Dragon Trail. 6. The 0.6-mile Lake Trail. 7. The 0.6-mile Wildlife Study Area Trail. 8. The 0.6-mile Whitetail Trail. 9. The 0.7-mile Sierra Club Trail. 10. The 1.3-mile North Woods Loop Trail.

WAURIKA LAKE U.S. Army Corps of Engineers, Waurika Project Office, P.O. Box 29, Waurika, OK 73573; (405)963-2111. Constructed and managed by the Army Corps of Engineers, this 10,100-acre man-made lake in south-central Oklahoma is on dammed Beaver Creek. The lake is 11 miles long and has many small coves and bays. Surrounding terrain is gently hilly with tallgrass prairie, wildflowers, and oak-forested areas. White-tailed deer, coyote, raccoon, rabbit, mourning dove, quail, wild turkey, and canvasback are among the wildlife.

• *Suggested Trails for Nature Walks:* 1. The 1-mile Beaver Creek Trail. 2. The 13-mile Walker Creek Trail, a loop trail which follows the lake shoreline.

BEAVERS BEND STATE PARK P.O. Box 10, Broken Bow, OK 74728; (405)494-6300. Beavers Bend State Park is situated next to Hochatown State Park on Broken Bow Reservoir, in southeastern Oklahoma. In this area are the mountains of the "Little Smokies," featuring tall pines, creeks, and the Mountain Fork River. Wildlife includes white-tailed deer, fox, raccoon, beaver, wild turkey, great blue heron, and bald eagle. The park has a nature center, and guided walks are available.

• *Suggested Trails for Nature Walks:* 1. The Cedar Bluff Nature Trail. 2. The Big Oak Nature Trail. 3. The Pine Ridge Nature Trail (loop). 4. The 24-mile David Boren Trail (easy-moderate), which links Beavers Bend with Hochatown State Park. 5. The 1-mile Beaver Lodge Nature Trail, which is on Corps of Engineers lands next to the park.

OOLOGAH LAKE U.S. Army Corps of Engineers, P.O. Box 700, Oologah, OK 74053; (918)443-2250. 50,000 acres. Site of the childhood home of Will Rogers, this man-made, 29,500-acre lake is 18 miles long and lies northeast of Tulsa. The area around the lake include hills and limestone bluffs, creeks, and open pastures and grasslands with shrubs, as well as forests of oak and hickory. Among the wildlife are white-tailed deer, fox, raccoon, cottontail rabbit, common bobwhite, owl, hawk, and wild turkey.

• *Suggested Trails for Nature Walks:* 1. The 2.4-mile Skull Hollow Nature Trail, consisting of three loops. 2. The 18-mile Will Rogers Centennial Trail, which includes 5 miles of side trails.

ARROWHEAD STATE PARK HC 67, Box 57, Canadian, OK 74425; (918)339-2204. 2,200 acres. This state park occupies lands alongside 102,500-acre Lake Eufaula, a man-made lake in east-central Oklahoma. Terrain is hilly with prairie grasslands, prickly pear cactus, and forests of oak, hickory, redcedar, and elm. Wildlife includes deer, coyote, fox, opossum, raccoon, and rabbit, along with quail, owl, and vulture.

• *Suggested Trails for Nature Walks:* 1. The 0.8-mile Outlaw Nature Trail. 2. The 3-mile Hiking Trail.

GREENLEAF STATE PARK Route 1, Box 119, Braggs, OK 74423; (918)487-5196. 565 acres. Greenleaf State Park is in the Cookson Hills of eastern Oklahoma, next to the Cherokee Wildlife Management Area and the Gruber State Game Management Area. The park features hills, small mountains, Greenleaf Creek, and 900-acre, man-made Greenleaf Lake, with wildlife that includes deer and wild turkey. The park has a nature center, and guided walks are available.

• *Suggested Trails for Nature Walks:* The 18-mile Greenleaf Trail, which consists of two loops and includes some steep hills, begins and ends in the park.

Other Suitable Locations for Nature Walks in Oklahoma

A number of Oklahoma's fifty-five state parks have nature trails. Information: Oklahoma State Parks, 2401 North Lincoln Boulevard, Suite 500, Oklahoma City, OK 73105; (800)654-8240.

Ouachita National Forest, based in Arkansas, has two large tracts in southeastern Oklahoma with trails. Information: Ouachita National Forest, P.O. Box 1270, Hot Springs, AR 71902; (501)321-5202.

The U.S. Army Corps of Engineers manages many lakes in the state that have trails. Information: Corps of Engineers, Tulsa District, P.O. Box 61, Tulsa, OK 74121; (918)581-7349.

Four national wildlife refuges in Oklahoma feature trails. Information: U.S. Fish and Wildlife Service, P.O. Box 1306, Albuquerque, NM 87103.

OREGON

Recommended Areas for Nature Walks

CRATER LAKE NATIONAL PARK P.O. Box 7, Crater Lake, OR 97604; (503)594-2211. 183,200 acres. This national park in the Cascades of southwest Oregon is centered around 6-mile-wide and 1,932-feet-deep Crater Lake, which sits inside volcanic Mt. Mazama at an elevation of 6,176 feet. The crater rim stands 1,000 feet above the lake's surface, and the highest point in the park is 8,929-foot Mt. Scott.

There are canyons and streams, shrubs and wildflowers, as well as an old-growth forest of ponderosa and lodgepole pine, subalpine and Douglas fir, with hemlock. Wildlife includes Roosevelt elk, black bear, mule and black-tailed deer, mountain lion, gray wolf, coyote, bobcat, fox, and wolverine, along with ruffed grouse, red-tailed hawk, golden eagle, and peregrine falcon. Ranger-led interpretive walks are offered in the summer.

• *Suggested Trails for Nature Walks:* 1. The 0.3-mile Sun Notch Viewpoint Trail. 2. The 1-mile Godfrey Glen Trail. 3. The 1-mile Castle Crest Wildflower Garden Trail (loop). 4. The 1.3-mile Discovery Point Trail. 5. The 1.7-mile Annie Creek Canyon Trail (loop). 6. The 0.7-mile Watchman Trail (moderate). 7. The 1.1-mile Cleetwood Cove Trail (moderate). 8. The 1.7-mile Garfield Peak Trail (moderate).

SIUSLAW NATIONAL FOREST P.O. Box 1148, Corvallis, OR 97339; (503)750-7000. 630,395 acres. Situated in the Coast Range of western Oregon, Siuslaw National Forest includes the 40-mile-long, 25,658-acre Oregon Dunes National Recreation Area, with 400-foot sand dunes and ocean beaches. There are also small mountains with steep ridges. Highest point is 4,097-foot Marys Peak, and three designated wilderness areas total 22,457 acres.

Throughout the area are creeks and waterfalls, lakes and marshes, meadows and forests of Douglas fir and spruce, with hemlock and cedar, including old-growth stands, as well as rhododendron and huckleberry bushes. Among the wildlife are Roosevelt elk, black-tailed deer, black bear, beaver, great blue heron, osprey, bald eagle, and whale offshore.

• *Suggested Trails for Nature Walks:* 1. The 1-mile Overlook Beach Trail. 2. The 1-mile Giant Spruce Trail. 3. The 1-mile Lagoon Trail. 4. The 1-mile Sweet Creek Trail. 5. The 1-mile Bluebill Trail (loop). 6. The 1.5-mile Waxmyrtle Trail. 7. The 2-mile Tahkenitch Dunes Trail. 8. The 2.5-mile Siltcoos Lake Trail. 9. The 3-mile Threemile Lake Trail. 10. The 6-mile Sutton Trail.

MT. HOOD NATIONAL FOREST 2955 NW Division Street, Gresham, OR 97030; (503)666-0700. 1,060,000 acres. Located in the Cascades of northern Oregon, this national forest is dominated by 11,235-foot Mt. Hood. There are also many other mountains, rock formations, canyons, glaciers, meadows with wildflowers, thousands of miles of streams,

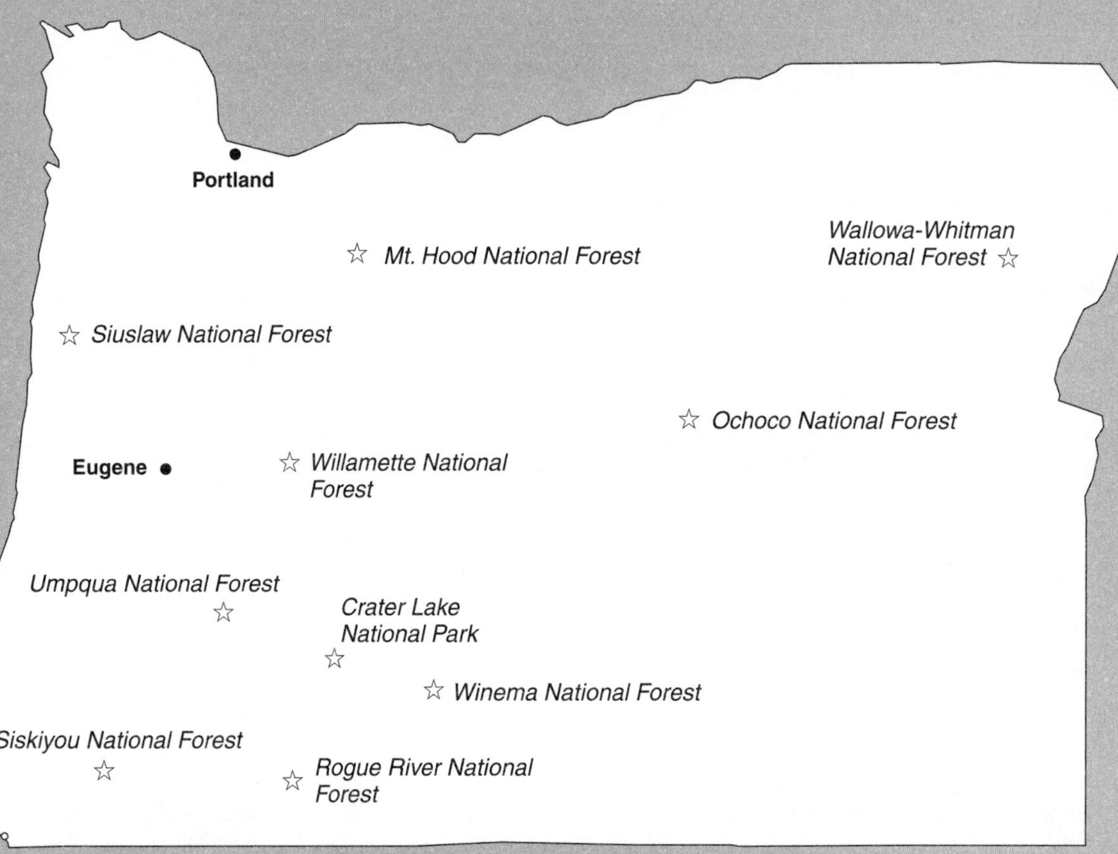
OREGON
Portland
Mt. Hood National Forest
Wallowa-Whitman
National Forest
Siuslaw National Forest
Ochoco National Forest
Eugene
Willamette National
Forest
Umpqua National Forest
Crater Lake
National Park
Winema National Forest
Siskiyou National Forest
Rogue River National
Forest

waterfalls, some hot springs, and over 150 lakes.

Six designated wilderness areas total 660,000 acres. The forest consists of Douglas and grand fir, with ponderosa pine and western hemlock, including old-growth stands, as well as rhododendron, bear grass, and huckleberry. Among the wildlife are elk, mule deer, black bear, mountain lion, bobcat, mountain goat, porcupine, snowshoe hare, skunk, marmot, and bat.

• *Suggested Trails for Nature Walks:* 1. The 0.5-mile Little Zigzag Falls Trail. 2. The 2-mile Jackpot Meadows Trail. 3. The 2-mile Mountaineer Trail. 4. The 4-mile Mirror Lake Trail. 5. The 4-mile Hidden Lake Trail. 6. The 4-mile Still Creek Trail. 7. The 4-mile Flag Mountain Trail. 8. The 5-mile "Ole" Salmon River Trail. 9. The 6-mile East Fork Trail. 10. The 7.5-mile Ramona Falls Loop.

ROGUE RIVER NATIONAL FOREST P.O. Box 520, Medford, OR 97501; (503)858-2200. 628,752 acres. Rogue River National Forest consists of two tracts in the Cascades and Siskiyou Mountains of southwestern Oregon, with one area adjacent to Crater Lake National Park. Elevations range from 1,600 to 9,495-foot Mt. McLoughlin, which is a volcanic cone. There are three designated wilderness areas totaling 92,800 acres.

It's a place of lofty, rocky mountain ridges and deep canyons with cliffs, many lakes, 1,140 miles of streams, and the Rogue and Applegate rivers. There are mixed hardwood and evergreen forests, including old-growth stands, with ponderosa and white pine, Douglas fir, spruce, and hemlock, as well as oak, maple, alder, and dogwood. Wildlife includes elk, black bear, mule deer, mountain lion, gray fox, raccoon, and beaver.

• *Suggested Trails for Nature Walks:* 1. The 0.5-mile Ashland Nature Trail. 2. The 1-mile Little Squaw Trail. 3. The 2.1-mile Beaver Dam Trail. 4. The 3.5-mile Rogue Gorge Trail. 5. The 3.9-mile Muir Creek Trail. 6. The 4.8-mile Da-Ku-Be-Te-De Trail. 7. The 5-mile Fish Lake Trail. 8. The 5.3-mile Little South Fork Trail. 9. The 6.1-mile Middle Fork Trail. 10. The 9.2-mile Payette Trail.

UMPQUA NATIONAL FOREST P.O. Box 1008, Roseburg, OR 97470; (503)672-6601. 984,880 acres. Stretching north and west of Crater Lake National Park in southwestern Oregon, this national forest features the North Umpqua Wild and Scenic River, three designated wilderness areas, and 9,182-foot Mt. Thielson, which is the highest point. Terrain includes mountains and steep canyons, with rock outcroppings and formations, cliffs and caves.

The forest consists of Douglas and Shasta fir, ponderosa and lodgepole pine, and western redcedar, including some old-growth trees, along with dogwood and rhododendron. Throughout the area are lakes and ponds, creeks and waterfalls, as well as alpine meadows with wildflowers. Among the wildlife are Roosevelt elk, mule and black-tailed deer, black bear, coyote, bobcat, fox, golden eagle, peregrine falcon, and waterfowl.

• *Suggested Trails for Nature Walks:* 1. The 0.9-mile Nature Trail. 2. The 0.7-mile Yakso Falls Trail. 3. The 1-mile Twin Lakes Loop Trail. 4. The 1-mile Susan Creek Falls Trail. 5. The 1.5-mile Calamut Lake Trail. 6. The 1.5-mile Canton Creek Falls Trail. 7. The 2.5-mile Twin Lakes Trail. 8. The 2.6-mile Fish Creek Trail. 9. The 3.7-mile Donegan Prairie Trail. 10. The 8.7-mile North Crater Trail.

WINEMA NATIONAL FOREST 2819 Dahlia Street, Klamath Falls, OR 97601; (503)883-6714. 1,045,000 acres. Winema National Forest in the southern Cascades includes lands directly east of Crater Lake National Park. It's an area of volcanic peaks, rocky ridges, and canyons, with many ponds and alpine lakes, streams, and rivers, including the Sycan Wild and Scenic River.

There are three designated wilderness areas. Along with wildflowers and open meadows, much of the region is forested with lodgepole and ponderosa pine, mountain hemlock, Douglas fir, and Englemann spruce. Wildlife includes mule deer, elk, black bear, mountain lion, coyote, bobcat, beaver, and wolverine.

• *Suggested Trails for Nature Walks:* 1. The 1.5-mile Lost Creek Trail. 2. The 1.6-mile South Rock Creek Trail. 3. The 1.9-mile Sevenmile Trail. 4. The 2.5-mile Twin Ponds Trail. 5. The 2.7-mile Cold Springs Trail. 6. The 0.8-mile Donna Lake Trail. 7. The 5.2-mile Badger Creek Trail. 8. The 5.3-mile Isherwood Trail. 9. The 6-mile Sky Lakes Trail.

SISKIYOU NATIONAL FOREST 200 NE Greenfield Road, P.O. Box 440, Grants Pass, OR 97526; (503)471-6500. 1,092,302 acres. This national forest is in the Siskiyou Mountains of southwestern Oregon. Amid the mountains and canyons here are many streams, lakes, and segments of the Rogue, Elk, and Illinois wild and scenic rivers.

Five designated wilderness areas add up to 232,495 acres. The region's forests are made up of ponderosa pine, Douglas fir, spruce, and cedar, with a few groves of old redwoods. Roosevelt elk, black bear, mule deer, mountain lion, gray fox, porcupine, beaver, red-tailed hawk, and great blue heron are among the wildlife.

• *Suggested Trails for Nature Walks:* 1. The 0.5-mile Southard Lake Trail. 2. The 1-mile Shrader Old Growth Trail (loop). 3. The 1-mile Redwood Nature Trail (loop). 4. The 1.8-mile Big Pine Nature Trail, consisting of four loops. 5. The 2.6-mile Babyfoot Lake Trail. 6. The 2.5-mile Sucker Creek Trail. 7. The 4-mile Tannen Lakes Trail. 8. The 5-mile Pine Grove Trail. 9. The 5-mile Lake Mountain Trail (easy-moderate). 10. The 12-mile Lower Rogue River Trail (easy-moderate).

WILLAMETTE NATIONAL FOREST P.O. Box 10607, Eugene, OR 97440; (503)465-6521. 1,675,407 acres. Located in the western Cascades of west-central Oregon, Willamette National Forest encompasses a number of rugged mountain peaks, steep slopes, high cliffs, and rock formations. Loftiest elevation is 10,495-foot Mt. Jefferson. Eight designated wilderness areas add up to 380,805 acres.

There are many streams and rivers, including the McKenzie Wild and Scenic River, over 350 lakes, alpine meadows, and forests of Douglas and Pacific silver fir, mountain hemlock, Englemann spruce, and western redcedar, including some old-growth stands. Among the wildlife are Roosevelt elk, black-tailed and mule deer, black bear, cougar, bobcat, fox, and wolverine, along with red-tailed hawk, bald eagle, and waterfowl.

• *Suggested Trails for Nature Walks:* 1. The 0.5-mile Delta Nature Loop Trail. 2. The 0.8-mile Hackleman Old-Growth Loop Trail. 3. The 0.8-mile House Rock Loop Trail. 4. The 1-mile Humbug Flats Trail. 5. The 1.9-mile Indigo Lake Trail. 6. The 2-mile Bobby Lake Trail. 7. The 4.2-mile Little North Santiam Trail. 8. The 5-mile Middle Fork Trail. 9. The 6.3-mile Larison Creek Trail. 10. The 27-mile McKenzie River National Recreation Trail.

WALLOWA-WHITMAN NATIONAL FOREST P.O. Box 907, Baker City, OR 97814; (503)523-6391. 2,383,159 acres. Consisting of two large tracts in northeastern Oregon, Wallowa-Whitman National Forest includes a multitude of rugged mountain peaks, jagged cliffs, and steep canyons, with elevations from 875 to 9,845 feet. Especially notable is the 652,488-acre Hells Canyon National Recreation Area, featuring the Snake Wild and Scenic River in the country's deepest gorge, which is 8,000 feet deep at one point.

There are four designated wilderness areas, with scores of lakes, countless streams, alpine meadows, wildflowers, some desertlike vegetation, as well as forests of lodgepole and ponderosa pine, subalpine and Douglas fir, Englemann spruce and western larch. Wildlife includes elk, mule deer, bighorn sheep, mountain goat, black bear, mountain lion, bobcat, coyote, porcupine, beaver, bat, falcon, and golden eagle.

• *Suggested Trails for Nature Walks:* 1. The 1-mile Anthony Lake Shoreline Loop. 2. The 1-mile Black Lake Trail. 3. The 1-mile Stud Creek Trail. 4. The 4.8-mile Hells Canyon Reservoir Trail. 5. The 1-mile Hoffer Lakes Loop (easy-moderate). 6. The 1.6-mile Crawfish Lake Trail (easy-moderate). 7. The 11-mile Saddle Creek Trail. 8. The 23.2-mile Elkhorn Crest Trail (moderate). 9. The 37.4-mile Western Rim Trail (moderate).

OCHOCO NATIONAL FOREST P.O. Box 490, Prineville, OR 97754; (503)447-6247. 956,877 acres. This national forest is in the high-desert country of central Oregon, with elevations ranging from 2,241 to 7,163 feet on Snow Mountain. Three wilderness areas here total 36,200 acres, and the forest includes the 111,379-acre Crooked River National Grassland.

Terrain consists of foothills, mountains, and deep canyons with cliffs and creeks, rock formations and talus. There are areas of sagebrush and juniper, wildflowers, and stands of ponderosa and lodgepole pine, white and Douglas fir, Englemann spruce and western larch. Among the wildlife are Rocky Mountain elk, pronghorn, mule deer, wild horse, coyote, pileated woodpecker, goshawk, and eagle.

• *Suggested Trails for Nature Walks:* 1. The 0.7-mile Sugar Creek Trail. 2. The 1-mile Walton Lake Trail. 3. The 1.4-mile Ponderosa Loop. 4. The 1.5-mile Rimrock Springs Trail (loop). 5. The first 4 miles of the South Prong Trail.

Other Suitable Locations for Nature Walks in Oregon

There are four additional national forests in the state, and all have trail systems. Information: 1. Deschutes National Forest, 1645 Highway 20 East, Bend, OR 97701; (503)388-2715. 2. Fremont National Forest, 524 North G Street, Lakeview, OR 97630; (503)947-2151. 3. Malheur National Forest, 139 Northeast Dayton Street, John Day, OR 97845; (503)575-1731. 4. Umatilla National Forest, 2517 Southwest Hailey Avenue, Pendelton, OR 97801; (503)276-3811.

Oregon has well over 200 state parks, and many of these locations feature nature or hiking trails. Information: Oregon Parks and Recreation Department, 1115 Commercial Street Northeast, Salem, OR 97310; (503)378-6305.

Nine national wildlife refuges in the state have trails. Information: U.S. Fish and Wildlife Service, 911 Northeast 11th Avenue, Portland, OR 97232; (503)231-6121.

John Day Fossil Beds National Monument has several short trails. Information: John Day Fossil Beds National Monument, 420 West Main Street, John Day, OR 97845; (503)987-2333.

There are trails at some U.S. Army Corps of Engineers lakes in Oregon. Information: Corps of Engineers, Portland District, P.O. Box 2946, Portland, OR 97208; (503)326-6075.

Trails are available at a number of Bureau of Land Management areas in the state. Information: Bureau of Land Management, P.O. Box 2965, Portland, OR 97208; (503)280-7001.

PENNSYLVANIA

Recommended Areas for Nature Walks

ALLEGHENY NATIONAL FOREST P.O. Box 847, Warren, PA 16365; (814)723-5150. 506,000 acres. Pennsylvania's only national forest is located in the Allegheny Mountains, in the northwestern part of the state. This large natural area includes the 23,000-acre Allegheny National Recreation Area, which is alongside the Allegheny River and Reservoir, as well as the 8,337-acre Hickory Creek Wilderness and three small national scenic areas.

Some of the terrain is mountainous, with rock ledges and outcroppings offering vistas, rivers and streams with waterfalls, lakes and wetlands, meadows, and hardwood forests with some stands of old-growth pine and hemlock. Wildlife includes white-tailed deer, black bear, coyote, wild turkey, and bald eagle.

• *Suggested Trails for Nature Walks:* 1. The 0.8-mile Buckaloons/Seneca Trail. 2. The 1-mile Tionesta Scenic Trail. 3. The 1.1-mile Longhouse Trail. 4. The 1.3-mile Hearts Content Trail. 5. The 1.5-mile Campbell Mill Trail. 6. The 1.6-mile Black Cherry National Recreation Trail. 7. The 1.7-mile Songbird Sojourn Trail. 8. The 7.1-mile Beaver Meadows Trail System, consisting of five easy trails. 9. The 12-mile Buzzard Swamp Trail System. 10. The 6.6-mile Minister Creek Trail (moderate).

DELAWARE WATER GAP NATIONAL RECREATION AREA Bushkill, PA 18324; (717)588-2451. 70,000 acres. Lying along the eastern border of Pennsylvania, with a portion in New Jersey, this national recreation area protects 38 miles of the Delaware River as well as adjacent lands. Best-known feature is the Delaware Water Gap, a deep gap in the Kittatinny Mountains cut by the river. Elevations range from 300 to over 1,500 feet.

Within the area is the Pocono Environmental Education Center, site of some of the trails. There are steep mountain ridges with streams and many waterfalls, and a forest of eastern hardwoods with hemlock and redcedar. Wildlife includes white-tailed deer, black bear, raccoon, opossum, muskrat, beaver, river otter, hawk, and bald eagle. Naturalist-led walks are available. See the New Jersey chapter for the area's trails in that state.

• *Suggested Trails for Nature Walks:* 1. The 1-mile Arrow Island Trail. 2. The 1-mile Toms Creek Trail. 3. The 1-mile Egypt Hills Pond Trail. 4. The 1-mile Adams Falls Trail. 5. The 0.5-mile George W. Childs Trail. 6. The 1.5-mile Dingmans Falls Trail. 7. The 1.5-mile Hidden Lake Trail (loop). 8. The 2-mile Scenic Gorge Trail. 9. The 3-mile Sunrise Trail. 10. The 3-mile Tumbling Waters Trail (easy-moderate).

COOK FOREST STATE PARK P.O. Box 120, Cooksburg, PA 16217; (814)744-8407. 6,668 acres. Bordering on the Clarion River in northwestern Pennsylvania, this state park has rock outcroppings, streams, and forests of maple and birch, with mountain laurel and rhododendron, as well as three tracts of virgin pine and

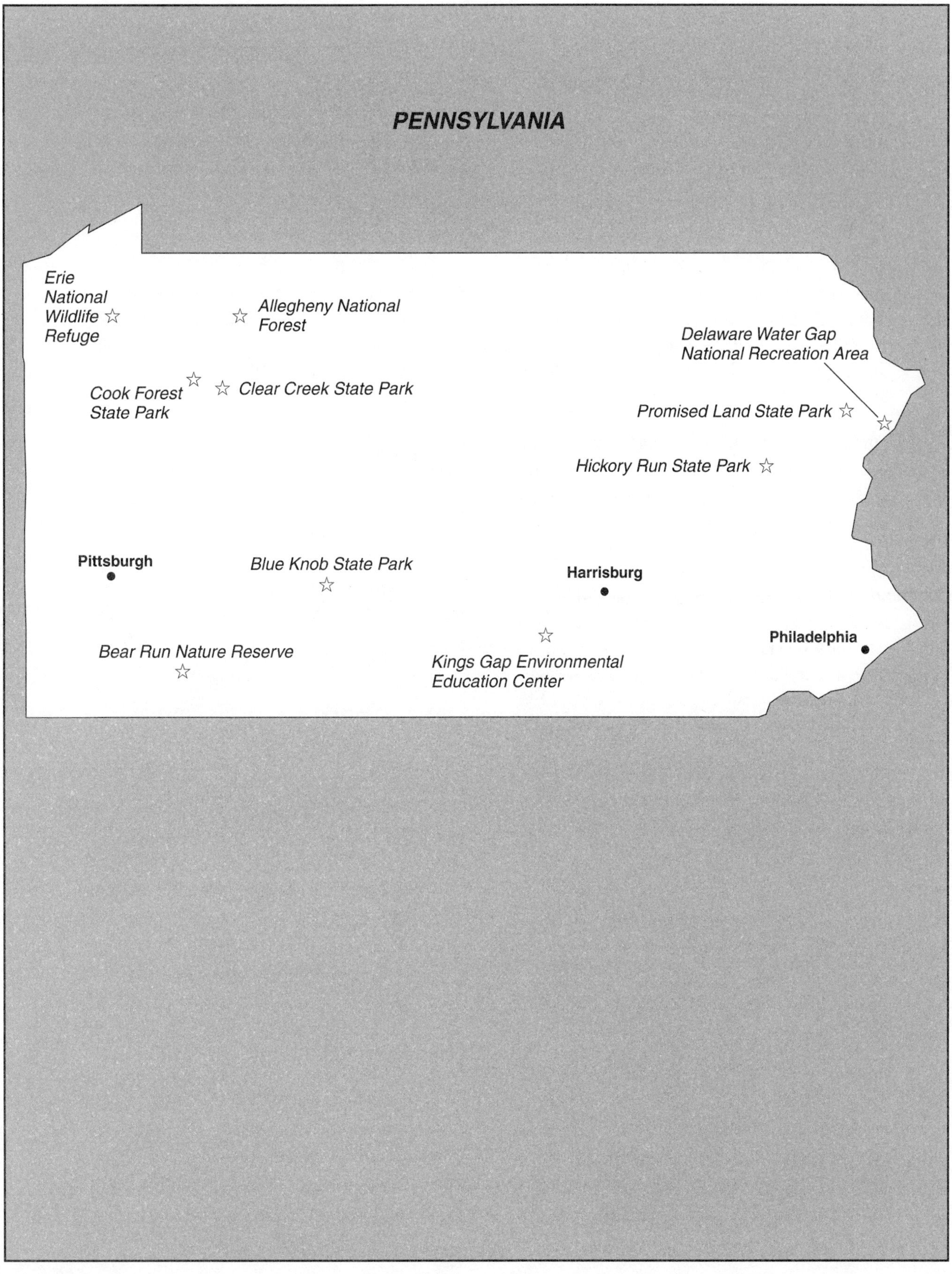
PENNSYLVANIA
Erie National Wildlife Refuge
Allegheny National Forest
Delaware Water Gap National Recreation Area
Cook Forest State Park
Clear Creek State Park
Promised Land State Park
Hickory Run State Park
Pittsburgh
Blue Knob State Park
Harrisburg
Philadelphia
Bear Run Nature Reserve
Kings Gap Environmental Education Center

hemlock, including some 300-year-old trees. Among the wildlife are white-tailed deer, black bear, porcupine, raccoon, skunk, and rabbit, along with wild turkey, heron, loon, osprey, and golden eagle. Guided trail walks are offered in the summer.

• *Suggested Trails for Nature Walks:* 1. The 0.5-mile Hemlock Trail. 2. The 0.9-mile Deer Park Trail. 3. The 1.1-mile Birch Trail. 4. The 1.2-mile Longfellow Trail. 5. The 1.5-mile CCC Trail. 6. The 1.5-mile Joyce Kilmer Trail. 7. The 1.5-mile River Trail. 8. The 1.8-mile Mohawk Trail. 9. The 2-mile Liggett Trail. 10. The 3-mile Brown's Run Trail.

HICKORY RUN STATE PARK RD 1, Box 81, White Haven, PA 18661; (717)443-0400. 15,500 acres. This large state park is in the foothills of the northeastern Pennsylvania's Pocono Mountains, a region of low ridges with some relatively flat areas. The Lehigh River runs along the western border of the park. There's a huge boulder field, along with streams, waterfalls, and several lakes, including Sand Spring Lake, which has a sand beach. Wildlife includes black bear, white-tailed deer, raccoon, opossum, and wild turkey. Nature walks are available in summer.

• *Suggested Trails for Nature Walks:* 1. The 0.5-mile Lake Trail. 2. The 0.5-mile Beach Trail. 3. The 0.5-mile Deer Trail. 4. The 0.8-mile Hawk Falls Trail. 5. The 1-mile Blue Trail. 6. The 1.5-mile Hickory Run Trail. 7. The 2-mile Manor House Trail. 8. The 2-mile Fireline Trail. 9. The 2.5-mile Orchard Trail. 10. The 4.5-mile Stage Trail.

PROMISED LAND STATE PARK RR 1, Box 96, Greentown, PA 18426; (717)676-3428. 2,971 acres. Promised Lane State Park is in the Pocono Mountains of northeastern Pennsylvania, at an elevation of 1,800 feet, amid lands of the 8,039-acre Delaware State Forest. Terrain is relatively flat but rocky, with creeks and waterfalls, swamps and peat bogs, 422-acre Promised Land Lake, 173-acre Lower Lake, and the 2,765-acre Bruce Lake Natural Area. The forest consists of mixed hardwoods, with oak, maple, and beech, plus hemlock and pine, as well as rhododendron, mountain laurel, and blueberry. Wildlife includes bear, deer, raccoon, and beaver.

• *Suggested Trails for Nature Walks:* 1. The 1-mile Conservation Island Nature Trail. 2. The 0.8-mile Whittaker Trail. 3. The 0.8-mile Lower Lake Trail. 4. The 1.8-mile Burley Inlet Trail. 5. The 0.5-mile Snow Shanty Trail. 6. The 1-mile Little Falls Trail. 7. The 1-mile Panther Swamp Trail. 8. The 1-mile 1800 Trail. 9. The 1.8-mile Rock Oak Ridge Trail. 10. The 5-mile Bruce Lake Trail.

CLEAR CREEK STATE PARK RD1, Box 82, Sigel, PA 15860; (814)752-2368. 1,209 acres. This state park sits alongside the Clarion River, next to Kittanning State Forest, in west-central Pennsylvania's Clear Creek Valley. The area is forested with oak and other hardwoods, as well as white spruce and pine, mountain laurel and rhododendron, and the streams include Clear Creek. White-tailed deer, black bear, and wild turkey are among the park's wildlife. Guided walks are offered in summer.

• *Suggested Trails for Nature Walks:* 1. The 0.4-mile Big Spring Trail. 2. The 0.4-mile Korb Trail. 3. The 0.5-mile Big Coon Trail. 4. The 0.8-mile Oxshoe Trail. 5. The 0.8-mile Radcliffe Trail. 6. The 0.9-mile Zerby Trail. 7. The 1-mile Saw Mill Trail. 8. The 1.5-mile Clear Creek Trail (easy-moderate). 9. The 1.6-mile River Trail (easy-moderate).

BEAR RUN NATURE RESERVE P.O. Box R, Mill Run, PA 15464; (412)329-8501. 4,200 acres. Located on land owned by the Western Pennsylvania Conservancy, Bear Run Nature Reserve occupies the slope of Laurel Ridge, alongside the Youghiogheny River, in the southwestern part of the state. There are wildflowers in season, stands of oak, hemlock, and pine, with rhododendron, and two major streams, Bear Run and Laurel Run.

• *Suggested Trails for Nature Walks:* 1. The 0.3-mile Kinglet Trail. 2. The 0.3-mile Saddle Trail. 3. The 0.4-mile Wintergreen Trail. 4. The 0.6-mile Aspen Trail. 5. The 0.9-mile Arbutus Trail. 6. The 1-mile Pine, Wagon, Poetry, and Tree Trails. 7. The 1.1-mile Snow Bunny Trail. 8. The 1.2-mile Warbler Trail. 9. The 2.3-mile Laurel Run Trail (easy-moderate).

KINGS GAP ENVIRONMENTAL EDUCATION CENTER 500 Kings Gap Road, Carlisle, PA 17013; (717)486-5031. 1,443 acres. Administered by the Bureau of State Parks, this environmental center is situated on South Mountain, next to Michaux State Forest, in south-central Pennsylvania. These lands feature ridges with rock outcroppings and formations, wetlands, and a pond and stream. Also here are a pine plantation and a deciduous forest of oak, maple, and tulip tree, along with Douglas fir and larch, mountain laurel, ferns and mosses, huckleberries and blueberries. Wildlife includes woodchuck and turkey vulture.

• *Suggested Trails for Nature Walks:* 1. The 0.3-mile Whispering Pines Trail (loop). 2. The 0.3-mile White Oaks Trail (loop). 3. The 0.6-mile Woodlands Ecology Trail (loop). 4. The 0.6-mile Pine Plantation Trail (loop). 5. The 1.7-mile Kings Gap Hollow Trail. 6. The 1.3-mile Maple Hollow Trail (easy-moderate). 7. The 1.5-mile Boundary Trail (easy-moderate). 8. The 1.6-mile Forest Heritage Trail (easy-moderate). 9. The 1.9-mile Rock Scree Trail (easy-moderate). 10. The 2.5-mile Scenic Vista Trail (easy-moderate).

ERIE NATIONAL WILDLIFE REFUGE RD 1, Wood Duck Lane, Guys Mills, PA 16327; (814)789-3585. 8,750 acres. Erie National Wildlife Refuge consists of two separate tracts of land about 35 miles south of Lake Erie. These are low-lying areas with 2,500 acres of wetlands, including a number of creeks, marshes, swamps, and ponds, along with meadows, grasslands, and forests. Among the wildlife are white-tailed deer, woodchuck, and beaver, as well as great blue heron, sandpiper, red-tailed hawk, bald eagle, and migratory waterfowl including ducks and Canada geese.

• *Suggested Trails for Nature Walks:* 1. The 1-mile Beaver Run Trail. 2. The 1-mile Muddy Creek Holly Trail. 3. The 2.8-mile Tsuga Nature Trail, consisting of two loops. 4. The 3-mile Deer Run Trail.

BLUE KNOB STATE PARK RR 1, Box 449, Imler, PA 16655; (814)276-3576. 5,614 acres. Perched in the Allegheny Mountains of south-central Pennsylvania, this park features 3,146-foot Blue Knob, second highest elevation in the state, with fine vistas. Terrain is ruggedly mountainous with streams as well as forests of northern hardwoods including oak and hickory, maple and birch, cherry and beech, plus eastern hemlock. White-tailed deer, grouse, and wild turkey are among the wildlife.

• *Suggested Trails for Nature Walks:* 1. The 0.9-mile Mountain View Trail Loop. 2. The 1.8-mile Homestead Trail. 3. The 0.9-mile Crist Ridge Trail. 4. The 3.5-mile Sawmill Trail. 5. The 5-mile Three Springs Trail. 6. The 2.8-mile Rock 'N' Ridge Trail (easy-moderate). 7. The 5-mile Mountain View Trail (moderate).

Other Suitable Locations for Nature Walks in Pennsylvania

Pennsylvania has 114 state parks, 97 of which have nature or hiking trails. Information: Bureau of State Parks, P.O. Box 8551, Harrisburg, PA 17105; (800)63-PARKS.

A number of Pennsylvania's state forests have trails. Information: Bureau of Forestry, P.O. Box 8552, Harrisburg, PA 17105.

The Nature Conservancy manages twenty-one preserves in Pennsylvania, and many of these locations feature trails. Information: The Nature Conservancy, 1211 Chestnut Street, 12th Floor, Philadelphia, PA 19107; (215)963-1400.

Trails are available at some U.S. Army Corps of Engineers lake sites in the state. Information: Corps of Engineers, Philadelphia District, U.S. Custom House, 2nd and Chestnut Streets, Philadelphia, PA 19106, (215)597-4741; Corps of Engineers, Baltimore District, P.O. Box 1715, Baltimore, MD 21203, (410)962-3693; Corps of Engineers, Pittsburgh District, 1000 Liberty Avenue, Pittsburgh, PA 15222, (412) 644-4191.

Information about trails on all public and private lands throughout the state is also available from the Pennsylvania Trails Program, P.O. Box 1467, Harrisburg, PA 17120.

RHODE ISLAND

Recommended Areas for Nature Walks

ARCADIA MANAGEMENT AREA 260 Arcadia Road, Hope Valley, RI 02832; (401) 539-2356. 12,000 acres. Located in western Rhode Island, this is the state's largest undeveloped area, a region of low hills and valleys with a number of ponds, swamps, streams, and a waterfall. There are rock ledges, outcroppings, and boulder fields amid forests of mixed hardwoods with oak, maple, hickory, beech, pine, and hemlock, as well as dogwood, rhododendron, mountain laurel, and blueberry. Among the wildlife are white-tailed deer, fox, coyote, raccoon, beaver, otter, and snowshoe hare, along with grouse, quail, and woodcock.

• *Suggested Trails for Nature Walks:* 1. The 1.7-mile John B. Hudson Trail. 2. The 1.6-mile Dye Hill Trail. 3. The 1.7-mile Ben Utter Trail. 4. The 2-mile Escoheag Trail. 5. The 1.7-mile Brushy Brook Trail (loop). 6. The 2.4-mile Deep Pond Trail. 7. The 4.9-mile Breakheart Trail. 8. The 8.9-mile Tippecansett Trail. 9. The 3.9-mile Mt. Tom Trail (easy-moderate). 10. The 6.7-mile Arcadia Trail (easy-moderate).

NORMAN BIRD SANCTUARY 583 Third Beach Road, Middletown, RI 02842; (401)846-2577. 450 acres. The Norman Bird Sanctuary borders on two large ponds near the Atlantic Ocean in southeastern Rhode Island. It's an area of low rocky ridges and valleys, woodlands and shrublands, open fields and meadows, marshes and swamps, small ponds and streams. Among the trees are black locust, black cherry, oak, beech, hickory, red maple, redcedar, and pine. Wildlife includes fox, rabbit, woodcock, pheasant, and great horned owl.

• *Suggested Trails for Nature Walks:* 1. The 0.5-mile Woodcock Trail. 2. The 0.4-mile Quarry Trail. 3. The 1.1-mile Woodland Trail. 4. The 0.3-mile Blue Dot Trail. 5. The 1-mile Gray Craig Trail. 6. The 1-mile Hanging Rock Trail. 7. The 1.2-mile Red Fox Trail. 8. The 1.2-mile Valley Trail. 9. The 1.4-mile Nelson Pond Trail.

FISHERVILLE BROOK WILDLIFE REFUGE c/o Audubon Society of Rhode Island, 12 Sanderson Road, Smithfield, RI 02917; (401) 231-6444. 772 acres. Situated in west-central Rhode Island, this Audubon Society wildlife refuge comprises open fields, swamps, brooks, a mill pond, and a forest of upland hardwoods with oak, beech, red and white pine, and white cedar. The bird life here includes great blue heron and hooded merganser.

• *Suggested Trails for Nature Walks:* 1. The 1.3-mile Blue Trail (loop). 2. The 0.3-mile Cedar Swamp Loop. 3. The 1.2-mile Split Rock Trail (loop). 4. The 0.9-mile Inner Loop. 5. The 1.4-mile Outer Loop.

GEORGE WASHINGTON MANAGEMENT AREA c/o Division of Forest Environment, 2185 Putnam Pike, Chepachet, RI 02814; (401)568-6700. 3,200 acres. This area in northwestern Rhode Island includes George Washington Memorial State Forest and Pulaski State

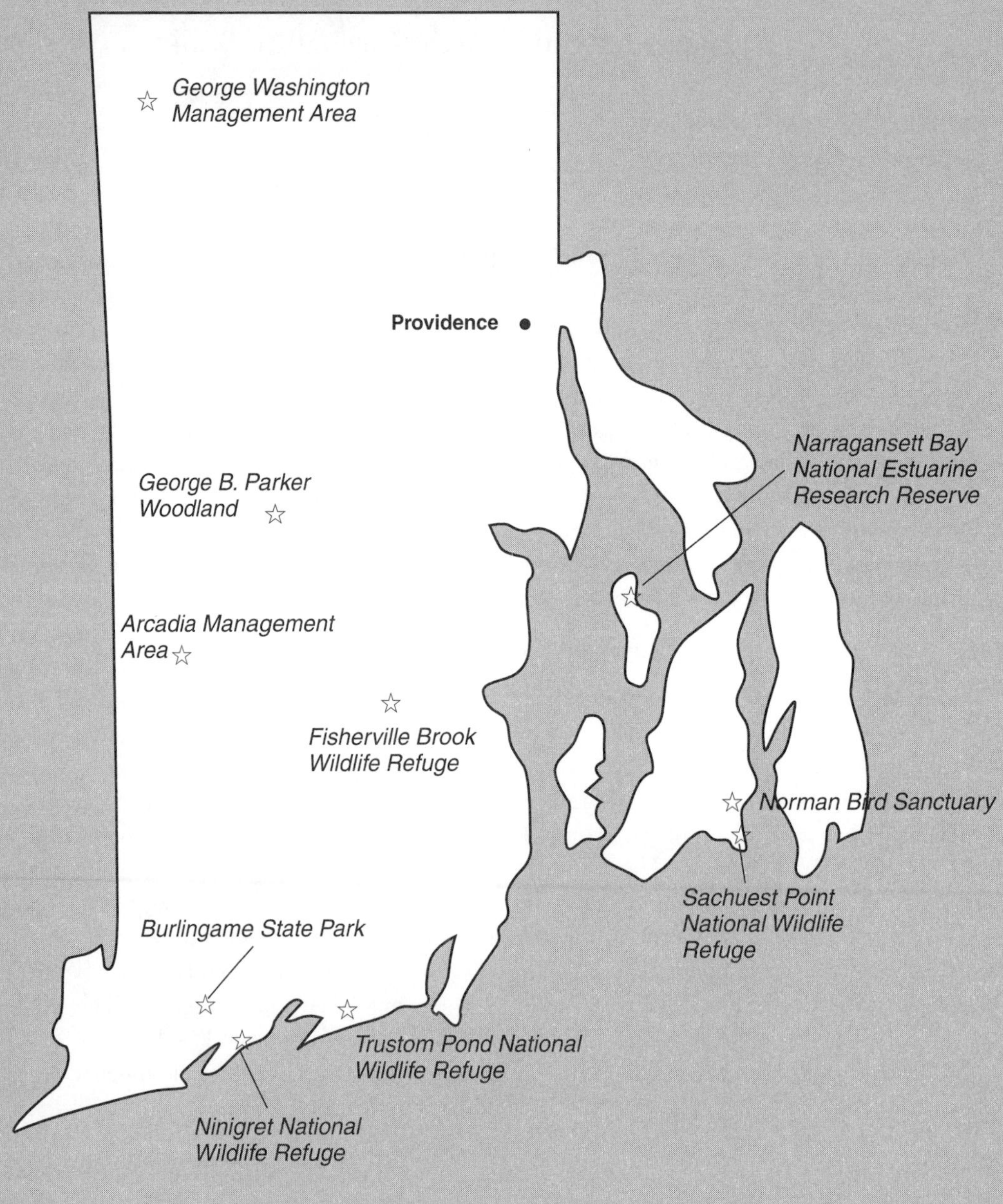
RHODE ISLAND
George Washington Management Area
Providence
Narragansett Bay National Estuarine Research Reserve
George B. Parker Woodland
Arcadia Management Area
Fisherville Brook Wildlife Refuge
Norman Bird Sanctuary
Sachuest Point National Wildlife Refuge
Burlingame State Park
Trustom Pond National Wildlife Refuge
Ninigret National Wildlife Refuge

Park. Terrain is hilly with rock ledges and outcroppings, the Bowdish Reservoir, several ponds and streams, marshes and a white cedar swamp. The forest consists of hardwoods and hemlocks, with beech and maple, birch and hickory, as well as mountain laurel and wildflowers. Among the wildlife are white-tailed deer, raccoon, muskrat, woodchuck, and snowshoe hare, along with woodcock, quail, owl, and hawk.

• *Suggested Trails for Nature Walks:* The 8-mile Walkabout Trail (loop), with two cut-off trails that make shorter loops possible.

BURLINGAME STATE PARK Route 1, Charlestown, RI 02813; (401)322-8910. 2,100 acres. Occupying the southwest corner of Rhode Island, next to the Kimball Bird Sanctuary, Burlingame State Park is centered on 600-acre Watchaug Pond, with streams, marshes, bogs, and a forest of mixed hardwoods. Wildlife includes white-tailed deer, snowshoe hare, woodcock, grouse, and waterfowl.

• *Suggested Trails for Nature Walks:* The 8.5-mile Vin Gormley Trail, which loops around Watchaug Pond.

GEORGE B. PARKER WOODLAND c/o Audubon Society of Rhode Island, 12 Sanderson Road, Smithfield, RI 02917; (401)231-6444. 690 acres. Owned by the Rhode Island Audubon Society, and located in the west-central part of the state, George B. Parker Woodland is known for its old stone cairns, walls, and other remnants of an earlier time. It's an area of hills and ravines with rocky terrain, brooks, open fields and old pastures with wildflowers, mosses and ferns, as well as a forest of maple, chestnut oak, hickory, beech, redcedar, pine, aspen, and gray birch. Wildlife includes white-tailed deer, fox, bobcat, raccoon, skunk, rabbit, and mink. The trails are very rocky.

• *Suggested Trails for Nature Walks:* 1. The 3-mile Coventry Loop. 2. The 3-mile Foster Loop.

TRUSTOM POND NATIONAL WILDLIFE REFUGE P.O. Box 307, Charlestown, RI 02813; (401)364-9124. 640 acres. Trustom Pond National Wildlife Refuge lies a few miles east of the Ninigret Refuge in southwest Rhode Island. It's a place of open fields and woodlands with swamps, ponds including 160-acre Trustom Pond, and a barrier beach on Block Island Sound. Among the diverse wildlife are gray fox, raccoon, and river otter, along with hawk, osprey, piping plover, and least tern.

• *Suggested Trails for Nature Walks:* The refuge has a 3-mile network of foot trails, with three observation platforms.

NINIGRET NATIONAL WILDLIFE REFUGE P.O. Box 307, Charlestown, RI 02813; (401)364-9124. 400 acres. Situated on the state's southwest coast, alongside 1,700-acre Ninigret Pond, this national wildlife refuge encompasses forests, grasslands, and wetlands with swamps and ponds. Wildlife includes osprey, hawk, and many songbirds, along with white-tailed deer, coyote, and opossum. There's an observation platform along each trail.

• *Suggested Trails for Nature Walks:* 1. The 1-mile Grassy Point Trail (loop). 2. The 1-mile Foster Cover Trail (loop).

SACHUEST POINT NATIONAL WILDLIFE REFUGE P.O. Box 307, Charlestown, RI 02813; (401)847-5511. 242 acres. Located on a peninsula in southeastern Rhode Island that extends into the Atlantic Ocean, Sachuest Point National Wildlife Refuge features sand beaches and dunes, some rocky shoreline, grasslands, and freshwater as well as saltwater marshes. Among the wildlife are red fox and cottontail, migratory birds including raptors, ducks, owl, common tern, and sandpiper.

• *Suggested Trails for Nature Walks:* There's a 3-mile system of interconnecting trails, with three observation platforms.

NARRAGANSETT BAY NATIONAL ESTUARINE RESEARCH RESERVE P.O. Box 151, Prudence Island, RI 02872; (401)683-5061. 2,626 acres. This reserve is located on 25-mile-long Narragansett Bay, southeast of Providence.

It consists of 1,035 acres of land at the northern end of Prudence Island—which is accessible by ferry—plus 92-acre Hope Island, Patience Island, and 1,591 acres of water. The reserve was established to protect an estuary (where freshwater and saltwater meet), and is used for research and recreation.

It's an area of salt marshes and tidal flats, freshwater ponds and streams, rocky shoreline with bluffs, meadows and fields, along with forests of pitch pine, sycamore maple, black locust, and redcedar. Wildlife includes white-tailed deer, little and great blue heron, glossy ibis, snowy egret, and osprey. Naturalist-led walks are scheduled in summer.

- *Suggested Trails for Nature Walks:* There's a network of several miles of trails at Prudence Island's northern end.

Other Suitable Locations for Nature Walks in Rhode Island

Rhode Island has thirteen state parks, and six of them have trails. Information: Division of Parks and Recreation, 2321 Hartford Avenue, Johnston, RI 02919; (401)277-2632.

The Audubon Society of Rhode Island has nine refuges that are open to the public, and most have trails. Information: Audubon Society of Rhode Island, 12 Sanderson Road, Smithfield, RI 02917; (401)231-6444.

There are trails in several state wildlife management areas. Information: Division of Fish and Wildlife, Box 218, West Kingston, RI 02892; (401)789-0281.

SOUTH CAROLINA

Recommended Areas for Nature Walks

SUMTER NATIONAL FOREST 4931 Broad River Road, Columbia, SC 29210; (803)561-4000. 353,800 acres. This national forest consists of three separate tracts in northwestern South Carolina, including lands alongside the Georgia and North Carolina borders. Terrain here ranges from rolling hills to mountains with elevations as high as 3,400 feet. There's one designated wilderness area, the 9,015-acre Ellicott Rock Wilderness.

Sumter also has lakes, many streams with waterfalls, and several rivers, among them the Chattooga National Wild and Scenic River along the Georgia line, as well as a forest of oak and hickory, maple and gum, hemlock and pine, with dogwood and redbud. Among the wildlife are white-tailed deer, black bear, fox, bobcat, raccoon, opossum, beaver, quail, and wild turkey.

• *Suggested Trails for Nature Walks:* 1. The 0.5-mile Parson's Mountain Interpretive Trail. 2. The 0.5-mile Yellow Branch Nature Trail. 3. The 0.5-mile Cherry Hill Nature Trail. 4. The 0.5-mile Living on the Land Trail. 5. The 0.7-mile Kings Creek Falls Trail. 6. The 1-mile Woods Ferry Trail (loop). 7. The 1.1-mile Parson's Mountain Lake Connector Trail. 8. The 20-mile Turkey Creek Trail. 9. The 29-mile Long Cane Horse and Hiking Trail (loop). 10. The 28-mile Buncombe Horse and Hiking Trail.

CONGAREE SWAMP NATIONAL MONUMENT 200 Caroline Sims Road, Hopkins, SC 29061; (803)776-4396. 22,200 acres. Stretching alongside the Congaree River in central South Carolina, this national monument protects a major stand of old-growth riverbottom hardwoods. There are two lakes, creeks, small bluffs by the river, and ninety species of trees including baldcypress, sycamore, oak, sweetgum, and holly. White-tailed deer, bobcat, raccoon, osprey, and barred owl are among the wildlife.

• *Suggested Trails for Nature Walks:* 1. The 1.1-mile Bluff Trail (loop). 2. The 2-mile Boardwalk Loop Trail. 3. The 4.2-mile Weston Lake Loop Trail. 4. The 6.2-mile Oakridge Trail. 5. The 10.3-mile River Trail. 6. The 10.6-mile Kingsnake Trail.

FRANCIS MARION NATIONAL FOREST 4931 Broad River Road, Columbia, SC 29210; (803)561-4000. 250,500 acres. Francis Marion National Forest is located on the flat coastal plain of southeastern South Carolina. It features several major rivers with limestone outcroppings, reservoirs, swamps with cypress and gum trees, and low ridges with forests of longleaf and loblolly pine, as well as oak and hickory, beech and elm. There are four designated wilderness areas totaling 14,173 acres; wildlife includes white-tailed deer, wild turkey, and alligator. The trails are frequently wet, and sections are sometimes under water.

• *Suggested Trails for Nature Walks:* 1. The 21-mile Swamp Fox National Recreation Trail. 2. The 19-mile Jericho Horse and Hiking Trail (loop).

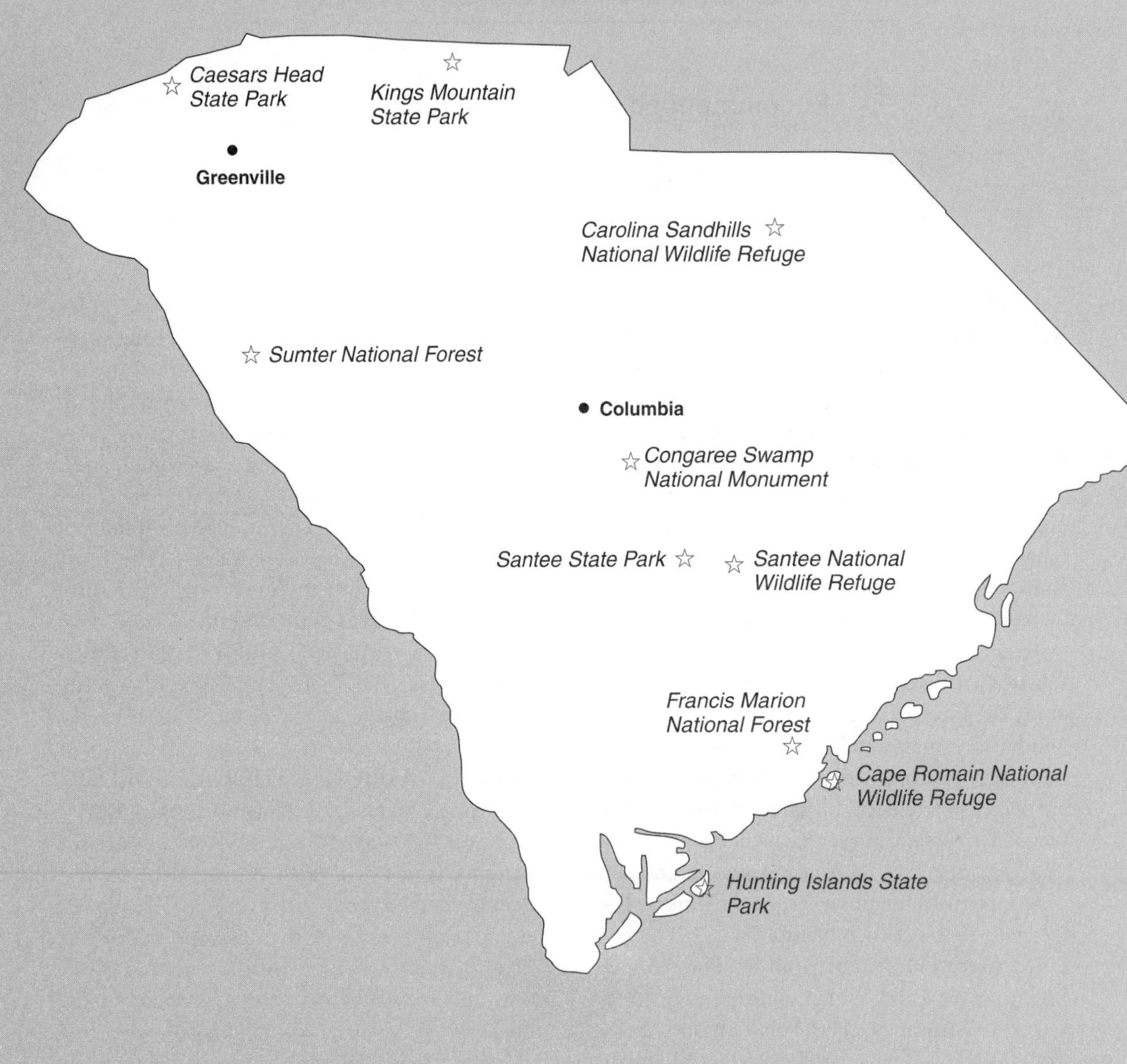
SOUTH CAROLINA
Caesars Head
State Park
Kings Mountain
State Park
Greenville
Carolina Sandhills
National Wildlife Refuge
Sumter National Forest
Columbia
Congaree Swamp
National Monument
Santee State Park
Santee National
Wildlife Refuge
Francis Marion
National Forest
Cape Romain National
Wildlife Refuge
Hunting Islands State
Park

HUNTING ISLAND STATE PARK 2555 Sea Island Parkway, Hunting Island, SC 29920; (803)838-2011. 5,000 acres. Situated on a barrier island off the southern coast of South Carolina, this state park has sandy beaches, salt marshes, a few dunes, a lagoon, and forests of slash pine, cabbage palmetto, and live oak. Wildlife includes white-tailed deer, raccoon, alligator, and sea turtle, with brown pelican, least tern, heron, and egret among the bird life. Nature walks are offered year-round.

• *Suggested Trails for Nature Walks:* 1. The 0.3-mile Garden Hammock National Recreation Trail. 2. The 1-mile Lighthouse Trail. 3. The 2-mile Nature Trail. 4. The 1-mile trail which leads from the park entrance to the camping area.

CAESARS HEAD STATE PARK 8155 Geer Highway, Cleveland, SC 29635; (803)836-6115. 10,204 acres. In association with nearby Jones Gap State Park, Caesars Head State Park is part of the ruggedly mountainous 40,000-acre Mountain Bridge Wilderness, near the North Carolina border in northwestern South Carolina. Included are steep cliffs, Table Rock and other granite outcroppings, 420-foot Raven Cliff Falls, Table Rock Reservoir, and major streams including Mathews Creek, Cold Spring Branch, and the Middle Saluda River. The forest consists of mixed hardwoods with oak, hickory, hemlock, and birch, as well as rhododendron and mountain laurel. White-tailed deer, raccoon, hawk, and turkey vulture are among the wildlife. Guided nature walks are available.

• *Suggested Trails for Nature Walks:* 1. The 0.8-mile Frank Coggins Trail. 2. The 3.3-mile Gum Gap Trail. 3. The 2-mile Raven Cliff Falls Trail (moderate).

SANTEE STATE PARK 251 State Park Road, Santee, SC 29142; (803)854-2408. 2,364 acres. Santee State Park lies alongside Lake Marion, a huge man-made lake in south-central South Carolina. The park includes lakes and ponds, creeks and wetlands, plus mixed forests of pine and hardwoods, with oak, cypress, and dogwood. Naturalist-led walks are available.

• *Suggested Trails for Nature Walks:* 1. The 0.4-mile Sinkhole Pond Trail. 2. The 0.8-mile Limestone Trail. 3. The 1-mile Oakpinolly Trail. 4. The 3.4-mile Bicycle Trail, which is open to foot travel.

KINGS MOUNTAIN STATE PARK 1277 Park Road, Blacksburg, SC 29702; (803)222-3209. 6,141 acres. This park is located in the eastern foothills of the southern Appalachians, adjacent to 3,945-acre Kings Mountain National Military Park, near the state's northern border. There are two man-made lakes, many streams, and forests of oak, hickory, maple, and pine, along with dogwood and mountain laurel.

• *Suggested Trails for Nature Walks:* 1. The 3-mile Clarks Creek Nature Trail. 2. The 16-mile Kings Mountain National Recreation Trail (easy-moderate loop), which circles around the national military park and includes the Clarks Creek Trail.

CAROLINA SANDHILLS NATIONAL WILDLIFE REFUGE Route 2, Box 330, McBee, SC 29101. 46,000 acres. Carolina Sandhills National Wildlife Refuge in northeastern South Carolina has hilly terrain with sandy soil, a forest of longleaf pine and scrub oak, many creeks, and thirty man-made lakes and ponds. Wildlife includes white-tailed deer, bobcat, fox, raccoon, opossum, red-tailed hawk, and bald eagle, with many species of ducks and geese.

• *Suggested Trails for Nature Walks:* 1. The 1-mile Woodland Pond Trail. 2. The 2-mile Tate's Trail.

PINCKNEY ISLAND NATIONAL WILDLIFE REFUGE Parkway Business Center, Suite 10, 1000 Business Center Drive, Savannah, GA 31405; (912)652-4415. 4,053 acres. Consisting of several islands, and accessible by highway, this national wildlife refuge is one of seven refuges clustered along the southeastern coast of Georgia. Pinckney Island has extensive salt marshes, creeks, and freshwater ponds, with tidal hammocks (little islands), areas of pine forest, brushlands, and a variety of grasses. Wildlife includes white-tailed deer, raccoon, and alligator, along with heron, egret, wood stork, and wading and shorebirds.

• *Suggested Trails for Nature Walks:* The refuge has a 14-mile network of nature trails, some of them grassy and others gravel-surfaced.

CAPE ROMAIN NATIONAL WILDLIFE REFUGE 5801 Highway 17 North, Awendaw, SC 29429; (803)928-3368. 64,000 acres. This large national wildlife refuge in southeastern South Carolina includes a 22-mile stretch of Atlantic coastline, with many bays, creeks, salt marshes, ponds, islands, and wild beaches. The best place for walks is 5,000-acre Bulls Island, which is accessible by ferry and has a forest of oak, pine, and magnolia. Among the area's bird life are egret, heron, ring-necked and wood duck, canvasback, brown pelican, and peregrine falcon; the refuge is home to such other wildlife as alligator, loggerhead sea turtle, white-tailed deer, red wolf, bobcat, and raccoon.

• *Suggested Trails for Nature Walks:* 1. The 2-mile Bulls Island National Recreation Trail. 2. There are 16 miles of old roads on Bulls Island that are suitable for walks.

Other Suitable Locations for Nature Walks in South Carolina

South Carolina has forty-eight state parks, and all but four feature nature or hiking trails. Information: South Carolina State Parks, 1205 Pendleton Street, Columbia, SC 29201; (803)734-0156.

There are trails at two other national wildlife refuges: 1. Ace Basin National Wildlife Refuge, P.O. Box 848, Hollywood, SC 29449; (803)889-3084. 2. Santee National Wildlife Refuge, Route 2, Box 66, Summerton, SC 29148; (803)478-2217.

The Audubon Society's Francis Beidler Forest has a long boardwalk trail. Information: Francis Beidler Forest, 336 Sanctuary Road, Harleyville, SC 29448; (803)462-2150.

SOUTH DAKOTA

Recommended Areas for Nature Walks

BADLANDS NATIONAL PARK P.O. Box 6, Interior, SD 57750; (605)433-5361. 244,000 acres. This national park in southwestern South Dakota protects an area of dramatic, eroded, and fossil-filled badlands with knife-edge ridges, rock formations including spires and knobs, steep canyons, and buttes.

It's also an area of prairie grasslands with cottonwood trees, juniper, skunkbush sumac, wild rose, and yucca. Among the wildlife here are bison, bighorn sheep, pronghorn, mule deer, coyote, prairie dog, jackrabbit, badger, porcupine, and bat, along with rock wren, cliff swallow, owl, and golden eagle. Naturalist-guided walks are available in the summer.

• *Suggested Trails for Nature Walks:* 1. The 0.3-mile Fossil Exhibit Trail (loop). 2. The 0.3-mile Door Trail. 3. The 0.5-mile Cliff Shelf Nature Trail (loop). 4. The Medicine Root Trail. 5. The 5-mile Castle Trail. 6. The 0.8-mile Notch Trail (easy-moderate).

BLACK HILLS NATIONAL FOREST RR 2, Box 200, Custer, SD 57730; (605)673-2251. 1,200,000 acres. Located in western and southwestern South Dakota, this huge national forest encompasses mountainous terrain with steep slopes, huge rock outcroppings, spires, pinnacles, and canyons. Included is 7,242-foot Harney Peak, highest elevation east of the Rockies.

Of special interest within forest boundaries are the 35,000-acre Norbeck Wildife Preserve and the 9,800-acre Black Elk Wilderness. There are many scenic vistas, forests of ponderosa pine and aspen, open meadows, mountain lakes and ponds, creeks, and wildlife that includes deer, elk, and mountain goat.

• *Suggested Trails for Nature Walks:* 1. The 2-mile Iron Creek Trail. 2. The 3-mile section of the Deerfield Trail alongside Rapid Creek. 3. The 8-mile segment of the 111-mile Centennial Trail, north of the Custer State Park boundary, in the Black Elk Wilderness and the Norbeck Wildlife Preserve. 4. The 10-mile Lake Loop Trail. 5. The 11-mile Flume National Recreation Trail. 6. The 2.8-mile Horsethief Lake Trail (easy-moderate).

WIND CAVE NATIONAL PARK RR 1, Box 190, Hot Springs, SD 57747; (605)745-4600. 28,292 acres. This relatively little known national park lies west of Black Hills National Forest and south of Custer State Park. It's most notable for an impressive underground cave system with over 70 miles of passageways, and famous for the honeycomb "boxwork" and other unique formations. Guided cave walks of varying lengths are available.

Above ground there's rolling mixed-grass prairie with limestone cliffs, several creeks, ponderosa pine and spruce forest, and wildlife including bison, mule deer, pronghorn, coyote, prairie dog, and golden eagle.

• *Suggested Trails for Nature Walks:* 1. The 1.8-mile Wind Cave Canyon Trail. 2. The 2-mile

SOUTH DAKOTA

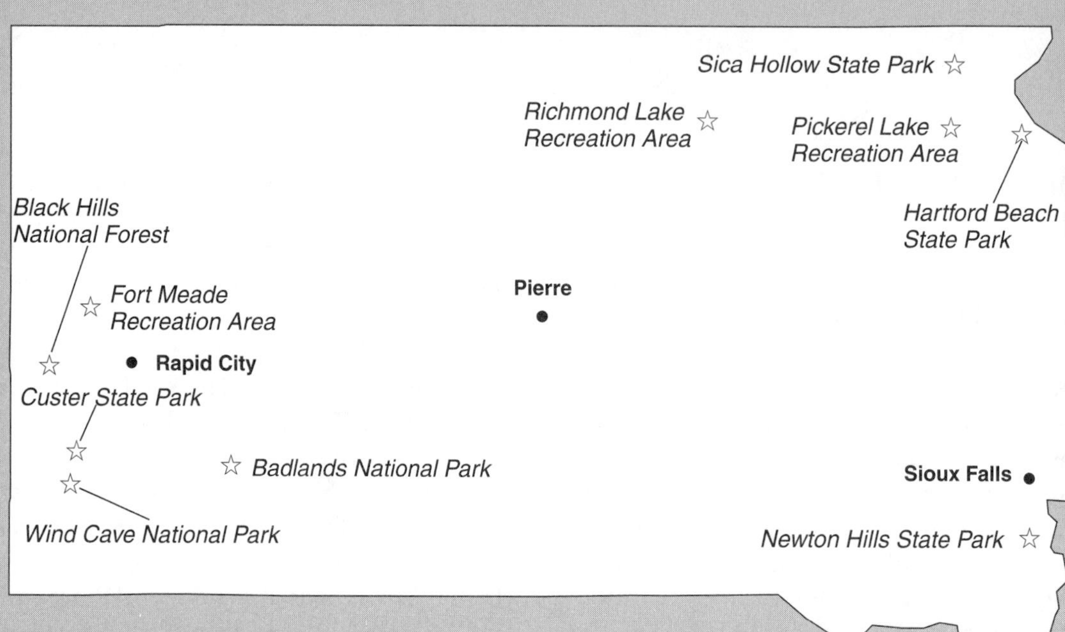

East Bison Flats Trail. 3. The 3.6-mile Sanctuary Trail. 4. A 6-mile stretch of the 111-mile Centennial Trail, which passes through the park.

CUSTER STATE PARK HC 83, Box 70, Custer, SD 57730; (605)255-4515. 73,000 acres. Largest by far of South Dakota's state parks, Custer is located north of Wind Cave National Park and south of Black Hills National Forest. Terrain here consists of rolling prairie grasslands along with mountains and canyons, huge granite rock formations and spires.

There are several lakes and streams amid forests of ponderosa pine, spruce, and hardwoods. Among the wildlife are bison, elk, mule deer, pronghorn, bighorn sheep, mountain goat, coyote, raccoon, skunk, and prairie dog. Guided nature walks are available in summer.

• *Suggested Trails for Nature Walks:* 1. The 1-mile Sylvan Lake Shore Trail (loop). 2. The 3-mile Grace Coolidge Creek Trail. 3. The 1-mile Badger Clark Historic Trail (easy-moderate loop). 4. The 1.5-mile Stockade Lake Trail (easy-moderate loop). 5. The 3.5-mile Prairie Trail (easy-moderate loop). 6. The 9-mile section of the Centennial Trail from Badger Hole to Black Hills National Forest (moderate).

NEWTON HILLS STATE PARK Route 1, Box 162, Canton, SD 57013; (605)987-2263. 948 acres. Occupying the northern shore of Lake Lakota, near the southeastern corner of the state, this park has rugged hills with streams, prairie grasslands, and hardwood forests of bur oak, basswood, ironwood, ash, cottonwood, and redcedar. White-tailed deer, red and gray fox, raccoon, beaver, opossum, and marmot are among the wildlife.

• *Suggested Trails for Nature Walks:* 1. The 0.8-mile Woodland National Recreation Trail. 2. The 0.8-mile Coteau Trail. 3. An additional walking option in the area is the Arboretum Trail in Union County State Park, southwest of Newton Hills State Park.

FORT MEADE RECREATION AREA c/o Bureau of Land Management, 310 Roundup Street, Belle Fourche, SD 57717; (605)892-2526. 6,700 acres. Fort Meade Recreation Area is on federal lands managed by the Bureau of Land Management. It preserves a historic fort directly north of Black Hills National Forest, in western South Dakota. Terrain ranges from flat to rolling, with pine-covered hills, grasslands, and streams including Bear Butte Creek.

• *Suggested Trails for Nature Walks:* 1. The 4.5-mile section of the Centennial Trail from the Bear Butte Lake trailhead to the Ft. Meade trailhead. 2. The 4-mile section of the Centennial Trail from the Ft. Meade trailhead to the Alkali Creek trailhead (easy-moderate).

HARTFORD BEACH STATE PARK RR 1, Box 50, Corona, SD 57227; (605)432-6374. 331 acres. Located in northeastern South Dakota, near the Minnesota border, this state park sits on the western shore of 22,000-acre, 38-mile-long Big Stone Lake, which at 960 feet is the lowest elevation in the state. Included are some prehistoric Indian burial mounds, along with bluffs and rock outcroppings, prairie grasslands, and a forest of bur oak, basswood, aspen, ironwood, cottonwood, and dogwood, along with shrubs and wildflowers. Wildlife includes white-tailed deer, fox, beaver, raccoon, muskrat, badger, rabbit, marmot, and mink.

• *Suggested Trails for Nature Walks:* 1. The 0.5-mile Aspen Springs Trail. 2. The 0.8-mile Robar Trail (loop). 3. The 0.3-mile Prehistoric Village Trail.

PICKEREL LAKE RECREATION AREA RR 1, Box 113, Grenville, SD 57239; (605)486-4753. 368 acres. Consisting of two units on Pickerel Lake, in the Glacial Lakes Region of northeastern North Dakota, this recreation area is characterized by hilly terrain with some large boulders and outcroppings, creeks, native prairie, shrubs, and wildflowers. There are also stands of bur oak, boxelder, and green ash, little and big bluestem grasses, as well as wild raspberry and serviceberry.

• *Suggested Trails for Nature Walks:* 1. The 0.8-mile Glacial Mounds Trail. 2. The 1.5-mile Campground-Beach Trail. 3. The 1-mile West Unit Trail (loop).

RICHMOND LAKE RECREATION AREA 37908 Youth Camp Road, Aberdeen, SD 57401; (605)225-5325. 368 acres. This state recreation area comprises three units on man-made, 1,012-acre Richmond Lake in northeastern South Dakota. Here are hilly prairie grasslands with bluffs, as well as a forest of hardwoods and conifers including cottonwood, willow, elm, hackberry, ash, pine, and spruce.

• *Suggested Trails for Nature Walks:* 1. The 0.3-mile Richmond Trail. 2. There's a 4.3-mile network of cross-country ski trails that are suitable for walking.

SICA HOLLOW STATE PARK c/o Roy Lake State Park, RR 2, Box 94, Lake City, SD 57247; (605)448-5701. 800 acres. Located on a 2,000-foot plateau in the northeast corner of the state, this park has forested hills and hollows, with Roy Creek, prairie grasslands, and a range of wildlife that includes white-tailed deer, raccoon, beaver, marmot, and wild turkey.

• *Suggested Trails for Nature Walks:* 1. The 0.5-mile Trail of the Spirits. 2. There are 14 miles of other trails in the park.

Other Suitable Locations for Nature Walks in South Dakota

South Dakota has thirteen state parks, twenty-five recreation areas, and three so-called nature areas. All but ten of the above areas feature trails. Information: Parks and Recreation Division, 523 East Capitol Avenue, Pierre, SD 57501; (605)773-3391.

Jewel Cave National Monument has short trails as well as gravel roads suitable for walks. Information: Jewel Cave National Monument, Route 1, Box 60AA, Custer, SD 57730; (605) 673-2288.

There are four national wildlife refuges in the state with trails. Information: U.S. Fish and Wildlife Service, Box 25486, Denver Federal Center, Denver, CO 80225.

Some U.S. Army Corps of Engineers lakes in South Dakota have trails. Information: Corps of Engineers, Omaha District, 215 North 17th Street, Omaha, NE 68102; (402)221-4137.

TENNESSEE

Recommended Areas for Nature Walks

GREAT SMOKY MOUNTAINS NATIONAL PARK 107 Park Headquarters Road, Gatlinburg, TN 37738; (615)436-1200. 520,004 acres (244,100 acres in Tennessee). Straddling the border of Tennessee and North Carolina, this national park is named for the imposing and often misty mountains that dominate the landscape. It features one of the largest wilderness areas in the eastern United States, with an extraordinary range of flora and fauna and over 100,000 acres of virgin forest—more than any other eastern location.

This is also the most frequently visited national park in the country. Elevations range from 840 to 6,643 feet on Clingman's Dome, second highest mountain in the East. It has a temperate deciduous forest, with redbud and dogwood, rhododendron and mountain laurel, as well as spruce and fir trees at higher elevations. Streams and waterfalls are ubiquitous. Among the wildlife are white-tailed deer, black bear, wild boar, bobcat, mountain lion, and red fox. Naturalist-led walks are available. See the North Carolina chapter for Smokies trails in that state.

• *Suggested Trails for Nature Walks:* 1. The 0.8-mile Cove Hardwood Trail. 2. The 1-mile Sugarlands Trail. 3. The 1-mile Cosby Trail. 4. The 1-mile Porters Creek Trail. 5. The 2.5-mile Laurel Falls Trail. 6. The 5-mile Alum Cave Trail. 7. The 1.3-mile Arch Rock Trail (easy-moderate). 8. The 1.5-mile Grotto Falls Trail (easy-moderate). 9. The 2.8-mile Cucumber Gap Trail (easy-moderate). 10. The 3-mile Upper Little River Trail (easy-moderate).

CHEROKEE NATIONAL FOREST P.O. Box 2010, Cleveland, TN 37320; (423)476-9700. 630,000 acres. Cherokee National Forest consists of two separate tracts north and south of Great Smoky Mountains National Park, along the state's eastern border. Terrain includes rugged mountains, ridges, "balds" (treeless mountains), knobs, rock outcroppings, steep gorges, and open valleys.

There are many rivers, streams, waterfalls, and some lakes, with meadows, wildflowers, as well as mixed hardwood and conifer forests, with pine and hemlock, mountain laurel and rhododendron. Wildlife includes black bear, white-tailed deer, wild boar, and raccoon, along with ruffed grouse, pileated woodpecker, and wild turkey.

• *Suggested Trails for Nature Walks:* 1. The 0.4-mile Pondview Loop. 2. The 0.4-mile Chilhowee Forest Walk. 3. The 0.7-mile Arbutus Trail. 4. The 1.4-mile Fisherman Trail. 5. The 1.5-mile Benton Falls Trail. 6. The 2-mile Azalea Trail. 7. The 3.2-mile Coker Creek Falls Trail. 8. The 3.2-mile Rocky Flats Trail. 9. The 3.8-mile Turtletown Creek Trail. 10. The 5.6-mile Bald River Trail.

SOUTH CUMBERLAND RECREATION AREA Route 1, Box 2196, Monteagle, TN 37356; (615)924-2980. 12,000 acres. The South

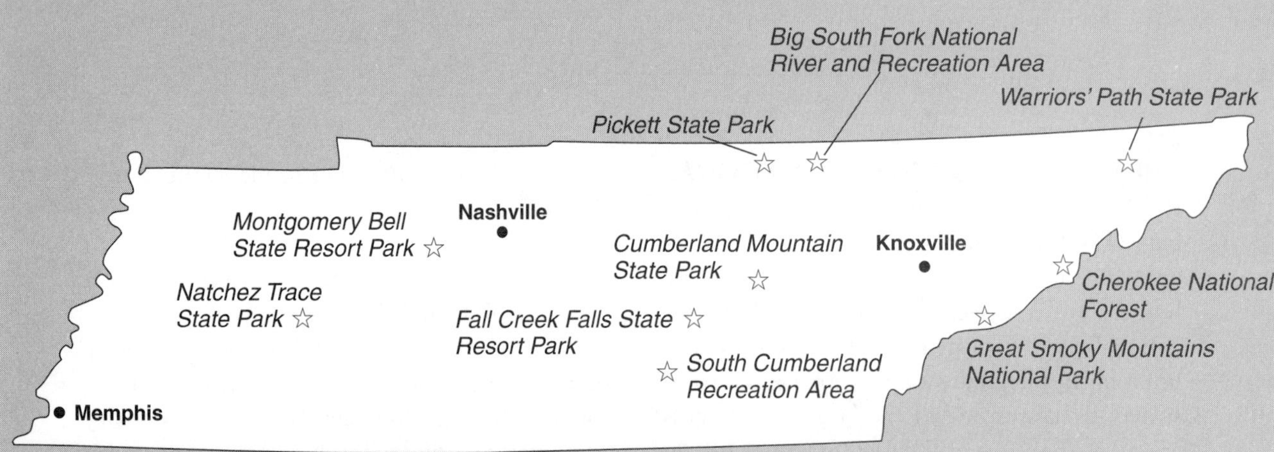
TENNESSEE
Big South Fork National
River and Recreation Area
Warriors' Path State Park
Pickett State Park
Montgomery Bell
State Resort Park
Nashville
Cumberland Mountain
State Park
Knoxville
Natchez Trace
State Park
Cherokee National
Forest
Fall Creek Falls State
Resort Park
Great Smoky Mountains
National Park
South Cumberland
Recreation Area
Memphis

Cumberland Recreation Area is made up of eight separate tracts in south-central Tennessee. The area most suitable for easy walks is the Savage Gulf State Natural Area, which lies on the western edge of the Cumberland Plateau, with a number of 800-foot gorges, sandstone and limestone cliffs, streams and waterfalls. The region is forested with oak, maple, hickory, poplar, hemlock, and pine, including old-growth stands, and there are shrubs, vines, ferns, and wildflowers. Among the wildlife are white-tailed deer, fox, bobcat, woodchuck, skunk, owl, and hawk.

• *Suggested Trails for Nature Walks:* 1. The 0.4-mile Ranger Falls Trail. 2. The 0.9-mile Stone Door Trail. 3. The 1.6-mile Stagecoach Historic Trail. 4. The 2.9-mile Laurel Trail. 5. The 3.2-mile Big Creek Rim Trail. 6. The 4.2-mile Savage Day Loop Trail. 7. The 5.8-mile South Rim Trail. 8. The 6.3-mile North Rim Trail. 9. The 7.1-mile North Plateau Trail. 10. The 1.4-mile Greeter Trail (easy-moderate).

BIG SOUTH FORK NATIONAL RIVER AND RECREATION AREA Route 3, Box 401, Oneida, TN 37841; (615)879-3675. 105,000 acres. Located on the Cumberland Plateau in northeastern Tennessee and extending into Kentucky, this area protects over 80 miles of the Big South Fork of the Cumberland River, which flows through a canyon gorge.

In the region are many creeks and waterfalls, cliffs and bluffs with overlooks, sandstone arches and rock shelters, boulders and caves, amid a forest of hemlock and pine. Wildlife includes white-tailed deer, bobcat, coyote, fox, muskrat, raccoon, beaver, opossum, skunk, mink, river otter, and bat.

• *Suggested Trails for Nature Walks:* 1. The 1-mile Sunset Overlook Trail. 2. The 1.3-mile Bandy Creek Campground Loop Trail. 3. The 2-mile Angel Falls Trail. 4. The 3.2-mile West Entrance Trailhead to Bandy Creek Campground. 5. The 3.2-mile Oscar Blevins Loop. 6. The 3.5-mile Middle Creek Loop. 7. The 0.8-mile Buffalo Arch Trail (easy-moderate). 8. The 3.2-mile Slave Falls Loop (easy-moderate).

MONTGOMERY BELL STATE RESORT PARK P.O. Box 39, Burns, TN 37029; (615)797-9052. 3,782 acres. Situated in central Tennessee, Montgomery Bell State Park is a place of rolling hills and hollows with meadows, marshes, several streams, a mixed hardwood forest with stands of pine, wildflowers, and several lakes, including 35-acre Acorn Lake, which has a sandy beach. White-tailed deer, fox, opossum, raccoon, and beaver are among the park's wildlife. Guided nature walks are offered year-round.

• *Suggested Trails for Nature Walks:* 1. The 0.3-mile McAdow Trail. 2. The 0.3-mile Spillway Trail. 3. The 0.8-mile Ore Pit Trail. 4. The 0.8-mile J. Bailey Trail (loop). 5. The 1-mile Wildcat Trail. 6. The 1.7-mile Creech Hollow Trail. 7. The 11.7-mile Montgomery Bell Overnight Trail (easy-moderate loop).

PICKETT STATE PARK Rock Creek Route, Jamestown, TN 38556; (615)879-5821. 11,752 acres. Pickett State Park is in the upper Cumberland Mountains of north-central Tennessee, next to the Big South Fork National River and Recreation Area. The park is notable for its unusual rock formations, bluffs, caves, and natural sandstone bridges. Also here are 15-acre Arch Lake with a sandy beach, wildflowers, dense rhododendron groves, mountain laurel, holly, and huckleberry, as well as forests of pine, hemlock, poplar, birch, and magnolia. Wildlife includes white-tailed deer, wild hog, pileated woodpecker, and barred owl.

• *Suggested Trails for Nature Walks:* 1. The 0.3-mile Indian Rockhouse Trail. 2. The 0.5-mile Island Loop Trail. 3. The 0.8-mile Lake View Trail. 4. The 1-mile Bluff Trail. 5. The 1.3-mile Natural Bridge Loop. 6. The 2.5-mile Lake Loop. 7. The 2.5-mile Hazard Cave Trail (loop). 8. The 3-mile Ridge Trail (loop). 9. The 1-mile Double Falls Trail (moderate). 10. The 4-mile Sheltowee Trace Trail (moderate).

FALL CREEK FALLS STATE RESORT PARK Route 3, Pikeville, TN 37367; (615)881-3297.

15,800 acres. This state park is located at the western end of the Cumberland Plateau, in central Tennessee. It features 256-foot Fall Creek Falls, several other waterfalls, streams including Cane Creek, and a lake. There are hills and gorges, rock ledges and overlooks, fields and wildflowers, with a forest of oak, hickory, hemlock, and poplar, plus rhododendron and mountain laurel. Among the wildlife are white-tailed deer, bobcat, fox, woodchuck, skunk, grouse, owl, and hawk.

• *Suggested Trails for Nature Walks:* 1. The 0.5-mile Fall Creek Falls Trail. 2. The 0.5-mile Trail to the Foot of Fall Creek Falls. 3. The 0.8-mile Woodland Trail. 4. The 1.1-mile Gorge Overlook. 5. The 4.6-mile Paw Paw Loop. 6. The 12-mile Cane Creek Lower Loop (easy-moderate). 7. The 13-mile Cane Creek Upper Loop (moderate).

WARRIORS' PATH STATE PARK P.O. Box 5026, Kingsport, TN 37663; (615)239-8531. 870 acres. Named after a path once used by the Cherokee, Warriors' Path State Park in northeast Tennessee sits on the shore of Patrick Henry Reservoir and the dammed Holston River. The park includes meadows, wildflowers, forests, hills, ridges, and high river bluffs.

• *Suggested Trails for Nature Walks:* 1. The 0.5-mile Lakeshore Trail. 2. The 0.5-mile Riverbank Trail. 3. The 0.5-mile Overlook Trail. 4. The 0.8-mile Lake Hollow Trail. 5. The 0.8-mile Holston Bluffs Trail loop. 6. The 0.8-mile Connector Trail. 7. The 2-mile Woodland Ridge Trail (loop). 8. The 2.5-mile Devil's Backbone Trail (easy-moderate).

NATCHEZ TRACE STATE PARK Wildersville, TN 38388; (901)968-3742. 14,073 acres. Surrounded by lands of 48,000-acre Natchez Trace State Forest in west-central Tennessee, this state park features four lakes, including 690-acre Pin Oak Lake, as well as sandy ridges, streams, open fields, and an oak-hickory forest with poplar and pine, maple and beech, sweetgum and boxelder. There's also an 118-foot pecan tree. White-tailed deer, bobcat, fox, raccoon, and beaver are among the wildlife.

• *Suggested Trails for Nature Walks:* 1. The 0.5-mile Twin Ridge Trail (loop). 2. The 1-mile Fern Trail. 3. The 1.5-mile Pin Oak Lake Trail. 4. The 3-mile Fairview Gullies Trail (loop). 5. The 4-mile Deer Trail. 6. The 3.5-mile Cub Lake Trail (moderate). 7. The 32-mile Red Leaves Trail (moderate).

CUMBERLAND MOUNTAIN STATE PARK Route 8, Box 322, Crossville, TN 38555; (615) 484-6138. 1,720 acres. Cumberland Mountain State Park is located on the Cumberland Plateau in east-central Tennessee. It's a place of pine and hemlock forests, streams including Byrd Creek, and man-made Byrd Lake.

• *Suggested Trails for Nature Walks:* 1. The 0.7-mile Byrd Lake Trail. 2. The 1-mile Cumberland Plateau Trail. 3. The 2-mile Pioneer Short Loop. 4. The 3-mile Pioneer Trail. 5. The 2.1-mile Byrd Creek Trail (easy-moderate loop). 6. The 6-mile Cumberland Overnight Trail (easy-moderate loop).

Other Suitable Locations for Nature Walks in Tennessee

Tennessee has forty-nine state parks, state recreation areas, and state natural areas, and forty-five of these locations feature foot trails. Information: Tennessee State Parks, 401 Church Street, Nashville, TN 37243; (615)532-0001.

Five national wildlife areas in the state have trails. Information: U.S. Fish and Wildlife Service, 1875 Century Boulevard, Atlanta, GA 30345.

There are trails at several Tennessee lakes managed by the U.S. Army Corps of Engineers. Information: Corps of Engineers, Nashville District, P.O. Box 1070, Nashville, TN 37202; (615)736-5115.

Some areas administered by the Tennessee Valley Authority include trails. Information: Tennessee Valley Authority, 17 Ridgeway Road, Norris, TN 37828; (615)632-1805.

The Land Between the Lakes National Recreation Area, which is divided between Kentucky and Tennessee, has a number of trails (see the Kentucky chapter). Information: Land Between the Lakes, 100 Van Morgan Drive, Golden Pond, KY 42211; (502)924-5602.

TEXAS

Recommended Areas for Nature Walks

BIG BEND NATIONAL PARK Big Bend National Park, TX 79834; (915)477-2251. 708,200 acres. Located in the Chihuahuan Desert and Chisos Mountains of southwestern Texas, this national park is named for the great bend in the Rio Grande, which forms the southern boundary of the park for 118 miles. The mountainous terrain here includes cliffs, canyons, and badlands with rock formations. Highest elevation is 7,825-foot Emory Peak.

The desert vegetation includes yucca, mesquite, and prickly pear cactus, with grasslands, cottonwood, and willow along the river, and juniper, oak, pinyon pine, as well as fir and aspen at higher elevations. Among the wildlife are white-tailed and mule deer, black bear, mountain lion, coyote, jackrabbit, peregrine falcon, and golden eagle. Ranger-led nature walks are available.

• *Suggested Trails for Nature Walks:* 1. The 0.5-mile Chihuahuan Desert Nature Trail. 2. The 0.5-mile Bottom of Burro Mesa Pouroff. 3. The 0.8-mile Rio Grande Village Nature Trail. 4. The 0.8-mile Santa Elena Canyon Trail. 5. The 0.7-mile Boquillas Canyon Trail. 6. The 1.6-mile Chisos Basin Loop Trail. 7. The 1.7-mile Mule Ears Spring Trail. 8. The 2.4-mile Chimneys Trail. 9. The 2.6-mile Window Trail (easy-moderate). 10. The 2.4-mile Lost Mine Trail (moderate).

GUADALUPE MOUNTAINS NATIONAL PARK HC 60, Box 400, Salt Flat, TX 79847; (915)828-3251. 76,920 acres. The Guadalupe Mountains are part of the 400-mile-long Capitan Reef, uplifted from an ancient ocean bed, with elevations surpassing 8,000 feet. Located in the Chihuahuan Desert along the New Mexico border, Guadalupe Mountains National Park protects a portion of the area. Highest point is 8,749-foot Guadalupe Peak.

There are a number of steep canyons here, among them forested McKittrick Canyon, which has maple, ash, oak, and walnut trees, as well as other lush vegetation. Cactus, cholla, and yucca are found elsewhere in the desert, and ponderosa pine, fir, and aspen grow at higher elevations. Wildlife includes mule deer, elk, black bear, mountain lion, coyote, gray fox, porcupine, jackrabbit, and peregrine falcon.

• *Suggested Trails for Nature Walks:* 1. The 0.6-mile Indian Meadow Nature Loop. 2. The 0.8-mile Pinery Trail. 3. The 0.9-mile McKittrick Canyon Nature Loop. 4. The 2.1-mile Devil's Hall Trail. 5. The 2.3-mile Smith Springs Loop Trail. 6. The 2.3-mile Bush Mountain Trail to Marcus Overlook. 7. The 3.4-mile McKittrick Canyon Trail. 8. The 5.5-mile Frijole-Foothills Trail (loop). 9. The 5.7-mile El Capitan Trail.

BIG THICKET NATIONAL PRESERVE 3785 Milam, Beaumont, TX 77701; (409)839-2689. 86,000 acres. Consisting of a cluster of twelve separate units of land in east Texas, this national preserve was established to protect an area of exceptional biological diversity. Four of the units have established trails.

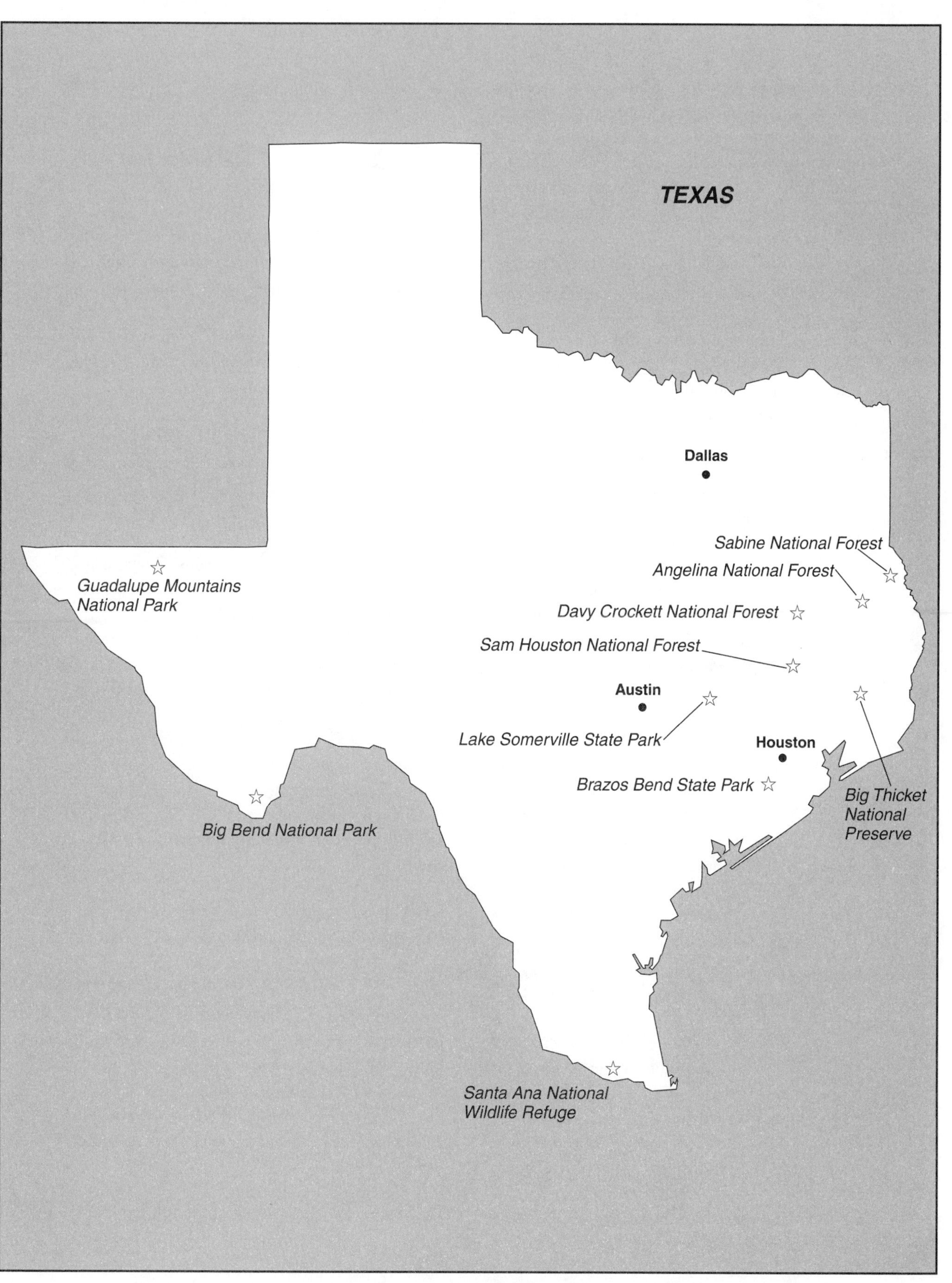
TEXAS
Dallas
Sabine National Forest
Angelina National Forest
Guadalupe Mountains
National Park
Davy Crockett National Forest
Sam Houston National Forest
Austin
Lake Somerville State Park
Houston
Brazos Bend State Park
Big Thicket
National
Preserve
Big Bend National Park
Santa Ana National
Wildlife Refuge

The region includes savannas and swamps, bayous and sloughs, creeks, and the Neches River. There are hardwood forests with cypress and stands of virgin pine, as well as beech, magnolia, holly, and sweetgum. Bobcat and coyote are among the wildlife here, and naturalist-led walks are available.

• *Suggested Trails for Nature Walks:* 1. The 0.4-mile Pitcher Plant Trail. 2. The 1-mile Sundew Trail (loop). 3. The 1-mile Beech Woods Trail (loop). 4. The 1.5-mile Beaver Slide Trail (loop). 5. The 4.1-mile Kirby Nature Trail (loop). 6. The 5.4-mile Woodlands Trail (loop). 7. The 15-mile Turkey Creek Trail.

SAM HOUSTON NATIONAL FOREST Homer Garrison Federal Building, 701 North First Street, Lufkin, TX 75901; (409)639-8501. 158,650 acres. Sam Houston National Forest in east Texas features small ridges and bottomlands with lakes and streams as well as hardwood and pine forests. Included within the forest are the 3,810-acre Little Lake Creek Wilderness and the 1,460-acre Big Creek Scenic Area. White-tailed deer, gray fox, bobcat, and armadillo are among the wildlife.

• *Suggested Trails for Nature Walks:* 1. The 0.5-mile Double Lake Trail. 2. The 0.5-mile Big Magnolia Trail. 3. The 0.8-mile Pine Trail. 4. The 1.5-mile White Oak Trail. 5. The 2-mile Big Creek Trail. 6. The 1.1-mile Stubblefield Interpretive Trail. 7. The 1.7-mile Lake Shore Trail. 8. The 5-mile Big Creek-Double Lake Trail. 9. The 140-mile Lone Star National Recreation Trail, which includes several loops.

SANTA ANA NATIONAL WILDLIFE REFUGE Route 2, Box 202A, Alamo, TX 78516; (210)787-3079. 2,080 acres. Situated alongside the Rio Grande near the southern tip of Texas, this national wildlife refuge has nearly flat terrain with subtropical riparian woodlands, several lakes, and 265 species of butterflies. Among the trees and shrubs are elm, hackberry, persimmon, ebony, and mesquite. Wildlife includes mountain lion, bobcat, gray fox, coyote, javelina, armadillo, beaver, opossum, and bat, as well as blue-winged teal, chachalaca, great horned owl, American kestral, and red-shouldered hawk. Four-mile guided bird walks are offered.

• *Suggested Trails for Nature Walks:* 1. The 0.3-mile Mesquite Trail. 2. The 0.6-mile Highland Trail. 3. The 0.8-mile Terrace Trail. 4. The 0.9-mile Vireo Trail. 5. The 1-mile Resaca Trail. 6. The 1.4-mile Jaguarundi Trail. 7. The 1.5-mile Cattail Trail. 8. The 1.6-mile Santa Ana Communities Trail. 9. The 2-mile Owl Trail. 10. The 2-mile Wildlife Management Trail.

ANGELINA NATIONAL FOREST 1907 Atkinson Drive, P.O. Box 756, Lufkin, TX 75901; (409)639-8620. 156,150 acres. Angelina National Forest stretches out on both sides of enormous Sam Rayburn Reservoir in east Texas. The forest includes some streams, rivers, lakes, and two designated wilderness areas, the 12,423-acre Upland Island Wilderness and the 5,286-acre Turkey Hill Wilderness. Vegetation consists of piney woods with longleaf and loblolly pine, baldcypress, magnolia, and dogwood.

• *Suggested Trails for Nature Walks:* 1. The 0.2-mile Board Foot Forest Walk. 2. The 0.5-mile Caney Creek Recreation Area Trail. 3. The 0.7-mile Boykin Springs Trail. 4. The 5.5-mile Sawmill Hiking Trail, which includes a 0.8-mile spur trail.

SABINE NATIONAL FOREST Homer Garrison Federal Building, 701 North First Street, Lufkin, TX 75901; (409)639-8501. 189,450 acres. Located west of huge Toledo Bend Reservoir along the Louisiana border, Sabine National Forest has a number of creeks, lakes, and high bluffs, and includes the 10,917-acre Indian Mountains Wilderness, with a forest of pine, oak, beech, and other hardwoods. Among the wildlife are white-tailed deer, raccoon, opossum, osprey, and bald eagle.

• *Suggested Trails for Nature Walks:* 1. The 0.3-mile Willow Oak Forest Walk. 2. The 0.5-mile

Tower Trail. 3. The 1-mile Mother Nature's Trail. 4. The 28-mile Trail Between the Lakes, a new trail which extends from Sam Rayburn Reservoir to Toledo Bend Reservoir.

DAVY CROCKETT NATIONAL FOREST Homer Garrison Federal Building, 701 North First Street, Lufkin, TX 75901; (409)639-8501. 161,480 acres. Davy Crockett National Forest is a place of rolling terrain with some bluffs, creeks, lakes, bogs, man-made ponds, and pine and hardwood forests, with white-tailed deer among the wildlife. There's one designated wilderness area, the 3,584-acre Big Slough Wilderness.

• *Suggested Trails for Nature Walks:* 1. The 2-mile Tall Pines Trail. 2. The 3-mile Tramway Trail. 3. The 20-mile 4 C National Recreation Trail.

LAKE SOMERVILLE STATE PARK Rt. 1, Box 499, Somerville, TX 77879; (409)535-7763. This park in east-central Texas consists of two separate units alongside 11,460-acre Lake Somerville, the 640-acre Birch Unit and the 300-acre Nails Unit. Terrain is rolling, with stands of oak, hickory, and yaupon. Wildlife includes white-tailed deer, coyote, fox, and raccoon.

• *Suggested Trails for Nature Walks:* 1. The 5-mile Birch Nature Trail, consisting of several loops. 2. The 3-mile Nails Nature Trail. 3. The 21.6-mile Lake Somerville Trailway, a multiuse trail that connects the park's two units.

BRAZOS BEND STATE PARK 21901 FM 762, Needville, TX 77461; (409)553-3243. 4,897 acres. Located alongside the Brazos River in east Texas, south of Houston, this state park features the Brazos River floodplain, with Big Creek, bayous, sloughs, and oxbow lakes, as well as tallgrass coastal prairie with Indian grass, little bluestem, and switch grass. There are also stands of oak, pecan, elm, cottonwood, sycamore, and black willow trees. Among the wildlife are white-tailed deer, bobcat, gray fox, raccoon, armadillo, and alligator, along with a diverse bird population. Guided walks are offered on weekends.

• *Suggested Trails for Nature Walks:* 1. The 0.5-mile Creekfield Lake Nature Trail. 2. The 0.5-mile Observation Tower Trail. 3. The 0.6-mile Elm Lake Trail. 4. The 2-mile Red Buckeye Trail. 5. The 2.4-mile White Oak Trail (loop). 6. The 2.5-mile Bluestem Trail. 7. The 4.1-mile Elm Lake-Forty Acre Lake Loop.

Other Suitable Locations for Nature Walks in Texas

Texas has eighty-one state parks and seven state natural areas. The majority of these locations have nature or hiking trails. Information: Texas Parks & Wildlife, 4200 Smith School Road, Austin, TX 78744; (800)792-1112.

There are ten national wildlife refuges in the state that have trails. Information: U.S. Fish and Wildlife Service, P.O. Box 1306, Albuquerque, NM 87103.

The U.S. Army Corps of Engineers administers a number of lakes in Texas where there are trails. Information: Corps of Engineers, Fort Worth District, P.O. Box 17300, Fort Worth, TX 76102; (817)334-2705.

UTAH

Recommended Areas for Nature Walks

ZION NATIONAL PARK Springdale, UT 84767; (801)772-3256. 147,000 acres. Located in southwestern Utah, Zion National Park is renowned for its striking reddish-brown cliffs, deep and narrow canyons, high plateaus, and slickrock scenery including sculpted mesas and rock formations, as well as sandstone arches—including 310-foot Kolob Arch, said to be the world's largest stone arch. Dominating the park is Zion Canyon, with walls 2,000 to 3,000 feet high and the Virgin River flowing through.

There are also streams and waterfalls, a petrified forest, and stands of pinyon-juniper with ponderosa pine, Douglas fir, and aspen at higher elevations, cottonwood and willow along the rivers, and other desert vegetation including cacti, yucca, and wildflowers. Among the wildlife are mule deer, mountain lion, ringtail, coyote, fox, porcupine, beaver, and jackrabbit, along with green-winged teal, great horned owl, and peregrine falcon. Naturalist-led walks are scheduled from March-November.

• *Suggested Trails for Nature Walks:* 1. The 0.3-mile Weeping Rock Trail. 2. The 0.5-mile Canyon Overlook Trail. 3. The 0.6-mile Lower Emerald Pools Trail. 4. The 1-mile Riverside Walk Trail. 5. The 1-mile Middle Pool Loop Trail. 6. The 1.8-mile Coalpits Wash Trail. 7. The 2.1-mile Northgate Peaks Trail. 8. The 2.5-mile East Mesa Trail. 9. The 8.1-mile Chinle Trail. 10. The 1-mile Watchman Trail (easy-moderate).

CANYONLANDS NATIONAL PARK 2282 South West Resource Boulevard, Moab, UT 84532; (801)259-7164. 337,570 acres. Stretching across the Colorado Plateau in southeastern Utah, this national park features two huge canyons and dozens of smaller ones, with buttes and mesas, rock arches and spires, castles and fins, towers and rock walls. The Green and Colorado rivers meet in the park.

Two areas of special interest are the Maze, a profusion of clustered canyons, and the Needles, a place of sculpted and colored rock pinnacles and arches. Also in the park are ruins of Anasazi Indian cliff dwellings. There's desert vegetation including pinyon-juniper and wildflowers, with desert bighorn sheep, mule deer, pronghorn, coyote, fox, bobcat, long-eared owl, snowy egret, and sharp-shinned hawk among the wildlife.

• *Suggested Trails for Nature Walks:* 1. The 0.5-mile Mesa Arch Trail (loop). 2. The 0.5-mile Aztec Butte Trail. 3. The 0.6-mile Pothole Point Trail (loop). 4. The 0.6-mile Cave Spring Trail (loop). 5. The 1-mile Whale Rock Trail. 6. The 1.3-mile Murphy Point Trail. 7. The 1.5-mile White Rim Overlook Trail. 8. The 2-mile Grand View Point Trail. 9. The 2.4-mile Slickrock Foot Trail (loop). 10. The 5-mile Neck Spring Trail (loop).

ARCHES NATIONAL PARK P.O. Box 907, Moab, UT 84532; (801)259-8161. 73,389 acres.

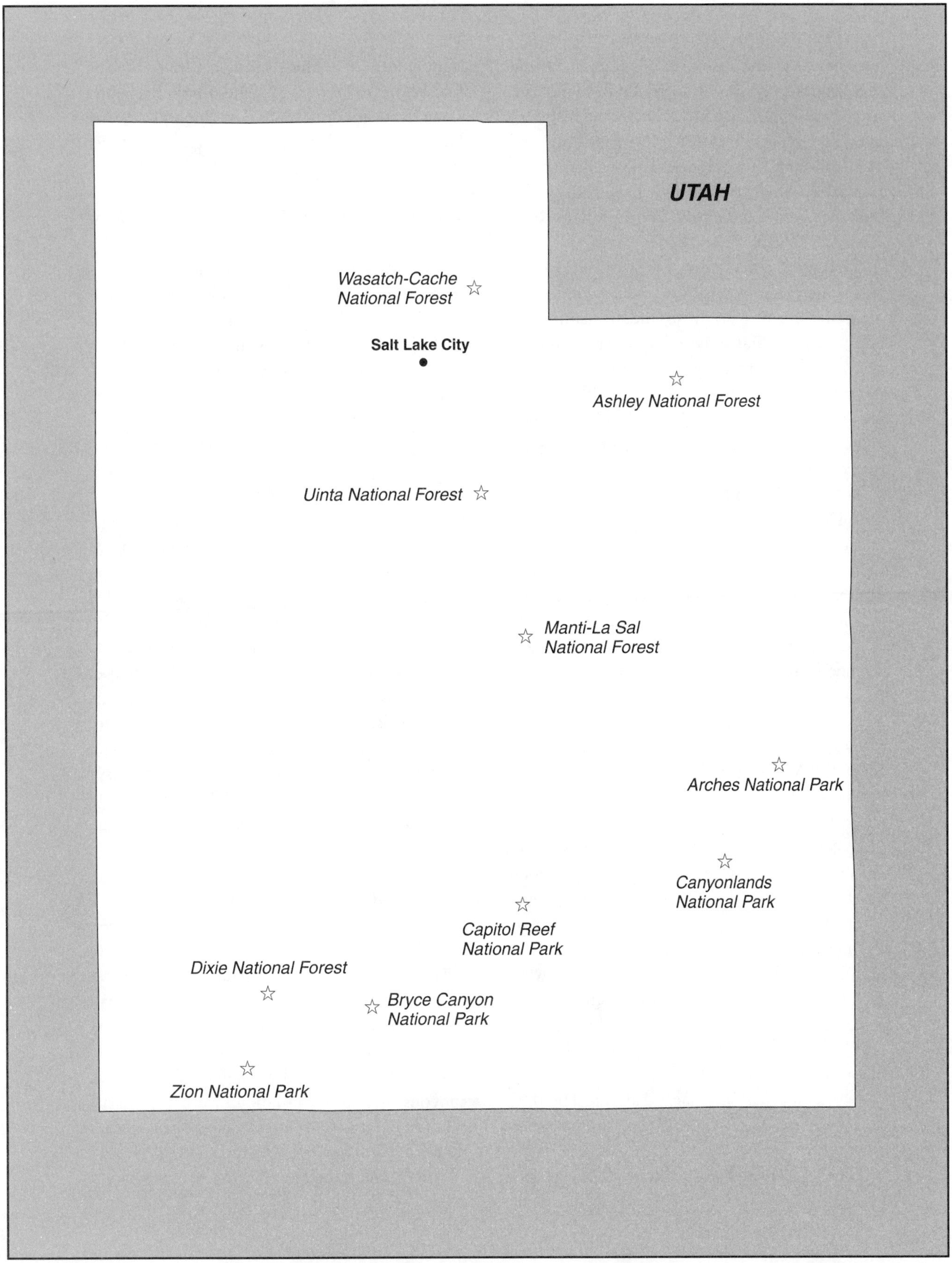

UTAH

Wasatch-Cache National Forest

Salt Lake City

Ashley National Forest

Uinta National Forest

Manti-La Sal National Forest

Arches National Park

Canyonlands National Park

Capitol Reef National Park

Dixie National Forest

Bryce Canyon National Park

Zion National Park

This national park sits north of Moab in the red rock country of southeastern Utah. The park protects a sculpted slickrock landscape featuring over 200 arches, including 291-foot-long and 105-foot-high Landscape Arch, as well as spires, pinnacles, fins, monoliths, balanced rocks, bluffs, canyons, and caves. The Colorado River runs along the southern border.

Elevations range from 4,000 to over 5,600 feet. There are desert flora with wildflowers including evening primrose, Indian paintbrush, and wild rose, plus pinyon and juniper. Among the wildlife are mule deer, kit fox, porcupine, jackrabbit, and cottontail, along with pinyon jay, mountain bluebird, screech owl, golden eagle, and red-tailed hawk. Ranger-led walks are offered in summer.

• *Suggested Trails for Nature Walks:* 1. The 0.2-mile Desert Nature Trail. 2. The 0.2-mile Balanced Rock Trail (loop). 3. The 0.2-mile Sand Dune Arch Trail. 4. The 0.2-mile Skyline Arch Trail. 5. The 0.3-mile Double Arch Trail. 6. The 0.5-mile Broken Arch Trail. 7. The 0.9-mile Windows Trail (loop). 8. The 1-mile Park Avenue Trail. 9. The 1-mile Tower Arch Trail (easy-moderate). 10. The 1.5-mile Delicate Arch Trail (easy-moderate).

BRYCE CANYON NATIONAL PARK Bryce Canyon, UT 84717; (801)834-5322. 37,102 acres. Bryce Canyon National Park in southern Utah is known for its colored and endlessly varied pinnacles and spires, other rock formations and badlands, cliffs, canyons, and plateaus. There are forests of ponderosa pine and aspen, fir and spruce, with sagebrush, pinyon and juniper, bitterbrush and manzanita. Wildflowers include wild iris, blue columbine, evening primrose, and Indian paintbrush. Mule deer, mountain lion, fox, coyote, bobcat, prairie dog, and marmot are among the wildlife.

• *Suggested Trails for Nature Walks:* 1. The 0.9-mile Queen's Garden Trail. 2. The 1-mile Bristlecone Loop Trail. 3. The 5.5-mile Rim Trail. 4. The 1.4-mile Navajo Loop Trail (easy-moderate). 5. The 1.5-mile Tower Bridge Trail (moderate). 6. The 1.9-mile Trail to the Hat Shop (moderate). 7. The 3-mile Peekaboo Loop Trail (moderate). 8. The 8-mile Fairyland Loop Trail (moderate). 9. The 22-mile Under the Rim Trail (moderate).

CAPITOL REEF NATIONAL PARK Torrey, UT 84775; (801)425-3791. 241,865 acres. This desert national park in south-central Utah protects most of the 100-mile-long, 2,000-foot-high Waterpocket Fold, an uplifted and eroded cliff. The park features many steep, rainbow-colored slickrock canyons, cliffs and ledges, domes and mesas, sandstone pinnacles and formations, natural bridges and arches.

Vegetation consists of desert flora and wildflowers, sagebrush and rabbitbrush, as well as pinyon-juniper woodlands, with stands of Douglas fir, oak, and cottonwood. Wildlife includes mule deer, black bear, mountain lion, red fox, bobcat, coyote, badger, porcupine, skunk, jackrabbit, marmot, and mink. Ranger-guided walks are offered from May to September.

• *Suggested Trails for Nature Walks:* 1. The 0.1-mile Goosenecks Trail. 2. The 0.3-mile Sunset Point Trail. 3. The first 0.5 mile of the 1.3-mile Fremont River Trail. 4. The 1-mile Capitol Gorge Trail. 5. The 2.3-mile Grand Wash Trail. 6. The 1-mile Hickman Bridge Trail (easy-moderate). 7. The 3.5-mile Old Wagon Trail (moderate). 8. The 2.3-mile Fremont Gorge Overlook Trail (moderate).

WASATCH-CACHE NATIONAL FOREST 8236 Federal Building, 125 South State Street, Salt Lake City, UT 84138; (801)524-5030. 1,219,748 acres. Located directly north and east of Salt Lake City in northern Utah, with a small area in southwest Wyoming, this national forest includes portions of the Wasatch and Uinta mountains as well as the Stanbury Range, with canyons, streams, lakes, and Great Basin Desert. Highest point is 13,442-foot Gilbert Peak. Seven designated wilderness areas total 612,000 acres.

There are mountain meadows, grasses and sedges, bitterbrush and sagebrush, and such wildflowers as cliffbrake, blue lupine, coneflower, Indian paintbrush, and cinquefoil, along with gooseberry, elderberry, and honeysuckle. The forest consists of subalpine fir and Englemann spruce, with limber pine and quaking aspen, willow and birch. Among the wildlife are mule deer, moose, elk, mountain goat, porcupine, muskrat, and beaver, plus spotted sandpiper, American kestrel, golden eagle, and peregrine falcon.

• *Suggested Trails for Nature Walks:* 1. The Tony Grove Lake Nature Trail (loop). 2. The Hidden Hollow Nature Trail (loop). 3. The Limber Pine Nature Trail (loop). 4. The 1.5-mile Riverside Nature Trail. 5. The 1.8-mile Little Water Trail. 6. The 2-mile Terraces-Elbow Fork Trail. 7. The 3-mile Big Water Trail. 8. The 5.5-mile Pipeline Trail. 9. The 2.8-mile Grandeur Peak Trail (moderate). 10. The 4-mile Bowman Fork Trail (moderate).

UINTA NATIONAL FOREST P.O. Box 1428, Provo, UT 84603; (801)377-5780. 949,848 acres. Uinta National Forest in north-central Utah features lofty rugged peaks including 11,877-foot Mt. Nebo and 11,750-foot Mt. Timpanogos, with high deserts, steep canyons and basins, foothills and valleys, springs, creeks, and lakes. Three designated wilderness areas total 69,000 acres.

There are open meadows, ferns, wildflowers including glacier lily, western coneflower, and columbine, as well as forests of Douglas fir, spruce, limber pine, subalpine and white fir, plus maple, oak, cottonwood, boxelder, and aspen. Among the wildlife are elk, mule deer, black bear, moose, Rocky Mountain goat, mountain lion, and hawk.

• *Suggested Trails for Nature Walks:* 1. The 0.6-mile Cascade Springs Interpretive Trail. 2. The 1-mile Trappers Cove Interpretive Trail. 3. The first mile of the 2-mile Silver Lake Trail. 4. The first 1.5 miles of the 5.3-mile Aspen Grove Trail. 5. The first 1.5-miles of the 8.6-mile Fifth Water Trail. 6. The 2-mile Stewart Cascades Trail. 7. The 2.6-mile Cottonwood Canyon Trail (easy-moderate). 8. The 1.7-mile Forest Lake Trail (moderate).

ASHLEY NATIONAL FOREST 355 North Vernal Avenue, Vernal, UT 84078; (801)789-1181. 1,384,131 acres. Occupying the northeast corner of Utah and extending into southwest Wyoming, Ashley National Forest is in the Uinta Mountains and includes 13,528-foot Kings Peak, highest elevation in the state. In addition to mountains there are plateaus, glacial basins, steep canyons, rock formations, and desert badlands.

Of special interest are the 200,000-acre Flaming Gorge National Recreation Area and much of the 460,000-acre High Uintas Wilderness, which extends into Wasatch-Cache National Forest. There are meadows and grasslands, pinyon-juniper woodlands, and forests of ponderosa and lodgepole pine, Douglas fir, spruce, and aspen. Mule deer, pronghorn, moose, elk, bear, mountain lion, and bighorn sheep are among the wildlife.

• *Suggested Trails for Nature Walks:* 1. The 1.5-mile Bear Canyon-Bootleg Trail. 2. The first mile of the 5-mile Dowd Mountain-Hideout Canyon Trail. 3. The 5-mile Canyon Rim Trail. 4. The 7.3-mile Little Hole National Recreation Trail. 5. The 1.5-mile Tamarack Lake Trail (easy-moderate). 6. The 2-mile Ute Mountain Trail.

MANTI-LA SAL NATIONAL FOREST 599 West Price River Drive, Price, UT 84501; (801)637-2817. 1,327,600 acres. Manti-La Sal National Forest is made up of four separate tracts in southeast and central Utah, a region of desert mountains, ridges, red-rock plateaus, mesas, precipitous cliffs, canyons, and arches, along with high lakes, mountain meadows with wildflowers, and grasslands with sagebrush and manzanita.

There are also areas of pinyon-juniper, as well as forests of ponderosa pine, alpine and Douglas fir, Englemann spruce, and aspen, with huckleberry and gooseberry. Wildlife includes mule deer, black bear, elk, moose, mountain lion, coyote, fox, porcupine, jackrabbit, prairie dog, and bat, as well as black tern, snowy egret, nighthawk, prairie falcon, and red-tailed hawk.

• *Suggested Trails for Nature Walks:* 1. The 3-mile Scad Valley Trail. 2. The 6-mile Lake Trail. 3. The 3-mile Oowah-Warner Trail (easy-moderate). 4. The 5.5-mile Tuerto Canyon Trail (easy-moderate). 5. The 8-mile Silver Creek Trail (easy-moderate). 6. The 10-mile Fish Creek National Recreation Trail (easy-moderate). 7. The 4-mile Mill Canyon Trail (moderate). 8. The 4-mile East Mountain Trail (moderate). 9. The 4-mile Left Fork of Huntington Canyon Trail (moderate). 10. The 9-mile Castle Valley Ridge Trail (moderate).

DIXIE NATIONAL FOREST 82 North 100 East, P.O. Box 580, Cedar City, UT 84721; (801)865-3700. 1,900,000 acres. Comprising several units of land in southwestern Utah, near Zion and Bryce Canyon national parks, this national forest has a landscape of mountains and ridges, canyons and red-rock formations, cliffs and mesas, streams and lakes. Elevations range from 3,500 to over 11,000 feet.

Vegetation includes alpine meadows with wildflowers, grasses, sagebrush, stands of bristlecone pine, and forests of spruce, fir, ponderosa pine, aspen, mahogany, oak, and juniper. Among the wildlife are elk, pronghorn, black bear, mule deer, mountain lion, bobcat, fox, coyote, snowshoe hare, jackrabbit, and bat, along with wild turkey, grouse, great blue heron, and bald eagle.

• *Suggested Trails for Nature Walks:* 1. The 0.5-mile Bristlecone Pine Trail. 2. The 0.5-mile Old Ranger Trail. 3. The 0.5-mile Singing Pine Trail. 4. The 0.7-mile Bear Valley-Willow Trail. 5. The 0.8-mile Cascade Falls Trail (easy-moderate). 6. The 32-mile Virgin River Rim Trail (easy-moderate). 7. The 2.5-mile Trail Creek Trail (moderate). 8. The 3-mile Left Fork Bunker Trail (moderate). 9. The 6-mile Dark Hollow Trail (moderate). 10. The 7.5-mile Willow Creek Trail (moderate).

Other Suitable Locations for Nature Walks in Utah

Utah has forty-five state parks, and some of these locations feature suitable trails. Information: Utah Division of Parks and Recreation, 1636 West North Temple, Suite 116, Salt Lake City, UT 84116; (801)538-7220.

An additional national forest in Utah has a network of trails: Fishlake National Forest, 115 East 900 North, Richfield, UT 84701; (801)896-9233.

A number of Bureau of Land Management areas in the state have trails. Information: BLM, Utah State Office, P.O. Box 45155, Salt Lake City, UT 84145; (801)539-4001.

There are trails at Natural Bridges National Monument. Information: Natural Bridges National Monument, Box 1, Lake Powell, UT 84533; (801)259-5174.

Cedar Breaks National Monument has trails. Information: Cedar Breaks National Monument, P.O. Box 749, Cedar City, UT 84720; (801)586-9451.

VERMONT

Recommended Areas for Nature Walks

GREEN MOUNTAIN NATIONAL FOREST 231 North Main Street, Rutland, VT 05701; (802)747-6700. 350,000 acres. Stretching along the spine of the Green Mountains, this national forest consists of two large tracts in southern and west-central Vermont. Here are a multitude of mountains and deep valleys, rugged ridges with cliffs and overhangs, meadows, and many streams, waterfalls, lakes, and ponds. Elevations range as high as 4,000 feet.

Six designated wilderness areas total 58,539 acres. Most of the region is hardwood-forested with oak and birch, maple and beech, along with spruce, hemlock, and pine, and there are many shrubs and wildflowers. Wildlife includes white-tailed deer, black bear, moose, coyote, bobcat, fox, beaver, raccoon, and porcupine, plus grouse, peregrine falcon, and red-tailed hawk.

• *Suggested Trails for Nature Walks:* 1. The 0.6-mile Goshen Trail. 2. The 0.8-mile Hapgood Pond Trail. 3. The 1-mile Robert Frost Interpretive Trail. 4. The 1.2-mile Texas Falls Nature Trail. 5. The 1.2-mile Minnie Baker Trail. 6. The 1.3-mile Hancock Branch Trail. 7. The 1.7-mile Chittenden Brook Campground Loop. 8. The 2.5-mile Silver Lake Interpretive Trail (loop). 9. In the Grout Pond Area are 10 miles of easy loop trails.

GROTON STATE FOREST Vermont Department of Forests, Parks and Recreation, 103 South Main Street, Waterbury, VT 05671; (802) 241-3655. 25,645 acres. Groton State Forest in north-central Vermont encompasses hills and small but rugged mountain peaks and ridges with ledges and rock outcroppings, old fields, bogs, marshes, swamps, streams, ponds, and several sizable lakes including 414-acre Lake Groton.

Within the state forest boundaries is the 700-acre Peacham Bog Natural Area, and there's a nature center. It's a forest of maple, birch, beech, and other northern hardwoods, along with pine, spruce, and fir. Among the wildlife are white-tailed deer, black bear, moose, fox, porcupine, beaver, fisher, otter, and mink, as well as grouse, heron, and loon.

• *Suggested Trails for Nature Walks:* 1. The 0.6-mile Nature Trail. 2. The 0.9-mile Little Loop Trail. 3. The 0.5-mile New Discovery Campground to Osmore Pond Trail. 4. The 1.5-mile Owl's Head Trail. 5. The 2-mile Osmore Pond Loop Trail. 6. The 3-mile Kettle Pond Trail. 7. The 1.3-mile Hosmer Brook Trail (easy-moderate). 8. The 1.7-mile Big Deer Mountain Trail (easy-moderate). 9. The 1.9-mile Coldwater Brook Trail (moderate). 10. The 2.5-mile Peacham Bog Trail (moderate).

BOMOSEEN STATE PARK c/o Vermont Department of Forests, Parks, and Recreation, RR #2, Box 2161, Pittsford, VT 05763; (802)483-2314. 2,878 acres. This state park is located alongside 2,360-acre Lake Bomoseen in the northern Taconic Mountains of west-central

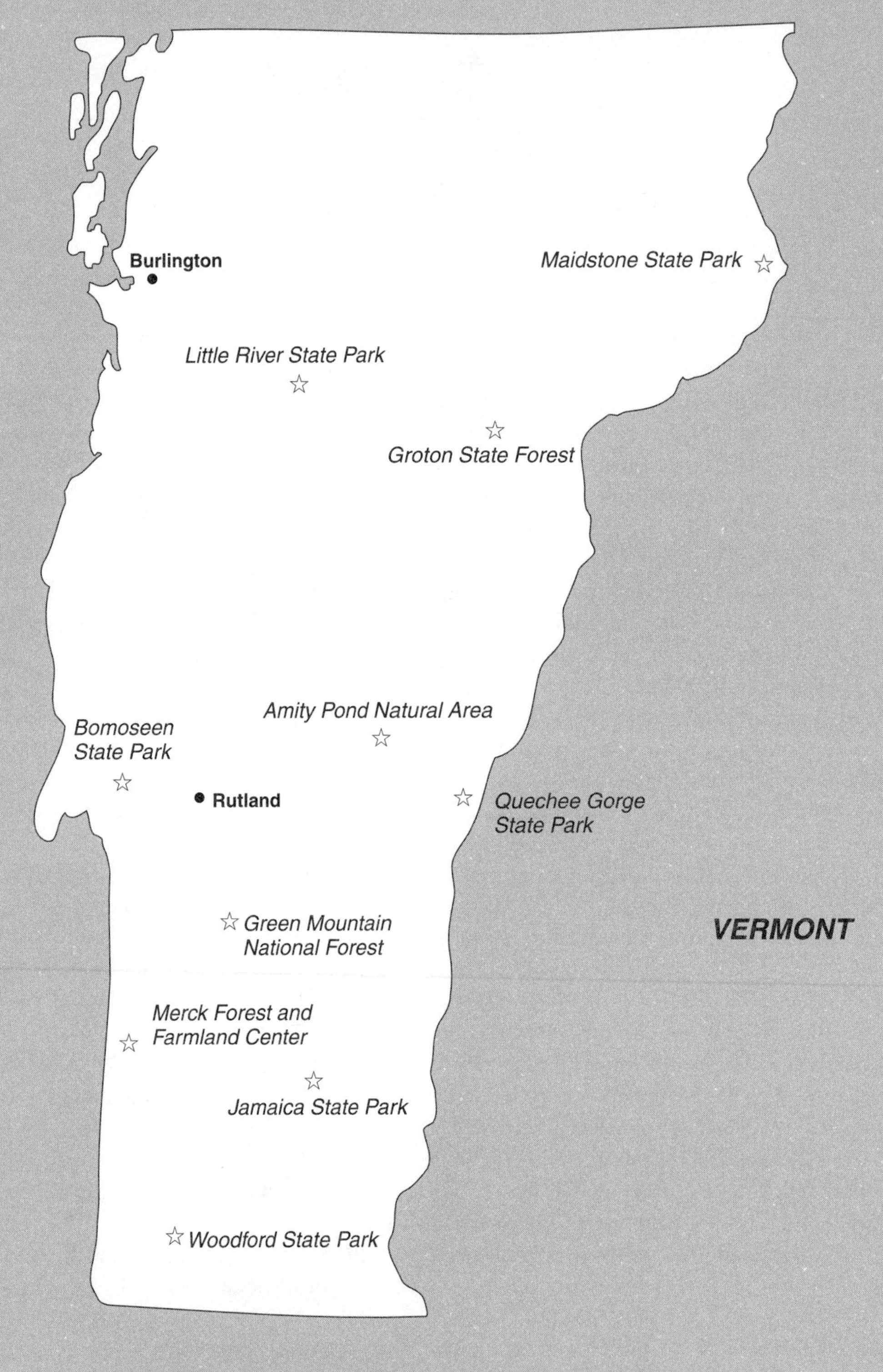
Burlington
Maidstone State Park
Little River State Park
Groton State Forest
Amity Pond Natural Area
Bomoseen
State Park
Rutland
Quechee Gorge
State Park
Green Mountain
National Forest
VERMONT
Merck Forest and
Farmland Center
Jamaica State Park
Woodford State Park

Vermont. Elevations here range from 450 to 700 feet. There are hills and ridges with slate bluffs, open fields and grassy areas, meadows and marshes, hardwood forests of oak and hickory, with hemlock and pine, plus several lakes and ponds, including 202-acre Glen Lake. White-tailed deer and beaver are among the wildlife.

• *Suggested Trails for Nature Walks:* 1. The 0.3-mile Half Moon Park Trail. 2. The 0.8-mile Daniel Coffey Memorial Trail. 3. The 1.5-mile Bomoseen Hiking Loop. 4. The 0.8-mile Slate History Trail. 5. The 4.5-mile Glen Lake Trail (easy-moderate).

WOODFORD STATE PARK c/o Department of Forests, Parks and Recreation, RR 2, Box 2161, Pittsford, VT 05763; (802)483-2314. 400 acres. Woodford State Park lies adjacent to Green Mountain National Forest's 5,060-acre George Aiken Wilderness, in southern Vermont. It's features 23-acre Adams Reservoir, and has marshes and bogs, small ponds and brooks, ferns and grasses, amid a forest of northern hardwoods and conifers. Maple, birch, beech, fir, and spruce are among the most common trees, and wildlife includes moose, white-tailed deer, black bear, beaver, and otter.

• *Suggested Trails for Nature Walks:* 1. The 0.5-mile Atwood Trail (loop). 2. The 2.7-mile trail around the reservoir.

MERCK FOREST AND FARMLAND CENTER P.O. Box 86, Rupert, VT 05768; (802)394-7836. 2,820 acres. Situated in southwestern Vermont's Taconic Mountains, with terrain ranging from hilly to mountainous, this privately owned forest is maintained for educational and other purposes including recreation. There's a demonstration farm with organic gardens and farm animals, along with meadows and grassy clearings, streams, two ponds, and a forest of oak, sugar maple, birch, aspen, fir, and spruce, Among the wildlife are white-tailed deer, porcupine, raccoon, snowshoe hare, and ruffed grouse.

• *Suggested Trails for Nature Walks:* 1. The 0.3-mile Long Tree Identification Trail. 2. The 0.8-mile Discovery Trail. 3. The 1.5-mile walk via several trails to the View Point (easy-moderate). 4. The forest has over 25 miles of other trails, ranging in difficulty from easy to strenuous.

JAMAICA STATE PARK c/o Department of Forests, Parks and Recreation, RR 1, Box 33, North Springfield, VT 05150; (802)886-2215. 772 acres. Consisting of two separate blocks of land in southern Vermont, Jamaica State Park includes small mountains as well as the West River, Branch and Cobb brooks, and 125-foot Hamilton Falls, one of the highest waterfalls in the state. There's a hardwood and hemlock forest with sugar maple and red oak, birch and beech, ash and elm, red spruce and white pine. White-tailed deer, beaver, and grouse are among the wildlife.

• *Suggested Trails for Nature Walks:* 1. The 3-mile Railroad Bed Trail. 2. The 1-mile Hamilton Falls Trail (moderate). 3. The 2-mile Overlook Trail (moderate).

QUECHEE GORGE STATE PARK c/o Department of Forests, Parks and Recreation, RR 1, Box 33, North Springfield, VT 05150; (802)886-2215. 612 acres. This state park in east-central Vermont protects 165-foot deep Quechee Gorge, which is a mile long and has steep rock walls, ledges, and the Ottauquechee River flowing through. There are also meadows, marshes, a mill pond, and a hardwood and conifer forest with maple, birch, hemlock, pine, and spruce.

• *Suggested Trails for Nature Walks:* 1. The 1.1-mile Quechee Gorge Trail (loop). 2. Several other short trails lead into the gorge, alongside the river, and past the mill pond.

MAIDSTONE STATE PARK c/o Department of Forests, Parks and Recreation, 324 North Main Street, Barre, VT 05641; (802)479-4280. 469 acres. This park lies alongside 796-acre Maidstone Lake near the Connecticut River, in Vermont's Northeast Kingdom. There are hills with streams, wildflowers, and a forest of red spruce and balsam fir, hemlock and cedar, maple and birch. Wildlife includes moose, white-tailed deer, black bear, porcupine, raccoon, beaver, and river otter, along with loon, black-backed woodpecker, owl, and hawk.

• *Suggested Trails for Nature Walks:* 1. The 0.5-mile Shore Trail. 2. The 0.5-mile Loon Trail (loop). 3. The 0.8-mile Moose Trail.

LITTLE RIVER STATE PARK RFD #1, Waterbury, VT 05676; (802)479-4280. 1,100 acres. Little River State Park is located on the Waterbury Reservoir within north-central Vermont's 40,333-acre Mt. Mansfield State Forest. It's a previously settled area that has reverted to a more natural state, with old stone walls, foundations, and other remnants of an earlier time. It's a place of high hills and brooks, grassy clearings and overgrown fields, and a forest of hemlock and white pine, basswood and white birch.

• *Suggested Trails for Nature Walks:* 1. The 0.5-mile Stevenson Brook Nature Trail. 2. The 0.3-mile Sawmill Loop Trail (easy-moderate). 3. The 1-mile Stevenson Brook Trail (easy-moderate). 4. The 2-mile Hedgehog Hill Loop Trail (easy-moderate). 5. The 2.8-mile Dalley Loop Trail (easy-moderate). 6. The 12-mile Little River Trail (moderate).

AMITY POND NATURAL AREA c/o Department of Forests, Parks and Recreation, RR 1, Box 33, North Springfield, VT 05150; (802)886-2215. 183 acres. Amity Pond Natural Area in east-central Vermont was given to the state with the requirement that motorized use be prohibited. It consists of old pastures and grassy areas with limestone outcroppings, brooks and swamps, shrubs and ferns, blackberry and raspberry bushes, and a hardwood forest with hemlock and other conifers. White-tailed deer, hare, and grouse are among the wildlife here.

• *Suggested Trails for Nature Walks:* The 2.7-mile Amity Pond Trail, which consists of a loop with some short spur trails (easy-moderate).

Other Suitable Locations for Nature Walks in Vermont

Vermont has forty state parks and a number of state forests, and the majority of these areas have at least short trails. Information: Vermont Department of Forests, Parks and Recreation, 103 South Main Street, Waterbury, VT 05676; (802)244-8711.

The Nature Conservancy manages thirty-three preserves and dozens of other small properties in Vermont. Some have trails and are open to the public. Information: The Vermont Nature Conservancy, 27 State Street, Montpelier, VT 05602; (802)229-4425.

The U.S. Army Corps of Engineers manages several lakes in Vermont with trails. Information: Corps of Engineers, New England District, 424 Trapelo Road, Waltham, MA 02254; (617)647-8107.

VIRGINIA

Recommended Areas for Nature Walks

SHENANDOAH NATIONAL PARK Route 4, Box 348, Luray, VA 22835; (703)999-2299. 194,200 acres. Overlooking the Shenandoah River Valley at the northern end of the Blue Ridge Mountains, in northern Virginia, this long and narrow national park features round-topped mountains and ridges with a number of cliffs and rock formations, hollows and ravines, and dozens of streams with waterfalls. The highest point is 4,051-foot Hawksbill Mountain.

There are open meadows with wildflowers and blueberries, and forests of oak, hickory, maple, birch, hemlock, and pine, along with mountain laurel and pink azalea. Among the wildlife are white-tailed deer, black bear, bobcat, gray fox, raccoon, opossum, and woodchuck, plus ruffed grouse, wild turkey, barred owl, and red-tailed hawk. Guided nature walks are available.

• *Suggested Trails for Nature Walks:* 1. The 1.3-mile Fox Hollow Nature Trail. 2. The 1.3-mile Deadening Nature Trail (loop). 3. The 1.3-mile Limberlost Trail (loop). 4. The 1.6-mile Stony Man Nature Trail (loop). 5. The 1.7-mile Traces Nature Trail (loop). 6. The 1.8-mile Story of the Forest Nature Trail. 7. The Appalachian Trail to Calf Mountain Summit (1.1 miles). 8. Other sections of the Appalachian Trail, which runs 95 miles through the park with gentle grades, are easy or easy-moderate. 9. The 0.9-mile Hawkbill Summit Trail (moderate). 10. The Whiteoak Canyon Trail to the Upper Falls (moderate 2.3 miles).

GEORGE WASHINGTON NATIONAL FOREST Harrisonburg Service Center, 101 North Main Street, P.O. Box 233, Harrisonburg, VA 22801; (540)564-8300. 1,330,000 acres. Currently in the process of being merged with Jefferson National Forest, and extending into the state of West Virginia, this national forest in the western part of Virginia encompasses portions of the Allegheny and Blue Ridge mountains, with rugged mountain ridges and rock ledges, hills and valleys. The highest point is 4,463-foot Elliott Knob.

Six designated wilderness areas total 32,000 acres. It's a forest of mixed hardwoods and pine, with oak, hemlock, beech, poplar, maple, and black cherry, as well as mountain laurel and rhododendron. There are also open meadows and grassy areas, lakes and ponds, streams with waterfalls, and several rivers. Wildlife includes white-tailed deer, black bear, bobcat, fox, raccoon, woodchuck, skunk, quail, wild turkey, owl, and hawk.

• *Suggested Trails for Nature Walks:* 1. The 0.5-mile Wildflower Trail. 2. The 0.5-mile Whispering Waters Nature Trail. 3. The 1-mile Lakeside Trail. 4. The 1-mile Unaka Nature Trail. 5. The 1-mile Stony Fork Nature Trail. 6. The 2-mile Craig Creek Trail (loop). 7. The 2.5-mile White Rock Gap Trail. 8. The 4-mile Trimble Mountain Trail (loop). 9. The 3.6-mile Sawmill Trail. 10. The 5.7-mile Hidden Valley Trail.

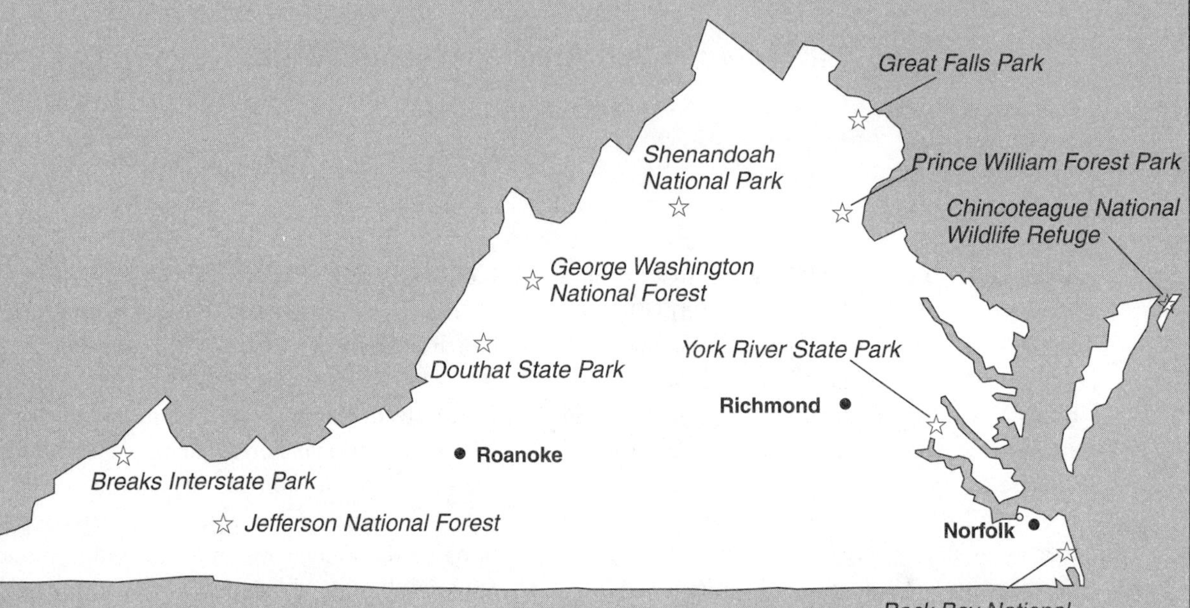
VIRGINIA
Great Falls Park
Shenandoah National Park
Prince William Forest Park
Chincoteague National Wildlife Refuge
George Washington National Forest
Douthat State Park
York River State Park
Richmond
Roanoke
Breaks Interstate Park
Jefferson National Forest
Norfolk
Back Bay National Wildlife Refuge

JEFFERSON NATIONAL FOREST Harrisonburg Service Center, 101 North Main Street, P.O. Box 233, Harrisonburg, VA 22801; (540)564-8300. 709,000 acres. This national forest in southwest Virginia is now being co-administered with George Washington National Forest. The landscape includes some rugged and steep mountains, rock ledges and outcroppings, highland plateaus and valleys. Eleven designated wilderness areas total more than 50,000 acres.

Elevations range from 600 to over 5,700 feet. Loftiest of the mountains is 5,729-foot Mt. Rogers, the highest elevation in Virginia, located in the 114,000-acre Mt. Rogers National Recreation Area. Throughout the forest are streams and waterfalls, swamps and woodlands, hardwood forests with hemlock and spruce, pine and fir, including some virgin stands, as well as rhododendron and azalea. Among the wildlife are white-tailed deer, black bear, fox, hawk, and wild turkey.

• *Suggested Trails for Nature Walks:* 1. The 0.8-mile Beartree Lake Trail (loop). 2. The 1-mile Phillips Creek Loop Trail. 3. The 1.1-mile Hurricane Knob Nature Trail. 4. The 1-mile Pandapas Pond Trail (loop). 5. The 1.5-mile Polecat Trail. 6. The 2.3-mile White Tail Trail. 7. The 4-mile Tract Fork Trail. 8. The 4-mile Lake Keokee Loop Trail. 9. The 2.8-mile Little Stony National Recreation Trail. 10. The lower 4-mile loop of the 9-mile Hoop Hole Trail.

PRINCE WILLIAM FOREST PARK P.O. Box 209, Triangle, VA 22172; (703)221-7181. 17,000 acres. Located in northern Virginia, Prince William Forest Park is a unit of the national park system. It occupies a valley with low ridges, streams including Quantico Creek and South Fork Quantico Creek, and Piedmont hardwood forest of red and white oak, yellow poplar, and beech, along with wild azalea. White-tailed deer, fox, beaver, raccoon, and wild turkey are among the wildlife. Naturalist-led walks are available.

• *Suggested Trails for Nature Walks:* 1. The 0.8-mile Pine Grove Trail. 2. The 0.7-mile Little Run Loop Trail. 3. The 1-mile Farms to Forest Trail (loop). 4. The 1.3-mile Laurel Trail Loop. 5. The 1.6-mile Oak Ridge Trail. 6. The 1.8-mile Birch Bluff Trail. 7. The 2.1-mile High Meadows Trail. 8. The 2.7-mile Farms to Forest Extension Trail. 9. The 2.6-mile North Valley Trail. 10. The 9.7-mile South Valley Trail.

GREAT FALLS PARK P.O. Box 66, Great Falls, VA 22066; (703)285-2966. 800 acres. Administered by the National Park Service, this Potomac River park lies on Virginia's northern border, northwest of Washington, D.C. It features Great Falls, where the river flows through a narrow, rocky gorge, and includes an abandoned canal system. Terrain is hilly with rocky cliffs and formations, wetlands, wildflowers, and a hardwood forest of oak and ash, poplar and sycamore, with redbud and dogwood. Ranger-led walks are available.

• *Suggested Trails for Nature Walks:* 1. The 1.3-mile Patowmack Canal Trail. 2. The 1.6-mile Old Carriage Road. 3. The 0.9-mile Swamp Nature Trail. 4. The 1.1-mile Matildaville Trail. 5. The 1.5-mile Ridge Trail.

BREAKS INTERSTATE PARK P.O. Box 100, Breaks, VA 24607; (540)865-4413. 4,500 acres. Situated on the Virginia-Kentucky border in southwestern Virginia, with a small area in Kentucky, this park features the 1,600-foot canyon of the Russel Fork River, which has pools and rapids. There are rugged mountains with sandstone formations, overlooks, and caves, along with marshes, Grassy Creek, and 12-acre Laurel Lake. The forest is of mixed hardwoods including oak, hickory, and maple, plus hemlock and pine, rhododendron and mountain laurel, yellow lady's-slipper, and other wildflowers. Among the wildlife are white-tailed deer, bobcat, raccoon, opossum, wild turkey, and red-tailed hawk.

• *Suggested Trails for Nature Walks:* 1. The 0.2-mile Tower Tunnel Trail. 2. The 0.4-mile Loop Trail. 3. The 0.5-mile Lake Trail. 4. The 0.5-mile Cold Spring Trail. 5. The 1.3-mile Laurel Branch Trail from Laurel Lake to the Notches. 6. The 0.4-

mile Geological Trail (easy-moderate). 7. The 0.5-mile Grassy Overlook Trail (easy-moderate). 8. The 0.8-mile Overlook Trail (easy-moderate). 9. The 0.5-mile Grassy Creek Trail (easy-moderate). 10. The 1.5-mile Prospector's Trail (moderate).

CHINCOTEAGUE NATIONAL WILDLIFE REFUGE P.O. Box 62, Chincoteague, VA 23336; (804)336-6122. 9,460 acres. Chincoteague National Wildlife Refuge occupies the southern portion of 37-mile-long Assateague Island, between Chincoteague Bay and the Atlantic Ocean, and next to Assateague Island National Seashore. This sandy barrier island has beaches and dunes, marshes and pine forests, with wildlife that includes white-tailed and sika deer, red fox, raccoon, muskrat, and a herd of wild horses. The refuge also protects such wintering waterfowl as snow goose and mallard, along with egret, heron, sandpiper, tern, piping plover, and peregrine falcon. Guided walks are available.

• *Suggested Trails for Nature Walks:* 1. The 0.3-mile Lighthouse Trail. 2. The 1-mile Freshwater Marsh Trail. 3. The 1.6-mile Woodland Loop. 4. The 3.2-mile Wildlife Loop, which is closed to vehicles daily until 3 p.m. 5. Ten miles of wild beach are also available for walks.

DOUTHAT STATE PARK Route 1, Box 212, Millboro, VA 24460; (703)862-7200. 4,493 acres. Surrounded by lands of George Washington National Forest, Douthat State Park is in the Allegheny Mountains of western Virginia. Included here are mountains and woodlands, Wilson Creek and other streams, as well as 50-acre Douthat Lake with a beach. There's a forest of oak, hickory, maple, poplar, hemlock, and pine, along with rhododendron and mountain laurel, sassafras and huckleberry. Among the wildlife are white-tailed deer, black bear, red fox, woodchuck, raccoon, rabbit, owl, and wild turkey. Guided walks are available.

• *Suggested Trails for Nature Walks:* 1. The 0.3-mile Buck Lick Trail. 2. The 0.8-mile Heron Run Trail. 3. The 0.9-mile YCC Trail. 4. The 0.9-mile Backaway Hollow Trail. 5. The 1-mile Beards Gap Hollow Trail. 6. The 1-mile Middle Hollow Trail. 7. The 1.2-mile Wilson Creek Trail. 8. The 1.2-mile Huffs Trail. 9. The 1.9-mile Laurel View Trail. 10. The 2-mile Locust Gap Trail.

BACK BAY NATIONAL WILDLIFE REFUGE 4005 Sandpiper Road, P.O. Box 6286, Virginia Beach, VA 23456; (804)721-2412. 7,732 acres. Located on the Atlantic Ocean in the southeast corner of the state, this national wildlife refuge includes barrier coastline with beaches and dunes, fields and marshes, islands in Back Bay, and a maritime forest of loblolly pine and live oak, with black cherry and blueberry. Nature walks are available. Among the birds here are piping plover, snow goose, osprey, bald eagle, and peregrine falcon, along with other wildlife including white-tailed deer, wild horse, red fox, raccoon, opossum, muskrat, mink, river otter, marsh rabbit, loggerhead sea turtle, and snapping turtle.

• *Suggested Trails for Nature Walks:* 1. The 0.3-mile Seaside Trail. 2. The 0.4-mile Bay Trail. 3. The 0.5-mile Dune Trail. 4. The East Dike Trail to B/C Cross Dike (2 miles). 5. The East Dike Trail to A/B Cross Dike (2.5 miles). 6. The East Dike Trail to False Cape State Park (4.3 miles). 7. Several trails are also available in False Cape State Park directly to the south, and these are accessible only through the refuge.

YORK RIVER STATE PARK 5526 Riverview Road, Williamsburg, VA 23188; (804)566-3036. 2,505 acres. This state park is situated on Chesapeake Bay's York River. It includes Taskinas Creek, sand flats and swamps, marshes and forest, with pine, cedar, oak, beech, maple, and gum, plus mountain laurel and holly. A 525-acre portion of the park has been designated a Chesapeake Bay National Estuarine Research Reserve, one of four such sites along the York River. Great blue heron, Virginia rail, spotted sandpiper, American woodcock, and bald eagle are among the bird life here. Interpretive nature walks are available.

- *Suggested Trails for Nature Walks:* 1. The 0.6-mile Beaver Trail. 2. The 0.8-mile Pamunkey Trail. 3. The 1-mile Majestic Oak Trail. 4. The 1.3-mile Woodstock Pond Trail. 5. The 1.3-mile Backbone Trail. 6. The 1.4-mile Powhatan Forks Trail. 7. The 1.4-mile Mattaponi Trail. 8. The 1-mile Dogwood Lane Trail. 9. The 1.6-mile Taskinas Creek Trail. 10. The 1.5-mile Riverview Trail.

Other Suitable Locations for Nature Walks in Virginia

Virginia has forty-three state parks and state natural areas, and there are established nature and hiking trails in all but a few areas. Information: Division of State Parks, 203 Governor Street, Suite 302, Richmond, VA 23219; (804)786-1712.

There are eleven state forests, and some of them have trails. Information: Department of Forestry, Route 1, Box 250, Cumberland, VA 23040; (804)492-4121.

Five national wildlife refuges in the state feature trails. Information: U.S. Fish and Wildlife Refuge, 300 Westgate Center Drive, Hadley, MA 01035.

Trails are common in northern Virginia's regional parks. Information: Northern Virginia Regional Park Authority, 5400 Ox Road, Fairfax Station, VA 22039; (703)352-5900.

A number of locations along the Blue Ridge Parkway in Virginia and North Carolina have trails. Information: Blue Ridge Parkway, 200 BB&T Building, One Pack Square, Asheville, NC 28801; (704)259-0779.

Several U.S. Army Corps of Engineers areas in the state have trails. Information: Corps of Engineers, Wilmington District, P.O. Box 1890, Wilmington, NC 28402, (919)251-4827; Corps of Engineers, Norfolk District, 803 Front Street, Norfolk, VA 23510, (804)441-7641; Corps of Engineers, Huntington District, 502 Eighth Street, Huntington, WV 25701, (304)529-5607.

WASHINGTON

Recommended Areas for Nature Walks

MOUNT RAINIER NATIONAL PARK Tahoma Woods, Star Route, Ashford, WA 98304; (360)569-2211. 235,404 acres. This national park in west-central Washington is centered around massive, 14,410-foot Mt. Rainier. The mountain is home to many glaciers, along with canyons, ridges and valleys, mountain lakes and rivers, streams and waterfalls, as well as subalpine meadows, wildflowers, ferns, and old-growth forests.

Common trees include Douglas fir, western redcedar, Sitka spruce, white pine, western hemlock, and red alder, and there are rhododendron and huckleberry bushes. Among the wildlife are elk, black bear, mule deer, coyote, mountain lion, mountain goat, beaver, raccoon, porcupine, marmot, snowshoe hare, kestrel, and red-tailed hawk. Guided nature walks are available.

• *Suggested Trails for Nature Walks:* 1. The 0.5-mile Trail of the Shadows (loop). 2. The 0.5-mile Life Systems Trail (loop). 3. The 1-mile Sourdough Ridge Trail (loop). 4. The 1.2-mile Nisqually Vista Trail. 5. The 1.3-mile Bench and Snow Lakes Trail. 6. The 1.3-mile Grove of the Patriarchs Trail (loop). 7. The 3-mile Silver Falls Trail (loop). 8. The 3.5-mile Naches Peak Loop. 9. The 3.5-mile Glacier Basin Trail. 10. The 3.5-mile Carbon Glacier Trail.

OLYMPIC NATIONAL PARK 600 East Park Avenue, Port Angeles, WA 98362; (360)452-0330. 908,720 acres. Situated on northwest Washington's Olympic Peninsula and nearly surrounded by the lands of Olympic National Forest, this national park features the Olympic Mountains, plus 57 miles of wild Pacific coastline with rocky cliffs and beaches. Highest point is 7,965-foot Mt. Olympus.

There are many glaciers, ridges, and valleys with rivers, streams, and several lakes, as well as alpine meadows, rare temperate rain forest of spruce and western redcedar, and lowland forest of hemlock and Douglas fir. Some of the trees are old-growth. Wildlife includes Roosevelt elk, black bear, black-tailed deer, mountain lion, coyote, raccoon, river otter, puffin, loon, cormorant, and bald eagle. Guided nature walks are available.

• *Suggested Trails for Nature Walks:* 1. The 0.5-mile Maple Glade Rain Forest Trail (loop). 2. The 0.5-mile Ancient Groves Nature Trail. 3. The 0.6-mile Second Beach Trail. 4. The 0.8-mile Hall of Mosses Trail. 5. The 1-mile Graves Creek Nature Trail (loop). 6. The 1-mile Marymere Falls Trail. 7. The 1.3-mile Spruce Nature Trail. 8. The 2-mile Heart of the Forest Trail. 9. The 3-mile Sand Point Trail. 10. The 4-mile Spruce Railroad Trail.

NORTH CASCADES NATIONAL PARK 2105 State Route 20, Sedro Woolley WA 98284; (360)856-5700. 505,000 acres. This national park in the Cascades of northwest Washington protects an area of rugged, jagged peaks, with pinnacles and spires, precipitous cliffs, deep and narrow valleys, glaciers and snowfields. The

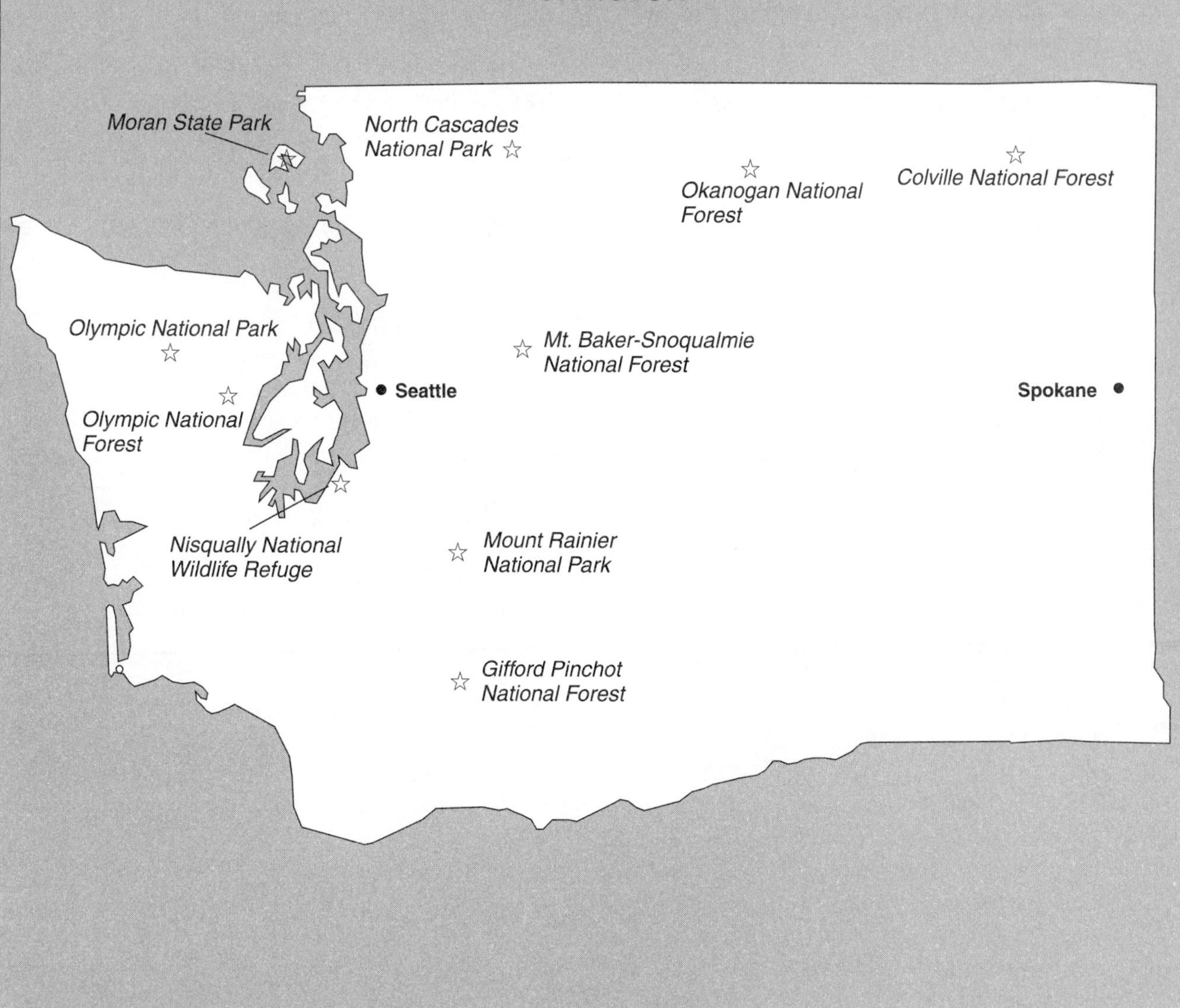
WASHINGTON
Moran State Park
North Cascades National Park
Okanogan National Forest
Colville National Forest
Olympic National Park
Mt. Baker-Snoqualmie National Forest
Seattle
Spokane
Olympic National Forest
Nisqually National Wildlife Refuge
Mount Rainier National Park
Gifford Pinchot National Forest

Stephen Mather Wilderness constitutes 92 percent of the total acreage, and within park boundaries are the 117,000-acre Ross Lake National Recreation Area and the 62,000-acre Lake Chelan National Recreation Area.

There are over 127 alpine lakes, many streams with waterfalls, 318 glaciers, meadows with wildflowers, and dense forests of Douglas fir and western redcedar. Mule deer, black bear, mountain lion, wolf, mountain goat, bobcat, red fox, wolverine, mink, owl, hawk, falcon, and bald eagle are among the wildlife. Naturalist-led walks are available in the summer.

• *Suggested Trails for Nature Walks:* 1. The 0.3-mile Horseshoe Bend Nature Trail (loop). 2. The 0.3-mile Picture Lake Trail (loop). 3. The 0.5-mile Ladder Creek Falls Trail (loop). 4. The 0.5-mile Shadow of the Sentinels Nature Trail (loop). 5. The 0.8-mile Blue Lake Trail. 6. The 1-mile Rainy Lake Trail. 7. The 1.5-mile Elbow Lake Trail. 8. The 1.8-mile Thunderwoods Nature Trail (loop). 9. The 2.5-mile Baker River Trail. 10. The 4-mile East Bank Trail.

OLYMPIC NATIONAL FOREST 1835 Black Lake Boulevard SW, Olympia, WA 98512; (360)956-2300. 632,000 acres. Located on the Olympic Peninsula in northwest Washington, the lands of this national forest surround Olympic National Park. The region includes steep, rugged mountains and canyons, lakes and rivers, streams, alpine meadows, and lush, low-lying rain forests. Five designated wilderness areas add up to 88,481 acres.

The forest is dominated by Douglas fir and western redcedar, Sitka spruce and western hemlock. There are also clubmoss-covered maples as well as wildflowers and ferns. Among the wildlife are Roosevelt elk, black bear, mule and black-tailed deer, Rocky Mountain goat, mountain lion, coyote, porcupine, and beaver, along with ruffed grouse, red-tailed hawk, and golden eagle.

• *Suggested Trails for Nature Walks:* 1. The 0.5-mile Maple Glade Nature Trail (loop). 2. The 0.5-mile Quinault Rain Forest Nature Trail (loop). 3. The 0.8-mile Ranger Hole Trail. 4. The 4-mile Quinault Loop Trail. 5. The 1.1-mile Elk Lake Trail. 6. The 11.7-mile Lower South Fork Skokomish Trail. 7. The 12-mile Wynoochee Lake Shore Trail. 8. The 3.5-mile Lena Lake Trail (moderate). 9. The 6-mile Lower Big Quilcene Trail (moderate).

MT. BAKER-SNOQUALMIE NATIONAL FOREST 21905 64th Avenue West, Mountlake Terrace, WA 98043; (206)775-9702. 1,700,000 acres. This national forest in the western Cascades has a number of prominent rocky peaks and ridges, including 10,778-foot Mt. Baker, along with glaciers, hundreds of alpine lakes, high basins, mountain meadows, and old-growth forests. There are eight designated wilderness areas, which constitute 42 percent of the total land area.

The most common trees are Douglas fir and western hemlock, red alder and western redcedar, lodgepole and white pine, with dogwood, rhododendron, huckleberry, and yew, as well as ferns and a profusion of wildflowers. Wildlife includes Roosevelt and Rocky Mountain elk, grizzly and black bear, mule deer, mountain goat, gray wolf, bobcat, red fox, and wolverine.

• *Suggested Trails for Nature Walks:* 1. The 0.8-mile John Muir Nature Trail. 2. The 1-mile Franklin Falls Trail. 3. The 1.6-mile Sunday Lake Trail. 4. The 1.3-mile Ashahel Curtis Nature Trail (loop). 5. The 3-mile Old Sauk Trail. 6. The 3.5-mile Ashland Lakes Trail. 7. The 4-mile Boulder River Trail. 8. The 6.5-mile White Chuck Bench Trail (moderate).

GIFFORD PINCHOT NATIONAL FOREST 6926 East 4th Plain Boulevard, P.O. Box 8944, Vancouver, WA 98668; (360)750-5009. 1,251,160 acres. Gifford Pinchot National Forest in southwest Washington features the 110,000-acre Mount St. Helens National Volcanic Monument, established to protect the well-known 8,365-foot volcano that erupted in 1980. Access to some of the area is restricted. There are also other volcanoes with extensive lava beds.

The forest consists of mixed hardwoods and conifers, including some old-growth stands, with Douglas fir, western redcedar, western hemlock, and white pine, as well as meadows with wildflowers, lakes, ponds, streams, and over 150 waterfalls. Wildlife includes Roosevelt elk, black bear, mule deer, mountain goat, mountain lion, and coyote. Guided walks are available.

• *Suggested Trails for Nature Walks:* 1. The 1.1-mile Takhlakh Loop Trail. 2. The 2.5-mile Woods Creek Watchable Wildlife Trail. 3. The 1.5-mile Iron Creek Campground Trail. 4. The first 1.5 miles of the 4-mile Lava Canyon Trail. 5. The 1.4-mile River View Trail. 6. The 1.5-mile Meadow Trail. 7. The 2.8-mile Sheep Canyon Trail. 8. The 4.5-mile Silver Creek Trail. 9. The 14-mile Lewis River Trail. 10. The 16.7-mile Valley Trail (moderate).

COLVILLE NATIONAL FOREST 755 South Main, Colville, WA 99114; (509)684-4557. 1,095,368 acres. Bordering on the Coulee Dam National Recreation Area and the Columbia River, this northeast Washington national forest includes hills and valleys, mountains and canyons, with rock cliffs and talus slopes, lakes, streams, and waterfalls. There are also meadows, shrubs, wildflowers, and old-growth trees, with ponderosa pine and western larch, Douglas fir and western hemlock. Among the wildlife are mule and white-tailed deer, black bear, moose, elk, mountain lion, bobcat, coyote, porcupine, skunk, and mink.

• *Suggested Trails for Nature Walks:* 1. The 0.5-mile Log Flume Interpretive Trail (loop). 2. The 0.5-mile Sherman Pass Trail. 3. The 0.8-mile Pierre Lake Trail. 4. The 1-mile Wolf Donation Trail (loop). 5. The 1.2-mile Long Lake Trail. 6. The 1.6-mile Swan Lake Trail. 7. The 1.6-mile Leona Trail. 8. The 1.3-mile South Skookum Trail (loop). 9. The 4.9-mile Frater Lake Trail. 10. The 5.9-mile Bead Lake Trail (easy-moderate).

OKANOGAN NATIONAL FOREST 1240 South Second Avenue, Okanogan, WA 98840; (509)826-3275. 1,706,000 acres. Located in the Cascades of northern Washington, alongside North Cascades National Park and the Ross Lake National Recreation Area, Okanogan National Forest features rugged alpine peaks, steep ridges, and deep canyon gorges, with numerous streams and lakes. Highest point here is 8,974-foot North Gardner Mountain.

There are forests of Douglas fir as well as ponderosa pine, subalpine fir, and Englemann spruce, including old-growth stands, as well as meadows and grasslands with many species of wildflowers. Wildlife includes mule deer, mountain lion, black bear, coyote, raccoon, skunk, and marmot, along with great blue heron, great horned owl, teal, Canada goose, and golden eagle.

• *Suggested Trails for Nature Walks:* 1. The 0.9-mile Big Tree Trail. 2. The 2-mile Lone Fir Interpretive Trail. 3. The 1-mile Beaver Lake Trail. 4. The 1-mile Mutton Creek Trail. 5. The 1.9-mile Beth Lake Trail. 6. The 2-mile Holman Creek Trail. 7. The 3.2-mile Louis Lake Trail. 8. The 3.1-mile Maple Pass Trail. 9. The 4-mile Early Winters Trail. 10. The 8.3-mile Blue Buck Trail.

MORAN STATE PARK Star Route, Box 22, Eastsound, WA 98245; (206)376-2326. 5,000 acres. Moran State Park occupies Orcas Island, off Washington's northwest coast, and is accessible by ferry. Terrain consists of hills and mountains with steep slopes, and there are several lakes, bogs, streams, waterfalls, and a forest of Douglas fir, western hemlock, lodgepole pine, western redcedar, and red alder. Highest point is 2,408-foot Mt. Constitution. Among the wildlife are deer, raccoon, muskrat, river otter, great blue heron, bald eagle, and osprey.

• *Suggested Trails for Nature Walks:* 1. The 0.3-mile Cascade Falls Trail. 2. The 1.3-mile Trail from the Picnic Area to Cascade Falls. 3. The 2.5-mile Cascade Loop. 4. The 2.2-mile Twin Lakes Trail. 5. The 3.9-mile Mountain Lake Loop. 6. The 2.3-mile Little Summit Trail (easy-moderate). 7. The 4.3-mile Cascade Creek Trail (easy-moderate).

NISQUALLY NATIONAL WILDLIFE REFUGE 100 Brown Farm Road, Olympia, WA 98506; (206)753-9467. 2,800 acres. Situated at the southern end of Puget Sound, in west-central Washington, this national wildlife refuge covers the Nisqually River Delta, with Red Salmon Creek, McAllister Creek, and the Nisqually River. There are saltwater and freshwater marshes, mudflats and estuaries, freshwater ponds, sandy beaches, open fields, and mixed conifer forests with cottonwood, maple, and alder. Among the birds protected by the refuge are great blue heron, green-winged teal, short-eared owl, peregrine falcon, bald eagle, and red-tailed hawk; the mammals here include black-tailed deer, coyote, raccoon, muskrat, beaver, river otter, and sea lion.

• *Suggested Trails for Nature Walks:* 1. The 0.5-mile Nisqually River Trail (loop). 2. The 1-mile Twin Barns Trail (loop). 3. The 5.5-mile Farm Dike Trail (loop).

Other Suitable Locations for Nature Walks in Washington

Washington has 141 state parks, many of which feature trails appropriate for nature walks. Information: Washington State Parks and Recreation Commission, P.O. Box 42650, Olympia, WA 98504; (360)902-8563.

One additional national forest in the state has a network of trails: Wenatchee National Forest, P.O. Box 811, Wenatchee, WA 98807; (509) 662-4335.

There are several state forests and multiple-use areas with trails. Information: Department of Natural Resources, P.O. Box 47001, Olympia, WA 98504; (360)902-1000.

Trails are available at thirteen national wildlife refuges in Washington. Information: U.S. Fish and Wildlife Service, 911 Northeast 11th Avenue, Portland, OR 97232; (503)231-6121.

Some U.S. Army Corps of Engineers areas in the state include trails. Information: Corps of Engineers, Seattle District, P.O. Box 3755, Seattle, WA 98124, (206)764-3442; Corps of Engineers, Walla Walla District, City County Airport, Walla Walla, WA 99362, (509)522-6714.

Statewide trail information is available from the Washington Trails Association, 1305 4th Avenue, #518, Seattle, WA 98101; (206)625-1367.

WEST VIRGINIA

Recommended Areas for Nature Walks

MONONGAHELA NATIONAL FOREST 200 Sycamore Street, Elkins, WV 26241; (304)636-1800. 908,000 acres. Largest of West Virginia's natural areas, Monongahela National Forest is located near and alongside the state's eastern border. This mountainous region includes 4,862-foot Spruce Knob, highest point in West Virginia, and the rugged Seneca Rocks, which rise 900 feet above the North Fork River, in the Spruce Knob-Seneca Rocks National Recreation Area.

There are rocky plains and heath barrens, highland bogs, the headwaters of five river systems, hundreds of miles of streams, and forests of mixed hardwoods and conifers—cherry, maple, oak, and poplar, plus cedar, spruce, and hemlock—along with rhododendron and mountain laurel. Among the wildlife are white-tailed deer, black bear, fox, bobcat, and wild turkey.

- *Suggested Trails for Nature Walks:* 1. The 0.5-mile Northland Loop Nature Trail. 2. The 0.5-mile Cranberry Glades Boardwalk Trail. 3. The 0.5-mile Whispering Spruce Trail. 4. The 1.1-mile Tablerock Overlook Trail. 5. The 1.1-mile Buffalo Fork Lake Trail. 6. The 1.8-mile Summit Lake Trail. 7. The 3-mile Williams River Trail. 8. The 3-mile Canyon Rim Trail. 9. The 3.7-mile Lake Sherwood Trail. 10. The 7.9-mile East Fork Trail.

NEW RIVER GORGE NATIONAL RIVER P.O. Box 246, Glen Jean, WV 25846; (304)465-0508. 63,000 acres. This is a corridor of land in southern West Virginia that protects 53 miles of the New River and 40 miles of its two tributaries, the Gauley and Bluestone Rivers. Five state parks preserve additional riverside lands. Included here are the deep New River Gorge, rock formations, creeks, waterfalls, and mixed hardwood forests with birch, sycamore, and rhododendron. White-tailed deer, bobcat, and wild turkey are among the wildlife.

- *Suggested Trails for Nature Walks:* 1. The 0.5-mile Sandstone Falls Trail (loop). 2. The 0.7-mile Big Buck Trail (loop). 3. The 0.8-mile Woodland Loop Trail. 4. The 1-mile Laing Loop Trail. 5. The 2-mile Canyon Rim Trail. 6. The 3.2-mile Thurmond-Minden Trail. 7. The 1.8-mile Big Branch Trail (easy-moderate loop). 8. The 2.5-mile Fayetteville Trail (easy-moderate). 9. The 5.6-mile Glade Creek Trail (easy-moderate).

NORTH BEND STATE PARK Route 1, Box 221, Cairo, WV 26337; (304)643-2931. 1,405 acres. Bordering on the North Fork of Hughes River, in northwestern West Virginia, this state park features ridges offering vistas, with valleys and ravines, rock formations and caves, streams and a pond, ferns and seasonal wildflowers, as well as hardwood forests of oak, poplar, and beech, plus white pine. The park's wildlife includes white-tailed deer.

- *Suggested Trails for Nature Walks:* 1. The 0.4-mile Giant Tree Trail. 2. The 0.5-mile Extra Mile Trail. 3. The 0.5-mile Overhanging Rock Trail

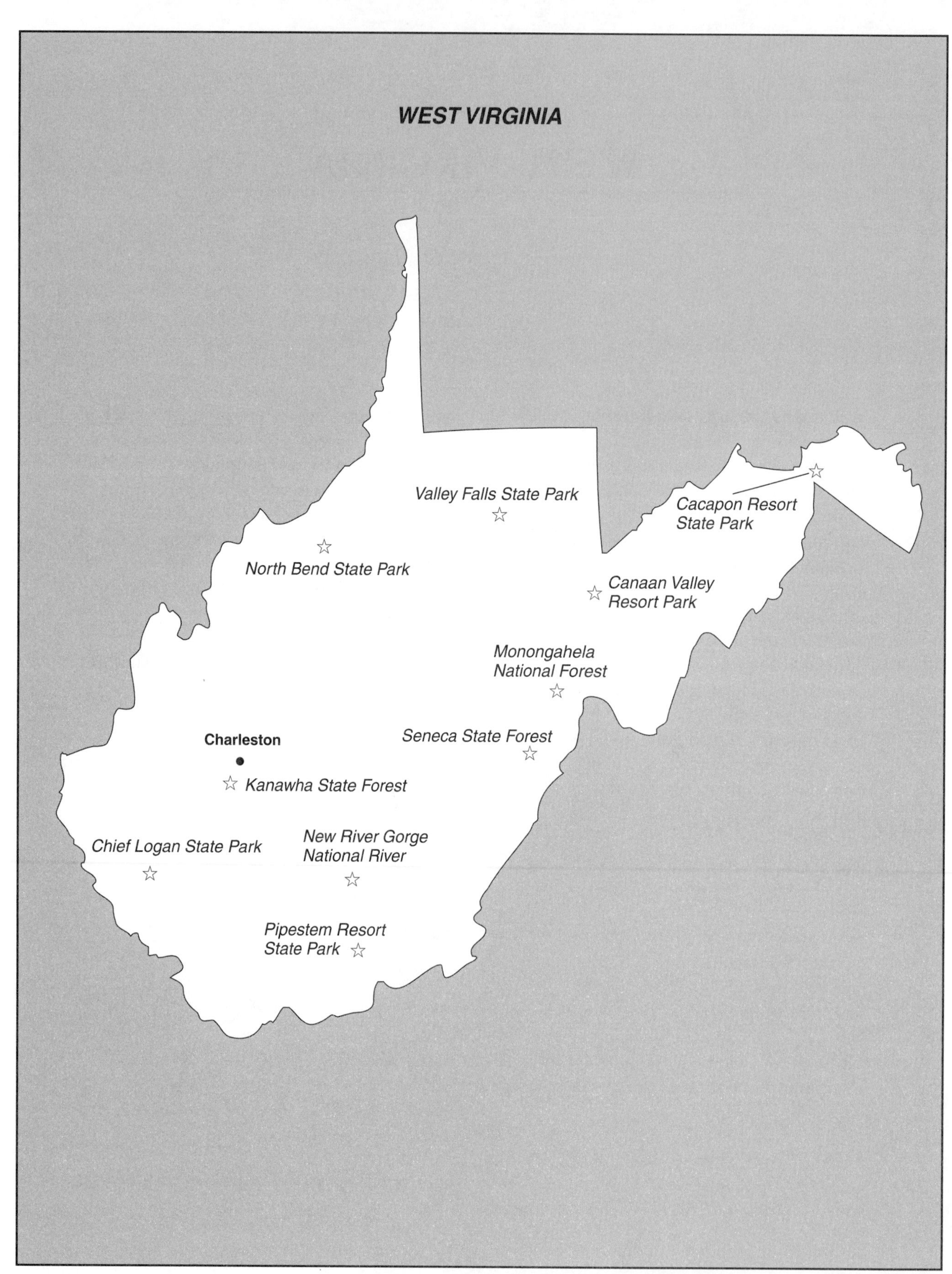

WEST VIRGINIA
Valley Falls State Park
Cacapon Resort State Park
North Bend State Park
Canaan Valley Resort Park
Monongahela National Forest
Seneca State Forest
Charleston
Kanawha State Forest
Chief Logan State Park
New River Gorge National River
Pipestem Resort State Park

(loop). 4. The 0.5-mile Southern Railroad Trail. 5. The 1-mile Hibbs Cemetery Trail. 6. The 1-mile Access Trail. 7. The 1.5-mile Giant Pine Trail (loop). 8. The 4.5-mile Nature Trail (loop). 9. The 2-mile Castle Rock Trail (easy-moderate loop). 10. A section of the 61-mile North Bend Rail Trail lies across the river, just outside the park.

PIPESTEM RESORT STATE PARK P.O. Box 150, Pipestem, WV 25979; (304)466-2804. 4,027 acres. Situated in the southeastern part of the state, Pipestem Resort State Park includes the Bluestone River Gorge, with rock outcroppings and vistas, oak-hickory forests, and 16-acre Long Branch Lake. Elevations range from 1,500 to 3,000 feet. White-tailed deer, black bear, bobcat, red fox, and golden eagle are among the wildlife. There's a nature center, and guided walks are scheduled year-round.

• *Suggested Trails for Nature Walks:* 1. The 0.5-mile North Side Trail. 2. The 0.6-mile Den Tree Trail. 3. The 0.6-mile Dogwood Trail. 4. The 0.5-mile Law Hollow Trail. 5. The 0.6-mile South Side Trail. 6. The 1.6-mile Lick Hollow Trail. 7. The 2.2-mile Lake Shore Trail.

KANAWHA STATE FOREST Route 2, Box 285, Charleston, WV 25314; (304)346-5654. 9,250 acres. Kanawha State Forest is just south of Charleston in the southwestern part of the state. It encompasses mountain ridges and hollows, cliffs and rock outcroppings, creeks and a small lake, with orchids and other wildflowers, as well as a forest of oak, birch, maple, beech, hickory, and hemlock. Wildlife includes white-tailed deer, black bear, bobcat, wild turkey, and songbirds.

• *Suggested Trails for Nature Walks:* 1. The 0.8-mile CCC Snipe Trail. 2. The 0.8-mile Pigeon Roost Trail. 3. The 1.5-mile Beech Glen Trail. 4. The 2.5-mile Davis Creek Trail. 5. The 0.8-mile Logtown Trail (easy-moderate). 6. The 0.8-mile Johnson Hollow Trail (easy-moderate). 7. The 0.8-mile Mossy Rock Trail (easy-moderate). 8. The 1.5-mile Polly Trail (easy-moderate). 9. The 1.5-mile White Hollow Trail (moderate). 10. The 1.5-mile Pine Ridge Trail (moderate).

SENECA STATE FOREST Route 1, Box 140, Dunmore, WV 24934; (304)799-6213. 11,684 acres. Located near the Virginia border in central West Virginia, Seneca State Forest lies alongside the Greenbrier River, which is said to be the longest remaining freeflowing river in the East. Included are small mountains with rock formations and outcroppings, streams, and a small lake, with a forest of oak, pine, and hemlock, along with rhododendron, mountain laurel, and huckleberry. Among the wildlife are white-tailed deer, black bear, beaver, grouse, and wild turkey.

• *Suggested Trails for Nature Walks:* 1. The 0.5-mile Scarlet Oak Trail. 2. The 0.5-mile Great Laurel Trail. 3. The 1-mile Little Mountain Trail. 4. The 1.5-mile Black Oak Trail. 5. The 1.5-mile Horseshoe Trail. 6. The 2-mile Hilltop Trail. 7. The 2.5-mile Crestline Trail. 8. The 5-mile Thorny Creek Trail. 9. The 75-mile Greenbrier River Trail lies across the river.

CHIEF LOGAN STATE PARK Logan, WV 25601; (304)792-7125. 3,300 acres. Chief Logan State Park is in the mountains of southwestern West Virginia. This is a place of forested hills and hollows, ridges and cliffs, with maple, oak, hickory, beech, birch, and sycamore trees. There are wildflowers including the endangered guyandotte beauty, ferns, meadows and grassy areas, a diverse wildlife, old coal mine sites, streams, and a small lake.

• *Suggested Trails for Nature Walks:* 1. The 1-mile Self-Guiding Interpretive Trail. 2. The 1.1-mile Lake Shore Trail. 3. The 1.1-mile Cliffside Trail. 4. The 2.3-mile Woodpecker Trail. 5. The 2.2-mile Buffalo Trail (easy-moderate). 6. The 3-mile Backbone Trail (easy-moderate). 7. The 1.1-mile Guyandotte Beauty Trail (moderate).

CANAAN VALLEY RESORT PARK Route 1, Box 330, Davis, WV 26260; (304)866-4121. 6,015 acres. This state park is situated in broad Canaan Valley, in east-central West Virginia. It includes hills and ridges, streams and swamps, northern bogs and heath barrens, mixed hardwood forests with beech and aspen, and a stretch of the Blackwater River. Black bear, bobcat, and beaver are among the wildlife. The park has a nature center and a wildlife observation area.

• *Suggested Trails for Nature Walks:* 1. The 0.8-mile Abe Run Trail. 2. The 1-mile Blackwater River Trail (loop). 3. The 1-mile Mill Run Trail (loop). 4. The 1.5-mile Club Run Trail (loop). 5. The 0.4-mile Ridge Top Trail. 6. The 1.5-mile Deer Run Trail. 7. The 2.5-mile Middle Ridge Trail (loop). 8. The 3-mile Railroad Grade Trail.

VALLEY FALLS STATE PARK Route 6, Box 244, Fairmont, WV 26554; (304)367-2719. 1,145 acres. Located in the Tygart Valley of northern West Virginia, Valley Falls State Park features 30-foot-high Great Falls and the Tygart River, which flows through a narrow canyon with sandstone ledges and giant boulders. The area is forested with oak and ash, maple and beech, rhododendron, ferns, and wildflowers. Wildlife includes white-tailed deer, grouse, and wild turkey.

• *Suggested Trails for Nature Walks:* 1. The 0.2-mile Tygart Valley River Trail. 2. The 2.1-mile Deer Trail. 3. The 3.2-mile Rhododendron Trail. 4. The 0.8-mile Dogwood Trail (easy-moderate). 5. The 2-mile Red Cardinal Trail (easy-moderate). 6. The 1.2-mile Wild Turkey Trail (moderate).

CACAPON RESORT STATE PARK Route 1, Box 304, Berkeley Springs, WV 25411; (304)258-1022. 6,000 acres. This state park is in the northeastern part of the state, near the Virginia and Maryland borders. It features 2,300-foot Cacapon Mountain, with sandstone outcroppings and boulders, as well as Cacapon Lake. There are several streams including the North, Middle, and South Fork Indian Run, and mixed hardwood forests with oak, maple, pine, dogwood, and mountain laurel. White-tailed deer are among the wildlife, and guided walks are available.

• *Suggested Trails for Nature Walks:* 1. The 1-mile Piney Ridge Trail. 2. The 1.5-mile Ridge Trail. 3. The 2-mile Laurel Trail (loop). 4. The 5-mile Central Trail (moderate).

Other Suitable Locations for Nature Walks in West Virginia

West Virginia has thirty-three state parks and nine state forests, and all but a handful of these locations have nature or hiking trails. Information: West Virginia Parks and Recreation, State Capitol Complex, Charleston, WV 25305; (800)CALL WVA.

Trails are available at several lakes managed by the U.S. Army Corps of Engineers. Information: Corps of Engineers, Huntington District, 502 Eighth Street, Huntington, WV 25701; (304)529-5607.

WISCONSIN

Recommended Areas for Nature Walks

NICOLET NATIONAL FOREST Federal Building, 68 South Stevens Street, Rhinelander, WI 54501; (715)362-1300. 661,000 acres. This national forest in northeastern Wisconsin encompasses an area of rolling hills and ridges with rock outcroppings, along with flatlands, wetlands including swamps and bogs, some 1,200 lakes, 1,100 miles of streams, and several sizable rivers.

There are 33,200 acres of designated wilderness. The forest is composed of northern hardwoods with maple, birch, ash, and oak, as well as conifers including hemlock, pine, spruce, fir, and aspen. Among the wildlife are white-tailed deer, black bear, and timber wolf, along with ruffed grouse, loon, and bald eagle.

• *Suggested Trails for Nature Walks:* 1. The 1-mile Phelps Trail (loop). 2. The 1.1-mile Franklin Nature Trail (loop). 3. The 1-mile Halley Creek Bird Trail. 4. The 1.3-mile Perch Lake Trail (loop). 5. The 1.8-mile Sam Campbell Trail (loop). 6. The 2-mile Sevenmile Lake Trail (loop). 7. The 2.5-mile Spectacle Lake-Kentuck Lake Trail. 8. The 2-mile Boulder Lake Campground Trail. 9. The 4-mile Luna-White Deer Trail (loop). 10. The 2.3-mile Laura Lake Trail (easy-moderate).

CHEQUAMEGON NATIONAL FOREST 1170 4th Avenue South, Park Falls, WI 54552; (715)762-2461. 857,000 acres. Consisting of several tracts of land in northern Wisconsin, Chequamegon National Forest is characterized by rolling hills, meadows, and hardwood as well as pine forests—including some old-growth trees—plus marshes and wetlands, 373 lakes, many streams, waterfalls, and rivers.

There are small mountains, ridges, and high bluffs with rock outcroppings. Two designated wilderness areas total 11,000 acres, and eleven semiprimitive, nonmotorized areas make up an additional 52,000 acres. Wildlife includes white-tailed deer, black bear, timber wolf, coyote, red fox, and bald eagle.

• *Suggested Trails for Nature Walks:* 1. The 0.5-mile Day Lake Campground Trail. 2. The 0.9-mile Birch Grove Trail. 3. The 1-mile Lake Namekagon Trail. 4. The 1.2-mile Long Lake Trail. 5. The 1.2-mile Mondeaux Trail. 6. The 1.5-mile Pigeon Lake Trail. 7. The 4-mile Black Lake Trail. 8. A network of 10.8 miles of trails at Round Lake. 9. The 13.6-mile Rock Lake National Recreation Trail, which consists of several loops.

WYALUSING STATE PARK 13342 County Highway C, Bagley, WI 53801; (608)996-2261. 2,674 acres. Wyalusing State Park is located at the confluence of the Mississippi and Wisconsin rivers in the southwestern part of the state. There are 600-foot bluffs and ridges of sandstone and dolomite, limestone outcroppings, crevices and small caves, ancient Indian burial mounds, streams, open fields and brushlands, grasses and wildflowers, with a hardwood forest of oak, elm, hickory, maple, ash, and cherry.

WISCONSIN
Chequamegon
National Forest
Nicolet National Forest
Newport State Park
Lake Wissota State Park
Peninsula State Park
Whitefish Dunes
State Park
Hartman Creek
State Park
Devil's Lake State Park
Governor Dodge
State Park
Madison
Wyalusing State Park
Milwaukee

Among the wildlife are white-tailed deer, gray and red fox, coyote, raccoon, beaver, muskrat, skunk, and mink, along with hawk, bald eagle, and turkey vulture.

• *Suggested Trails for Nature Walks:* 1. 0.5-mile Sentinel Ridge Nature Trail Loop. 2. The 1.5-mile Sugar Maple Nature Trail Loop. 3. The 0.9-mile Bluff Trail. 4. The 0.8-mile Old Wagon Wheel Trail. 5. The 1.5-mile Old Immigrant Trail. 6. The 1.6-mile Sentinel Ridge Trail. 7. The 1.7-mile Sand Cave Trail. 8. The 2.6-mile Walnut Springs Trail. 9. The 3.2-mile Turkey Hollow Trail. 10. The 0.5-mile Indian Trail (easy-moderate).

PENINSULA STATE PARK P.O. Box 218, Fish Creek, WI 54212; (414)868-3258. 3,763 acres. Situated on northeastern Wisconsin's Door County Peninsula, which extends into Green Bay, this state park has rolling terrain with some rocky high cliffs and sand beaches, marshes and meadows, mixed hardwood forests with maple and beech, as well as a northern forest of cedar and spruce, hemlock and balsam. There are two small designated Natural Areas, and wildlife includes white-tailed deer, raccoon, and skunk. The park has a nature center, and naturalist-led walks are offered.

• *Suggested Trails for Nature Walks:* 1. The 0.5-mile White Cedar Nature Trail (loop). 2. The 0.7-mile Minnehaha Trail. 3. The 0.8-mile Hidden Bluff Trail. 4. The 0.8-mile Trail Trampers' Delight. 5. The 1.5-mile Skyline Trail. 6. The 1.8-mile Hemlock Trail. 7. The 2-mile Sentinel Trail (loop). 8. The 2.2-mile Nicolet Bay Trail. 9. The 2-mile Eagle Trail (easy-moderate).

DEVIL'S LAKE STATE PARK S5975 Park Road, Baraboo, WI 53913; (608)356-8301. 8,434 acres. Stretching across the Baraboo Hills of south-central Wisconsin, and including a nature center, this state park features Devil's Lake, with its rugged 500-foot bluffs, rock formations, and boulders. There are also streams and marshes, open fields and prairie, forests of oak, hickory, maple, and birch, as well as some ancient Indian mounds. Among the wildlife are white-tailed deer, black bear, mountain lion, bobcat, fox, skunk, and turkey vulture. Naturalist-guided walks are available.

• *Suggested Trails for Nature Walks:* 1. The 0.5-mile Devil's Doorway Trail. 2. The 0.7-mile Grottos Trail. 3. The 0.4-mile Group Camp Trail. 4. The 0.8-mile Tumbled Rocks Trail. 5. The 0.8-mile Parfrey's Glen Trail. 6. The 2.5-mile Steinke Basin Loop Trail. 7. The 2.5-mile Johnson Moraine Loop Trail. 8. The 1.3-mile East Bluff Trail (easy-moderate). 9. The 1.3-mile East Bluff Woods Trail (easy-moderate). 10. The 4-mile Ice Age Loop Trail (easy-moderate).

WHITEFISH DUNES STATE PARK 3701 Clark Lake Road, Sturgeon Bay, WI 54235; (414)823-2400. 863 acres. This northeastern Wisconsin state park stretches between the shores of Lake Michigan and Clark Lake, a large inland lake. There are 90-foot sand dunes, beaches, rock ledges and cliffs, small creeks, and forests of pine and hemlock, beech and maple, cedar and birch. Wildlife includes white-tailed deer and wild turkey. The park has an interpretive center, with guided walks available in summer.

• *Suggested Trails for Nature Walks:* 1. The 1.5-mile Brachiopod Trail. 2. The 1.8-mile Green Trail. 3. The 0.7-mile Clark Lake Spur Trail. 4. The 2.5-mile White Trail. 5. The 2.8-mile Red Trail. 6. The 4.2-mile Yellow Trail. 7. The 1-mile Whitefish Creek Spur.

NEWPORT STATE PARK 475 South Newport Lane, Ellison Bay, WI 54210; (414)854-2500. 2,400 acres. Newport State Park is near the tip of the Door County Peninsula in northeastern Wisconsin. Terrain here is mostly flat. There are 11 miles of Lake Michigan shoreline, some of it rocky and rugged, with beaches and dunes, a large inland lake, wetlands, meadows, and forests. White-tailed deer, coyote, fox, raccoon, and porcupine are among the wildlife. Guided nature walks are available.

• *Suggested Trails for Nature Walks:* 1. The 2-mile Meadow Loop. 2. The 2.2-mile Lynd

Point/Fern Loop. 3. The 4-mile Rowley Bay Loop. 4. The 5-mile Newport Loop. 5. The 7-mile Europe Bay Loop.

LAKE WISSOTA STATE PARK Route 8, Box 360, Chippewa Falls, WI 54729; (715)382-4574. 1,062 acres. This state park is on man-made, 6,300-acre Lake Wissota, in the Chippewa Valley of west-central Wisconsin. It's an area of gently rolling hills with meadows and prairie grasslands, marshes, and a beaver pond, as well as mixed conifer and hardwood forest with pine and oak. Guided nature walks are available in summer.

• *Suggested Trails for Nature Walks:* 1. The 1-mile Beaver Meadow Nature Trail. 2. The 1-mile Jack Pine Trail. 3. The 1.9-mile Eagle Prairie Trail. 4. The 1.5-mile Red Pine Trail. 5. The 1.4-mile Lake Trail. 6. The 0.8-mile Plantation Trail. 7. The 2.3-mile Staghorn Trail.

HARTMAN CREEK STATE PARK N 2480 Hartman Creek Road, Waupaca, WI 54981; (715)258-2372. 1,363 acres. Hartman Creek State Park is located on the Upper Waupaca Chain of Lakes in the central part of the state, adjacent to the Emmons Creek Fishery and Wildlife Area. There are some creeks, a 300-foot beach on Hartman Lake, and seven lakes within park boundaries. The 1,000-mile Ice Age National Scenic Trail passes through the park.

• *Suggested Trails for Nature Walks:* 1. The 0.4-mile Glacial Trail. 2. The Deer Path Trail. 3. The 1-mile Dike Trail. 4. The 1-mile Pope Lake Trail. 5. The 1.5-mile Windfeldt Trail. 6. The 4.7-mile Oak Ridge Trail, consisting of several loops.

GOVERNOR DODGE STATE PARK 4175 Highway 23 North, Dodgeville, WI 53533; (608)935-2315. 5,029 acres. Southwestern Wisconsin's Governor Dodge State Park features steep hills and valleys with 450-million-year-old sandstone bluffs and rock overhangs. There are also streams, meadows, prairie remnants, ferns, wildflowers, and an oak-hickory forest with pine. Wildlife includes deer, coyote, red and gray fox, raccoon, muskrat, beaver, and woodchuck, along with pileated woodpecker, barred owl, ruffed grouse, wild turkey, and red-tailed hawk. Naturalist-led walks are scheduled in summer.

• *Suggested Trails for Nature Walks:* 1. The 0.3-mile Stephens Falls Trail. 2. The 2.5-mile Gold Mine Trail (loop). 3. The 3.3-mile Mill Creek Trail (loop). 4. The 2-mile Pinecliff Nature Trail (easy-moderate loop). 5. The 4.5-mile White Oak Trail (easy-moderate). 6. The 6.8-mile Meadow Valley Trail (easy-moderate). 7. The 8.1-mile Lost Canyon Trail (easy-moderate).

Other Suitable Locations for Nature Walks in Wisconsin

Wisconsin has forty-three state parks, ten state forests, and four state recreation areas. All but one of these locations feature nature or hiking trails. In addition, there's a system of state trails that extends beyond park boundaries. Information: Bureau of Parks and Recreation, Box 7921, Madison, WI 53707; (608)266-2181.

There are trails alongside the St. Croix National Scenic Riverway. Information: St. Croix National Scenic Riverway, P.O. Box 708, St. Croix Falls, WI 54024; (715)483-4384.

Trails are available on some of the islands at Apostle Islands National Lakeshore. Access is by excursion boat or water taxi. Information: Apostle Islands National Lakeshore, Route 1, Box 4, Bayfield, WI 54814; (715)779-3397.

The Ice Age National Scientific Reserve includes trails at several of its nine units. Information: Ice Age Reserve, DNR Box 7921, Madison, WI 53707.

Four national wildlife refuges in the state have trails. Information: U.S. Fish and Wildlife Service, 1 Federal Drive, Federal Building, Fort Snelling, MN 55111.

WYOMING

Recommended Areas for Nature Walks

YELLOWSTONE NATIONAL PARK P.O. Box 168, Yellowstone National Park, WY 82190; (307)344-7381. 2,200,000 acres. Occupying the northwest corner of the state, Yellowstone is our largest national park outside of Alaska, and it's most famous for the unmatched assortment of geysers and hot springs—including Old Faithful and Mammoth Hot Springs—as well as the Grand Canyon of the Yellowstone River and enormous Yellowstone Lake.

There are also rugged mountains and wild forests, with shrubs and wildflowers, meadows and sagebrush desert, rivers and streams. Elevations range from 5,300 to nearly 11,358 feet on Eagle Peak. Parts of the park are forested with Douglas fir, lodgepole pine, Englemann spruce, aspen, and juniper. Wildlife includes bison, pronghorn, elk, moose, mule deer, grizzly and black bear, bighorn sheep, bobcat, red fox, river otter, and red-tailed hawk. Guided walks are led by ranger-naturalists.

• *Suggested Trails for Nature Walks:* 1. The 0.3-mile Wraith Falls Trail. 2. The 0.5-mile Harlequin Lake Trail. 3. The 0.5-mile Artist Paintpots Trail. 4. The 0.5-mile Lost Lake Trail. 5. The 2-mile Storm Point Trail (loop). 6. The 2-mile Canyon Rim Trail. 7. The 2.5-mile Riddle Lake Trail. 8. The 2.5-mile Cascade Lake Trail. 9. The 2.5-mile Lone Star Geyser Trail. 10. The 5-mile Beaver Ponds Loop Trail.

GRAND TETON NATIONAL PARK P.O. Drawer 170, Moose, WY 83012; (307)733-2880. 310,520 acres. This park encompasses northwestern Wyoming's Teton Range, which rises up dramatically from the valley of Jackson Hole. Several of the glacier-sculpted and snow-covered mountains surpass 12,000 feet, and there are twelve glaciers, numerous canyons, and many lakes large and small, along with a stretch of the Snake River.

The park includes conifer forests of lodgepole and limber pine, subalpine and Douglas fir, and Englemann spruce, as well as sagebrush flats and meadows with wildflowers. Among the wildlife are moose, bison, a large herd of elk, grizzly and black bear, mule deer, bighorn sheep, pronghorn, and coyote, along with great blue heron, green-winged teal, red-tailed hawk, bald eagle, and osprey. Ranger-led walks are available in summer.

• *Suggested Trails for Nature Walks:* 1. The 0.5-mile Lunchtree Hill Trail. 2. The 0.5-mile Snake River Trail. 3. The 0.8-mile Cunningham Cabin Trail. 4. The 1-mile Leigh Lake Trail. 5. The 2-mile Lakeshore Trail (loop). 6. The 3-mile Heron Pond and Swan Lake Trail (loop). 7. The 3.3-mile String Lake Trail (loop). 8. The 6.4-mile Two Ocean Lake Trail (loop). 9. The 6.6-mile Jenny Lake Trail (loop). 10. The 8.8-mile Hermitage Point Trail (loop).

MEDICINE BOW NATIONAL FOREST 2468 Jackson Street, Laramie, WY 82070; (307)745-2300. 1,093,618 acres. Consisting of several units of land in southeastern Wyoming,

WYOMING

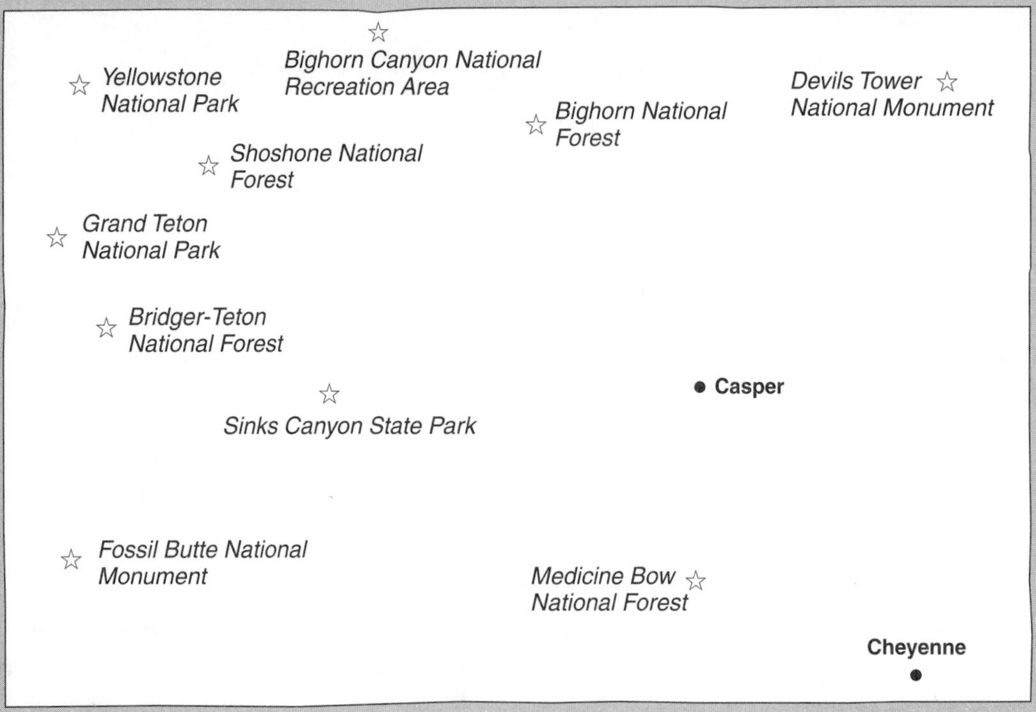

Bighorn Canyon National Recreation Area

Yellowstone National Park

Devils Tower National Monument

Bighorn National Forest

Shoshone National Forest

Grand Teton National Park

Bridger-Teton National Forest

Casper

Sinks Canyon State Park

Fossil Butte National Monument

Medicine Bow National Forest

Cheyenne

this national forest includes portions of the Medicine Bow, Sierra Madre, and Laramie mountain ranges, with elevations from 5,500 to 12,013 feet on Medicine Bow Peak. Four wilderness areas total 79,135 acres.

There are steep canyons and rock formations, high plateaus and meadows, many glacial lakes and streams, and vegetation that ranges from alpine tundra to subalpine fir and Englemann spruce forests, with lodgepole pine and aspen at lower elevations, as well as grasses, sagebrush, and wildflowers. Wildlife includes elk, mule and white-tailed deer, pronghorn, black bear, bighorn sheep, mountain lion, coyote, and prairie dog.

- *Suggested Trails for Nature Walks:* 1. The 0.5-mile Deep Lake Trail. 2. The 1.5-mile 296 Lakes Trail. 3. The 1.6-mile Lost Lake Trail. 4. The 2-mile LaBonte Creek Trail. 5. The 2.8-mile Turtle Rock Trail. 6. The 3-mile Headquarters National Recreation Trail. 7. The 3-mile Queely Lake Trail. 8. The 4.1-mile North French Creek Canyon Trail. 9. The 9.5-mile Douglas Creek Trail. 10. The 4-mile North Gap Lake Trail (easy-moderate).

BRIDGER-TETON NATIONAL FOREST P.O. Box 1888, Jackson, WY 83001; (307)739-5500. 3,400,000 acres. Located in northwestern Wyoming, with lands adjacent to Yellowstone and Grand Teton national parks, Bridger-Teton is the second largest national forest in the lower 48 states. It's home to the Wind River Mountains, the Tetons, and the Gros Ventre and Wyoming ranges, with elevations from 5,900 to 13,785 feet. Three large wilderness areas total 1,300,000 acres.

There's alpine scenery with high ridges and peaks, some enormous glaciers, a huge number of lakes—1,300 in the Bridger Wilderness alone—as well as streams and the Snake, Yellowstone, and Green rivers. Vegetation includes grasslands and sagebrush, meadows with flowers, and forests of spruce and pine, with fir and aspen. Among the wildlife are elk, grizzly and black bear, deer, bighorn sheep, pronghorn, mountain goat, lynx, wolverine, great horned owl, sharp-shinned hawk, and bald eagle.

- *Suggested Trails for Nature Walks:* 1. The Snow King Nature Trail (loop). 2. The first mile of the Sheep Creek Ridge Trail. 3. The first 3 miles of the Horsetail Creek Trail. 4. The first 2 miles of the Swift Creek Trail. 5. The first 3 miles of the Lower Cache Creek Trail. 6. The first part of the Mosquito Creek Trail. 7. The first 6 miles of the Cliff Creek Trail. 8. The first few miles of the Cabin Creek Trail. 9. The Wolf Creek Trail (easy-moderate). 10. The first 4 miles of the Granite Creek Trail (easy-moderate).

SHOSHONE NATIONAL FOREST 808 Meadow Lane, Cody, WY 82414; (307)527-6241. 2,466,586 acres. Shoshone National Forest lies east and south of Yellowstone National Park, in northwestern and west-central Wyoming. It features a landscape of high peaks and canyons, pinnacles and rock formations, plateaus and deep valleys. Within forest boundaries are portions of the Wind River, Beartooth, and Absaroka ranges, including the crest of the Continental Divide.

Elevations range from 4,600 to 13,804 feet on Gannett Peak, which is the highest elevation in Wyoming. Five designated wilderness areas total 1,379,596 acres. The forest has 236 mountains over 12,000 feet, more than 500 lakes, many streams, and 156 glaciers, the most of any area in the country outside of Alaska. Vegetation varies from sagebrush flats to alpine tundra, and wildlife includes elk, grizzly and black bear, moose, deer, bighorn sheep, and mountain goat.

- *Suggested Trails for Nature Walks:* 1. The 1.8-mile Silas Lake Trail. 2. The 3.5-mile Yellowstone Trail. 3. The 1.5-mile Twin Lakes Trail (easy-moderate). 4. The 3-mile Sheep Bridge Trail (easy to moderate). 5. The 4-mile Christina Lake Trail (easy-moderate). 6. The 5-mile Night Lake Trail (easy-moderate). 7. The 7.5-mile Smith Lake Trail (easy-moderate). 8. The 14.4-mile Beartooth Loop National

Recreation Trail (easy-moderate). 9. The 6-mile Crazy Lakes Trail (moderate).

BIGHORN NATIONAL FOREST 1969 South Sheridan Avenue, Sheridan, WY 82801; (307)672-0751. 1,107,671 acres. This national forest is in the Bighorn Mountains of north-central Wyoming, with elevations from 4,000 to 13,167 feet on Cloud Peak. Terrain consists of rugged mountain peaks, U-shaped valleys, and canyons, with streams, rivers, and hundreds of lakes.

Included are the 195,000-acre Cloud Peak Wilderness and the Medicine Wheel National Historic Landmark. There are meadows, grasslands, areas of alpine tundra, and a forest of lodgepole pine and Douglas fir, Englemann spruce and aspen. Among the wildlife are moose, bison, elk, mule and white-tailed deer, black bear, bighorn sheep, mountain lion, and coyote, along with great horned owl, rough-legged hawk, and peregrine falcon.

• *Suggested Trails for Nature Walks:* 1. The 6.1-mile Dutch Oven Pass Trail. 2. The 1.5-mile Lily Lake Trail (easy-moderate). 3. The 3-mile Stull Lakes-Coney Lake Trail (easy-moderate). 4. The 6.4-mile Shell Creek Trail (easy-moderate). 5. The 6.8-mile Sherd Lake Trail (easy-moderate). 6. The 12-mile Dry Fork Trail (easy-moderate). 7. The 13-mile Solitude Loop Trail (easy-moderate). 8. The 18-mile Littlehorn Trail (easy-moderate). 9. The 6.5-mile Misty Moon Trail (moderate). 10. The 7-mile Lost Twin Lakes Trail (moderate).

BIGHORN CANYON NATIONAL RECREATION AREA P.O. Box 7458, Fort Smith, MT 59035; (406)666-2412. 65,000 acres (30,000 in Wyoming). Bighorn Canyon National Recreation Area is on the Wyoming-Montana border, with lands in both states. The South District is accessible only from Wyoming. It features 71-mile-long Bighorn Lake, which was created by damming the Bighorn River, with steep-walled canyons, desert shrublands, shortgrass prairie, wildflowers, and juniper woodlands, as well as fir and pine forests. Wildlife includes elk, mule deer, wild horse, black bear, mountain lion, bighorn sheep, coyote, porcupine, beaver, and cottontail.

• *Suggested Trails for Nature Walks:* 1. The 0.3-mile Crooked Creek Nature Trail. 2. The 0.4-mile Lockhart Ranch Trail. 3. The 1-mile Hillsboro Trail. 4. The 1.8-mile Medicine Creek Trail. 5. The 0.2-mile Beaver Pond Nature Trail (North District). 6. The 3-mile Om-Ne-A Trail (easy-moderate/North District).

SINKS CANYON STATE PARK 3079 Sinks Canyon Road, Lander, WY 82520; (307)332-6333. 600 acres. This state park in west-central Wyoming includes Sinks Canyon, with limestone and sandstone formations, cliffs, caverns, and the Middle Fork of the Popo Agie River, which disappears underground for a half mile before reemerging.

Much of the vegetation consists of meadows with sagebrush and bitterbrush, prickly pear cactus, and stands of Rocky Mountain juniper, maple, quaking aspen, Douglas fir, limber and lodgepole pine, cottonwood, willow, and dogwood. The wildlife includes bighorn sheep, elk, mule deer, moose, black bear, muskrat, beaver, and marmot, along with ruffed grouse, American kestrel, sharp-shinned hawk, turkey vulture, and golden eagle.

• *Suggested Trails for Nature Walks:* 1. The short Visitor Center Trail. 2. The 0.9-mile Popo Agie Nature Trail (loop). 3. The 6.2-mile Sinks Canyon Volksmarch Trail (loop).

DEVILS TOWER NATIONAL MONUMENT P.O. Box 10, Devils Tower, WY 82714; (307)467-5283. 1,347 acres. Located in the northeast corner of Wyoming, in the western edge of the Black Hills, this national monument is centered on Devils Tower, a distinctive volcanic rock column 867 feet high, 1,000 feet wide at the base, and 5,117 feet above sea level. In the area are grasslands, pine and oak forests, and the Belle Fourche River. Wildlife includes white-tailed and mule deer, prairie dog, porcupine, bald and golden eagle, and turkey vulture. Nature walks are offered in summer.

• *Suggested Trails for Nature Walks:* 1. The 1.3-mile Tower Trail (loop). 2. The 0.6-mile Valley View Trail (easy-moderate). 3. The 0.6-mile Southside Trail (easy-moderate). 4. The 1.5-mile Joyner Ridge Trail (easy-moderate). 5. The 2.8-mile Red Beds Trail (moderate) loop.

FOSSIL BUTTE NATIONAL MONUMENT
P.O. Box 592, Kemmerer, WY 83101; (307)877-4455. 8,198 acres. This national monument in southwestern Wyoming protects a fossil-laden butte that was once an ancient lake. Thousands of fossils have been uncovered here. Elevations range from 6,600 to more than 8,000 feet, and the terrain includes flat buttes and ridges, rock formations and talus slopes. There's desert vegetation with sagebrush grasslands and stands of pine and fir, with willow and aspen. Among the wildlife are mule deer, elk, pronghorn, moose, coyote, prairie dog, beaver, and bald eagle. During the summer guided walks are available.

• *Suggested Trails for Nature Walks:* 1. The 1.5-mile Fossil Lake Trail (easy-moderate). 2. The 2.5-mile Historic Quarry Trail loop (moderate).

Other Suitable Locations for Nature Walks in Wyoming

Wyoming has twenty-two state parks, state recreation areas, and state historic sites. Twelve of these locations feature trails. Information: Wyoming State Parks, 2301 Central Avenue, Barrett State Office Building, Cheyenne, WY 82002; (307)777-6323.

Some Bureau of Land Management areas in the state include trails. Information: BLM, Wyoming State Office, P.O. Box 1828, Cheyenne, WY 82003; (307)775-6256.

INDEX

READER RESPONSE

Your feedback can help make future editions of this book even better. Is there a park, forest, preserve, or other natural site that you believe belongs in this book? Is ther a location that should possibly be removed? Have you spotted an error? Is any of the information we've provided out of date now? We'll be very grateful for your suggestions and corrections. Please write to:

Charles Cook
Essential Guide to Nature Walking
P.O. Box 655
Pomona, NY 10970

TRIP INFORMATION

Charles Cook leads nature walks, hikes, wilderness camping trips, and other outings to natural areas throughout the northeastern United States from March through November each year. Day trips are offered to parks and forests in southeastern New York, western Connecticut, and northern New Jersey. Overnight trips are to wilderness areas in New York's Adirondacks and the northern New England states. For further information please write to:

Charles Cook / Trip Information
P.O. Box 655
Pomona, NY 10970